Taxation: Policy and Practice

29th Edition

2022/23

D1339201

Taxation
Policy and Practice

29th edition
2022/2023

Andy Lymer
Professor of Personal Finance & Taxation
Aston University

Lynne Oats
Professor of Taxation & Accounting
University of Exeter

FISCAL
PUBLICATIONS

Taxation: Policy and Practice – 29th Edition 2022/2023

Copyright © Andy Lymer & Lynne Oats

For more information, contact Fiscal Publications at info@fiscalpublications.com or visit: http://www.fiscalpublications.com

ISBN 9781906201654   (also available as an ebook – ISBN 9781906201661)

Edition	Year	Edition	Year
First edition	1993	Sixteenth edition	2009
Second edition	1994	Seventeenth edition	2010
Third edition	1995	Eighteenth edition	2011
Fourth edition	1996	Nineteenth edition	2012
Fifth edition	1997	Twentieth edition	2013
Sixth edition	1999	Twenty first edition	2014
Seventh edition	2000	Twenty second edition	2015
Eighth edition	2001	Twenty third edition	2016
Ninth edition	2002	Twenty fourth edition	2017
Tenth edition	2003	Twenty fifth edition	2018
Eleventh edition	2004	Twenty sixth edition	2019
Twelfth edition	2005	Twenty seventh edition	2020
Thirteenth edition	2006	Twenty eighth edition	2021
Fourteenth edition	2007	Twenty ninth edition	2022
Fifteenth edition	2008		

Cover design by Filter Design Ltd

 Typesetting and production by Mac Bride, Southampton.

Contents

*   Page xi shows how to access the Additional Contents on our website where purchasers of the book can access these chapters in full.

P Preface to the 29th Edition

Philosophy and history of the book

This book was initially created at a time when there was a significant gap in the market for tax textbooks. Excellent material already existed which covered a legal approach to tax, an economic/public sector approach and very detailed technical materials. What was missing, however, was an introductory level text that took a combined, interdisciplinary view on the subject, written in a readable style. Dora Hancock produced the first six editions of the text until Andy Lymer (Aston University) took over producing the text. Since the eleventh edition, authorship has rested entirely with Andy and Lynne Oats (University of Exeter).

Our aim is to provide a complete, but readable, general UK tax textbook that also covers the requirements of professional level introductory UK tax courses. This book is therefore suitable as a supplement to the UK accounting and business professional examinations, particularly in providing greater depth to the courses you may be undertaking towards professional exams to enhance your understanding of this topic.

A number of key changes were made in this edition including:

1. Updating the book fully for the various changes brought about this year in the March 2022 Spring Statement and the various Finance and other Acts in the last year including:

    - Adjustments for 2022/23 to dividend tax rates;

    - Revisions to the National Insurance Contribution rates (to include the new Health and Social Care Levy until April 2023);

    - Further amendments to the car linked benefit in kind and capital allowance rules;

    - Impact of the extension of the Annual Investment Allowance to 31 March 2023 before reversion to its base level from April 2023;

    - Temporary extension of carry-back of trading losses from one year to three years;

- Outline details of important changes that were announced in the March 2022 Spring Statement but will not apply until at least April 2023 – including significant increases to Corporation tax (other than for small businesses) and Diverted Profits tax from April 2023.

2. Further development of the Quick Quiz questions for all computational chapters. We also have added this year clearer signposting in the text to indicate when you should be ready to attempt the various questions in the Quick Quiz and Full questions section. The Quick Quiz questions allow students to practice their skills before tackling the more difficult, Full questions that then we provide (some of which have answers only available through the course lecturer).

3. A number of new computational questions in all chapters for use by both students and lecturers both in the book and on the website. Many of these questions are based on recent professional examination questions.

4. Updating and widening of the range of Fiscal Facts added throughout the text to contextualise further the material being discussed.

5. Updating of the tax glossary.

Other well liked features of the book have been updated and developed where necessary, based on user feedback received and reviews of how tax is taught in the UK at present.

How to use this text

This textbook is not written as a reference text, although the detailed indices and glossary it contains will help direct you to specific areas of material when you need this help. It is instead written to be read. To gain the most from this text we would advise you to read chapters in their entirety, preferably starting at the beginning of the chapter!

Regular activities are included in the text to illustrate the important points you will need to understand and to give you a chance to practice what you are learning as you go through the book. Although there may be a significant 'urge' to jump straight from the activity to the feedback provided, you will miss much of the benefit of the activities if you do not first attempt them yourself.

You will also find a number of quick quizzes, longer self-test and full exam style questions at the end of each chapter that cover the material explained in the chapter. Some of these have answers provided in the back of the book but for others you will have to obtain the answers from your lecturer or teacher, as they will only be provided to them via their section of the website.

As you read the text you will regularly meet new tax terms. You will find all the terms you will need to be familiar with in the glossary at the back of the book. Use this resource as you come across the terms so you can gradually build up your tax vocabulary as you learn new tax ideas and techniques. To help you in this process we put words in italics when we introduce new terms that so you can easily spot you need to take special note and make sure you are aware of their meaning.

Website

A comprehensive website is available to all purchasers of this book to support your use of this text (**http://www.fiscalpublications.com/lymerandoats/2022**. This site is enhanced and updated each year and you should consider it as a direct extension to the book. It contains a range of materials and resources that will help you gain the most from your studying of the UK's taxation system. The site includes:

- several extra chapters for this book (for the print version – these are included in the etext version of the book) providing discussion of environmental taxation (Chapter 13) and of the impacts of the UK tax system (Chapter 14),
- two additional chapters online providing greater details on UK tax system history and more detail on inheritance taxation,
- extensive multiple choice based self-test questions for each chapter,
- extensions to many areas of the text to allow you to go deeper into particular topics if you need to (watch out for the pointers to this as you work through the text – these are marked with the computer symbol in the left hand margin), and
- a range of links and other resources to help with your wider reading for this subject and any assignments/dissertations you may need to undertake associated with a course you may be taking.

The website is frequently updated throughout the year so check it from time to time for changes.

Acknowledgements

We acknowledge the permission granted us by CIMA, ICAS and ACCA to use past examination questions in this text, and on the website.

CIMA, the Chartered Institute of Management Accountants, is the world's leading and largest professional body of management accountants, with 172,000 members and students operating in 168 countries, working at the heart of business.

The Institute of Chartered Accountants of Scotland (ICAS) is the world's first professional accountancy body. It was the first to adopt the designation

'Chartered Accountant', and the letters 'CA' can only be used in the UK by ICAS members. ICAS has been training CAs for over 150 years and is highly regarded throughout the world for the high calibre of its members.

ACCA (the Association of Chartered Certified Accountants) is the global body for professional accountants. They aim to offer business-relevant, first-choice qualifications to people of application, ability and ambition around the world who seek a rewarding career in accountancy, finance and management.

You can find out more about these bodies at the following links:
- CIMA at www.cimaglobal.com or www.cimaglobal.com/Students/
- ICAS at www.icas.com or www.icas.com/become-a-ca and
- ACCA at www.accaglobal.com or www.accaglobal.com/en/qualifications.html

The Fiscal Facts notes added throughout the text were sourced from various public online resources including the Institute for Fiscal Studies, HM Treasury and HMRC websites.

We would particularly like to thank Nicky Thomas (Senior Lecturer in Tax and Accounting, University of Exeter) for her continued technical assistance in the development of this year's text, and various others, particularly our students and adopting lecturers, who have provided helpful suggestions and ideas included in this edition as they do every year and for which we are most grateful.

Please note, however, that whilst every attempt has been made in writing this text to be accurate and true to the current UK tax system, it should not be solely relied upon as a definitive source of information on current tax rules. Readers are advised to seek specific professional advice in their tax affairs. Neither the authors nor the publishers accept any legal responsibility for any loss related to actions taken based on material contained in this book.

This book is improved year on year in part on the basis of feedback people provide to us as the authors. We are most grateful for this and very much welcome comments you wish to make about the book or suggestions for future development of the book, or the associated website. The authors can be contacted for this purpose at:

lymer&oats@fiscalpublications.com

Andrew Lymer and Lynne Oats
July 2022

Taxation: Policy & Practice – website

https://www.fiscalpublications.com/lymerandoats/2022

Fiscal Publications, and the authors of this text, have created a website to be used in conjunction with this textbook.

Visit the above address to find:

1   Answers to questions at the end of each chapter (note – some are reserved for lecturer use only as teaching aids – if you want copies of these please ask your lecturer).
2   Extension materials for many parts of the text allowing you to go deeper into these topics than are covered in the book.
3   An extensive tax term glossary (included in the ebook version of the book).
4   Extra chapters to the book (for all versions) on UK tax system history and inheritance taxation, and (included in the ebook version), environmental taxation and impacts of the UK tax system.
5   Multiple choice questions – self test questions for each chapter.
6   A large extra question and answer bank for self or classroom managed extra practice and illustration of tax computations.
7   A large list of tax related links for further reading, dissertation etc.
8   Easy to print rates and allowance pages.

Whilst the lecturer area of the website is only available to bona fide teachers, the student area is open to all purchasers of this book. Basic registration will be required for this access.

Please use your unique user ID and password, as listed below, to gain access to this part of the site.

User ID: 2022student419876
Password: 2022er!77kp

Do not provide these details to others. Fiscal Publications reserves the right to block your access to the site if it suspects this has occurred.

Fiscal Publications

Other useful books to aid your study of UK and international taxation

This text is produced by a UK-based publishing house that specialises in taxation and public economics texts. See below for some of their other books that will enhance your understanding of UK taxation and help prepare you for any assessments you have to face.

Taxation: incorporating the 2022 Finance Act

by Alan Combs and Ricky Tutin

ISBN   978 1 906201 67 8
Ebook 978 1 906201 68 5

This is the companion text for Taxation: Policy and Practice. It provides many further examples and 100s of questions and answers for additional explanation and practice of all the topics covered in this book.

UK Income Tax Practice Questions – 2nd edition

by Alan Combs

Ebook 978 1 906201 69 2

This Income Tax question bank is linked directly to the Lymer & Oats text, providing for you more than 50 extra full questions and answers that thoroughly cover all the materials covered in this book. The perfect way to prepare for your exams.

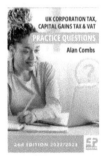

UK Corporation Tax, Capital Gains Tax and VAT Practice Questions – 2nd edition

by Alan Combs

Ebook 978 1 906201 70 8

This question bank focuses on Corporation Tax, Capital Gains Tax and VAT questions. It provides more than 50 full questions and answers, many of full exam level, that will fully prepare you for any assessment you are facing of the level covered by the Lymer & Oats textbook. Each question is directly linked to this text so the reader can easily see what questions link with which parts of this book.

For further details see **http://www.fiscalpublications.com** – including a large bank of extra questions and answers and other student and lecturer materials for purchasers of this book. **Student discounts available for many titles** – see website for details.

ALL of our titles are also available as **EBOOKS** available via Kortext (**https://store.kortext.com**) or Vital Source (**https://www.vitalsource.com**)

1 The framework of UK taxation

Introduction

1.1 Taxation has played an important role in civilised (and not so civilised) societies for thousands of years. The earliest written records of how such societies formed and were organised illustrate the importance of taxation in their successes, but also some of their downfalls. Taxation continues to play an important role in modern societies, as we will see throughout this chapter.

Ever since people began to gather together in groups and share resources as communities, taxes in some form or another have been raised to pay for services to benefit the community as a whole, rather than specific individuals or groups, including, for example, provision of defence for the whole community.

In the 21st century taxes are now used to achieve a number of government objectives as well as to raise revenue to fund public spending and to repay borrowing. In modern Britain taxation has become completely embedded in our society. Whilst few people would say they like to pay taxes, their presence provides the foundation for an orderly, well managed, country. It also provides the basis on which we can support each other in times of crisis, as we have seen since early 2020 due to the far-reaching effects of the COVD-19 pandemic.

At the end of this chapter you will be able to:

- outline the need for tax in a civilised society;
- discuss the historical background of taxation, particularly in the UK;
- describe the main features of UK tax policy making; and
- understand the structure of the current UK tax system.

Objectives of taxation

1.2 Taxation is used as a tool by the UK government to support its basic functions. These basic functions include:

- Managing the economy – including employment levels, the nature, type and location of business activity, levels of inflation, the balance of payments and relationships with our trading partners;
- Regulation – protection of the environment, the public generally or of groups within society who might otherwise be exploited;
- Developing society – providing a social welfare and health system to improve the standards of living for the whole society. This includes providing for the country's needs in times of crisis;
- Providing public goods – provision of products and services for common consumption that may not be adequately provided by the private sector. These include defence and education systems for example.

The primary purpose of imposing a tax on society is to raise money to pay for public (government) spending in performing the basic functions listed above. This can be achieved by covering costs as they are incurred, or by funding repayment of government debt.

However, taxes are also used to influence the behaviour of taxpayers directly for the benefit of society. For example, taxes are charged on petrol, alcohol and tobacco (in part at least) to increase their cost so as to discourage their consumption in order to improve the environment and health of the country.

Tax reliefs can also be offered by a government to encourage activity that might not otherwise occur but that is considered beneficial for society in some way. For example, creating freeports or enterprise zones which have lower than normal taxes to persuade businesses to locate in particular areas. We will look more closely at how taxes are used to influence behaviour in the UK in Chapter 14.

Taxation, therefore, is a very important feature of a modern society and the nature of a particular tax system reflects the views of its society, and government, at a point in time. Tax systems change regularly as society modifies its views on how best to balance the various aspects of the basic functions of government listed above. They also change as society's views of the relative importance of particular issues in the society, such as environmental protection, change over time. Key changes in the tax system often occur when government philosophies change, such as when power in the Government shifts from one political party to another after an election.

What is a tax?

1.3   Before we study the history of tax and examine the current UK rules for taxation in detail, we must understand what a tax is. All taxes have some features in common. They are a compulsory levy, imposed by government or other tax raising body, on income, consumption, wealth or people, for which the taxpayer receives nothing specific in return.

Not all payments to a government are taxes however. Charges, fees for services, costs for provision of goods supplied by a government entity (e.g. electricity if the supply if state owned), tolls and other levies could be paid to a government, but where they are paid simply to cover the cost of providing something specific in return then they are not strictly taxes.

The collection of all the taxes in operation in an economy at a specific point in time, and the rules related to these taxes, is called a 'tax system'.

A brief history of taxation

1.4   Before we look at how the UK tax system currently operates, it is important to look back at history. Tax systems evolve slowly over time, with often fairly small changes each year. Therefore, understanding the tax system of today requires at least some appreciation of the tax system of the past. By understanding why particular taxes were created as they were, you be able to appreciate some of the complexities of the current system you are learning about. Most taxes made sense at the time they were introduced, even if they seem strange later!

Throughout history tax has been a sensitive issue between rulers or governments and their subjects or citizens. Significant civil unrest and even wars, have resulted from disputes about tax. This section briefly reviews some of these events both in ancient history, and more recent British history, illustrating the dynamic nature of tax systems over time and how methods and mechanisms for taxing people have changed.

The following is a condensed version of a longer discussion of the history of tax that is available on the website.

As you read this section, note how the complexity of the tax system generally increases over time but at the same time, yet many of the basic features of taxation have actually remained fairly constant. There is a saying that 'an old tax is a good tax', which reflects the idea that once a particular form of tax is in place, it can be very difficult to remove later.

Taxation in the past: an overview

1.5 Taxes have been levied on societies for just about as far back in history as we have records (e.g. taxes feature in ancient Egyptian, Chinese and Central American societies). In Roman times, for example, only indirect taxes were imposed, although from time to time the Emperor would demanding extra from citizens as *tributum*, or direct taxes. There is also evidence of poll taxes, or *capitato*, and land taxes, or *jugatio*, imposed at various times.

1.6   In the Middle Ages, or medieval times, (1066 – 1540), kings and queens, via their Treasuries, had access to revenue from three main sources.

1. Income from Crown property;
2. Feudal rights, where the ruler received income (in various forms) from land owners, who in turn extracted it from their tenants; and
3. Customs duties and other levies, imposed in times of emergency.

1.7   In the early modern period (1540 – 1750) taxation became a particularly contentious issue during the first reign of the Stuarts (1603-1649) leading to differences (both tax related and others) between the King and Parliament, which became insurmountable and ended with Charles' execution in 1649.

The late modern period, from 1750 – 1945 saw more dramatic changes with a shift away from taxing a very wide range of items of consumption and wealth to income tax, which was introduced in the UK in 1799. Over the course of the 19th century, a more recognisable tax system emerged as the free trade movement led to repeal of many taxes on consumption and to supplement income tax, taxes on land and inheritances.

At the beginning of the 20th century tax was paid on earned income by fewer than a million people. Hence it was paid only by the better off in UK society.

Fiscal Fact

Approximately 59% of working age adults (25.7m of 43.5m people) paid at least some income tax in 2019.

[Source – HMRC Table 2.1 Number of individual income tax payers and ONS Overview of the UK Population Jan 21)

The contemporary tax system

1.8 After World War 2, significant changes to the UK tax system included the extension of income tax to a wider range of taxpayers, introduction of pay as you earn collection for employment income and the national insurance contribution system. A purchase tax was used to tax spending for a large part of the 20th century until it was replaced in 1973 by Value Added Tax (VAT), as a precursor to Britain becoming part of the European Economic Community (now the European Union) and became primary tax on consumption in the UK (we will discuss UK VAT in Chapter 10).

In 1965 two new taxes, corporation tax (see Chapter 9) and capital gains tax (see Chapter 8) , were introduced and in 1984 the previous capital transfer tax was replaced by Inheritance Tax (also discussed in Chapter 8). For the remainder of the 20th century, the overall structure of the UK tax system in terms of the types of taxes and their relative importance, was quite stable.

Taxation in the 21st century

1.9 As we have moved into the 21st century various key changes face the UK's tax system. This includes changes that come from leaving the European Union, and other geopolitical upheavals, the impact of the Covid-19 pandemic and also opportunities and threats from increased digitalisation.

In the case of Brexit, Europe had various powers over how our tax system operates, including the rates we could use for VAT as we will explore in Chapter 10. Departure from Europe has allowed the UK to revisit rules and we are beginning to see some changes, for example reductions in VAT rates that would not have been possible if we had stayed in Europe.

In coming years we will, of course, need to address the economic effects of Covid-19 pandemic and the huge associated cost the country has taken on to deal with it. We are already seeing some tax changes as a result of this health (and its resulting economic) crisis, which are discussed further in section 1.13 below.

Changes related to digitalisation are almost certainly going affect more of us however. For example, HMRC are keen to be one of, if not the, most technologically advanced tax authorities in the world. The increased use of technology in dealing with our tax affairs started some years ago electronic filing of tax returns and changes to back-office data processing to improve the auditing capabilities of HMRC. 'Making Taxes Digital' started in earnest from April 2019. This has seen many of those who have to file VAT returns move completely online for their interactions with HMRC. This is affecting all aspects of how taxpayers keep their business or personal accounting records, and how they send and receive information from the tax authority.

Current tax legislation and regulation

1.10 Tax rules are currently created in the UK by a combination of law, regulation and cases, and to a lesser degree rulings and best practice guidance from HMRC. There are a number of sources of tax law. Table 1.1 below lists the key tax laws that contain the rules we will examine in this book.

Table 1.1: UK Tax Legislation

Source	Key Relevant Act
Income Tax	
Earned income/pensions	Income Tax (Earnings and Pensions) Act 2003 (ITEPA)
Other sources	Income Tax (Trading and Other Income) Act 2005 (ITTOI) and Income Tax Act 2007 (ITA)
Corporation tax	Income and Corporation Taxes Act 1998 (ICTA), Corporation Tax Act 2009 (CTA), Corporation Tax Act 2010 and Corporation Tax (Northern Ireland) Act 2015.
Capital Allowances	Capital Allowances Act 2001 (CAA)
National Insurance Contributions	Social Security & Benefits Act 1992, National Insurance Contributions Act 2011 and 2015
Capital Gains	Taxation of Chargeable Gains Act 1992 (TCGA)
Value Added Tax	Value Added Tax Act 1994 (VATA)
Inheritance Tax	Inheritance Tax Act 1984 (IHTA)
Stamp Duty	Stamp Act 1891 and Electronic Communications Act 2000 (ECA),
Land Tax	Stamp Duty Land Tax Act 2015 and Land and Buildings Transactions Tax 2015 (LBTT –Scotland only), Land Transactions Tax 2018 - Wales Only).
Administration of direct tax	Taxes Management Act 1970 (TMA) and Commissioners for Revenue and Customs Act 2005 (CRCA)

Regular Finance Acts that bring into UK law the plans of the Chancellor announced in the Budget each year. In most years only one Finance Act is passed and it is given the date of that year – i.e. this year it is the Finance Act 2022. However, in some years there can be more than one Finance Act if this proves necessary, for example a Finance Act (No 2) 2022 has not been enacted at the time of writing, but may become necessary in the current economic climate. Other regulations and laws (such as Statutory Instruments) can also be used by the Government to amend or extend these various Acts.

Some tax aspects can also be found in more general, non-tax specific, Acts of Parliament. For example, in November 2016 an Act redefining rules on charity regulation came into force which included various details about the taxation of charities.

Whilst we look at the current law as we examine each tax issue, this text does not include a detailed consideration of these laws and therefore does not make reference to particular parts of these Acts or regulations. This is a deliberate policy to reduce the complexity of our explanation. However, it is very important that you remember that legislation underpins all the detail we describe and you may need to refer to this at some point to fully understand how the tax rules work for a particular issue.

In addition to UK tax law, the UK's tax system is shaped by a number of other laws, cases and guidance statements from HMRC. This can make for a complex web of rules in many areas of tax.

Many of the rules that applied in the UK as a result of being a member of the EU have now been brought into UK law following exit from the union.

The UK's tax system is a common law system. This means that specific tax related laws created by Parliament are interpreted by judges in courts as disputes are brought before them to be settled. Throughout this book you will meet a number of legal cases that determine how legal principles should be applied to specific circumstances.

The UK's tax authority (HMRC) also periodically issues guidance of various types for taxpayers and their advisors. Whilst this is not legally binding on taxpayers and can be challenged, it does provide useful advice on the tax authority's view on how specific tax issues should be handled. Taking a look at HMRC's website for example, you will find guidance on a range of issues as well as access to HMRC's internal manuals which explain how the authority approaches specific aspects of the taxes it administers.

National v local taxation

1.11 Like many other countries, the UK suffers from 'vertical fiscal imbalance'. This means that lower levels of government, which in the UK is local (e.g. city, district or county councils) or regional government (e.g. Welsh or Northern Irish Assemblies and the Scottish Parliament), don't raise enough money of their own to meet their spending obligations and instead need to rely on central government for extra funds, usually paid in the form of grants. In the UK, local government currently only raises about 25% of its own revenue needs and has to get the rest from central government. This balance of funding between the two levels of government hasn't always been this way. Before 1992, local government used to raise between 45% and 60% of its own revenue, mainly from taxes. After this date however, capping systems imposed on local governments by central government have prevented local governments raising higher percentages of their spending from taxation. The current degree of vertical fiscal imbalance is considered to be a problem.

The main tax levied by local government is *council tax*, which was introduced in 1993. Before considering how this tax works, we will briefly review the local taxes that existed before 1993.

For many years, the main local tax in the UK was *domestic rates*. This was based on a percentage of the value of property (both residential and non-residential) located in the area of control of the local government. In the 1980s there was growing concern that rates were unfair, and in 1990, the rates system for residential property was replaced with a new tax, the *community charge*, sometimes referred to as the *poll tax*. The community charge was extremely unpopular (as we will see in Chapter 2) and so in 1993 the Government was forced to and replace it with the *council tax*.

Council tax is made up of two elements, which makes it a 'hybrid tax'. Half of the tax bill relates to the value of the property, and the other half is based on a charge of 25% for each of the first two adults living in the property. This means that a single adult household will only pay 75% of the usual bill.

Council tax is set locally and therefore it was, until recent new powers given to the regions, the only personal tax in the UK that varied according to where you lived. Property values are placed into 8 bands (9 bands in Wales after 2005) and the local government sets the rate for one of them, the others then are a proportion of that rate.

Large increases in the rate of council tax cause a lot of dissatisfaction, which is one of the reasons why local government funding is regularly under review.

Devolved Taxation

1.12 Despite local government having legal powers to use council tax to raise some of their funding, historically the only regional government with legal rights to raise taxes in the UK was the Scottish Parliament. They have the power to vary income tax by increasing or decreasing it up to 3% in either direction from the national levels for taxpayers in Scotland, and now have a different rate scale from the rest of the UK.

However, greater tax raising powers were granted to Scotland as part of the Scotland Act (2012). These cover areas such as land taxation (instead of the use of Stamp Duty, Scotland now operates a Land and Buildings Transaction Tax (LBTT) effective from April 2015), and a separate Scottish Landfill Tax (SLfT). They are collected by a body called *Revenue Scotland* (http://www.revenue.scot). The income tax varying powers were also formalised at the same time to enable a *Scottish Rate of Income Tax* (SRIT) to be created. This came into force in April 2016 and Scottish income taxpayers now pay different rates of personal income tax (albeit not significantly) to those in the rest of the UK. Other taxes will also become more directly under the Scottish Parliament's control as part of the devolution process currently underway following the Independence vote at the end of 2014.

Also in 2014 Northern Ireland was given powers to set its own Corporation tax (this was due to commence in April 2018 but has been delayed). This was to enable it to compete more effectively in this area with the Republic of Ireland that has a lower rate of corporation tax.

Wales did not historically have any of these same powers, however, from April 2018 it has been allowed to collect its own Land Transaction Taxes, paid via a new body entitled the *Welsh Revenue Authority* (http://www.beta.gov.wales/welsh-revenue-authority). Now, much like the situation in Scotland, land transactions-based taxes are different in this region to other parts of the UK. The Welsh government also has the power to vary income tax for Welsh residents, but has yet to do so. The income tax rates in Wales remain the same as those in England and Northern Ireland.

Tax policy making in the UK

1.13 Tax policy is the preserve of Her Majesty's Treasury. This is a Ministerial Department – the Minister being the Chancellor of the Exchequer, supported by the Chief Secretary to the Treasury, the Financial Secretary to the Treasury, the Economic Secretary to the Treasury and Exchequer Secretary to the Treasury.

The most critical event of the annual taxation calendar in the UK (most years) is the annual Budget Statement made by the Chancellor of the Exchequer. This used to be made during March, but from 2017 this switched to November each year (although this was again held in March in 2021 due the Covid-19 pandemic). This statement outlines the Government's budget plans for the year, which correspondingly have to be balanced with how they will raise the money to finance these plans. It is in this annual statement that most tax changes for the year are therefore to be found. (Summary details of this year's Budget, and summaries of those of the last few years, can be found online at the Tax Student website as Appendix B.)

In June 2010, the Government issued a document alongside an emergency budget, called *Tax Policy Making: A new approach.* This document discussed several proposals for improving the policy making process for the UK, which had long been criticised for a lack of consultation and ad hoc changes without sufficient warning. Since then, tax policies are usually announced with time for consultation, and draft legislation published for comment before being introduced to Parliament. Changes in the law are now accompanied by Tax Information and Impact notes that explain the changes and their expected impact.

Two further important developments in tax administration were created in the early days of the Coalition Government in 2010. First, was the creation of an Office of Tax Simplification. This is an independent body, attached to the Treasury, charged with trying to find ways to simplify the UK tax system (we will consider why simplicity is considered to be important in designing a tax system in Chapter 3). This body has proven effective in getting a range of tax simplifications made to the UK tax system – including changes to the way tax is computed on employee expenses and benefits in kind as we show in Chapter 5.

Second, Government created the Office for Budget Responsibility. This body provides independent economic forecasting and analysis for the Government in an attempt to take political pressure out of important judgements of the state of the UK economy, and to ensure the Treasury is held to better account by independent expertise.

In January 2017 a further review of the process of tax policy setting was published by the Chartered Institute of Tax (CIOT) the Institute of Fiscal Studies (IFS) and the Institute for Government entitled 'Better Budgets: making tax policy better'. Another report by the Institute for Government, Overcoming the Barriers to Tax Reform, was published in April 2020 which suggested five reasons for the Government to publish a tax strategy with objectives:

1. Clear objectives would allow the Government to better explain tax reform to the public;

2. Objectives would allow Government to plan effectively over longer periods;

3. Declared objectives would enable other departments to engage better with Treasury and ensure consistency between policies;

4. Objectives would allow Members of Parliament to hold the Government to account; and

5. Clear objectives could help build cross party consensus.

In July 2020, the House of Commons Treasury Committee announced an inquiry into Tax After Coronavirus. Witnesses to the inquiry were unanimous that significant tax rises should not be imposed in the short term, but will be needed in the future. Amongst other things, the Committee recommended that the Government publish a tax strategy identifying high level objectives. In response, the Government declined to implement this and other recommendations from the Committee.

There is ongoing concern that tax policy is subject to less scrutiny in Parliament than other areas of public policy and that the split of policy making responsibility between HM Treasury and HMRC is not ideal.

Money raised and spent by the UK Government

1.14 The UK government finances its activities from a number of sources, primarily taxes. The Office for Budget Responsibility (OBR) expects the total revenue from taxes and other sources to be £987.5 billion for 2022/23, which is 39.3% of national income. Importantly, the national debt has increased significantly as a result of the Covid-19 pandemic is expected to be £2.5 trillion or 95.5% of national income.

Activity

The main taxes in the UK are income tax, corporation tax, VAT, council tax, national insurance contributions, business rates and fuel duty. Put these taxes in order according to how much revenue they each raise, from highest to lowest.

Feedback

The OBR publishes statistics that can help us do this. A brief guide to the public finances (as at March 2022) can be found here:

https://obr.uk/forecasts-in-depth/brief-guides-and-explainers/public-finances/

You will see that the largest revenue raiser is income tax together with national insurance contributions. After that comes VAT, then corporation tax, council tax, business rates and fuel duty.

For a more detailed analysis by the OBR of the UK's public finances, see the publication Economic and Fiscal Outlook March 2022 which is available here: https://obr.uk/efo/economic-and-fiscal-outlook-march-2022/.

This mix of taxes has been a feature of the UK system for many years, with only minor modifications. The current Government is constrained by its own election manifesto promises not to increase certain taxes but went ahead with an increase in national insurance contributions to help correct the health and social care crisis. Subsequently, in the Spring Statement of 2022, the Chancellor announced cuts to national insurance contributions and income tax in light of the increased cost of living. We will look at these changes more closely in Chapter 4.

How does the UK Government spend its money?

1.15   The OBR expect public spending in 2022/23 to be £1,087bn, or 43.2% of national income. Central government departments are expected to spend £407bn or 37% if public spending on current running costs.

Activity

Which three government departments will spend most on current running costs?.

Feedback

Once again the OBR brief guide to the public finances (as at March 2022) can help us answer this (*https://obr.uk/forecasts-in-depth/brief-guides-and-explainers/public-finances/*). You will see that the three largest items of spending are health and social care, education and defence. The biggest component of 'annually managed expenditure' is cash transfers through the welfare system.

The OBR guide also tells us that compared to other countries, the UK raises a bit less revenue than most other industrial countries and public spending is slightly above the average, which means that the UK has a budget deficit that is considerably higher than the average for industrial countries.

Summary

In this chapter we have laid the foundations that you will need to study taxation from this textbook, and beyond. We have drawn briefly on the lessons of history to try to illustrate how taxation affects all of us today. You are now able to trace the history of taxation over more than 2,000 years. The difficulties facing Parliament today have been faced by leaders throughout the centuries. Governments must raise revenues in ways which are seen by the electorate as being fair and equitable if they can reasonably expect them to be paid.

A modern Chancellor has to consider many conflicting objectives when setting out tax proposals in the annual budget. He or she must decide how much tax to raise and then determine how that tax should be raised from the different taxes available. To do this a Chancellor must be aware of the potential consequences of the legislation on individuals and businesses.

In this chapter we have been able to introduce the complex relationship between legislation and case law and understand the limitations of each and we illustrated how the Government uses the current tax system to raise revenue, and briefly how they spend this revenue.

In Chapters 2 and 3 we will consider in more detail the UK tax system and the nature of a 'good' tax. We will look at the administration of the UK tax system in Chapter 2, then the general principles of the design of tax systems in Chapter 3.

Project areas

There are a number of areas covered in this chapter which would provide good material for projects. These include the following:

- a comparison of the progressive nature of the tax systems of a number of countries,
- exploring the history of UK taxation,
- examining the consequences of Brexit for UK tax policy,
- assessing the relative use of different taxes in the UK tax system and the corresponding spending activity of the UK government,
- comparing the balance of local v national (federal) taxation in the UK with other countries. Why might these balances be different?
- discussing the impact of the devolving of more tax powers to regional governments in Scotland, Northern Island and Wales?

Discussion questions

1   Do you think that people will be more likely to work if they receive support through the tax system rather than a separate benefits system?

2   Is it right (and fair) that the UK is so dependent on income taxation as a source of tax revenue? What risks are involved in such a policy? Why might these risks be acceptable to assume?

3   What other unusual taxes can you discover that have existed in some point in history? How effective were they?

4   How is Lady Godiva connected with taxation? What other interesting events in history have been influenced by tax policy issues?

Further reading

History

Beckett, J.V., Land Tax & Excise: The levying of taxation in seventeenth and eighteenth-century England 100 *English Historical Review*, 285, 1985.

Daunton, M. J., *Trusting Leviathan: the politics of taxation in Britain*, 1799 – 1914, Cambridge University Press: Cambridge, 2001.

Daunton, M. J., *Just Taxes: the politics of taxation in Britain 1914 – 1979*, Cambridge University Press: Cambridge, 2002.

Dowell, S., *A History of Taxation in England* (4 volumes), Frank Cass & Co. Ltd: London, (1965 - 3rd Edition, first published in 1884).

Ezzamel, M., Accounting Working for the State: Tax Assessment and Collection During the New Kingdom, Ancient Egypt, *Accounting and Business Research*, 32/1:17-39, 2002.

Farnsworth, A., *Addington: Author of the Modern Income Tax*, Stevens & Sons Ltd: London 1951.

Harris, P., *Income Tax in Common Law Jurisdictions: from the origins to 1820*, Cambridge University Press, Cambridge, 2006.

Kennedy, W., *English Taxation 1640-1799*, G. Bell & Sons Ltd: London, 1913.

Monroe, H.H., *Intolerable Inquisition? Reflections on the Law of Tax*, Stevens & Sons: London, 1981.

Sabine, B.E.V., *A History of Income Tax*, George Allen & Unwin: London, 1966.

Soos, P., *The Origins of Taxation at Source in England*. IBFD Publications: Amsterdam, 1997.

Tax Reform

Sandford, C., *Successful Tax Reform: Lessons from an analysis of Tax Reform in six countries.* Fiscal Publications: Birmingham, 1993.

Steinmo, S., The Politics of Tax Reform, in Sandford, C. (ed.) *More Key Issues in Tax Reform*, Fiscal Publications: Birmingham, 1995.

Progressivity

James, S. and Nobes, C., *The Economics of Taxation: 18th Edition*, Chapter 2, Fiscal Publications: Birmingham, 2018.

Dilnot, A., The Income Tax Rate Structure, in Sandford, C., (ed.) *Key Issues in Tax Reform*, Fiscal Publications: Birmingham, 1993.

Scottish Taxation

Cooper, C., Danson, M., Whittam, G. & Sheridan, T. "The neoliberal project— Local taxation intervention in Scotland" *Critical Perspectives on Accounting,* Volume 21, Issue 3, March 2010, Pages 195-210.

Institute of Chartered Accountants of Scotland (ICAS), *Guide to Scottish Taxes,* https://www.icas.com/__data/assets/pdf_file/0004/578227/ICAS-GUIDE-TO-SCOTTISH-TAXES-2021-EDITION-MARCH-2021.pdf

Comparative Taxation

Evans, C., Hasseldine, J., Lymer, A., Ricketts, R. & Sandford, C. *Comparative Taxation: Why tax systems differ*, Fiscal Publications, Birmingham 2017.

For more information about local taxation see the Ministry of Housing, Communities and Local Government's website:

https://www.gov.uk/government/organisations/ministry-of-housing-communities-and-local-government

which also contains a section on local government finance:

https://www.gov.uk/government/collections/local-government-finance-reports

For further details on the Office for Budget Responsibility see their website:

http://obr.uk/

For further details on the Office of Tax Simplification see:

https://www.gov.uk/government/organisations/office-of-tax-simplification

For further details on Revenue Scotland see:

https://www.revenue.scot

For further details on the Welsh Revenue Authority see:

https://gov.wales/welsh-revenue-authority

---

2 Tax administration and compliance

Introduction

2.1   In the previous chapter we considered the historical development of the UK tax system and looked briefly at the current tax structure and tax policy making process. This chapter extends our understanding of the UK tax system by looking more closely at how it is administered by HMRC.

At the end of this chapter you will be able to:
- describe the main administrative features of the UK tax system today, including the systems for collecting taxes, penalties and dispute procedures;
- understand how HMRC operates to encourage taxpayers to voluntarily comply with their tax obligations; and
- discuss the issues that affect whether or not taxpayers comply with the tax rules.

Tax administration

2.2   Until April 2005 the UK tax system was mostly managed by two Government departments, Inland Revenue for direct taxes such as income tax and H.M. Customs and Excise for indirect taxes such as VAT.

Customs and Excise is one of the oldest Government departments (although they were only combined into one department in 1909) with a history dating back to the 13th century as a formal body working for the King to collect duties and prevent smuggling.

Following a lengthy consultation process, Inland Revenue and H.M Customs and Excise merged into one body with effect from 18 April 2005 and are now called Her Majesty's Revenue and Customs (HMRC). This was an important development as it brought the UK into line with most other developed countries. It is a non-Ministerial departments of the UK Government, which means it has no dedicated Minister to oversee its operation. There are 20 Non-Ministerial departments currently compared with 23 Ministerial departments. Having the tax authority as a non-ministerial department theoretically removes it from political influence.

As we saw in Chapter 1, in the UK tax policy is set by HM Treasury, not HMRC, although HMRC has input into operational aspects of policy development.

The tax year

2.3 Until the mid-18th century the Government used an accounting year which ended on Lady Day, 25 March, the first quarter day in the calendar year (and the date of the start of the church year, i.e. it was the old New Year's Day for most purposes, as the Feast of the Annunciation of the Virgin Mary – exactly nine months before Christmas Day). In 1752 the Government adopted the Gregorian calendar which required the loss of 11 days between the 2 and 14 of September to bring the calendar year back into line with the solar year. However, the Government was unwilling to have an accounting period which did not run for 365 days and so moved their year-end forward by 11 days to 5 April. Hence today a tax year (for an individual) runs from 6 April to the following 5 April: the tax year 2022/23 runs from 6 April 2022 to 5 April 2023. This is the year we will use for most of the examples in later chapters although for companies the tax year differs. It is 1 April – 30 March (we will cover corporation tax in Chapter 9).

The self assessment system

2.4 Self assessment is a system under which the taxpayer is responsible for working out his or her own tax liability and reporting it to the revenue authority –HMRC in the UK's case. Prior to the 1990's a number of UK taxes had official (direct) assessment system, where the tax authority works out the tax liability. Individual taxpayers are now required to use self assessment for income tax and capital gains tax, as are companies for corporation tax.

The key advantage of self assessment from the Government's point of view is that HMRC doesn't have to produce assessments for taxpayers. By putting the responsibility on the taxpayer to work out his or her own tax liability (i.e. to 'self' assess), HMRC can devote more of its resources to following up cases that might be inaccurate, providing more advice and offering other services to help taxpayers rather than having to check every tax return that is filed. So self assessment may reduce the cost to the Government of administering the tax system, but on the other hand, it increases the cost to the taxpayer of complying with the system as they can no longer rely on the tax authority to do some of the work for them. We look more at the compliance costs of the tax system in section 2.11.

Time limits apply to the operation of various parts of the tax system and penalties are possible if they are not adhered to. For example, a taxpayer may have forgotten to include something in their self assessment for income tax, perhaps an expense that qualifies as an allowable deduction, and need to ask for an amendment to be made. Another possibility is that HMRC may discover something about the taxpayer's affairs, perhaps some omitted income, that means that the self assessment is incorrect, and need to issue a new assessment. The time limits are harmonised across the different taxes and they are as follows:

For taxpayer claims	4 years
For ordinary assessments	4 years
Assessments where the loss of tax is due to carelessness	6 years
Assessments where the loss of tax is deliberate	20 years

Another important feature of the UK's self assessment system is online filing. The Government have for some years been encouraging taxpayers to file their annual tax returns online and provides free software to allow many taxpayers to do so. Online filing, or e-filing, has a number of advantages for both HMRC and taxpayers. For example, the online filing system has a number of checks automatically built in to its operation so that as a taxpayer completes his or her return form online, the system ensures that figures are put in the correct place and calculates the amount of tax due. For both parties the key advantage is speeding up the filing process. This includes for taxpayers getting any tax refunds due to them as soon as possible.

Fiscal Fact

HMRC predict that there will be 32.2 million individual income taxpayers in 2021-22 (Source: HMRC Table 2.1).

In 2014, HMRC launched a project that will eventually allow all self assessed taxpayers (whether individuals or small business taxpayers) to use a secure, personalised portal to view messages from HMRC, and receive email alerts. The scheme, promoted under the banner of '*Making Tax Digital*', will remove the need for many to file a tax return in the future. This will be possible because data HMRC holds on the taxpayer will be linked to a *Personal Tax Account* so that many taxpayers will just need to check and validate (or correct) this information, without needing to provide most data the tax return normally asks for. Only those who receive income, or incur tax deductible expenses, that HMRC do not know about from other sources, will need to provide additional information (as at present for most data). Taxpayers will be able to do this at any point in the year to update their account. It is proposed that this new approach will enable taxpayers to be able to pay their tax bill as they go – on a month by month basis if they wish.

The roll out of this new online account approach commenced in 2015/16. According to HMRC's 2018/19 Annual Report, 19 million people had been given access to their personal tax account by July 2019 and every small business customer had access to their own equivalent online account – called their *Business Tax Account*.

The plan proposes complete roll out country wide to all taxpayers over the next few years. The extension of this project beyond the pilot has been delayed for small businesses but all businesses that pay VAT (more than 1.2 million business) started to use this process in April 2019 to report their VAT returns online. All businesses that pay income or corporation tax will be eventually included. This is currently expected to be in operation by April 2023. Sole traders and landlords with income over £10,000 will join MTD in April 2024.

The HMRC Guide to personal tax accounts can be found here:

http://www.hmrc.gov.uk/courses/syob4/pta_guide/

More information on HMRC's plans for digital tax management can be found in their 'Making Tax Digital' strategy paper at:

https://www.gov.uk/government/publications/making-tax-digital

Table 2.1: Estimated number of UK taxpayers
(Source: HMRC website - Number of taxpayers and registered traders, Numbers: thousands)

	Income Tax	Corporation Tax	Capital Gains Tax[2]	Inheritance Tax[3]
2021/22	32,700[1,4]	NA	NA	37[1,4,5]
2020/21	31,600[1,4]	NA	NA	31[1,4,5]
2019/20	31,300[1,4]	1,590	265	29[1,4,5]
:	:	:	:	:
2015/16	31,000	1,345[4]	263[4]	29
:				
2000/01	29,300	520	200	24
:	:	:	:	:
1988/99	25,200	355	150	29
:	: :	:	:	
1983/84	24,000	230	115	30
:	: :	:	:	
1978/79	25,900	185	225	43
:	: :	:	:	
1973/74	23,100	175	285	47

[1] Projected estimates based upon using economic assumptions consistent with the OBR's March 2022 Economic and Fiscal Outlook.

[2] After 1990/91 married couples count as two if both have CGT liabilities as a result of independent taxation. Prior to this they only counted as one.

[3] Figures show the number of death estates paying inheritance tax, capital transfer tax or estate duty and the number of lifetime transfers paying tax.

4   Provisional

5   The transferable nil rate band introduced in October 2007 led to a significant reduction in the number of
     inheritance tax payers during 2007-08 and 2008-09. The introduction of the residence nil rate band in
     2017-18 reduced the number of estates liable to inheritance tax from 2016-17.

Table 2.1 summarises details of the number of UK taxpayers over nearly 50 years. It shows the number of people or entities paying the key four direct UK taxes assessed by self assessment. Inheritance taxpayer numbers had been falling year on year because of a large extra exemption that came into effect from April 2018 (the residence nil-rate band) but have increased subsequently.

Tax payments

2.5   Whilst the new digital account system proposes to eventually bring tax payments for different taxes together into one single bill, the current process for paying taxes due varies for the different types of taxes. For income tax, as we will see in more detail in Chapter 4, tax that is not collected throughout the year through deductions at source, or from your employer via pay as you earn (PAYE), is paid in instalments with an interim payment on 31 July during the tax year and a final payment on 31 January following the end of the relevant tax year. Capital gains tax is also mainly payable on 31 January following the end of the tax year. Companies' tax payments vary depending on their size; large companies pay tax in quarterly instalments (two during the course of the tax year and two after it has ended, and since 1 April 2019 earlier for very large companies) whereas small companies pay their entire tax bill 9 months after the end of their tax year (see Chapter 9 for more details). VAT for most traders is payable on a quarterly basis, although there are some variations for both very small and very large taxpayers (see Chapter 10).

Compliance checks

2.6   The merger of the former two revenue departments into HMRC led to a number of procedures that now apply to all the different types of tax that they administer. Under the self assessment system, taxpayers file their tax returns and do their own tax computation. HMRC accepts this information (and the payment of tax) at face value in the first instance, but then has the right to check that the information and calculations provided are correct.

Compliance checks apply to income tax, capital gains tax, national insurance contributions, VAT and PAYE, as well as student loans. HMRC provide online guidance explaining how the system of compliance checks works. HMRC can ask for information or documents by sending what is known as an 'information notice'. There are penalties for not supplying the information requested in such a notice. HMRC can also ask for information about a taxpayer's affairs from other people and if necessary, can visit the taxpayer either with a pre-arranged visit or sometimes unannounced.

If the result of a check is that the taxpayer has to pay additional tax, he or she will also have to pay interest on the additional tax not paid at the right time and may be subject to penalties.

HMRC have recently been carrying out a greater number of compliance checks and make use of a number of digital channels to gather information. In particular, the *Connect* tool allows HMRC to pull together a vast array of information about taxpayers with the aim of detecting undeclared income.

Penalties

2.7   The UK has a penalty regime that applies to all the taxes under the control of HMRC. Penalties are charged as an additional percentage of the tax involved (i.e. in addition to paying the tax due) and are linked to taxpayer behaviour. There are three levels of culpability as follows:

- *Careless* – where the taxpayer has failed to take 'reasonable care' (maximum penalty 30%).
- *Deliberate but not concealed* – where the inaccuracy is deliberate but the taxpayer has not tried to hide it from HMRC (maximum penalty 70%);
- *Deliberate and concealed* – where the taxpayer has made a deliberate mistake, and made arrangements to hide it from HMRC (maximum penalty 100%).

In deciding whether a taxpayer has taken reasonable care, the penalty system considers their particular situation, so, for example, HMRC expects a different standard of care from a large company than from a low income wage earner.

There is provision for the penalty to be discounted if the taxpayer makes an unprompted disclosure. In this situation the three levels of penalty become 0%, 20% and 30% for the three levels of culpability listed above.

Under self assessment, taxpayers have a duty to make enquiries if their tax position is not clear. In a 2013 case, *Timothy Harding v HMRC* [FTC 56/2013], the taxpayer received a payment when his employment was terminated early, and although he did try to check his tax situation using an article published on a reputable website, the Upper Tribunal held that the penalty for carelessness imposed by HMRC should stand.

Finance Act 2017 introduced two new rules relating to penalties for tax avoidance. The first rule says that taxpayers cannot rely on advice to demonstrate that they have taken reasonable care to avoid inaccuracy, and is designed to discourage entering into tax avoidance schemes. The second provides for penalties for enablers of abusive tax avoidance arrangements that are later defeated in court. We look at tax avoidance more closely in Chapter 11.

Disputing tax liabilities

2.8   What happens if the taxpayer and HMRC disagree about the amount of tax payable? Before changes introduced in 2009, a system to address tax disputes had been in operation since the end of the 1700's. This system involved initially appealing to so called 'General Commissioners' (non-experts operating part time and aided by tax accountants or lawyers) and if resolution wasn't found at this level, a further appeal to 'Special Commissioners' (legally trained experts who dealt with appeals or more complex cases) was available.

In April 2009 a tribunals system was created that now applies across many areas of the tax system (and more widely) in the UK to address disputes about tax liabilities. It has its own specialist judiciary and rules of procedure.

Importantly the tribunal system is independent of HMRC and appeal notices are sent directly to the Tribunals Service (they used to be sent to HMRC under the previous system). If a taxpayer disputes an assessment of tax, he or she has 30 days in which to appeal. There are two tiers of tax tribunal; a first tier tribunal that will hear the less complex cases, and an upper tribunal that will hear more complex cases, and also appeals from decisions of the first tier tribunal.

Appeals from the upper tribunal are to the Court of Appeal and then to the Supreme Court, but only on points of law, not questions of fact.

In 2007, HMRC introduced a Litigation and Settlement Strategy which describes the circumstances under which disputes can be settled, that is a tax liability agreed, without having to go to court.

HMRC also uses Alternative Dispute Resolution (ADR). ADR is common in the commercial world and has become HMRC's normal practice since 2013/14. This form of mediation might be appropriate, for example, where both HMRC and the taxpayer want to work collaboratively, but it is difficult to identify essential points of disagreement, or where a previously collaborative relationship has broken down. HMRC guidance contains a number of examples of cases that are suitable for mediation as a first step, rather than moving straight to litigation which is costly for both parties.

In August 2012, a Tax Assurance Commissioner was appointed, not to engage directly with taxpayers, but to oversee HMRC's decision making processes to make sure these are operated appropriately. The Commissioner produces an annual report to illustrate how their work is undertaken in a transparent way. In September 2012, a Tax Decision Review Board was established and in November of the same year, a Code of Governance for resolving disputes was published. These developments were partly in response to the criticism of HMRC's settlements with several large business taxpayers by the National Audit Office and the Public Accounts Committee that attracted very public criticism of the way some settlements had been arrived at.

Fiscal Fact

According to the latest Tax Assurance Commissioner's report, contained within HMRC's Annual Report 2021, in 2020-21 3,364 (6,808 in 2019-20) new appeals were made via the tribunal system. During the year (5,400 in 2019-20) were settled either by formal hearing or agreement before a hearing was required. Of the remainder, the outcome of appeal hearings (at first tier tribunal level) was:

Decided in HMRC's favour:	1,052
Decided partially in HMRC's favour	50
Decided in the taxpayer's favour	147

At the upper tribunal 53 tax appeal cases were heard in the year (43 found in HMRC's favour, with 23 more partially), 3 cases at the High Court (3 found in HMRC's favour), 18 cases at the Court of Appeal (9 found in HMRC's favour and 1 for the taxpayer) and 4 cases at the Supreme Court (2 found in HRMC's favour and 2 for the taxpayer).

Tax compliance

2.9   One of the key tasks of any revenue authority is to encourage taxpayers to comply with the tax rules and regulations. In an ideal world, the rules would be very clear, taxpayers would understand how much they have to pay, and would willingly pay the right amount at the right time. Unfortunately our world is not ideal, and the level of compliance among taxpayers is variable, to say the least.

There are many interesting research studies of tax compliance that try to understand what drives taxpayers to comply, or not comply, with the tax rules, and also what types of taxpayers are more likely not to comply. There has been a significant increase in the amount of research into taxpayer compliance in the past decade, and increasingly tax authorities around the world are sharing their experiences and ideas through fora such as the OECD.

A recent research study commissioned by HMRC (2019) considers the drivers of tax compliance behaviour among the wealthy and the ways that it can be improved. The study finds that wealthy individuals mainly use tax agents to manage their tax affairs and their tax behaviour reflects a balance between wanting to contribute to society, but being intolerant of an onerous tax regime.

The Tax Gap

2.10 HMRC calculates a 'tax gap' annually, as a way to monitor trends over time. The tax gap is the difference between the tax actually collected and the tax that should be collected (the theoretical liability). According to the 2022 report, the total tax gap is estimated to be £32bn in 2020/21, although it is admitted that all of the tax gap estimates for the different taxes are subject to error, and so need to be treated with some caution. It is important to note that the tax gap can never be completely eliminated.

The good news is that this gap is coming down from a peak of 7.5% of total tax liabilities in 2005/6 to 5.1% in 2020/21 (up from 4.9% in 2018/19 which was the lowest level at which it has been recorded)

For the VAT tax gap (estimated to be approximately £9bn or 7% of the theoretical VAT liability in 2020/21), and excise duty gap (estimated to be £3.5bn or 7.2% of theoretical excise tax liability in 2020/21), HMRC draws on national statistics such as household consumption figures, as well as internal data collected within HMRC. For personal income tax, national insurance contributions and capital gains tax, the gap is estimated to be approximately 12.7bn or 3.5% of theoretical liability. For corporation tax the gap is £5.6bn or 9.2% of theoretical liability.

HMRC uses a variety of data sources and techniques to arrive at the tax gap estimates, including random enquiries and data matching, which involves using data supplied by third parties such as banks to try to estimate undeclared income. This is difficult to do fully in the UK because not everyone has to fill in a tax return.

HMRC uses a risk based compliance strategy which means it tries to focus on areas of highest risk. This means identifying tax avoidance and evasion and those taxpayers who are most likely to engage in these activities. Tax evasion (where taxpayers deliberately omit or misrepresent information to reduce their tax liabilities), the hidden economy and criminal attacks, account for approximately 41% (or £13.2bn) of the net tax gap according to HMRC estimates.

HMRC are trying to organise their operations to minimise the tax gap, but at the same time to encourage as many taxpayers as possible to comply voluntarily with their tax obligations. As part of the process of trying to understand taxpayers better in order to make sure they are dealt with appropriately, HMRC is broken down into a number of specialist areas, including a high net worth individuals area, that focuses on very wealthy taxpayers, and a large business service that focuses on very large companies. It also 'segments' individual taxpayers into groups, recognising that not all taxpayers are out to avoid or evade their tax obligations.

Compliance costs

2.11   Compliance costs are the costs resulting from the need to comply with the tax rules such as paying for tax advice, employing someone to keep records for tax computations, time spent completing tax forms if you do it yourself or costs for paying someone else to do it for you, and so on. Such costs would not have been incurred if there was no tax to pay and so should be considered as part of the effective incidence of taxation. In 2005 the accounting firm KPMG undertook a study of compliance costs in the UK tax system. They discovered that these costs amount to around 0.45% of UK GDP (i.e. approximately £5 billion!). While this is a large amount of money, the situation in the UK is comparable to other developed countries where these costs are of a similar scale.

While all tax systems will produce some compliance costs, keeping them to a reasonable sum is a problem for any tax system and there are regular calls for these costs to be reduced. One possible way to do this is to make the tax system less complicated; therefore, hopefully, costing people less to comply with it. The Administrative Burden Advisory Board, was created in 2009 to look at, then implement, the best ways of achieving cost savings.

The Office of Tax Simplification (OTS) has also been targeting this issue since its creation in 2010. They produced a report in February 2012 providing suggestions to remove burdens that added significantly to tax compliance costs for small businesses where they thought these were unnecessary (OTS, 2012). At Budget 2012 the Treasury published a report, entitled 'Making tax easier, simpler and quicker for small businesses' on its planned responses to the initial suggestions of the OTS targeted at smaller businesses. (see Chapter 6 for details on the rules that were introduced following this report).

In 2018, the OTS (OTS 2018) produced recommendations for HMRC guidance to be improved to help taxpayers comply with the tax rules more easily, thus reducing compliance costs and in October 2019 they released a report detailing areas of complexity linked to 'life events' (getting married/divorced, having children, retiring etc) that they suggested should be addressed (OTS 2019). In the last year they have produced reports on making tax easier through smarter use of third party data (OTS 2021) and completed two reviews on ways to develop capital gains taxation (OTS 2020 & 2021b). The work of the OTS is currently being reviewed to look at whether its important work could be improved upon further.

Whenever new tax legislation to be administered by HMRC is introduced, a Tax Information and Impact Note (TIIN) is produced. In addition to showing the forecast tax revenue from the new rule, HMRC must also calculate the economic impact and the impact on individuals or households. This includes the cost to comply with the new rule. TIINs also record the impact on protected groups under the Equality Act 2010 and the impact on costs for business and civil society organisations. Finally, other impacts are recorded where relevant including the wider environmental impact and carbon assessment, and the impact on justice, competition and health.

Tax agents and advisers

2.12   In the UK, as in other countries, tax agents play an important role in the tax system. Tax agents are people who help taxpayers fulfil their tax obligations, and are sometimes referred to as tax intermediaries, because they operate between the taxpayer and HMRC. In recent years we have seen increasing attention being given to tax agents and how they operate. In the UK there is no formal requirement for tax agents to be registered with HMRC, but they are usually professionally qualified accountants or lawyers. It is estimated that around 30% of tax advisers are not members of a professional body.

Those tax agents that are members of professional bodies, must adhere to a code of conduct - the Professional Conduct in Relation to Taxation (PCRT). The guidance is prepared jointly with several professional bodies including Chartered Institute of Taxation (CIOT), ICAEW, ICAS and ACCA.

The PCRT states that the fundamental principles of professional conduct are as follows:

- Integrity;
- Objectivity;
- Professional competence and due care;
- Confidentiality; and
- Professional behaviour.

Fiscal Fact

According to the National Audit Office (2010), eight million UK taxpayers receive help from third parties in completing and filing their income and corporation tax returns each year. Around 43,000 professional tax agent firms, from international corporations to sole traders, help taxpayers to manage their tax affairs.

HMRC has been working on a Tax Agent Strategy, and related programme of activity, to enhance their relationship with tax agents. This has included developing an HMRC Standard for tax agents that aims to reach those advisers who are not members of a professional body. This standard does not go as far as the PCRT and contains three core principles: integrity, professional competency and professional behaviour.

An HMRC Tax agent blog (*https://taxagents.blog.gov.uk*) provides ongoing advice and support on a variety of issues and also access to a series of 'toolkits' to help agents identify the key areas where errors occur.

The HMRC Charter

2.13 Since 2009, it has been a legal requirement for HMRC to set out a Charter that must include the standards of behaviour and values that HMRC will aspire to. You can find the current version of the Charter, which was updated in November 2021 here:

https://www.gov.uk/government/publications/hmrc-charter/the-hmrc-charter.

In addition to setting out what each party can expect from the other, the HMRC Charter talks about keeping data secure and also what taxpayers can do if they believe these standards have not been adhered to. HMRC publish the indicators used to monitor performance, and performance data. There is also a Customer Experience Committee that monitors HMRC's performance against the Charter.

The language that is used is quite informal, suggesting that HMRC are an approachable department, in keeping with the view of taxpayers as being 'customers'. HMRC also elaborate on principles of support for customers who need extra help, for example low income and elderly customers.

HMRC Strategy

2.14 In the March 2020 Budget, the Chancellor set out the Government's intention to create a tax system fit for the 21st century. This led to a report entitled 'Building a trusted, modern tax administration system' in July 2021. The report focuses in particular on the advantages of digitalisation and technological innovation. It sets out a 10 year strategy covering the following areas:

- Making tax digital;
- Keeping pace with digital developments in other countries;
- Changing the frequency of reporting and payment of taxes;
- Changing the administration framework for example simplified registration processes and smarter use of data.

The process of developing a detailed strategy to achieve the overall aims will include wide consultation. HMRC recognises that modernising the UK's tax system should not be rushed and will entail incremental rather than radical reform. An important component is maintaining public trust in the way the tax system is administered.

Summary

In this chapter, we have extended our understanding of how the UK tax system works by looking at how it is administered by HMRC. As an organisation, HMRC has undergone considerable change in recent years, and continues to evolve to keep pace with modern developments not just in the UK, but overseas as well. Some of the administrative policies adopted by HMRC have been borrowed from other countries or from the research of supra national bodies such as the OECD, such as the segmentation of the taxpayer population so as to provide a different type of service or enforcement strategy to each category.

Before we move on to the detail of the individual taxes that make up the UK tax system in Chapters 4 onwards, in Chapter 3 we will first consider the nature of a good tax – if indeed any tax can be considered to be good – addressing firstly the principles of the design of tax systems. This means that you will be in a position to evaluate each of the UK's taxes according to these design principles.

Project areas

There are a number of areas covered in this chapter which would provide good material for projects. These include the following:

- exploring the effectiveness of a self assessment system for income tax assessment, and the impact the new digital accounts may have on taxpayer compliance and taxpaying behaviour,
- assessing the effectiveness of the Tribunals Service compared to the previous dual roles of the General and Special Commissioners,
- exploring what motivates taxpayers to comply, or not, with the tax rules and regulations,
- there has been significant work done over the last twenty years on assessing (as accurately as we can) the compliance costs of taxation. An exploration of how this can be done in practice by looking at this research would be an interesting project or dissertation.
- how tax gaps are measured and assessed – and the extent to which they provide a useful way to access the performance of tax administrations like the UK's.
- reviewing the performance of HMRC in its task of administering the UK tax system.

Discussion questions

1 What are the advantages and disadvantages of a system of self assessment under which taxpayers are responsible for working out their own tax liabilities?

2 What demographic characteristics play a role in tax compliance, for example, are women more or less likely to cheat on their taxes than men, or better educated taxpayers than uneducated taxpayers?

3 HMRC refer to taxpayers as 'customers'. What are the benefits for the department and for taxpayers of doing this?

4 What can be done in practice to address the tax gap?

5 What are the implications for taxpayers of being moved online for the management of their tax affairs and tax filing as part of the 'Making Tax Digital' processes?

Further reading

Dates in UK Tax System

J. Jeffrey-Cook, (2001), A year beginning on 6 April, *Taxation*, 5 April, p8.

Tax Administration

Sandford, C., M. Godwin & P. Hardwick, (1989), *Administrative and Compliance Costs of Taxation*. Fiscal Publications: Birmingham.

For more details of the administration of UK tax see the HMRC website (https://www.gov.uk/government/organisations/hm-revenue-customs).

Penalties

For the HMRC 2015 discussion document and other information – see https://www.gov.uk/government/consultations/hmrc-penalties-a-discussion-document

For a discussion of penalties in light of the introduction of 'Making Tax Digital' see: https://www.gov.uk/government/consultations/making-tax-digital-sanctions-for-late-submission-and-late-payment

Tax Compliance

Braithwaite, V., (2009), *Defiance in Taxation and Governance*, Edward Elgar: Cheltenham.

HMRC (2013), *Levelling the playing field: Compliance progress report – March 2013*, available at https://www.gov.uk/government/publications/levelling-the-tax-playing-field

HMRC (2019), *Researching the drivers of tax compliance behaviour among the wealthy and ways to improve it*, HMRC Research Report 537, available at: https://www.gov.uk/government/publications/researching-the-drivers-of-tax-compliance-behaviour-among-the-wealthy-and-ways-to-improve-it

HMRC (2022), *Measuring Tax Gaps 2022 edition: Tax gap estimates for 2020-21*, available at https://www.gov.uk/government/statistics/measuring-tax-gaps

Kirchler, E., (2007), *The Economic Psychology of Tax Behaviour*, Cambridge University Press: Cambridge.

Compliance Costs

Evans, C., Hasseldine, J., Lymer, A., Ricketts, R. & Sandford, C. (2017) *Compliance Costs (Chapter 11)* in Comparative Taxation: Why tax systems differ, Fiscal Publications: Birmingham.

Office of Tax Simplification (2012), Small business tax review – final report, available at:
  https://www.gov.uk/government/publications/small-business-tax-review

Office of Tax Simplification (2014), Review of employee benefits and expenses – final report, available at:
  https://www.gov.uk/government/publications/review-of-employee-benefits-and-expenses-final-report

Office of Tax Simplification (2017), Focus Paper – The OTS Complexity Project, – report available at:
  https://assets.publishing.service.gov.uk/government/uploads/system/uploads/attachment_data/file/603469/OTS_Focus_paper_on_complexity_final.pdf

Office of Tax Simplification (2018), Guidance for Taxpayers: a vision for the future, available at:
  https://assets.publishing.service.gov.uk/government/uploads/system/uploads/attachment_data/file/746076/OTS_Guidance_for_taxpayers_041018.pdf

Office of Tax Simplification (2019), Life events review: Simplifying tax for individuals, available at:
  https://assets.publishing.service.gov.uk/government/uploads/system/uploads/attachment_data/file/838130/Taxation_and_life_events_Oct_2019.pdf

Office of Tax Simplification (2020), Capital Gains Tax review – first report: Simplifying by design, available at:
https://www.gov.uk/government/publications/ots-capital-gains-tax-review-simplifying-by-design

Office of Tax Simplification (2021a), Making tax easier through smarter use of third party data, available at:
https://www.gov.uk/government/consultations/making-tax-easier-through-smarter-use-of-third-party-data

Office of Tax Simplification (2021b), Capital Gains Tax second report: Simplifying practical, technical and administrative issues, available at:
https://www.gov.uk/government/publications/ots-capital-gains-tax-review-simplifying-practical-technical-and-administrative-issues

Pope, J. (2002), *Administrative and compliance costs of international taxation*, in The International Tax System, Lymer, A. & J. Hasseldine (eds), Springer: Heidelberg.

Sandford, C. (1995), *Tax compliance costs measurement and policy*, Fiscal Publications: Birmingham.

Making Tax Digital

Overview of Making Tax Digital (updated 1 April 2022):
https://www.gov.uk/government/publications/making-tax-digital/overview-of-making-tax-digital

HMRC Charter

HMRC Charter:
https://www.gov.uk/government/publications/hmrc-charter

Tax Agents/Intermediaries

CIOT (2017), *Professional Conduct in Relation to Taxation (PCRT)*, available at:
https://www.tax.org.uk/professional-conduct-in-relation-to-taxation-pcrt

HMRC (2013), *Tax Agent Strategy*, available at:
https://www.gov.uk/government/publications/agents-strategy-an-overview

OECD (2008), *Study into the Role of Tax Intermediaries*, available at:
http://www.oecd.org/tax/administration/39882938.pdf

3 Principles of tax system design

Introduction

3.1 In Chapter 1 we considered the objectives of a tax system and determined that taxation is a tool used by government to manage the economy, regulate and develop society and provide public goods. We also noted that the nature of any particular tax system, which consists of a number of different types of tax, is constantly changing with the changing views of society as a whole.

In this chapter we will first discuss a number of ideas and concepts which are relevant to understanding how to design a tax system. We will then identify and explore the desirable characteristics of a tax system that underpin its design. These principles apply to any tax system - not just the UK's. Once we have done this we will evaluate various bases of taxation to illustrate the application of this theory in practice.

At the end of this chapter you will be able to:

- outline the key issues of tax system design;
- state and discuss the five desirable characteristics of a tax system;
- state the range of tax bases from which a tax system may be built; and
- discuss the merits and limitations of each of these tax bases.

Key issues in taxation design

3.2 In this section we will explore the key issues of tax system design that all tax systems must keep in balance to function properly:

- What to tax?
- Who to tax?
- What kind of rate structure?
- How should the tax burden be distributed? and
- What effect do taxes have on taxpayer behaviour?

What to tax?

3.3 We saw in the historical review of taxation in Chapter 1 that taxes have been imposed on all kinds of activities, goods and services throughout history.

The classification of taxes, however, comes down to three broad groups:

Income Taxes	taxes on a taxpayer's income earned or received between specific points in time;
Wealth/Capital Taxes	taxes on a taxpayer's accumulated wealth, its transfer or on its changing value;
Consumption Taxes	taxes on a taxpayer's spending.

The rules used to decide what is taxed, and what is not, under each of these categories is called the *tax base*. For example, what categories of income a taxpayer is taxed on will form the income tax base, and so on. For each of these bases, decisions must be made about what, if any, individual elements of the base should be taxed, exempted from tax, or relieved from tax in some other way.

In the case of income tax, the Government may choose to make income from particular activities, or for particular types of potential taxpayers, exempt from tax, thereby removing it from the tax base. For example, if an economic objective the Government set itself was to encourage people to save more, interest income could be exempted from tax, or be relieved in part, so a lower tax rate was paid on it than might otherwise be the case. As taxpayers who earn interest would then keep more of it for themselves they are likely to be incentivised to save more than they may have before the tax rule change.

The Government may also allow reductions in tax liability for particular types of expenditure. In some countries, (but not the UK anymore) taxpayers are allowed to deduct mortgage interest in calculating their income tax base, to encourage home ownership over other forms of accommodation, such as renting.

Wealth taxes can be difficult for governments to manage, in part because finding a correct value for assets can sometimes be hard. Some countries choose not to tax wealth ownership at all, and some do so using an annual wealth tax at a low rate. Many countries only tax wealth at the time it is transferred from one person to another, for example when a taxpayer dies or gives an asset away, or when an asset is sold and a profit (gain) is made. We have two taxes in the UK that cover these three areas – Inheritance Tax in the first two cases, and Capital Gains Tax in the third. We will look at both of these in Chapter 8. Governments that impose wealth taxes may choose not to tax particular types of asset, for example, a taxpayers' main home is not part of the tax base for wealth tax in many countries – although they often have to pay tax on second homes if they are wealthy enough to afford one!).

Consumption taxes may be comprehensive, which means they are imposed on the full range of goods and services that people buy. In most countries, however, there are certain items of consumption that are taxed differently or not at all. For example, it is common to exempt necessities such as basic food items from the tax base.

Tax bases also change over time as their rules of application are developed in response to a variety of factors including economic and social change.

Balancing the rules of the three tax bases to form the whole tax system is an important task carried out by the Government. Later in this chapter we will look at how the Government goes about deciding how this balance should be set, and how it changes over time. We look at the theoretical arguments for each of these three tax bases later in the chapter.

As we saw in Chapter 1, the primary current UK taxes under each of the bases are:

Income Taxes	For individuals: Income Tax
	For companies: Corporation Tax
Wealth/Capital Taxes	Capital Gains Tax
	Inheritance Tax
	Stamp Duty
	Council Tax
	Business Rates
Consumption Taxes	Value Added Tax
	Excise Duties (e.g. on alcohol, petrol or tobacco)

Who to tax?

3.4 In addition to deciding what to tax, Governments also have to decide who should be responsible for paying a tax, i.e., who should the taxpayer be for any particular tax? This is sometimes referred to as determining the tax 'unit'. For income tax, the taxpayer could be an individual or a family. If the Government chooses to tax a family unit, decisions then must be made about what 'family' means for this purpose. The individual is more commonly used as the tax unit for income taxation therefore to avoid this being needed. However, this decision in turn then has other implications – such as what to do about the fact that married couples can combine their economic decision making to potentially be more tax effective than two individuals acting independently. Decisions are also required about whether to impose a tax on other legal entities, such as companies and partnerships.

Tax rate structure

3.5   Let's now think about how a tax rate structure might work. A tax rate structure will either be:

- *proportional* – the rate of tax to be paid increases directly in line with increases in the tax base;
- *progressive* – the rate of tax to be paid increases faster than the increase in the tax base; or
- *regressive* – the rate of tax to be paid increases more slowly than increases in the tax base.

In most tax systems, including the UK's, there is a generally accepted principle that income tax should be progressive, i.e. taxpayers with larger incomes should pay a higher rate of tax than taxpayers with smaller incomes. Also, it is likely to be desirable that once all taxes that a taxpayer must pay are taken into account, that the system should overall also be progressive.

To be a progressive tax there doesn't necessarily have to be a steadily rising tax rate as the tax base rises. A tax can still be progressive even if it only has two rates of tax.

Activity

Ahmed and Belinda have income of £10,000 and £20,000 respectively. Both are liable for income tax and are entitled to a tax-free threshold of £5,000 after which the tax rate is 20%. How much income tax will Ahmed and Belinda pay?

Feedback

Ahmed will pay £1,000 ((£10,000 – 5,000) × 20%) tax. This equates to 10% of his income. Belinda will pay £3,000 ((£20,000 – 5,000) × 20%) tax or 15% of her income. Belinda pays a higher overall percentage of her income in tax because both have a fixed level of tax-free income (£5,000) before starting to pay tax. Belinda has to pay three times the tax that Ahmed has to pay, yet her income is only twice as much as his (i.e. the tax rate is rising faster than the rate of income). This simple tax system is therefore a progressive one even with only two rates (0% and 20%).

A proportional tax is where there is only one tax rate for all – irrespective of the level of the tax base. In turn a regressive system would produce the opposite effect to the progressive system – as the tax base (such as income) rose, the rate of tax would become lower. For example, in such a system those on higher incomes would pay a lower rate of tax on average to those on lower incomes.

A good rule of thumb for assessing whether a tax rate is progressive, proportionate or regressive is to compare the *average rate of tax (ART)* with the *marginal rate of tax (MRT)* faced by the taxpayer. The average rate is found by dividing the amount of tax payable by the value of the tax base. The marginal rate of tax is the rate the taxpayer would have to pay on an extra £1 of the tax base.

If the average rate of tax is less than the marginal rate of tax the system is progressive (at least for that particular taxpayer at that point). If the average rate of tax equals the marginal rate of tax the tax system is proportional, and if the average rate of tax is greater than the marginal rate of tax it is regressive.

To illustrate this with the example above, for Ahmed (with £10,000 income), the average rate of tax is 10%, and the marginal rate of tax is 20% (as he would pay 20p extra in tax if he earned £1 more) so the rate system is progressive for Ahmed (10% < 20%) on their current tax base. The same applies for Belinda (15% < 20%).

An exercise illustrating the relationship between personal allowances and progressivity can be found on the website. You could now attempt it to further develop this idea of tax burdens.

Distribution of the tax burden

3.6   The previous section was concerned with the structure of the tax rate scale that is applied to a tax base for a particular taxpayer. But there are other tax factors to take into consideration, for example tax relief on particular payments made by the taxpayer, or the combined effects with other taxes, when considering the burden of taxes. Even though the rules are the same for all, the tax system rules may affect one taxpayer differently to another. For example, not everyone will have the same income, and some may be allowed tax reliefs others can't claim.

The *tax burden* is the degree to which a tax, specific collection of taxes, or a tax system viewed in its entirety, affects a taxpayer or group of taxpayers. It is a question of who in society bears the impact, this is also called the *incidence*, of tax. Governments may try to spread this burden evenly throughout society, or may instead decide that it is fairer if the wealthy in society are asked to bear a higher burden than those who are poorer.

Progressivity and Regressivity

3.7   Confusingly, we also use the terms progressive and regressive when we talk about a tax and its burden or incidence. A progressive tax, or tax system, is one where wealthy taxpayers bear a higher burden of tax overall, not just a higher rate of tax, although of course these two things are connected.

A regressive tax on the other hand, is one that places a heavier burden on poorer taxpayers than wealthy taxpayers. For example, unlike most income taxes that are usually designed to be progressive, VAT is generally considered to be a regressive tax because everybody pays the same rate (most items are taxed at 20%). This means that poorer taxpayers will spend a higher proportion of their total income on VAT than richer people (who are usually able to save a higher percentage of their income and therefore pay less VAT as a proportion of their total income). In the UK, this problem is balanced to some extent by policies to reduce VAT on some essential goods, such as applying a zero rate (i.e. 0%) of VAT on most food. However, this zero-rate taxing does not apply to all basic items and therefore VAT is generally considered to be a regressive tax. We will explore more how the UK VAT system works in Chapter 10.

Taxpayer behaviour

3.8   As we discussed in Chapter 1 in considering the objectives of taxation, alongside raising revenue for Governments, tax systems can also be used to try and change taxpayers' behaviours in desired ways because people will react to changes in the taxes they are faced with.

It might seem strange, but we actually know very little about how taxpayers behave in response to the introduction of new taxes, or changes to the tax system. There are academic studies that attempt to match taxpayer behaviour with tax changes, but few are conclusive. This is perhaps to be expected because modern society is so complex. Creating even a moderately complex tax system makes it very difficult to comprehensively map the impact of changes in taxes and taxpayer responses, and even harder to predict this in advance as changes are designed. This makes designing tax systems a challenging activity. It is never entirely clear how people will react to any changes made.

A good example of the use of the tax system to influence taxpayers' behaviour in a positive way is the switch to taxing company cars by reference to their level of CO_2 emissions (rather than business miles driven as was previously the case). This made it more expensive to drive higher polluting cars relative to lower polluting cars for the same mileage.

When the Government introduced this new approach in 2002, it hoped that companies providing cars for their employees to drive would switch to using lower emission cars, which would be beneficial for the environment. Recent statistics suggest that this has been successful to some extent. By 2019 average emissions for new cars were down to 127.9g/km a huge 29% reduction on the 2000 levels and 20% lower than average cars in use. It certainly seems that the change in rules, working along with opinion changes in the wider society, has produced the desired impact of encouraging employers to provide greener vehicles for their employees. It has contributed effectively, with other initiatives, to make the whole sector more conscious of emission levels of cars. (You can find out more detail on company car taxation in Chapter 5)

The 'sugar tax' (or Soft Drinks Industry Levy to give it its proper title) on added sugar in drinks, commenced in April 2018. This is another example of how the Government uses a tax to try to change people's behaviour. The levy was initially set at 18p/litre for drinks with more than 5g/ml of added sugar, rising to 24p/litre where there is more than 8g/ml of added sugar. The Government hoped that this extra tax, increasing the price of these drinks compared to others, will mean fewer people will consume them. Further, it was hoped this will then motivate the drinks industry to lower the sugar content in their drinks. Together these effects should, it is hoped, lower the overall levels of sugar consumed in the UK. In October 2020, HMRC reported that soft drinks manufacturers and traders have paid an extra £719 million in tax since its introduction and that many manufacturers had indeed reduced the sugar content of many of their drinks in advance of the introduction of the tax.

Fiscal Fact

Just under 94% of Sugar Tax payments were declared at the higher rate during 2018/19, rising to just over 94% in 2019/20 and 96% in 2020/21. [Source: HMRC UK Soft Drink Industry Levy Statistics – September 2021]

Unfortunately, taxpayers don't always behave in the way the Government expects them to. An example in the UK of an unexpected change in taxpayer behaviour was the increased use of companies as the trading structure chosen for operating a business to take advantage of the lower tax rates that apply to corporations as compared to individuals. Following the introduction of a new 10% rate (later reduced to 0%) for companies with low profits, there was a significant increase in the number of businesses that switched to trading as companies. The intention of the policy was to encourage entrepreneurship, but many businesses switched only to reduce their tax bill, and so eventually the policy was reversed.

Tax avoidance and evasion

People have found imaginative ways of circumventing a liability to tax for as long as taxes have been used. Some evade tax, for instance by smuggling goods into the country from abroad rather than paying the correct import tax. Others may under-declare their incomes, or overstate their expenses, to reduce their income tax bill.

Fiscal Fact

The number of higher rate income taxpayers increased from 1.7 million in 1990/91 to 2.1 million in 1996/97. It is estimated this number will rise to 4.3 million in 2021/22 [Source: HMRC Statistics – Table 2.1]

Tax evasion is illegal and is punishable by fines and/or imprisonment. Tax avoidance on the other hand is legal and involves arranging your activities in ways that will reduce your tax bill. Some acceptable tax avoidance, sometimes called tax 'planning', is simple. For instance, saving money in an ISA (Individual Savings Account) rather than an ordinary building society account, has the result that income from the account is always paid without being subject to tax (subject to certain limits as we will see later) and therefore not even needing to be reported to HMRC on tax returns. This, therefore, is a sensible, and fully Government supported, arrangement which enables taxpayers to avoid paying tax on investment interest received.

Attitudes to tax avoidance have changed over the years and vary even at the same point in time depending on the perspective from which the question is considered. Indeed, the boundary between acceptable and (what to some will be) unacceptable tax avoidance is an issue of constant debate (we will explore this further in Chapter 11). Some tax avoidance schemes are highly artificial and involve changing the nature of transactions or creating artificial transactions to take advantage of concessions in the tax law. These are generally considered to fall into the unacceptable tax avoidance category (i.e. are likely to be proven not to be legal if challenged in the courts – HMRC has a very good track record in defeating these in court, although not with 100% success). Others are not so clearly on the wrong side of the boundary and may be viewed differently as to whether or not they are acceptable by taxpayers and the tax administrators.

Another topical example is exploiting the different tax rules that apply to employees and consultants (who are self-employed or use a small company structure with themselves as the main/only employee). This use of what are called 'personal service' companies, continues to be a tax avoidance issue of concern to HMRC, which we look at in more detail in Chapter 11.

In the next section we will review in more detail the foundation principles of tax system design that help us to find solutions to some of the problems faced in creating a working tax system.

The desirable characteristics of a tax system

3.9   Prior to the late eighteenth century, taxation was used mainly to raise revenue to fund military campaigns and defend the nation state against their enemies, whoever they happened to be at the time. Taxation was viewed as being the price paid for the protection of the state. Thomas Hobbes wrote in his famous book *Leviathan* in 1651:

> "For the impositions that are laid on the people by the sovereign power are nothing else but the wages due to them that hold the public sword, to defend private men in the exercise of their several trades and callings."

By the late eighteenth century, at the start of the industrial revolution, more consideration was being given to the ways in which taxes were raised and the most appropriate forms of tax to create effective tax systems.

Adam Smith was one of a number of early thinkers on this topic who considered the principles of how to design an effective tax system, and in his book, *The Wealth of Nations*, published in 1776, he outlined four desirable characteristics for a tax system:

1. "The subjects of every state ought to contribute to the support of the Government, in proportion to their respective abilities; that is in proportion to the revenue which they respectively enjoy under the protection of the state.

2. The tax which each individual is bound to pay ought to be certain, and not arbitrary.

3. Every tax ought to be levied at the time, or in the manner, most convenient for the contributor to pay it."

4. Every tax ought to be so contrived as both to take out, and keep out, of the pockets of the people, as little as possible over and above what it brings into the public treasury of the state. A tax may either take out or keep out of the pockets of the people a great deal more than it brings into the public treasury, and in four ways: a) by the number of officers who levy it; b) by obstructing the industry of the people; c) by penalties incurred in attempting to evade the tax; d) by subjecting the people to the frequent visits and examinations of the tax-gatherers."

It must be remembered, however, that at the time Adam Smith was writing, there was no income tax in Britain, so his comments are largely made in the context of a tax system made up predominately of capital/wealth and consumption taxes. In more modern terms these 'Canons of Taxation', as they became known, can be re-stated as:

1. *Equity*: a tax should be seen to be fair in its impact on all individuals. Taxes should be levied according to people's taxable capacity.

2. *Certainty*: taxes should not be arbitrary, the taxpayer should know his or her tax liability and when and where to pay it.

3. *Convenience*: it should be easy for the taxpayer to pay what they owe.

4. *Efficiency*: the tax system should not have an impact on the allocation of resources and it should be cheap to administer. Taxes which are too costly for the tax authority to administer should be avoided as much as possible. Costs to governments include administration costs, the cost of chasing up delinquent taxpayers through audits and the like, and the costs of considering disputes with taxpayers over the way in which the tax laws operate.

Other writers have subsequently proposed further characteristics to add to this list. Two common additions are *simplicity* and *flexibility*. Designing for simplicity would suggest that, where possible, the tax system should have as little complexity as possible (e.g. not having either elaborate nor large numbers of exceptions for particular activities or personal characteristics of the taxpayer). It is important for a tax to be simple to understand so that a taxpayer can easily calculate his or her liability.

Aiming for flexibility suggests that a tax system should be established in such a way as to be able to cope with changing economic circumstances over time without requiring substantial changes.

A problem with desirable characteristic lists, as given above, is that their authors usually do not order them in any practically useful way. Should each of the characteristics be allocated equal weight in the design of the tax system, or are some more important than others? Are some of the characteristics so important that any successful system of tax must have them? What happens when two desirable characteristics conflict with each other? We need to consider each of these characteristics in more detail before attempting to answer these questions.

Equity

3.10 A tax which is not seen to be equitable, or fair, is usually resented by the individuals asked to pay it and therefore equity is an important constituent of any tax system - as a government clearly needs people to pay the taxes they charge them with or the whole system will grind to a halt.

There are two aspects to the fairness of a tax system - *horizontal equity* and *vertical equity*:

- a tax system is horizontally equitable if taxpayers with equal taxable capacity bear the same tax burden;
- a tax system has vertical equity if those with greater capacity to pay tax bear a higher tax burden.

Horizontal equity

3.11 We have two problems of definition when considering horizontal equity. Firstly, how will we identify taxpayers with equal taxable capacity? Two individuals doing the same job for the same money with the same personal circumstances are likely to have the same taxable capacity in most tax systems, but how do you compare the taxable capacity of an individual, who has earned income, with another, who is not working but has substantial wealth? Equally, an individual who prefers to spend their leisure time drinking alcohol incurs a greater tax liability (because alcohol attracts VAT and excise duty) than an individual who spends the same amount of money on trips to the theatre, as this isn't as heavily taxed (only VAT, not excise duty, is charged on theatre tickets), regardless of their relative taxable capacities.

The second problem of definition relates to ensuring that in practice equal amounts of tax are paid by individuals with the same taxable capacity. For example, suppose we consider two individuals with the same lifetime income, one of whom earns the average UK income for each year of his working life of 40 years while the other earns 20 times as much as the average for only two years of her working life (i.e. both earn the same income in total). Under a progressive income tax system, like the one in operation in the UK at present, the first taxpayer will pay less tax than the second as the second taxpayer will pay a higher rate of tax on their income on average. For an income tax to have full horizontal equity it would therefore need to be based on the lifetime income of the taxpayer not on incomes from year to year. This would be difficult, if not impossible, to put into practice, and would, in turn, raise further knock-on difficulties. For example, how should individuals with different life spans be taxed? Women generally have a longer life expectancy than men. If income is to be spread over a taxpayer's lifetime should women pay less tax than men on their taxable capacity because they will need to support themselves for more years?

Vertical equity

3.12 What about vertical equity? Achieving this is also difficult in practice. There are at least three layers to this problem. To implement a tax system with vertical equity we must first decide who, in principle, should pay tax at higher rates. Then we must decide how much higher that rate should be than the rates paid by other taxpayers, and finally we must devise a tax system which achieves these objectives for the full variety of taxpayers.

Taxable capacity

3.13 An individual may be considered to have a greater taxable capacity or to have a higher level of economic well-being or to receive more benefits from government spending. Any of these criteria might be used to identify individuals who should pay the higher rate of taxation. However, which, or which combination, of these criteria should be used? So far, we have assumed that it is easy to determine what a person's taxable capacity is, so that we can make judgements about horizontal and vertical equity. In practice, however, it is extremely difficult to decide what factors should be taken into account in working out a person's taxable capacity. Most often we use the notion of 'ability to pay', which links directly to Adam Smith's notion of 'respective abilities'.

Ability to pay

3.14 There are some practical difficulties involved in measuring ability to pay.

Activity

What factors should be taken into account when measuring a person's ability to pay taxes?

Feedback

The first factor you probably thought of is the person's income level. But using this then raises further questions about how people earn their income. For example, suppose two individuals undertake the same job but the first chooses to work only the basic required hours, and spends more leisure time in their garden, while the second chooses to work overtime each week instead. If income alone is used to determine 'ability to pay' then the second individual will pay more tax than the first. But both employees had the same opportunity to earn extra money so is it really fair that one of them should pay more tax than the other? If we could assess the ability to earn an income, instead of simply taxing what is actually earned, then both could be made to pay the same amount of tax.

If we want to use the ability to pay as our criteria for assessing how much tax someone should pay we must therefore first decide whether we will use actual income or some measure of potential income. In practice, of course, it is actual income that is taxed because of the practical difficulties of reliably determining potential income. But even if we settle for only being able to tax the actual income of taxpayers, we will have still further problems with achieving vertical equity.

Suppose two individuals have the same income but the first saves money in order to provide for retirement while the second spends money as it is earned and depends on the state for support in their old age. The first individual will probably pay tax on the returns on savings, and so could well pay more tax in total than the second individual, while the second receives more benefits from the state in their old age. Can this be considered to be equitable? It is unlikely that, put this way, the first individual will agree!

In answering the above Activity question, you may also have considered a person's stock of wealth as part of their ability to pay. Some people are known to be "asset rich, but income poor" (for example, a person who may own and live in a large house with no mortgage, but whose only source of income may be government benefits), which raises the question of whether wealth holdings should be counted in deciding what ability to pay is.

What about family circumstances? There is an argument that a single person with no dependents has a larger capacity to pay tax than one who has numerous dependents, maybe a non-working partner and several children for example. There may be an argument that this should be factored into decisions about how much tax burden he or she should bear.

As a result of these difficulties in working out how to assess people's taxable capacity using a concept of ability to pay, both horizontal and vertical equity are therefore difficult to achieve in practice – even if in theory they sound appropriate.

Fiscal Fact

According to the Institute for Fiscal Studies, the top 10% of taxpayers received 34% of the pre-tax income of taxpayers and provided 61% of the revenue.

See https://ifs.org.uk/taxlab/taxes-explained/income-tax-explained.

The benefit principle

3.15 An alternative approach to the use of 'ability to pay' to achieve equity is to try to relate tax charged to the benefit received from the state. This implies creating a tax system where those who benefit most from the services provided by a government should pay the most tax. This might sound fair in principle but proves difficult to achieve practically.

In practice there are relatively few activities which can be effectively taxed using the benefit approach. For example, many services provided by a government cannot be opted out of if someone does not want to receive the benefit. Defence or law and order are, for example, benefits which are impossible for a citizen to choose whether to consume or not (these types of services or goods are referred to as *public goods*).

On the other hand, it may be undesirable for some services to be withheld from citizens who do not contribute to their cost, even if it were feasible. For example, there was a time when homeowners and businesses could subscribe to the fire service in the same way as a motorist can choose to join the roadside assistance agencies (like the AA or the RAC) today. While on the surface it seems this could work – the fire service would only show up for subscribers – however, if a non-subscriber suffered a fire and the fire services did not put the fire out it could spread to neighbours who had paid to have their property protected. A public service to put out fires for all makes more sense practically. In addition, it is likely to be unacceptable to the community as a whole that some members of society are not helped by the fire services when they are in need, for example, those who cannot otherwise afford to make a private contribution. Nowadays, this service is therefore provided largely as a public good.

Further problems with achieving equity via a benefit approach includes issues with how to value benefits received, over what time scale do you try to measure the benefit (e.g. over their whole life or only part of it?) and also what does this do to the redistribution objective of a government (an important element of the objectives for a tax system as we discussed in Chapter 1).

It therefore seems difficult to imagine that a significant part of the tax system could be organised on the basis of assessing, and taxing, benefit received. Taxes which are raised to pay for specific (usually predefined) activities are termed *earmarked* or *hypothecated* taxes. In the past they have been unpopular with the Treasury as it limits how they can use tax revenues received. We therefore have seen little use of such taxes in recent tax history.

However, there are several examples of hypothecated taxes in the UK. For example, Vehicle Excise Duties (VED) were originally intended to fund highway construction and maintenance. In practice, the receipts from these duties are now used for general expenditure i.e. they are no longer hypothecated.

In the past proposals have been outlined for the National Health Service (NHS) to be funded by way of a hypothecated tax on the basis that taxpayers would be willing to pay more taxes if a clear link between the tax and health care could be established. A new hypothecated tax of this kind was proposed by the then Chancellor, Kenneth Clarke, in his November 1993 budget but this was never implemented. The 2002 Budget, however, picked up on this idea, and announced a rise from April 2003 in National Insurance Contributions to pay for some of the growth in the NHS. More recently, the Government has introduced a new Health and Social Care Levy, initially implemented as an uplift in National Insurance Contributions. Presumably this was more politically acceptable than an increase in other taxes such as VAT or income tax.

The congestion charge now in operation in London (and more recently several other cities in the UK) is yet another example of a hypothecated tax as money raised from car users in the centre of London from this charge, over and above the cost of providing the collection service itself, is supposedly spent directly on improvements to the city's infrastructure and public transport system rather than paying for other services the Greater London Authority is responsible for.

The concept of equity is complex and we have done little more than introduce the subject in this section, however, you should now be able to see that it is an important concept that should be considered when examining the effectiveness of any tax system.

Certainty

3.16 Having explored the desirable characteristic of equity, and the difficulties that arise in putting it into practice, we will next examine the nature of certainty as a feature of good tax system design.

A country's citizens need to be fully informed about who will have to pay the taxes in the tax system and when they will have to be paid (called the *incidence of tax*). Taxes where the incidence is clear are to be preferred over taxes where there is disagreement and uncertainty over the ultimate payer of the tax and when the tax must be paid.

Under this criterion, as we will see in Chapter 9, corporation tax could be considered to be a poor tax, for example, because it is unclear whether the shareholders, employees, customers or others bear the ultimate burden of the tax. It is also argued by some that individuals are more aware of how much income tax they pay than how much VAT they pay, making income tax more certain than VAT. We can use the term '*salience*' to describe awareness of the tax burden, and say that income tax is more salient than VAT.

To achieve full certainty in designing a tax, the complete tax consequences of any transaction should be known in advance of the transaction being undertaken. It is difficult to achieve this in practice. This is due to both problems with interpreting the rules (particularly grey areas of the law), but also as rules need to change from time to time (e.g. because the ideas develop of how best to tax or economic conditions alter and so on) so perfect certainty can't be assured.

This characteristic has an important impact on how tax systems evolve over time. In part, because of the need to consider certainty when designing tax systems, tax rule changes are only rarely made retrospectively.

If imposing taxes retrospectively regularly occurred in a tax system, then certainty would be significantly decreased. A good example of how retrospective taxes can upset taxpayers was the suggestion to increase Vehicle Excise Duties on the most polluting cars that was announced in the 2007 Pre-Budget. These plans were to impose increased duties on all cars over a certain engine capacity . People who had already made the choice to own such cars were going to have to pay extra taxes they were not expecting to have to pay when they bought them. This rarely meets with taxpayer approval.

Certainty is therefore an important characteristic but tax systems do have to change from time to time and will often affect at least some previous decisions people have made.

We will consider the question of incidence more fully in Chapter 14, once you have learned more about how the UK tax system works in practice.

Convenience

3.17 The third 'Canon of taxation' is convenience, which relates to how people pay their taxes, or otherwise engage with the tax system. For example, it is usually more convenient for people to have tax deducted at source (i.e. withheld by the payer and paid directly to the Government on behalf of the taxpayer rather than having to pay a lump sum at some later time). Taxation at source has historically been an important feature of the UK's income tax and corporation tax but is less so now.

Activity

What are the advantages and disadvantage of collecting income tax at source, ie from the payer of income?

Feedback

The advantage to the Government is that the tax revenue is received earlier than by direct assessment. However, asking a payer of income to deduct tax creates an administration burden for them. So, while it may be convenient for the recipient to not have to worry about paying income tax, it creates inconvenience for the payer. Also tax withheld at source is normally calculated independently of the taxpayer's personal circumstances and may not represent the correct amount of tax due. There may need to be an adjustment by way of a repayment from HMRC or an extra payment. We will review how extra payments are collected in Chapter 4.

Pay As You Earn (PAYE) is a form of taxation at source, where an employee deducts income tax from employees' wages, which creates a significant administrative burden for employers. We'll review further how PAYE works in practice in Chapter 4.

Income tax collected via the self-assessment system is an example of *direct assessment* – the alternative to taxing at source. In the UK, any income subject to taxation which has not been fully taxed at source already will need to be directly assessed by filing a tax return. Tax due on this income is then paid directly to HMRC. Capital taxes are mostly paid by direct assessment in this way.

The burden of complying with rules for both taxation at source and direct assessment should not be underestimated when you are thinking about ways in which a tax system could be improved. This is captured by the Canon of convenience.

Efficiency

3.18 There are two separate aspects to efficiency derived from Adam Smith's Canons of taxation: economic efficiency and administrative efficiency.

Economic efficiency

3.19 A tax system is seen to be *economically efficient* if it does not distort the economic and commercial decisions which are made by individuals. Economic efficiency is sometimes referred to as *fiscal neutrality*, and the key idea is that taxes should, as far as possible, not interfere with the workings of the market including the decisions taxpayers make about their various activities. We will be considering economic efficiency in more detail in the Chapter 14 where we discuss the impact of the UK tax system on decision making. Here, however, we will consider the way in which the tax system affects people's behaviour more generally, referred to as "distortions", and therefore the extent to which a tax system is economically efficient by its design.

As we noted earlier in this chapter, tax can affect peoples' behaviour in many ways. Sometimes distortions resulting from particular taxes are deliberately intended by a government to affect individuals' behaviour.

Planned distortions include *tax reliefs*, *tax breaks* or *tax concessions*. These are a reduction in taxes theoretically due, sometimes also referred to as a *tax expenditure* as it represents tax revenue forgone by a government. An example is the tax reductions given to businesses for locating in a particular area the Government is seeking to regenerate or develop.

Taxes can also be explicitly used in a non-fiscally neutral way to dissuade particular behaviour. Such taxes are termed *corrective taxes* or *Pigouvian taxes*. They are designed to correct for externalities (costs imposed on others) and internalities (costs imposed on individuals themselves) in the market. Examples are environmental taxes (see Chapter 13), or taxes on socially harmful consumption such as alcohol.

In addition to the immediate effect of a tax change on taxpayer behaviour, there is also the problem of subsequent 'knock-on' (or so called 'second order') effects that are difficult to control.

Activity

Road pricing has been proposed for motorways to discourage their use for environmental and congestion-reducing purposes. What 'knock-on' effects could arise from such a measure?

Feedback

A problem of direct pricing for the use of some roads and not others is that some drivers might just reduce their total miles driven, but instead will just use different roads to avoid paying the taxes. The accident rate per mile driven is higher on roads which are not motorways, leading to fears of an overall increase in road traffic accidents if such a scheme was introduced. It also seems likely that congestion will increase on roads which do not carry a charge as road users switch to them more. This might increase journey times and fuel consumption for all road users and the accident rate might rise still further. To minimise these effects the Chancellor would have to set carefully the cost per mile travelled to a level that would deter enough road users from motorways but not simply to transfer too many journeys onto other roads or the effect may be to worsen the overall situation.

Knock-on effects like this, caused by the presence of taxes or resulting from changes in the tax system, are a common feature of many taxes and a constant headache for tax policy creators. Tax system changes which do not have a knock-on effect will not distort the decisions made by individuals and companies and are therefore referred to as 'fiscally neutral'.

The extent to which tax changes create behavioural changes depends in part on how heavy the tax burden is to start with, the higher the tax rate for example, the greater the incentive to avoid or evade paying tax.

The goal of fiscal neutrality can conflict with using taxation as an important tool to explicitly affect how people make decisions. A government will therefore sometimes use non-fiscally neutral taxes in a targeted way where they consider the knock-on impacts to be desirable (and manageable).

Taxes therefore regularly have distortionary effects on peoples' decisions – some planned and some not. Examining economic efficiency, or fiscal neutrality, provides a measure of the extent to which these distortions are created by the tax system, or changes to the tax system. Some distortions improve the system, but controlling these impacts can prove difficult in practice. The use of taxation as a behaviour influencing tool by governments is one of the key reasons the tax system is constantly changing.

We will return to the subject of fiscal neutrality again in Chapter 14, once you have learned more about the detail of how the UK tax system works.

Administrative efficiency

3.20   A second aspect of efficiency as a characteristic of a good tax system relates to the administration of taxation. The more a tax costs to administer (creating and checking returns, chasing non-payment etc.) the less of the money raised by the tax is available to the Government for their expenditure plans

Most tax authorities are constantly seeking new ways to increase the administrative efficiency of their tax systems. Advances in digital technologies are increasingly being used to improve efficiency as we saw in Chapter 2.

Simplicity

3.21   Simplicity was not specifically mentioned as one of Adam Smith's Canons of taxation, but this is perhaps not surprising since, at the time he was writing, the tax system was relatively simple. There was no income tax for example, only a variety of wealth and consumption taxes. The idea of simplicity as a goal for tax and tax system design is linked to certainty and convenience, and really only began to become popular as an explicit goal in the latter part of the twentieth century.

The rationale for stating that a good tax is a simple tax is that the more complex a tax or tax system is, the more difficult it is for everyone concerned, both taxpayers and tax administrators. It is also a commonly held view that too much complexity allows opportunities for more unacceptable tax avoidance activity and that if the system were simpler and easier to understand, tax avoidance opportunities would be reduced. Another cost of complexity is a lack of certainty.

The aim of simplifying the tax system has quite a long history in the UK, and includes rewriting direct tax legislation trying to make it easier to understand, and the establishment of the Office for Tax Simplification (OTS) (discussed in Chapter 2).

One of the difficulties, however, is that in order to simplify the tax system, or individual taxes within the tax system, policy makers have not only to be able to identify the causes of the complexity that need to be removed, but also to have the political and public will to address it. Often this is not sufficiently present to allow simplification to occur in practice at the pace that might otherwise be desirable.

Flexibility

3.22 A flexible tax is one which changes, or can be changed, easily in response to changes in the economic environment. A key aim of government is to reduce the fluctuations in economic activities caused by the economic cycle (the so called 'boom/bust' cycle) as this is often seem as good for an economy in the longer term. A flexible tax, designed properly, can have a stabilising effect on the economy to assist with this goal. For example, it can cause money to be taken out of a growing economy to keep its growth at a manageable level, and reduce the amount of money that is taken out of the economy when it enters a 'slow down' or a recession to soften any downward spiral effect.

Therefore, in times of recession a government might be content to see its tax receipts fall and increase its borrowing (as an alternative way to fund its expenditure plans) in order to give the economy a boost while during boom years a government might be happy to see its tax receipts increase, thus moderating the boom.

The modern income and corporation tax systems are good examples of relatively flexible tax systems. When incomes and business profits rise, the amount of tax raised increases without any direct action from government and equally when income or business profits fall, the amount of tax collected also falls. Because of the stepped progressive nature of most income tax systems the percentage change in the tax collected is greater than the percentage change in wages or profits. If wages increase by, say, 10% in a year income taxes will increase by more than 10% over the same period without a need for a change in the legislation. Taxes will increase by a greater percentage than wages because marginal rates of tax (the amount of tax you must pay if you earn an extra pound of income) are higher than average rates of tax for most income taxpayers in a progressive tax system).

In practice, there is often a time lag between the decision by the Government to take some fiscal action, the implementation of the policy and the full impact of the tax on the economy. For example, during the 1980s there was great pressure from environmentalists to reduce the lead emissions from petrol. In the late 1980s the duty on unleaded petrol was reduced to make it more attractive to use than leaded petrol. Demand for unleaded petrol increased as a result of the changes but there was a time delay while information about it was disseminated throughout the population and car owners arranged to have their engines modified or changed the type of car they drove. Ultimately, however, this has resulted in almost no new petrol cars being sold which do not use unleaded fuel.

This same trend is being seen in the gradual move to more environmentally friendly bio-fuels as extra tax concessions are again being used by the Government to encourage, albeit slowly, their wider use.

Smith's Canons revisited

3.23 Now that we have spent some time discussing each of Smith's desirable tax system characteristics (plus simplicity and flexibility) we can return to the question we asked at the start of this section – can we rank the factors by importance to make them more useful for tax system designers to use in practice? To do this we will use the historical example of a particular tax proposed and supported by the Government at the time, to illustrate the importance of understanding the different characteristics and considering their relative ranking: the community charge (or poll tax).

Community Charge (Poll Tax)

3.24 As was introduced in Chapter 1, the Community Charge replaced Domestic Rates in April 1990. The Rates had been a long-established, but unpopular, tax used as the primary form of local taxation for provision of many local services (like schools, roads, police, fire service etc.). Rather than levy local tax solely on homeowners as the rates system did, the Community Charge was instead levied on virtually all individuals over 18 years of age i.e. changed from being a property tax to an individual, personal, tax. The supporters of the Community Charge argued that it increased certainty (at least political accountability) by making the individuals who were eligible to vote in local government elections responsible for paying for their elected council's expenditure proposals – not just those individuals in the community who owned property there.

Opponents of the Community Charge, however, claimed that the tax was unfair because the majority of individuals were required to pay the same amount of tax regardless of their personal circumstances (i.e. it was regressive). It was considered vertically inequitable as it was less 'ability to pay' focused than the rates system had been and instead tried to focus more on a benefits approach to tax setting – i.e. followed the argument that everyone benefited from good local services so all should contribute to their cost. Some individuals, including students and the unemployed, were able to pay a reduced amount but little relief was available for the majority of individuals.

In practice the tax proved to be difficult to collect (i.e. administratively inefficient) with significant numbers of people simply disappearing from official records, like electoral rolls, to avoid having to pay the tax. With many missing taxpayers, equity was therefore compromised. In addition to the administrative problems, protests about the unfairness of the Community Charge (leading ultimately to the Poll Tax riots in March 1990) escalated until the Government backed down on the tax's imposition and it was replaced with the current system of Council Tax which, ironically, took us back to a property related, 'ability to pay' style, local tax system as the previous Rates system had been, despite its apparent faults and flaws.

The importance of equity

3.25 It would appear then that the Community Charge failed because it was difficult to collect once taxpayers considered it to be unfair (i.e was regressive). There is also other evidence that the most important characteristic of a good tax system, (in the UK at least), is that it should be seen to be (and ideally should actually be) fair, making equity important to get right in planning tax reform. This case illustrates that the most effective way of achieving acceptable equity is likely to be to use an ability to pay approach. It also illustrates the importance of perceptions of equity, taxpayers will be unhappy if they think a tax is unfair, even if a closer analysis shows that it is, in fact, equitable.

However, other characteristics should not entirely be ignored just to improve equity. Some consideration must at least be given to these other characteristics if the tax system is not to become unbalanced. What is clear from our examination of the desirable characteristics of the tax system is that there are overlaps between them, but also considerable tensions, or even conflicts, between them and it is not possible to design a system that addresses all characteristics at the same time. Over time, priorities change, and also different countries will have different priorities depending on social, cultural and economic conditions. The design of the tax system is likely therefore to evolve over time and the need will remain to continually review the desirable characteristics present in the planned changes.

The Mirrlees Review

3.26 In 2006, the Institute for Fiscal Studies embarked on a major review of the UK tax system to explore more options for the development for the tax base mix in the UK 30 years on from the creation of the Meade Committee. This review was chaired by Sir James Mirrlees and included various eminent economists who examined the UK system and recommended improvements and alterations to the core principles of the use of the all three tax bases in the UK. Its findings were released at the end of 2010. There are a number of recommendations including:

- Refining VAT to remove zero rating and low rates;
- Exempting savings income, i.e. interest, from income tax;
- Merging income tax and national insurance contributions;
- Merging welfare benefits with income tax; and
- Having the same tax burden regardless of whether you are employed, self-employed or operating through a company.

These recommendations clearly give priority to the criteria of economic efficiency (fiscal neutrality), based on the idea that tax should not influence decision making unless absolutely necessary. Implementing these ideas will create both winners and losers in society and therefore likely to affect the balance of equity that has previously dominated the design of the UK tax system, and to date little change has resulted from this analysis.

Alternative tax bases

3.27 We started this chapter by asking the question what should be taxed? We now return to that question with a more detailed look at the three main possible tax bases. A considerable amount of debate has been generated by the question of the tax base, or other method, which should be used to determine an individual's contribution to public funds. The above discussion of six desirable characteristics of a good tax system should now equip you to evaluate the relative merits of each of these tax bases. We have already discussed two ways of allocating the tax burden; the ability to pay and the benefit approaches. In this section we will consider the nature of the three possible tax bases to which these approaches can then be applied i.e.:

- wealth (or capital)
- income
- consumption.

In particular, we need to ask ourselves, if we were designing a tax system, should we use one, two or three tax bases in our tax system design to enable the six desirable characteristics of good tax system design to be delivered optimally? We conclude this section with a summary of some of the latest thinking on changes to the use of different tax bases.

Wealth

3.28 First, could we create a tax system just using a wealth tax (or taxes)? Wealth can be held in various forms so a tax system only using wealth taxes would need to include a focus on different forms of wealth to work effectively. These would include probably both what you have earned yourself (your accumulated income) and what you have been given (inheritances or gifts).

Wealth taxes are among the oldest forms of taxation. This is because wealth can, under some circumstances, be easier to tax than income, where wealth is held in forms you can see (e.g. tangible property).

A comprehensive wealth tax could be based on wealth ownership, which reflects the ability to pay of the taxpayer, as we discussed in section 3.14. At present, the few wealth taxes in the UK are imposed on a 'realisations' basis, that is they are applied when the taxpayer disposes of wealth, not throughout the period of ownership.

3.29 A tax on wealth is also useful as a tool for redistributing wealth, often a key goal of a government. However, there are a number of difficulties which arise when trying to value wealth which can make wealth taxes costly to administer.

Activity

List some of the things that may contribute to an individual's wealth.

Feedback

3.30 You have probably included some tangible assets in your list like land and buildings. Other assets include shares and securities and the market value of a business run by the individual. However, for many people the present value of their future earnings and the present value of their pension fund are probably their most valuable assets. Did you include these? Wouldn't these need to be included in any comprehensive wealth tax?

The present value of an individual's future earnings is the estimated positive cash flows arising from employment throughout their working life, restated in present value terms. However, we live in a rapidly changing world in which an individual may be faced with redundancy, retraining and second or even third careers during his or her working life. In practice it does not seem feasible to value the future earnings of every citizen for taxation purposes. Since future pension rights are generally dependent on earned income it would also be difficult to value the future pension of every citizen regularly. In addition, some may use other assets to save for retirement apart from pensions, so a wealth tax that excludes pension rights would not be horizontally equitable.

Some capital assets may provide additional benefits to their owner such as power and influence. For example, a wealthy individual is likely to have better access to borrowing. However, it would be extremely difficult to ascribe a value to these benefits to determine a comprehensive measure of wealth.

3.31 So, while some wealth taxes (for example, property based taxes like Council tax) have proven relatively cheap to collect in practice, a general wealth tax as the primary tax base for the country is likely to be expensive to administer compared to other tax bases because of the difficulties of assessing the values of assets not currently available for sale i.e. there is no market value that can be used. Other difficulties include the difficulty of disclosure and discovery – i.e. finding out who owns what assets so they can be taxed. However, if we believe that ability to pay is an appropriate way to distribute the overall tax burden across society, then wealth tax should form some part of the tax system, to increase equity and also to prevent tax avoidance by holding assets which grow in value over time but aren't easily captured by income or expenditure taxes.

Fiscal Fact

According to the OECD, between 1965 and 2019 the share of taxes on property fell from 7.9% to 5.5% of total tax revenues on average across the OECD. The UK is one of a few countries that raise more than 10% of total revenues from property taxes. [Source: OECD Revenue Statistics 2021]

To illustrate this idea, imagine you owned your own company. To take money out of the business you could either pay yourself a wage from its profits or you could instead leave the funds in the company which would increase the value of shares i.e. wealth gains rather than income. Measures may have to be introduced to restrict the scope for converting income into capital gains in order to limit the potential loss of income tax revenues or to create inequity between different citizens who earn wealth gains in different ways. In the UK, capital gains tax does this to some extent as you will see in Chapter 8.

Inheritance taxes are probably one of the best ways of achieving a redistribution of wealth, as at least once in a lifetime, money is taken from relatively richer people so that the Government can pass it on to others.

Activity

Could a comprehensive wealth tax be used to replace all other taxes? What would be the advantages or disadvantages of such an approach to taxation?

Feedback

3.32   It could be argued that a comprehensive wealth tax is most in keeping with the concept of using 'ability to pay' to design a tax system and is therefore likely to lead to a more equitable tax system overall than other taxes alone may be able to achieve. On the other hand, it is unlikely to raise enough revenue alone for most countries. It would need a rate so high that it would force taxpayers to sell off assets each time it is due in order to pay the tax, which may not be in the best interests of either the taxpayer concerned, or the wider society. There are also considerable measurement and assessment problems. For example, it is relatively easy for some items of wealth to be concealed from the tax authorities. Finally, as we have discussed, wealth is difficult to accurately value.

In the UK, a Wealth Tax Commission was established in 2020 to analyse proposals for a UK wealth tax. The Commission recommended that to raise taxes following Covid-19, a one-off wealth tax would be better than increasing taxes on work or spending. An annual wealth tax was not recommended, but there is scope to reform the way the UK taxes wealth. The Commission's website can be found here: *https://www.ukwealth.tax* .

Income

3.33 If wealth isn't a perfect tax base to use by itself, what about just taxing income? Income is used as a major tax base throughout the world and in many countries, including the UK, is the most important tax base in the tax system (at least in terms of revenue raised for the Government). However, this does not mean that the design and application of an income tax is without difficulties or that it is the best tax base to use in all cases. Our first problem arises when we try to define what we mean by 'income'.

Problem of definition

3.34 On the surface income might seem an easy concept – isn't it just what we earn between two dates? In reality it isn't as simple as that, at least when it comes to writing rules for a workable tax system. If you have studied any accounting, for example, you will know that profit for a business (their 'income') can be measured in various ways resulting in different 'profit' figures. Which one should we pick for tax purposes? The same applies to individuals' income measures. How comprehensive should it be? Should it include more than wages or salary? What if you aren't just paid in cash but also receive goods or services as part payment for your labour? Should they also be included in your taxable income? If so, at what value? Also, when should they be included? When you are given them or when you use them? Writing a set of rules that will work out the income to be taxed for a period of time is therefore not easy.

Hicks (1939) defined income as the maximum value which "a man can consume during a period and still expect to be as well off at the end of the period as he was at the beginning". Hence, if a tax system which taxes income is to be equitable it must allow for the inflation impacts, i.e. some value will be lost from the tax base each year just because of price increases. In times of inflation some of the income generated therefore must be retained within a business just in order to cover the loss in value of assets over the year due to inflation. Perhaps this inflation component shouldn't be included in income for tax purposes therefore? This sounds very reasonable but there are a number of difficulties which have probably deterred the Government from implementing such a system. These problems include:

- Determining how the value of the capital base should be measured.
- The use of the word 'expect' in Hick's definition. It does not tell us how much an individual can consume with certainty, only what he can

consume and expect to maintain his capital base. It does not help us, therefore, to determine how to tax unpredicted profits, or losses.

Governments are generally reluctant to allow inflation to become an integral part of the tax system. One area of the tax system you will find this, however, is for some thresholds and tax limits which are usually increased in line with the increase in inflation. Governments are perhaps reluctant to cater for inflation impacts for fear that it will itself then fuel further inflation.

Comprehensive Income Tax

3.35 At the same time as Hicks was coming up with a definition of income, in the US, the economists Simons (1938) and Haig (1921) were considering this same issue in relation to income tax. Concerned with equity, they recommended a broad tax base. Simons' classic book *Personal Income Taxation* (Simons 1938) recommended accrual taxation with a definition of income that didn't contain any exceptions and deductions. Under this system, income is the sum of the increases in a person's net wealth over a period of time plus the amount of that person's consumption during the period. This can be restated in terms of real events so that comprehensive income would be equal to the amount which is consumed plus/(less) any increase/(decrease) in the value of the individual's wealth. By using such a definition for the tax base, we have a clear picture of a person's taxable capacity, but don't need to be concerned with how that capacity came into being.

Like many theoretical approaches to tax, however, the idea of a comprehensive income tax sounds good, but is almost impossible to put into practice. The use of this type of comprehensive income tax would result in creating all the difficulties described in the section on a wealth tax above, as it links income measures to measures of wealth.

In 1978 a group of tax experts, called the Meade Committee, was set up to evaluate the UK's tax system. The report they produced was entitled *The Structure and Reform of Direct Taxation*. Among the assessments and proposals for change they examined, the Committee considered the possibility of using a comprehensive income tax – i.e. one that could exist as the only form of taxation in the UK removing the need for capital and expenditure taxes.

The Meade Committee rejected the possibility of using a comprehensive income tax of this kind, claiming that it was impracticable to introduce all the measures which would be necessary to adjust for inflation. Instead they supported the introduction of an extended expenditure tax, which we consider in the next section. Other more recent efforts have revisited this idea however, attempting to address these limitations in different ways. For example, the Taxpayers' Alliance's

Single Income Tax proposal published in 2012 as the result of its 2020 Tax Commission. A more comprehensive income tax was also a central element of the Institute for Fiscal Studies' Mirrlees Review of the UK tax system published in November 2010.

Activity

Explain why the use of a comprehensive income tax might result in undesirable impacts on the economy of the country that introduces it.

Flat taxes

3.36 Many of the problems with income tax arise because of the use of a progressive tax rate, in the interests of vertical equity. There are some countries, however, that adopt a 'flat tax'. The premise for this tax is that a progressive system of income tax rates is a disincentive to extra work, savings and reinvestment, whereas if a tax was imposed at a low, flat rate, people would have more incentive to work and invest which would then benefit the whole economy. This can be demonstrated using the so called 'Laffer Curve', proposed (although he argued not created) by Arthur Laffer in the US (see Laffer 2004), which shows a proposed relationship between tax revenue and the tax rate as follows:

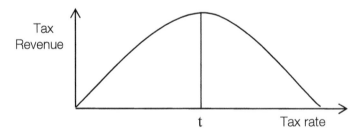

The graph proposes that tax revenues would be zero if the tax rate was 0% or 100%. It suggests tax revenues will rise with increases in tax rates when the tax rate is low, as this encourages growth of economic activities to compensate for the increased tax charges. A point is then reached (tax rate t) where a government is obtaining the maximum possible revenue. After this point, if the tax rate increases, a government actually gets less revenue because there is diminishing incentive to work harder or invest, and more incentive to avoid paying taxes – to the point that at a tax rate of 100%, it is argued that no-one would have any incentive to work or invest (from a pure economic reward perspective at least).

The difficult question is determining in reality where the point t might be both for individual taxes and for the tax system as a whole. This can vary due to a wide variety of factors in practice including:

- the types of taxes that make up the tax system more widely;
- if the economy is growing or not;
- how high tax rates are already;
- the ability for taxpayers to avoid the taxes,
- ... and other factors.

It is important that a government tries to understand what level t is, as below this point any lowering of tax rates will decrease tax revenues overall. As such, this model provides only a partial view of how to determine appropriate tax rates and can't be used to justify whether tax cuts or rises are good or bad by themselves, even though some use the Laffer curve do just that.

Much tax policy has looked to build on this basic principle to create optimal tax revenues. At one extreme, in a 1985 book by Hall and Rabushka called *The Flat Tax*, published in the US, a new system of flat taxes was proposed that looked to build on this idea. Under this system, wages and salaries would be taxed at a low flat rate after a personal allowance to seek to motivative economic activity. Business income would be taxed on:

- Total revenue from sales
- Less inputs purchased from other businesses (which are taxed in the hands of those other businesses)
- Less wages and pensions paid to workers (which are taxed in the hands of the employees)
- Less purchases of plant and equipment (so that investment is not discouraged by the tax system)

Notice that under this model it was proposed that savings and investment income would not be taxed at all.

There is some evidence that a flat tax works well as an incentive to economic activity, but so far it has only been tried in either tax haven countries such as Hong Kong and Jersey, or transitional economies such as Estonia. No other developed country has yet tried such a flat tax, despite its potential attractions.

Taxes are also used for other economy adjusting, market correcting and behaviour changing purposes than simply to maximise revenue at any point in time (see our discussion on the objectives of taxation in Chapter 1). Even with the use of a single tax within a tax system, such as a comprehensive income tax, these different motivations and purposes for taxation would make it very difficult to optimise all at the same point.

Consumption

3.37 Having illustrated important limitations with taxes on wealth and income as sole tax bases, we finally consider the possible use of consumption taxes as the key tax base in a tax system. A consumption tax taxes what an individual takes out of the economy, unlike an income tax which can really be said to tax what is contributed to society. If we only had a consumption tax there would no need to value wealth, which we have already concluded is difficult to do equitably in all circumstances. This problem is avoided as consumption tax is only levied when the taxpayer spends money, not on the wealth they hold on to in whatever form.

If we only taxed consumption, not only would wages, salaries and profits be tax free on receipt, but since a consumption tax does not tax the return on an investment until it is spent, there is a significant encouragement to save rather than spend with this type of tax system. As governments often see increasing savings as good for the long-term health of their economy, this would arguably be a good feature of this kind of tax system (and where spending rather than saving is needed, consumption tax can be adjusted to encourage more spending).

Theoretically, a consumption tax can be designed to incorporate personal allowances and varying rates of tax exactly as an income tax typically does. This would probably require some kind of tax return being filed to obtain refunds of overpaid tax, but could be possible to achieve with reasonable administrative efficiency. Hence, a consumption tax could be progressive and take account of a taxpayer's personal circumstances – if that is considered desirable.

However, because income and savings are not taxed directly under a consumption tax, the tax base will be narrower than for income tax and so the consumption tax rate will have to be set at a suitably higher rate to compensate for this narrowing in order to raise the same revenue for the Government.

One radical form of consumption tax was recommended by the Meade Committee in 1978, which suggested four alternative ways of operating a comprehensive expenditure tax system. In each case the main problem is how to approximate actual expenditure. The Committee proposed that this was to be resolved largely by measuring expenditure as a residual from gains in income or wealth (i.e. expenditure in a period = income received in that period +/– changes in wealth in that period) to avoid the impracticality of needing to track actual expenditure.

The Committee considered two forms of expenditure tax: a universal expenditure tax which is described below, and a two-tier expenditure tax which would collect a basic rate of tax through a system of value added tax (VAT) at the point of purchase and higher rates of tax directly from taxpayers periodically under a separate collection/repayment system such as an annual return detailing what the taxpayer spends in a period.

Under a universal expenditure tax, a taxpayer's consumption expenditure would be calculated by adding the taxpayer's total realised income to any capital receipts, including the sale of capital assets and any amounts borrowed, and deducting any expenditure which is not for the purposes of consumption, including expenditure on capital assets and amounts repaid. Then tax could be levied on consumption expenditure at a number of rates if desired.

Expenditure taxes, particularly in the form of value added taxes as the second of the Meade Committee's options above, have become popular with governments everywhere in recent years (albeit combining a VAT system with an income tax system rather than any form of more direct way of taxing expenditure as the second element of the system) but only a few countries have used this tax as their primary tax base. We'll review why this might be the case in the next section.

Mixture of bases?

3.38 Therefore, as none of the tax bases are adequate in their own right to form the only tax base for a balanced tax system, a combination of the bases is commonly used. In most cases these will usually involve all three bases to enable the advantages and limitations of each base to offset each other to the extent this is possible. This doesn't have to always be the case however, and some countries will sacrifice a rounded tax system design to focus on one or two tax bases. This may be seen, for example, in a tax haven where tax is used as a competitive tool to attract activity to the country. Lowering, or removing, taxes on one tax base can be used to achieve this although this must be applied carefully to ensure government spending needs can be fulfilled with the other tax bases, or alternative means, if a key tax base is not to be subjected to taxation.

The UK taxation system

3.39 To conclude this chapter we will briefly review how the theory of tax bases that we have just discussed in the previous section is directly translated into the UK's current tax system. Because the use of any one tax base alone creates practical difficulties for the effectiveness of tax systems (as we have seen) a mixture of income, wealth and expenditure taxes are often used to try and mitigate their individual limitations, create maximum flexibility in the system and address each of the other desirable characteristics of a good tax system.

As we saw in the section on how the UK raises its revenue in Chapter 1, the key taxes in operation in the UK at present are:

1. Income tax – direct tax on income base payable by individuals

2. Corporation tax – direct tax on income base payable by companies

3. VAT – indirect tax on consumption base payable by all

4. Capital Gains tax – direct tax on capital asset disposals/wealth payable by individuals

5. Inheritance tax – direct tax on wealth/capital asset transfers on death payable by individuals

6. Stamp Duty – direct tax on certain capital/wealth transfers payable by all

7. Customs and Excise Duties (Various) – indirect taxes on consumption payable either by all or on a selective basis on some purchases.

The rest of this book, in conjunction with the web site, provides more detail on most of the above taxes. It illustrates how the detailed rules for each, and the interaction of these taxes, are applied in practice.

As we examine the detail of the current rules for each tax, consider what we have learned so far about the desirable characteristics of a good tax system and ask yourself to what degree the UK's current tax system is effective in achieving these goals. You will see we are good in some areas and not so good in others, and hence the need for constant reappraisal of the tax system and regular adjustments to its operation even perhaps some radical changes.

Summary

In this chapter we explored what to tax and how to design a suitable tax system to tax it. This included thinking about issues such as: whether we should tax at source or to directly assess tax due, the role of hypothecated taxes, tax neutrality, distribution of the tax burden and issues of tax avoidance and evasion in tax system design.

We have also spent some time discussing desirable characteristics of taxation as the foundation principles for how a tax system should be designed. We then evaluated the feasibility of using wealth, income and consumption as a dominant tax base for the tax system before concluding with a brief summary of how the theory of tax bases is applied in current UK practice.

In this chapter we may have raised as many questions for you as we have given answers. We will attempt to answer many of these questions as we review the detail of the current UK tax system throughout the remainder of this book.

Project areas

There are many interesting questions which are inspired by the material dealt with in this chapter. For example,

- the potential role for hypothecated taxes;
- the impact on the UK economy of avoidance activity and corresponding anti- avoidance strategies;
- is progressivity always desirable in a tax?
- what is the appropriate mix of tax bases for the UK's tax system?
- how might the UK look to repay the economic costs incurred related to the Covid-19 pandemic and its related huge levels of government support to the economy and workers – while maintaining Smith's principles?

You may consider for a project the extent to which a particular tax, or tax system more generally, achieves one or more of Adam Smith's desirable characteristics, or how some countries can operate without a balance of income, wealth and expenditure taxes.

The question of the funding of higher education is topical. An interesting question is 'Should a graduate tax be used to fund higher education?' Would this comply with the characteristics of a good tax system?

Using the tax system as a way of influencing transport policy has been a recent focus of the current UK Government. For example:

- congestion charges have been introduced for vehicle traffic in London (and proposed for other UK cities),
- a number of new roads have been built in a way that allows for them to pay for themselves using tolls,
- the Government is considering replacing the Vehicle Excise Duty (VED) with a charge based on road use (and the 2006 Budget introduced more graduation to the levels of this duty in favour of low emissions producing vehicles and in 2008 increased Vehicle Excise Duty on higher polluting cars).

Why do you think taxes, and related charges, have become some popular as a way of influencing transport policy?

Discussion questions

1 Road fund licences were originally introduced to pay for road building and maintenance. This is a tax based not on an ability to pay but according to use. In practice much of the road fund licence is now used for other purposes. Is this a good way to raise taxes?

2 Would increased hypothecation be a better way to organise the Government's revenue and expenditure systems?

3 What corrective taxes, if any, might you introduce in the UK at present?

4 Do you think parents should pay more or less tax than childless individuals?

5 If a government wished to provide funding to increase the level of fitness of the population would it be better to provide subsidised facilities such as leisure centres or to give tax relief on the cost of getting and keeping fit, such as health club memberships?

6 Has the sugar tax led to a reduction in sugary drink consumption?

7 To what degree does the current UK tax system fulfil the characteristics of a desirable tax system?

8 Is an expenditure, income or wealth tax inherently fairer than the others?

9 Not all countries use all tax bases. Why might this be the case and what features of a country allow different mixes of tax bases to operate?

10 Have the Mirrlees Review or the Taxpayers' Alliance Single Income Tax proposals provided useful and practical suggestions for improving the UK's tax system?

Further reading

ACCA, (2008), Discussion Paper: *Perspectives on Fair Tax*, available at http://www.accaglobal.com/uk/en/technical-activities/technical-resources-search/2008/june/perspectives-on-fair-tax.html.

Haig, R., (1921), The concept of income – Economic and legal aspects, *The Federal Income Tax*. New York: Columbia University Press, pp. 1-28.

Hall, R. and Rabushka, A., (1985), *The Flat Tax*, Hoover Institution Press: Stanford, California, USA.

Hicks, J.R., (1939), *Value and Capital*, Oxford University Press: Oxford, UK (2nd Edition, 1974).

Laffer, A., (2004), *The Laffer Curve: Past, present and future*, https://www.heritage.org/taxes/report/the-laffer-curve-past-present-and-future

James, S. and Nobes, C., (2018), *The Economics of Taxation, 18th edition*, Fiscal Publications: Malvern, UK.

Meade Committee Report (1978), *The Structure and Reform of Direct Taxation*, IFS/Allen and Unwin: London, UK.

Mutén, L., (1998), "Minimising the Tax Effects of Inflation" in Sandford, C., (ed) *Further Key Issues in Tax Reform*, Fiscal Publications: Birmingham, UK.

O'Connell, J., (2012), *Total Lifetime Tax*, Report for the Taxpayers' Alliance, see http://www.taxpayersalliance.com/total_lifetime_tax .

Salin, P., (2020) *Tax Tyranny*, Edward Elgar publishing.

Sandford, C., (1995), "Taxing Wealth", in *More Key Issues in Tax Reform*, Fiscal Publications: Birmingham, UK.

Sandford, C., (1995), "Minimising Administrative and Compliance Costs", in *More Key Issues in Tax Reform*, Fiscal Publications: Birmingham, UK.

Shome, P., (2021) *Taxation History, Theory, Law and Administration*, Springer.

Simons, H., (1938), *Personal Income Taxation: The Definition of Income as a Problem of Fiscal Policy*, University of Chicago Press: Chicago, USA.

Smith, A., (1776), *An Inquiry in the Nature and Causes of the Wealth of Nations*, Ward, Lock & Co. Ltd: London, UK. (The World Library 1812 reprint).

Taxpayers' Alliance, (2012), *The Single Income Tax*, Final report of the 2020 Tax Commission, see https://www.taxpayersalliance.com/the_single_income_tax.

For detailed discussions of alternative tax bases and their application see:
Evans, C., Hasseldine, J., Lymer, A., Ricketts, R. and Sandford, C., (2017), *Comparative Taxation: Why Tax Systems Differ*, Fiscal Publications: Malvern, UK.

For a review of the potential for an annual wealth tax to be used in the UK, see *A wealth tax for the UK*, the Wealth Tax Commission (2020) led by A. Advani, E. Chamberlain and A. Summers - http://www.ukwealth.tax

For the Mirrlees Review publications, see: http://www.ifs.org.uk/mirrleesReview

Details on the work of the Office of Tax Simplification can be found at: https://www.gov.uk/government/organisations/office-of-tax-simplification

4 Personal income taxation

Introduction

4.1 In Section 1 of this book we examined the history of the UK tax system, outlined its administration and looked at the principles of tax system design. This foundation provides us with the background we need to now begin to examine the current UK tax system in detail.

This chapter introduces you to the personal income tax computation and explains the various elements that go into its make-up. Chapters 5, 6 and 7 review the sources of taxable income in more detail and show you how to calculate the correct values to enter into the respective parts of the income tax computation. Chapter 8 then introduces you to capital taxes particularly focusing on capital gains tax, a different tax to income tax, but one that is also paid by individuals. Throughout the chapters in this section the focus is on income taxation of the individual, either as an employed person, or as a self-employed person (as a sole trader). We will examine how the direct tax system operates for companies in Chapter 9.

Fiscal Fact

In 1938/39 there were only 3.8 million taxpayers liable for income tax (with married couples counting as one taxpayer, as that was how income taxpayers were assessed then) of 47.4 million people in the UK at that point i.e. only approx.15% of the population were income taxpayers (on the basis that around 50% of the total population were married then). By 2021/22 the number is expected to reach 32.2 million (of est. approximately 66.5 million people, i.e. 48%). Of these, 25.1 million are expected to be aged 65 or less, with 7.1 million therefore aged over 65; 18.5 million are male and 13.7 million are female. (Source: HMRC Income tax statistics and distributions - Table 2.1 ONS Historical UK Population Estimates)

In the UK, individuals pay tax on their income for a *tax year*. The tax year runs from 6 April to the following 5 April (the reason for these odd dates was described in Chapter 1).

A tax system rarely remains the same for long and over the years there have been a number of major changes to the way in which individuals are taxed in the UK. For example, key changes in the last 35 years have included the introduction of independent taxation in the 1990/91 tax year (separate taxation of men and women whether they are married or not) and self-assessment for personal taxation was introduced from 6 April, 1996. With all of the additional pressure on public finances as a result of Covid-19 we can expect more changes to the UK individual tax system in the next few years as the huge sums borrowed begin to be repaid.

In this chapter you will learn how to calculate the amount of an individual's income that is subject to income tax and learn about the reliefs and allowances that are available to reduce the tax due. Once you have deducted the allowances and reliefs from the taxable income you will learn how to compute a taxpayer's tax liability.

At the end of this chapter you will be able to:

- differentiate between income that is taxable and that which is exempt;
- describe the tax rules for the different categories under which individuals pay income tax;
- calculate the allowances and reliefs available to an individual;
- describe the system of national insurance and calculate any national insurance contributions payable by both employers and employees;
- prepare a personal tax computation for an individual;
- outline the system of self-assessment for individuals; and
- offer basic income tax planning advice to individuals and members of a family unit.

The tax computation

4.2   A tax computation for an individual can be set out in the following way. This structure is identical to the one used by HMRC when calculating income tax due and follows the computation steps of the Income Tax Act 2007. Laying out your computation this way therefore helps with real tax filing processes. It will also help ensure you include all the necessary stages in your computations and put things in the correct order. You are strongly advised to follow this proforma each time you do a personal tax computation.

We will outline the seven steps in this computation briefly for you first in this section before providing further details on each step of the calculation.

Thomas Lester's income tax computation for 2022/23:

	Non-savings £	Savings £	Dividends £	Total £
Income:				
Property Income	1,500			1,500
Trading Income	21,000			21,000
Employment Income	28,850			28,850
Savings Income:				
Bank interest received		3,500		3,500
Building Society interest		3,000		3,000
Dividend Income			1,500	1,500
Total Income	51,350	6,500	1,500	59,350
Less reliefs	(500)			(500)
Net Income	50,850	6,500	1,500	58,850
Less Personal Allowance	(12,570)			(12,570)
Total Taxable Income	38,280	6,500	1,500	46,280

Tax Due:				
Non savings income	37,700		@ 20%	7,540.00
	580		@ 40%	232.00
Savings income	500		@ 0%	
	6,000 (6,500 –500))		@ 40%	2,400.00
Dividend income	1,500		@ 0%	–
	46,280			
Tax Borne				10,172.00
Less:				
Tax reductions	(none apply for Thomas this year)			(0.00)
Add:				
Additional tax	(none applies for Thomas this year)			0.00
Tax Liability				10,172.00
Less tax already paid:				
PAYE				(3,400.00)
Tax Payable				6,772.00

In this section of the book you will find out how to produce a tax computation like this one, given basic facts about a taxpayer's situation.

You can see that Thomas receives his income from a number of sources. This includes income from owning property in the UK, income from being partly self-employed, income from employment and some interest and dividends. It is not uncommon to see multiple income sources like this in a tax computation. It is becoming more common than it was in the past to see both income from employment and from self-employment (trading income) in the same tax year as people's working lives become less traditionally structured and portfolio careers and working structures become more common.

The income tax computation is split into seven 'steps'. The first three aggregate a taxpayer's taxable income from all sources and then deducts any reliefs and allowances that are applicable to produce "taxable income". The remaining four steps then calculate the tax due on this taxable income. The way in which a component of income is taxed depends on the tax rules under which it is assessed.

The income tax system contains a number of tax reliefs which are special rules that reduce the amount of tax otherwise payable. These tax reliefs serve a number of purposes. They can be used by the government to help specific categories of individuals, products or services and can encourage particular activities by reducing the comparable post income tax cost of the activity. When used in this way they are effectively a replacement for direct public expenditure and therefore can be called *tax expenditures*. We will look at the concept of tax expenditures more closely in Chapter 14.

In this chapter you will meet several types of tax relief as we work through the steps of the income tax computation. There are a number of ways of providing tax reliefs and you will see that they can take the form of exemptions from tax (in step 1), deductions from the calculation of taxable income (steps 1 and 2) allowances which operate in a similar way to deductions (steps 1 and 3), adjustments to the rates of tax (step 4) and reductions in tax liability (step 6).

In the next section we summarise the seven steps of the tax computation, before looking more closely at step 4, how the tax rates are applied. We then come back to the remaining steps in more detail.

Computing taxable income

Step 1 – Aggregating the categories of income

4.3   All the taxable income Thomas has received or earned in the year, from all sources, is listed in his tax computation, grouped into various categories (or what the tax legislation calls 'components' of income). A few sources of income are exempt from income tax, as we will see later, but most have to be taxed and so must be listed here. For most categories of income we include what is due to Thomas, even though he may not have actually received it all yet (i.e. we use an *accruals basis* – we will explain further how this works later).

Note that we split up Thomas' income sources into different categories by using different rows and into different types by using four columns. This is important to help us calculate the correct rate of tax at step 4 of the tax computation; note how each of the three (non-total) columns in the first part of the computation becomes a row when computing tax borne – the fourth step.

Property, trading and employment income

4.4 Income from owning and renting out property, from being self-employed (trading) or from employment is listed in Thomas's tax computation first. Usually property and trading income have not had tax deducted by the payer (i.e. what we call 'taxed at source') so can just be listed here at the value the tax rules set out for each category (we'll show you how these rules work in Chapter 5, 6 and 7).

Income from employment, however, usually has some income tax deducted by the taxpayer's employer before it is paid via a system called 'Pay as You Earn' (PAYE) and so the taxpayer only receives the net amount after the tax is deducted. The employer then pays this tax to the Government on the employee's behalf. You will see that in Thomas' case his computation shows the total (gross) he has earned from employment during this year (£28,850) in step 1, but he is able to later deduct the PAYE already paid via his employer (£3,400 in this case) at the end of the computation when determining what tax may still be payable.

Savings and investment income

4.5 Bank deposit interest and the building society interest is usually received 'gross', which means that no tax is withheld by the payer of the interest. In Thomas' case you can see he received £3,500 of bank interest and £3,000 of building society interest.

Exempt income

4.6 Most income is potentially subject to income tax under the UK's tax system and therefore needs to be included in one or other of the categories of income calculations. There are, however, various exempted sources of income that can be received without any income tax becoming due. You should be aware of the most common of these, including:

- the increase in the value of National Savings & Investments savings certificates,
- premium bond prizes, betting and lottery winnings and other competition prizes,
- gifts,
- interest from Individual Savings Accounts (ISAs) or Junior ISAs,
- interest from Child Trust funds,
- some social security benefits, including child benefit and universal credit,
- shares allotted to employees under approved schemes such as share option plans,

- educational grants and scholarships (for the recipient),
- statutory redundancy pay, pay in lieu of notice and some other payments up to a maximum of £30,000 made when an employment is terminated.
- payments made by employers to employees for death in service or in respect of disability sustained at work (e.g. personal injury payments),
- lump sums received from approved pension schemes,
- qualifying care relief (fostering and shared lives carer income) – qualifying income up to an annual sum is exempt from income tax (the excess is taxable). Currently this sum is £10,000 per residence, plus £200 per week (for a child under 11 years of age) and £250 per week (for a child/adult older than 11).

Whether or not tax has to be paid on specific categories of income, and how much, is detailed in the tax legislation. We will review the rules for calculating these amounts throughout the remaining chapters of the book.

Fiscal Fact

Exempting income from tax, of course, costs the UK Government in foregone tax revenue (this is called 'tax expenditure'). For example, for 2021/22, the forecasted cost of exempting ISAs from income tax was £3.7 billion. For the same year the cost of allowing redundancy pay up to £30,000 to be tax free is estimated to be £900 million, exempting approved company share scheme option plans £50 million and exempting premium bond winnings could cost £10 million. In total, at October 2019, The National Audit Office reported the UK had a total of 1,190 different tax reliefs with a forecast total cost of £155 billion for the 2018/19 year representing a 5% real increase in costs since 2014/15. (See the table 'Non-structural costs estimates' on the HMRC website for further examples.)

Step 2 – Dealing with deductible reliefs

4.7   After you have computed the total income received by aggregating all categories of taxable income, any reliefs that are applicable can be deducted as step 2. In our example, Thomas made payments of £500 that can be treated as reliefs. An example of a relief is a trading loss, which we will cover in Chapter 7. Tax deductions available for any pension contributions paid gross are another example dealt with at this step (see further details in Chapter 5.3).

Total income minus reliefs produces *net income*.

Step 3 – Personal allowances

4.8   Most individuals are entitled to a certain amount of income each year free from income tax. This is called a *personal allowance* and is deducted from the net income figure to arrive at total taxable income. If a blind person's allowance is applicable, it is also deducted at this stage. Thomas does not appear to qualify for a blind person's allowance so no deduction is made in his case.

Net income minus personal allowances produces *taxable income*.

Having completed steps 1-3 and determined the taxable income of the taxpayer, you are now ready for the computation of tax liability using steps 4–7.

Computing tax liability

Step 4 - Income tax rates

4.9   The next stage of the tax computation is to calculate what rates of tax apply to the total taxable income. As part of step 1, the income categories were classified into one of three *types* – non-savings, savings income, and dividend income. This is necessary as each of these income types has its own tax rates. Later in the chapter we will examine exactly how these different rates are applied to a taxpayer's total income.

Step 5 - Tax borne

4.10   Tax borne is the outcome from applying the tax rates to the taxable income, and represents the amount of tax that the taxpayer is liable for on his or her taxable income before any tax reductions (which can reduce the tax borne) or additional tax on their income (that may increase it).

Step 6 – Tax reductions

4.11   At this step there is a deduction from the tax borne for any entitlements the taxpayer has for *tax reductions*. There is a limited range of special reductions that includes married couples' and civil partners' reduction for elderly taxpayers, qualifying maintenance payments and some special schemes for tax deductible investments. Tax relief for any foreign taxes paid at source (double tax relief) is given at this point in the computation – see Chapter 12 for more on this topic.

Step 7 – Additional tax

4.12   The final step in computing the *tax liability* for the taxpayer is to add in any extra tax that may be due. These are fairly rare but include, for example, extra tax where gift aid is claimed but insufficient tax has been paid to cover the claim.

We will discuss charitable donations, and where this situation may arise, later in this chapter at 4.38. Pension related surcharges are also applied here. We will talk about these in Chapter 5.

Tax payable

4.13 The result of completing all seven steps is the computation of the taxpayer's tax liability for the tax year. This is the sum that the taxpayer needs to pay to HMRC to settle their income tax bill for the year. In Chapter 2 we explained that some of this tax may have already been *deducted at source*, i.e. paid via the taxpayer's employer, or otherwise credited to the taxpayer directly, before this computation is done. The final (eighth) stage in the full computation therefore is to deduct from the overall tax liability for the year any sums that form part of this total liability but have already paid (or deemed paid) to HMRC during the tax year. This most commonly will include PAYE withheld by the taxpayer's employer but occasionally may include other things, such as tax paid at source on patent royalties.

If the taxpayer still owes any tax after deducting these sums already paid over, it must then be paid to HMRC directly. As outlined in Chapter 2, this is likely to be due by 31 January following the end of the tax year (this is also the latest date by which the tax return for the current year should be received by HMRC). However, in some cases sums may be due earlier in the tax year, as we will see in Chapter 6.

If the taxpayer has paid more tax during the year than the final tax liability, the taxpayer will receive a refund (repayment) from HMRC of the tax overpaid. This can happen from time to time, often associated with situations where the taxpayer's circumstances have changed during the year (e.g. they lost their job, or retired perhaps) and so the tax their employer deducted was too much once the whole year is taken into account. The taxpayer can request a refund of the overpayment.

Important: Note that the *taxable income* part of the calculation (steps 1 to 3) is always rounded down to the nearest pound (i.e. you can effectively chop off the pence at each step in your final computation). For the *tax due* part of the calculation (steps 4 to 7), you should always round down your figures to the *whole penny*. This is important to ensure you do not get rounding errors in your tax computation.

Basis of assessment

4.14 It is important when undertaking a tax computation to know at what point any income needs to be included in an income tax computation. The *basis of assessment* is the way in which income is allocated to the correct tax years for income tax payment purposes. The different categories of income each have different ways of working out what amount has to be included in any particular tax year although there are several common general bases of assessment that are used across the different income categories as follows:

Cash or *Accruals* basis – a cash basis is sometimes called a *receipts* basis, and is where the amount included in the tax computation for a particular tax year is the amount actually received during the year. An *accruals* basis on the other hand, includes the amount accrued during the tax year, regardless of whether it is actually received by the taxpayer or not i.e. it will include income owed to the taxpayer even if they haven't actually received it yet. The cash basis is most commonly used for employment income. The accruals basis has historically been mainly used for trading (business) income, in line with the method used for accounting purposes. From April 2013, however, small businesses have had the option to use the cash basis for this source of income too, as we will see in Chapters 5 and 6.

Whether the basis of assessment is cash or accruals can make a difference to the taxpayer. For example, employees are normally taxed on a cash basis. It would be theoretically possible, however, to tax employment income using an accruals basis. For most employees this would make little or no difference to their tax bills each year, but for those who receive performance-related bonuses, which are often paid in the tax year after the one in which they were earned, the tax on the bonus would then be payable before the bonus was actually received. Most people would not like this idea!

Arising or *remittance* basis – where UK taxpayers have income or profit from other countries, we need to decide when it will be taxed in the UK. An arising basis means that the overseas income or profit is taxed when it accrues, even if the money is not brought into the UK. The remittance basis means that it is not subject to UK tax until it is actually brought in (or 'remitted') to the UK. We will look at this more closely in Chapter 12.

Current year or *preceding year* basis – this difference relates to trading income computation. For many years in the past, businesses were taxed on the profit they earned during the previous tax year. Now, however, business profits are taxed on a current year basis i.e. what is accrued in the current tax year. For self-employed people this is linked to their business year (i.e. the period for which they produce accounts). We will see how this operates in practice in Chapter 6.

The system of income tax rules

4.15 There are four primary Acts that contain the main rules for income tax: the Income and Corporation Taxes Act (ICTA) 1988, the Income Tax (Earnings and Pensions) Act (ITEPA) 2003, the Income Tax (Trading and Other Income) Act (ITTOIA) 2005 and the Income Tax Act (ITA) 2007. The Finance Acts produced each year from the annual UK Budget amend these Acts. In this book we will look at the combined rules of the various tax Acts and any changes that have occurred to them as a result of any subsequent Finance Acts.

It is important to identify which set of tax rules any particular income stream is taxed under because each has its own specific rules for:

- the income to be taxed;
- allowable deductions, if any, from the income;
- the basis of assessment; and
- how the tax is collected.

We saw in Chapter 1.3, that ever since we started collecting income tax in the UK, the rules used a series of discrete categories to classify different income sources. There were referred to as 'Schedules', sometimes divided into subsections called 'Cases'. We no longer refer to these Schedules and Cases, although you may come across references to them when reading older case law.

The current system for determining UK income tax liability is structured as follows:

Employment income	Income from employment or office holding – Part 2 ITEPA 2003 (was Schedule E ICTA 1988);
Pension income	Income received from a pension – Part 9 ITEPA 2003;
Property income	Income, such as rent, from UK property – Part 3 ITTOIA 2005 (was Schedule A ICTA 1988);
Trading income	Income from a trade or profession – Part 2 ITTOIA 2005 (was Schedule D Cases I & II ICTA 1988);
Savings income	Interest income for example from banks and building societies – Part 4 ITTOIA 2005 (was Schedule D Case III ICTA 1988);
Dividend income	Income from UK dividends and other distributions from UK companies – Part 3 & 4 ITTOIA 2005 (was Schedule F ICTA 1988);
Miscellaneous income	Income not dealt with under any of the above categories – Part 5 ITTOIA 2005 (was Schedule D case VI ICTA 1988).

As we go through this section of the book we will look in detail at the most important tax rules for calculating what income is taxable. In this chapter we will determine the aggregated income which is subject to tax, the allowances and reliefs which can be set against the income for tax purposes and the date on which tax must be paid. Chapter 5 will look at income from employment and pensions. In Chapter 6 and Chapter 7 we will examine trading income and deductions for taxpayers who are carrying on business as sole traders, as well as property income.

Throughout this chapter we only discuss income from UK sources. The general rules for income tax change when the source of the income comes from outside the UK. We will examine these differences in Chapter 12.

Rates of tax

4.16   Having looked in outline at how we aggregate the categories of income in the top part of the individual taxpayer's tax computation (steps 1 – 3), let us jump ahead and examine the *tax due* part of the computation before we return to the top part for a more detailed examination in the following section.

Income tax bands

4.17   As we noted in the previous section, to determine the rate of tax to be paid on the taxable income (i.e. step 4 of the computation), we need to classify the taxable income into three broad types i.e. non-savings, savings and dividend income. This classification is important as each type of income has a different set of rates that will apply to it. Which rate is used will vary from person to person based on the band into which the income type falls. Someone receiving an additional £1 could therefore be taxed on it at different rates depending on the income type it is, and how much other income of that type, and other types, the taxpayer receives. Remember as we discussed in Chapter 3.5, this is called the *marginal* tax rate.

While this might sound confusing initially, it is fairly simple to apply in practice once understood – particularly if you follow the proforma we illustrated in Thomas Lester's income tax computation.

There are three bands (sometimes called *brackets*) that currently apply across the various income types: the basic rate band, the higher rate band, and the additional rate band. There is also a special starting rate for savings, but first we will deal with the three bands that apply to all income categories.

From April 2017 several differences exist between the income tax computations for taxpayers living in Scotland and those in the rest of the UK. If you need to know these rules you can find on the website a supplement covering the differences between the Scottish tax system and that of the rest of the UK.

The size of these bands is fixed each year. For 2022/23 this is set as:

	Tax Band
Basic rate	0 – 37,700
Higher rate	37,701 – 150,000
Additional rate	>150,000

All taxable income must be allocated to these bands to determine which rate to use to calculate the tax payable. The following sections show how this is done.

Fiscal Fact

HMRC believe there will be approximately 472,000 UK taxpayers who will have earned £150,000 or more in 2021/22 and 19,000 of these are expected to earn £1m of more. (Source: HMRC Statistics - Table 2.5: Income tax liabilities by income range)

Non-savings income

4.18   Let's look at how these tax bands apply to non-savings income first. This includes any employment, property, trading, foreign and miscellaneous incomes. For most people this is will be their main income type.

For the current tax year rates of tax for non-savings income are:

	Tax Band	Rate	Maximum amount payable in band
Basic rate	0 – 37,700	20%	£ 7,540.00
Higher rate	37,701– 150,000	40%	£ 44,920.00
Additional rate	>150,000	45%	

Activity

Calculate the income tax due on taxable incomes of:

(a)	£2,500
(b)	£10,000
(c)	£45,000
(d)	£175,000

(Assume all income is non-savings income. Don't forget that 'taxable income' means the amount remaining after the correct personal allowance has been deducted)

Feedback

		£
(a)	2,500 @ 20%	500.00
(b)	10,000 @ 20%	2,000.00
(c)	37,700 @ 20%	7,540.00
	(45,000 – 37,700) @ 40%	2,920.00
		10,460.00
(d)	37,700 @ 20%	7,540.00
	(150,000 – 37,700) @ 40%	44,920.00
	(175,000 – 150,000) @ 45%	11,250.00
		63,710.00

Note what happened in (c). Initially the basic rate band (first £37,700 of taxable income) was 'filled up' and taxed at 20%. Any amount falling into the higher rate band (taxable income between £37,700 and £150,000) is then taxed at 40%. In (d) the 45% rate applied to taxable income over £150,000 as the 40% band (between £37,700 and £150,000) was also filled up.

Fiscal Fact

In 2021/22 income tax of £97.9 billion is expected to be paid by taxpayers on non-savings income taxable within the basic rate band. A further £54.1 billion will be collected from those who have non-savings earnings falling into the higher rate band and £34.5 billion from those with these earnings falling in the additional rate band (a total from non-savings income of £186.5 billion). (Source: HMRC Table 2.6).

Savings income

4.19 Since 1996/97 a distinction has been drawn between savings and non-savings income for calculating tax due and a lower rate of tax used for some savings income to encourage people to save more. Savings income is treated as being the middle part of taxable income for the purposes of determining rates of tax to be applied, so you allocate this income to the tax bands only after you have allocated all the non-savings income to the bands as part of your computation.

Savings income includes:

- interest from a bank account (including from National Savings & Investments accounts);
- interest from a building society;
- interest from gilt edged securities (i.e. British Government stock);
- interest from debentures; and
- income from an annuity.

Under Islamic law, receipt or payment of interest is prohibited. Alternative finance arrangements have developed to accommodate this. For tax purposes, the profit element of purchase and resale arrangements, and profit share return arrangements, is treated the same as if it were interest.

For savings income only, there is an initial tax band that may apply – called the *starting rate for savings* band. Savings income in this band is taxed at 0%. For the current tax year rates of tax for savings income are:

Tax Band		Rate	Maximum amount payable in band*
	£		£
Starting rate	0 – 5,000	0%	–
Basic rate	5,001 – 37,700	20%	6,539.80
Higher rate	37,701 – 150,000	40%	44,920.00
Additional rate	>150,000	45%	

* only if all of the taxpayer's income is from savings.

Note that the starting rate for savings of 0% only applies if the non-savings income is less than £5,000. Savings income falling into the starting rate for savings band in this way is tax free.

Since 6 April 2016, a *personal savings allowance* (PSA) is available to taxpayers **in addition** to the starting rate for savings band and gives an additional zero rate sum of £1,000 to basic rate taxpayers and £500 to higher rate taxpayers. This means, irrespective of their non-savings income, they can receive the first £1,000 (if basic rate taxpayers) or £500 (if higher rate taxpayers) of any savings income without incurring any tax. Additional rate taxpayers are not entitled to a personal savings allowance.

Once the starting rate for savings band is full, and the personal savings allowance (if applicable) has been taken into account, any further savings income which falls within the basic rate band is then taxed at 20%, as for non-savings income. Also, like non-savings income, any savings income falling into the higher rate band is taxed at 40%, and that falling into the additional rate band is taxed at 45%. Note that, although the personal savings allowance carries a zero rate of tax, it is still taken into account to work out how much of each rate band has been used up. In this way it is different to the personal allowance we saw earlier.

Try the following activity to see how the bands, and this time two income types, interact. Note the order in which the taxable income is applied to the bands. Getting the order right is essential (i.e. non-savings income is always to be considered first before savings income when filling up the bands).

Activity

Calculate the income tax liability for an individual with total taxable income consisting of savings income of £2,500 and employment income of:
(a)   £3,800
(b)   £20,000
(c)   £50,000
(d)   £160,000
(Remember 'taxable income' means the correct personal allowance has already been applied)

Feedback

	£
(a) Non-savings income	
3,800 @ 20%	760.00
Savings income	
(5,000 – 3,800) @ 0%	–
1,000 PSA @ 0%	–
300 – (£2,500 – 1,200 – 1,000) @ 20%	60.00
	820.00
(b) Non-savings income	
20,000 @ 20%	4,000.00
Savings income	
1,000 PSA @ 0%	–
1,500 @ 20%	300.00
	4,300.00
(c) Non-savings income	
37,700 @ 20%	7,540.00
(50,000 – 37,700) @ 40%	4,920.00

Savings income	
500 PSA @ 0%	–
2,000 @ 40%	800.00
	13,260.00
(d) Non-savings income	
37,700 @ 20%	7,540.00
(150,000 – 37,700) @ 40%	44,920.00
(160,000 – 150,000)@ 45%	4,500.00
Savings income	
2,500 @ 45%	1,125.00
	58,085.00

In (a) £1,200 (i.e. £5,000 – £3,800) of savings income falls into the 0% tax free band as the savings starting rate band (of £5,000) is not used up by non-savings income. The PSA amount (£1,000 as this person is not a higher or additional rate taxpayer) is taxed at 0%. The remainder of the savings income then falls into the basic rate band and is taxed at 20%.

In (b), all of the starting rate for savings, and part of the general basic rate band is used up by non-savings income so the savings income above the basic rate PSA of £1,000 all falls into the basic rate band and is therefore taxed at 20%.

In (c) the PSA is only £500, because the taxpayer is higher rate taxpayer. The non-savings income uses all of the starting and basic rate bands so the savings income above the PSA must be taxed at the higher rate of 40%.

In (d) the savings income is pushed into the additional rate band of 45% by the high non-savings earnings. As an additional rate taxpayer, there is no entitlement to the PSA.

Fiscal Fact

Taxpayers paying tax on savings income at the basic rate in 2021/22 are expected to contribute £158 million, at the higher rate £264 million and the additional rate £388 million. This is a total of £810 million from savings income. (Source: HMRC Table 2.6)

Dividend income

4.20 Before 6 April 1999 dividends from UK company shares were treated in the same way as savings income. Since this time however, dividends have been subject to their own tax rules and so must be treated separately in the tax computation. They are treated as the third part of a person's taxable income when determining which rates of tax to apply. If you receive any dividend income it will be taxed at 8.75% (7.5% in 2021/22) if it falls into the basic rate band, 33.75% (32.5% in 2021/22) if it falls into the higher rate band or 39.35% (38.1% in 2021/22) if it falls into the additional rate band.

For the current tax year rates of tax for dividend income are:

	Tax Band	Rate	Maximum amount payable in band*
	£		£
Dividend allowance	0 - 2,000		
Basic Rate	2,001 - 37,700	8.75%	3,123.75
Higher Rate	37,701 - 150,000	33.75%	37,901.25
Additional Rate	>150,000	39.35%	

* only if all of the taxpayer's income is from dividends.

The special 8.75% rate for dividends is sometimes referred to as the *dividend ordinary rate*, the 33.75% rate the *dividend upper rate* and the 39.35% rate the *dividend additional rate*. We will look at the rules that describe how dividends from companies are taxed in more detail later.

Prior to 6 April 2016, dividends were included in tax computations at their gross value. They were treated in the taxpayer's computation as if 10% had been deducted by the company as a tax at source – although no deductions were actually made. From 6 April 2016 onwards, these rules changed. Instead, the actual amount of dividend received is included in the taxpayer's income tax computation and a *dividend allowance* was introduced to give all taxpayers (whatever rate of income tax they pay) the first £2,000 (unchanged from 2021/22) of dividends received tax free. Like the personal savings allowance we saw earlier, the dividend allowance is taken into account when deciding which band the dividends above the allowance will fall into.

Fiscal Fact

Collectively, all taxpayers are expected to pay £2 billion in taxes on dividends at the ordinary rate in 2021/22. Higher rate taxpayers however, are expected to pay an extra £4.89 billion in tax on their dividends and additional rate taxpayers an extra £5.25 billion. This represents a total of £12.14 billion from dividend income. [Source: HMRC Statistics Table 2.6]

Activity

Pat (aged 45) has earned the following income for the tax year:

	£
Taxable trading income from her business	20,850
UK Dividends	1,000
Income from UK property	1,000

Calculate Pat's income tax payable.

Feedback

Pat is entitled to a personal allowance of £12,570 which is deducted from her aggregated income before calculating tax due, as we saw in the Thomas Lester example earlier. (Personal allowances are discussed in more detail later in section 4.6). She is also entitled to a dividend allowance in this tax year.

Pat has three categories of income to include in her tax computation; trading income (taxable income for her business), dividend income and property income. These three categories fall into two types; non-savings (the trading and property incomes) and dividends. Pat has no savings income for this year.

	Non-savings £	Dividends £	Total £
Trading income	20,850		20,850
Dividend income		1,000	1,000
Property income	1,000		1,000
Net income	21,850	1,000	22,850
Less: Personal allowance	(12,570)		(12,570)
Taxable income	9,280	1,000	10,280
Tax due:			
Non-savings income: 9,280 @ 20%		1,856.00	
Dividend income: 1,000 @ 0%		–	
Tax payable		1,856.00	

Note that as Pat has a dividend allowance of £2,000 she has no tax to pay on the £1,000 dividends she received. She only has to pay tax on her non-savings income.

Activity

How would your answer to the previous activity differ if Pat had earned £45,350 income from her business and dividends of £6,000?

Feedback

	Non-savings £	Dividends £	Total £
Trading income	45,350		46,350
Dividend income		6,000	6,000
Property income	1,000		1,000
Net income	46,350	6,000	52,350
Less: Personal allowance	(12,570)		(12,570)
Taxable income	33,780	6,000	39,780

Tax due:

Non-savings income: 33,780 @ 20%	6,756.00
Dividend income	
2,000 @ 0%	–
1,920 @ 8.75%	168.00
2,080 (6,000 – 2,000 – 1,920) @ 33.75%	702.00
Tax payable	7,626.00

Notice that the first £2,000 of Pat's dividend income is covered by the dividend allowance, after this £1,920 of Pat's basic rate tax band still remains. So £1,920 of the dividend will be tax at 8.75% and the rest of the dividend would fall in the high rate tax band, taxed at 33.75%.

We will return to the taxation of dividends in more detail later in this chapter.

Summary

4.21 We have seen that there are seven rates of tax that may apply to an individual taxpayer's income: 0% (for savings and dividends) 8.75% (only for dividends), 20% (non-savings or savings), 33.75% and 39.35% (only dividends may be taxed at these rates), 40% (for non-savings and savings), or 45% (non-savings and savings). The order in which you include the different incomes in the computation can therefore affect the amount of tax paid because of these various tax rates. You are not allowed to pick the order you want to use unfortunately. You must always calculate the tax due in the following order:

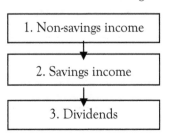

1. Non-savings income

2. Savings income

3. Dividends

Non-savings income must be included in the computation first (if the taxpayer has any), then savings (if they have any) and finally dividends (again, if they have any). Dividends can therefore be considered the top part of anyone's income for their income tax computation. As we saw earlier, this means a taxpayer will only be able to use the 0% rate on savings income if there is not more than £5,000 of taxable non-savings income, as non-savings income must come first in the computation.

Note that general reliefs and personal allowances do not necessarily have to be deducted in the same order i.e. from non-savings income first, then if not used up, from savings income and finally from dividends. They should be applied to the taxable income in the way **that best suits the circumstances of the taxpayer** – i.e. usually the one that minimises the taxpayer's total tax payable. Look back to the example computation at the start of this chapter to review how these rates applied to Thomas' income. In his case, they are both deducted from the non-savings income as neither will use up all of this band of income for this period. We will meet several instances later however, where this approach does not produce the lowest tax payable when applied in a different order to the specific incomes of taxpayers. Do watch out for this.

Let's now return to the top part of the personal income tax computation (steps 1 to 3) again to look at how we calculate taxable income in more detail.

Step 1: Categories of Income

4.22 The distinctions between the different income tax classifications are important because different rules will apply to a taxpayer having income classified under one category or another. This can have a significant impact on the overall amount of tax they have to pay and when it is paid.

Income taxed at source

4.23 Before we look at the different categories of income in a bit more detail, this section clarifies how deduction of income tax at source affects our computation. In Chapter 2 we discussed how income can be received in one of two forms:

1. already, at least partly, taxed at source, or
2. not taxed at all yet (to be taxed instead entirely by direct assessment).

Income that is taxed by direct assessment is paid to the recipient gross, while income taxed at source is paid after deduction of some income tax.

We saw in Chapter 1 that the procedure by which some income is paid to the recipient net of tax was introduced at the beginning of the 19th century as an anti-avoidance measure. This is administratively efficient as the payer of the income can then be made partly responsible for the tax due, not just the recipient.

The following income is taxed at source for individual taxpayers (the rules are different for companies as we will see in Chapter 9):

- patent royalties (but not copyright royalties); and
- annuities.

Income taxed at source has tax deducted at a flat rate – at the basic rate of 20% (i.e. the recipient only gets 80% of the gross amount due to them but of course can claim the extra 20% as a reduction in tax payable at 'step 8' i.e. when computing how much of their tax liability is still due).

If individuals who are not liable to income tax (e.g. perhaps because their income is less than the personal allowance) receive income which has been taxed at source, they can usually reclaim the tax which has been deducted directly from the HMRC. However, people who are higher, or additional, rate taxpayers may have to pay more tax at the end of the tax year to make up the full amount they should have paid on this income.

Income from earnings and pensions

4.24 Tax on employment income is collected using the PAYE (Pay-As-You-Earn), scheme, which means that the employer deducts the tax due on the income of employees before the payment is made to them. Unlike the use of a flat rate of tax at source for patent royalties and annuities, PAYE takes into account the taxpayer's personal circumstances. This means that for many employees the correct amount of tax is deducted by their employers so they won't have to complete a tax return unless they are higher rate taxpayers, have other income sources that aren't fully taxed or need to reclaim any overpaid tax. This feature of the UK tax system means relatively few people file tax returns in the UK each year compared to many other countries.

Fiscal Fact

Income tax receipts to the UK Government via PAYE as estimated to be £188.7 billion in 2021/22. This represents 84% of total net receipts from income tax for that year. [Source: HMRC Revenue and Customs Receipts]. 12.2 million taxpayers (i.e. only about 18% of UK citizens) were required to file income tax returns for the 2020/21 tax year and 11.3 of these had been received by the last filing date for that year (28 February 2022 – this is usually the end of January each year but was extended in 2022 due to the pandemic to give people a little more time to file these). [Source: HMRC Press Release 1 March 2022]

Remember that income from earnings and pensions must be included in Step 1 as a *gross* amount. If PAYE has been paid on this income already, the amount paid is then deducted from the tax computation at the very end of the tax due calculation (along with any other tax withheld) to determine what tax remains to be paid by the taxpayer.

Property income

4.25 All income from UK land and property is taxed using the property income rules. This includes rental income from such things as letting land, furnished or unfurnished houses, commercial properties, holiday cottages, caravans or houseboats on permanent moorings. Individuals, whether residents of the UK or not in the tax year, are taxed on any annual profits or gains related to land or property located in the UK. Taxable profits are calculated by deducting total allowable expenses from total income from land and property. The basis of assessment is the accrued income for the tax year for all items other than short lease premiums, although from 6 April 2013 the taxpayer can choose to use a cash basis instead if they so wish.

An allowance of £1,000 for individuals' property income (not available to those in partnerships) in 2017. This is an attempt to save potential taxpayers having to file tax returns for small sums of income tax due on small amounts of income, for example, letting accommodation on AirBnB.

The allowance is structured such that if an individual taxpayer's income received in the tax year from a property business (in total) was less than £1,000, then there would be no requirement to declare it and no tax is due. However, if the income from the property business exceeds the £1,000 allowance, the taxpayer has to declare the relevant income, but could either do so as before (by deducting allowable expenses from the income received) or by ignoring expenses actually incurred and just deducting the £1,000 allowance to determine how much should be declared from these sources.

We will examine the property income rules in more detail in Chapter 6, section 6.8. The following activity, however, illustrates the rules briefly for you.

Activity

Mary lets a house that she owns in London. Rent was £9,600 a year until 30 September 2022 when it was increased to £10,200. Rent is payable a month in advance on the first of the month. The rent due on 1 April, 2023 was not received until 10 April, 2023. Mary incurred allowable expenses of £1,000 during the year to 5 April, 2023. Determine Mary's property income for 2022/23 on the accruals basis.

Feedback

Income, using the accruals basis, is:

(6 × £800) + (6 × £850) = £9,900

Notice that it does not matter that one payment due in the tax year was actually paid in the following year – that is the point of the accruals basis.

Hence the property income is £8,900 (£9,900 – £1,000). This is the figure you should put in Mary's tax computation. (Note: strictly the income should be calculated on the daily basis, but this monthly basis is usually acceptable to HMRC).

Trading income

4.26 Trading income primarily includes all income earned from being self-employed. The normal basis of assessment for trading, or business, profit is the *current year* basis. Under this principle the basis period for a year of assessment is normally the 12 months to the accounting date ending in the tax year. However, there are a number of circumstances in which this simple rule cannot be applied, especially in the early years of trading, the final years of trading or years in which a business changes its accounting date. The rules that apply in most of these circumstances will be discussed in section 6.42. Expenses which are wholly and exclusively for the purpose of the trade are allowable deductions using the *accruals* basis to create a taxable profit figure to be used in the tax computation, although from 6 April 2013, taxpayers can choose to use a cash basis (as we will see in section 6.40).

As with property income, FA17 introduced a new allowance of £1,000 for trading income to remove very small traders from the income tax net. The allowance works in the same way as the property income allowance.

We will return to examine trading income computations in more detail in Chapters 6 and 7.

Savings and investment income

4.27 As discussed in the earlier section of this chapter, interest received is taxed as savings income.

The savings income assessable for income tax in a tax year is the interest received within the year of assessment without any deductions, which means either paid to the taxpayer or made available, for example, credited to his or her account. Note therefore, that the accruals basis is not used but instead we use a *cash basis* for savings income.

Activity

Elizabeth opened a savings account in 1991. Interest is credited on 31 December each year, interest in recent years has been:

	£
31 December, 2020	300
31 December, 2021	360
31 December, 2022	310

Determine Elizabeth's savings income for 2022/23.

Feedback

The assessable amount of savings is the interest arising in the tax year (i.e. the cash basis). Hence the savings income for 2022/23 is £360 as that is what was credited to her bank account in the tax year.

Dividend income

4.28 Dividends and other distributions from companies are taxed under this income category. All non-dividend distributions from companies (which are not specifically excluded from the general rule) are also taxed as if they were a dividend to help reduce an obvious tax avoidance strategy.

Miscellaneous income

4.29 This category is used to tax annual profits or gains not falling under any other category. In particular, income from casual commissions, enterprise allowance payments, some capital sums from the sale of patent rights and business income received after a business has ceased trading (called 'post cessation receipts') are taxed under this heading. The basis of assessment is the *receipts* basis.

Steps 2 & 3: Deductible reliefs and allowances

4.30 In steps 2 and 3 of our income tax computation, adjustments are made for deductible reliefs and some personal reliefs in the form of allowances. Look back at Thomas Lester's tax computation to see where these appear (steps 1 - 3) and the effect it has on his tax computation.

Deductible reliefs

4.31 A deductible relief is an amount the income tax law allows as a deduction from the payer's total income to calculate their net income (step 2 of the tax computation). The following are deductible reliefs:

- pension contributions (for self-employed people or for employed people under net pay arrangements for excess relief – see Chapter 5, section 5.38 for an explanation of these rules)
- loss reliefs that are chargeable against general incomes (these include, for example, trade losses of various types, some property losses if you are running a property business as a landlord – as we will see in Chapter 6, and employment losses)
- payments of eligible interest (see below);
- qualifying annual payments.

Deductions at this step are only possible if there is sufficient income to absorb them. However, where a choice exists, the order that is used for deducting reliefs should be one that gives the greatest reduction in the taxpayer's income tax liability.

Tax relief for these items is given at the taxpayer's marginal rate of tax. To achieve this all reliefs must be shown gross when they are entered into the tax computation and then relief will automatically be given at the taxpayer's marginal rate of tax. This is because the deduction will reduce the total tax liability to the extent of the tax relief i.e. less tax will then be due at the top marginal rate of tax. If the taxpayer's taxable income is close to a tax band boundary, it may even reduce the marginal rate of tax to a lower band.

The following activity illustrates how to include reliefs as step 2 in the tax computation and shows the impact a relief can have on marginal tax rates:

Activity

Catherine makes a pension contribution that is eligible for treatment as a tax relief of £500 (gross) and has non-savings income of

a) £15,850
b) £12,850

Calculate her tax liability for the tax year.

Feedback

		£
a)	Total income	15,850
	Less tax relief for pension contribution	(500)
	Net income	15,350
	Less: personal allowance	(12,570)
	Taxable income	2,780
	Tax due/liability 2,780 @ 20%	556

b)

Total income		12,850
Less tax relief for pension contribution		(500)
Net income		12,350
Less: personal allowance		(12,570)
Taxable income		0
Tax due/liability	£0 @ 0%	0

i.e. the presence of the tax relief has meant that Catherine is taken out of paying any income tax at all – her marginal rate of tax goes from 20% to 0%. She cannot, however, get a refund for the amount of personal allowance not used, as we will see in 4.35.

Payments of eligible interest

4.32   Some yearly interest payments can be treated as a relief for tax calculations. The payment of eligible interest is therefore relieved at the taxpayer's marginal rate of tax. Examples of eligible interest that can be treated as tax reliefs are limited but include:

- *Loans to purchase plant and machinery for use in a partnership or as an employee.* The loan must be used to purchase plant and machinery for which capital allowances are available (these rules will be discussed in Chapter 7). The relief is available to partners or employees only (i.e. not to self-employed people or to corporations), for a maximum of three years from the end of the tax year in which the loan was taken out. (Note that interest on loans to purchase plant and machinery is already an allowable deduction for a self-employed person or company for tax purposes, which is why they are not allowed this treatment).

- *Loans to invest in an employee-controlled company.* The loan must be used to acquire ordinary shares either before, or within 12 months of, a company first becoming employee-controlled. The company must be a UK resident, unquoted, trading company or the holding company of a trading group. A company is employee controlled if at least 50% of the issued ordinary share capital and voting power is owned by employees or their spouses. If one employee owns more than 10% of the shares he or she is deemed to own 10% when testing to see if the 50% employee-controlled rule is satisfied (i.e. the rest of their shares will be treated as if not in employee ownership). If any capital is repaid the relief will be reduced.

- *Loans to invest in a partnership.* The loan must be used to either purchase a share in a partnership or introduce capital into a partnership or make a loan to a partnership to be used wholly and exclusively for business purposes. The claimant must be a member of the partnership throughout the time the interest relief is claimed. Limited partners are not eligible for this relief.

Annual payments

4.33 Deductible relief is also available for a limited range of annual payments. Historically there were many payments that came into this category, but now there are only a few, which are beyond the scope of this book.

More examples can be found on the website to illustrate the impact of tax reliefs for taxpayers other than those paying at basic rate.

Personal reliefs

4.34 Throughout the 20th century there were numerous changes to the way the income tax system operates that relate to what personal reliefs from income tax could be claimed or how they were operated including recognition of married women as separate from their husbands and shifts in the way reliefs were provided for children.

Further details of these, and earlier, changes to the UK tax system historically can be found in the online Chapter *History of UK Taxation.*

Fiscal Fact

It is predicted that for 2021/22 the lowest earning 25% of the UK population will receive 10.5% of the share of total income before tax in the UK and will pay 2.2% of total income tax receipts between them on this income. The highest earning 25% will receive 53% of the share of total income received and pay 76% of all income tax (i.e. almost thirty-five times that of the lowest 25%). The highest earning 1% are expected to earn 12.1% of all income and will pay between them 28% of all income tax (nearly thirteen times the lowest 25%). There are 6,000 people are expected to earn over £2,000,000 in 2021/22 and will pay an average estimated rate of tax of 39.7% on this income. [Source: HMRC Statistics Tables 2.4 & 2.5]

In this section we will now review the allowances and reliefs currently available to UK income taxpayers.

Personal allowance (PA)

4.35 The personal allowance operates like a tax-free threshold, or zero rate tax band. Most people (whatever age they are) who are UK residents are entitled to this initial sum of income on which no income tax is due. This is called the *basic* personal allowance. For 2022/23 this tax-free sum is at least £12,570 (unchanged from 2021/22). This includes children, and those who are married as well as single people. However, not everyone gets a basic personal allowance. If a taxpayer's income in the tax year exceeds £100,000 this may be partly, or even fully, lost. We will examine how this occurs below.

Fiscal Fact

When the personal allowance rose to £12,500 in 2019/20 it meant that no-one earning the national minimum wage for at least 30 hours a week would have to pay any income tax on their earnings.

There is provision in statute for the personal allowance to increase at least in line with inflation each year (using the Consumer Prices Index (CPI) to measure this rise since Budget 2011), unless Parliament opts to waive the provision for a particular year (as the Chancellor did, for example, with no increase this year from the 2021/22 level). However, sometimes the increase can exceed this measure for example in 2019/20 in lifting the personal allowance to £12,500 from £11,850 the previous year. Budget 2021 provides that the current personal allowance will be frozen until April 2026.

While increases in personal allowances benefit all taxpayers that are entitled to them, they benefit those paying tax at higher rates more than those on lower rates, in absolute terms because the actual tax saving is at a higher marginal rate.

If we look at *average* rates of tax, on the other hand, an increase in personal allowance will give a greater reduction in the average rate of tax for a lower income taxpayer than a higher rate taxpayer. The impact of changes in personal allowance or other tax rate bands is quite complicated. You may want to refresh your understanding of the difference between marginal and average rates of tax by looking at section 3.5.

If wages are rising because of inflation, then freezing the personal allowance means people will pay more tax when they may not be any better off in real terms. This is sometimes called fiscal drag, or bracket creep. Of course,, increases in personal allowance do not benefit those whose income is below the personal allowance threshold.

In 2012/13 and 2013/14 the Government went further to expressly recognise where the benefits lay when personal allowances were increased by making the extra basic rate personal allowances only beneficial to basic rate taxpayers. They did this by lowering the start of the higher rate band by the same amount it increased the personal allowance. This meant throughout this period higher rate taxpayers were no better off by any increases, even though basic rate taxpayers were.

Increases to the higher rate band have, however, occurred again in the past few years – although not always at the same rate as the rise in the personal allowance. For example, in 2019/20 the rise of £3,000 in the higher rate band starting point (from £34,500 to £37,500) was 4.6 times that of the rise in the personal allowance (of £650 from £11,850 to £12,500). These recent changes have undone most of the impact of the previous policy to focus personal allowance increases on the less well off.

Personal allowances are usually only available to be used by the person who is directly entitled to them – they couldn't historically be transferred to anyone else. However, this basic principle changed in 2015/16 with some allowance becoming transferrable under limited circumstances. Between a couple (married or in a civil partnership), one partner can now transfer up to £1,260 (no change from 2021/22) of their un-used personal allowance to the other, providing neither pays tax on their income above the basic rate. This will clearly be beneficial if one is a taxpayer and the other isn't using all their personal allowance, as moving un-used allowance to the taxpaying spouse will enable the couple to have more of their combined income tax-free. The receiving partner's personal allowance is simply increased by the total transferred to them (i.e. if the full transfer was made then their personal allowance for 2022/23 would rise to £13,830). This £1,260 limit is called the *Marriage Allowance*.

Fiscal Fact

When first introduced it was anticipated that up to 4 million households could benefit from the new Marriage Allowance rules. This will include up to 15,000 couples in civil partnerships.

Any personal allowance that is not used (or transferred) in the year is lost if that person's income is insufficient to use the allowance in full in any particular year. They also can't be rolled forward from year to year – but a new personal allowance can be claimed each year of course.

The 2009 Budget announced an important change to the longstanding philosophy of everyone getting at least some tax-free income, irrespective of their income levels. From April 2010, personal allowances are tapered down to zero for those with an adjusted net income more than £100,000. Adjusted net income starts with "net income", which is the total of the individual's income subject to income tax less certain deductions (for example, trading losses and payments made gross to pension schemes). This is then reduced by the grossed-up amounts of any Gift Aid contributions (charitable donations – see section 4.38 below) and pension contributions which have received tax relief at source (see section 5.38). Relief for any payments to trade unions or police organisations that was deducted in arriving at the individual's net income is then added back to arrive at the adjusted net income.

The tapering of personal allowances for those earning over £100,000 is at the rate of £1 for every £2 earned over £100,000 i.e. you will lose all of your personal allowance when you earn over £125,140 (£100,000 + (2 x £12,570)).

Note, you can't end up with a negative personal allowance, so for taxable incomes, after reliefs, above this sum the personal allowance just becomes zero.

Activity

Joe's net income for the tax year is £106,728 from various sources (after reliefs but before personal allowances). He has made no gift aid or personal pension payments in the year nor paid subscriptions to any trade union or police organisation. What will his personal allowance be for 2022/23?

Feedback

Joe's personal allowance will be:

£12,570 – (1/2 x (£106,728 – £100,000) = £9,206

This is the figure you should then use in Joe's tax computation at Step 3 instead of the full £12,570. Had Joe earned over £125,140 his personal allowance would be zero.

Fiscal Fact

The estimated cost to the Treasury in tax revenue foregone of allowing personal allowances was a huge £115 billion for 2021/22 – up from £72 billion for 2012/13. [Source: HMRC Statistics – Structural tax reliefs]

A quirk of the reduction in the personal allowances for higher earners is that people falling into this high-earning category suffer a higher than normal effective marginal tax rate on this extra income. The following activity illustrates this.

Activity

Calculate the marginal rate of tax of a single person with net income of £100,000 and compare it with the marginal rate of tax if they earn £8 more in the same period. What is the effective marginal rate on this difference?

Feedback

	£	£
Net income	100,000	100,008
Less personal allowance	(12,570)	
£12,570 – (100,008 – 100,000)/2		(12,566)
Taxable income	87,430	87,442

Hence an increase of £8 in total income leads to an increase of £12 in taxable income. If the marginal rate of tax in both situations is 40% (i.e. assuming the income is non-savings or savings income), the extra £8 of income results in an extra £4.80 (£12 × 40%) of tax, which is an effective marginal rate of tax of 60% (£4.80 ÷ £8).

Therefore, those in the lucky position to be earning between £100,000 and £125,140 are facing an effective 60% marginal tax rate. This falls to 40% again when they reach £125,140 income per annum and their personal allowance is fully used up.

Blind person's allowance (BPA)

4.36 This allowance is given to taxpayers who are registered as blind under local government rules. The allowance is £2,600 for this tax year (£2,520 in 2021/22) and is available in addition to the personal allowance. Unlike the personal allowance however, if the blind person has insufficient income to use the allowance in full the excess may all be transferred to their spouse or civil partner so they get a larger tax-free allowance than they would otherwise.

 You can now attempt Quick Quiz questions 1-6 and Full questions 2, 3 & 5.

Steps 4 & 5: Charging Taxable Income

4.37 Income tax is charged under steps 4 and 5 on the taxpayer's taxable income, after deducting the allowable payments in step 2 and personal reliefs in step 3 discussed above. We saw how this is done earlier in 4.16 – 4.20. In this section we look at an additional complication that arises when taxpayers make an allowable gift, or donation, to a charity.

Donations to charity

4.38 Since 6 April, 2000 most gifts to charities by individuals, however small and however regular, have been eligible for tax relief at the marginal rate of the taxpayer under the so-called 'Gift Aid' rules.

All that is necessary to operate this scheme is that the donor gives to the charity a Gift Aid declaration (a simple form, or even an oral statement will do) saying that they are giving money to the charity using the Gift Aid rules. The charity can then use this declaration to get back from HMRC at least some of the income tax paid (the basic rate tax) by the taxpayer related to the donation. Charities can reclaim 25p for every £1 you donate (£1 x 100/(100–20) = £1.25, so you pay £1 and HMRC pays 25p thereby returning to the charity 20% on the total £1.25 received).

This does not vary however with the marginal tax rate of the donor, i.e. the charity gets 25p for every £1 donated whatever rate the donor pays tax at. However, taxpayers can claim tax relief if their marginal rate is more than 20% so the cost of the donation to them is less. They do this via declaring the charitable donation as part of their tax return. We will see how this works in practice below.

The rules that apply when companies donate to charities are different to the rules for individuals. We will look at the rules for companies in Chapter 9.

Gift relief is also available for donations to community amateur sports clubs (CASCs) as well as to registered charities. The system for receiving the relief is identical to donations to charities. The Budget 2010 extended Gift Aid relief to certain EU based charities for gifts made by UK taxpayers. The same computation rules apply as for donations to UK based charities.

To be eligible for tax relief on charitable donations the donor must have paid at least the amount in tax on their taxable income that HMRC will be asked for by the charity or charities they donate to in the tax year. Either income tax or capital gains tax paid can be used to cover the tax (but not others taxes such as VAT). Where a taxpayer has not paid enough of these taxes to cover this, HMRC will ask the taxpayer to pay back the extra money the charity claims from them if gifts are made via Gift Aid rules. Taxpayers should beware in using these rules therefore when giving to charities or they may get a bill from HMRC they aren't expecting.

Fiscal Fact

In 1990/91, income tax repayments totalling £470 million were made to charities. In 2020/21 total repayments via gift aid totalled £1.38 billion. Charities also receive money related to individual donor's gifts via other tax reliefs including inheritance tax relief which provided £1.04 billion to the sector in 2020/21. In total from all tax reliefs available to charities, they reclaimed £5.7 billion in the year. [Source: HMRC UK Charity Tax Relief Statistics –Tables 1 and 2]

Tax relief is given to the taxpayer when making Gift Aid donations by increasing their basic rate band by the gross amount of the gift. This process ensures that relief is given at higher or additional rates to taxpayers who are higher or additional rate taxpayers (as their higher rate bands then start at a higher taxable income level). Similarly, basic rate taxpayers will get the deduction at 20% as their marginal rate (increasing their higher rate band start point of course makes no difference as they don't earn at the level at which this limit begins to affect their tax paid).

If a donor receives a benefit in return for their gift, the gift aid reclaim is restricted. Provided the benefit does not exceed the limits below, however, then gift aid can still be reclaimed by the charity. The current limits of value of any associated benefits (applicable since April 2019) are:

Donation	Permitted benefits value
£0 – £100	25% of the donation
£100+	£25 + 5% of the amount of the excess gift value over £100

A charitable gift paid under Gift Aid rules does not in fact need to appear in the taxpayer's tax computation and so for basic rate taxpayers these can be ignored when doing their tax computation. However, adjustments to the computation need to be made under certain circumstances, particularly for higher and additional rate taxpayers. The next activity shows you how this may occur.

Activity

In this tax year Andrew, an employee, makes a Gift Aid donation of £1,000 (net) to his favourite charity. What would his income tax computation be if his only income was non-savings income of:

a) £30,570
b) £12,620
c) £53,570
d) £200,000

Feedback

Andrew's payment, grosses up to £1,250 (£1,000 × 100/80). The charity collects the extra £250 from HMRC via the Gift Aid scheme. We need to check that Andrew has paid enough basic rate tax to cover the repayment to the charity.

a)

	£
Earnings from employment	30,570
Less personal allowance	(12,570)
	18,000
Tax due: 18,000 @ 20%	3,600.00

Nothing else needs to be done in this case as Andrew's income easily covers the reclaiming of the £250 from HMRC. He also is a basic rate taxpayer so no higher rate band adjustment is needed. In such a situation you would not normally need to list this gift aid payment in Andrew's tax computation as it will have no impact on his calculation.

b)

	£
Earnings from employment	12,620
Less personal allowance	(12,570)
	50
Tax due: 50 @ 20%	10.00

In this case Andrew is not paying enough tax to cover the £250 that the charity would reclaim on his donation. He will therefore need to pay another £240 (£250 − £10) to HMRC as extra income tax or he can inform the charity not to treat this as gift aided if he doesn't want to pay the extra to HMRC.

c)

	£
Earnings from employment	53,570
Less personal allowance	(12,570)
	41,000

Tax due:

(37,700 + 1,250) @ 20%	7,790.00
(41,000 – 38,950) @ 40%	820.00
	8,610.00

In this case as Andrew is a higher rate taxpayer his basic rate band is extended by the gross amount of his charitable donation (£1,250) so that he receives relief for this payment at the higher rate. This means £1,250 extra of his income is taxed at 20% instead of at 40% as would have otherwise been the case, saving him £250 (20% × £1,250) in tax.

d)

	£
Earnings from employment	200,000
Less personal allowance	(nil)
	200,000

Tax due:

(37,700 + 1,250) @ 20%	7,790.00
((150,000 + 1,250) – 38,950) @ 40%	44,920.00
200,000 – 151,250 @ 45%	21,937.50
	74,647.50

In this case both the basic rate band and the higher rate bands are extended by the gross amount of the gift aid payment, so Andrew has saved £312.50 (20% x £1,250) + (5% x £1,250) in tax.

Gift Aid donations do not necessarily have to be dealt with in the tax year in which the payment is made. Since 2003, provided a claim is made before the tax return for that year is presented to HMRC, a taxpayer can opt to 'carry back' their payment so that it is treated as if it had been paid in the previous tax year. This will then affect the taxpayer's tax computation for that previous year, not for the current year.

Another form of tax relief for gifts to charities is the *Payroll Giving Scheme*, set up in the Finance Act 1986. The scheme applies to employees who pay tax under the PAYE scheme and whose employer runs a scheme, approved by HMRC. The scheme operates by withholding sums from their pay. The taxpayer can instruct their employer to make a donation to the charity of their choice. The advantage of doing this for the taxpayer, is that donations are made before PAYE deductions meaning tax relief at their marginal rate is automatically applied and will not need any further adjustments to be made via a tax return even if they are higher or additional rate taxpayers. This means they would not have to file a tax return to get the extra tax paid back if they didn't need to file one for any other reason.

Fiscal Fact

In recent years the sums given via payroll deduction have plateaued at around £130 million per year (£132 million in 2019/20). Around 1.1 million individuals give to charities this way each year. This has however, more than doubled (in sums given and in number of donors using this scheme) since 2000/01. [Source: HMRC UK Charity Tax Relief Statistics –Table 8]

In 2013, the National Audit Office undertook a study of the Gift Aid system, to consider the costs and effectiveness of the scheme and also to see if it was being abused for fraud or tax avoidance purposes. The report states (at p11):

"Tax relief on donations reflects a long-held principle... that charitable income should be exempt from taxation where that income is used for charitable purposes. Gift aid and other reliefs on donations are current mechanisms for achieving this. They encompass a wider set of objectives, such as making the tax system simpler for charities and donors to use and encouraging more giving by making donations more tax efficient."

We look further at the broader question of tax reliefs for charities in section 14.28 and also on how to address company charitable donations in section 9.11.

Step 6: Tax reductions

4.39   After calculating the tax borne (steps 4 & 5) a taxpayer may be entitled to various reliefs in the form of tax reductions, taken into account in step 6. As with step 3, these are a mixture of personal and activity based reliefs and include:

- tax reduction for elderly married couples and civil partners;
- venture capital trust (VCT) reduction;
- enterprise investment scheme (EIS) and seed enterprise investment scheme (SEIS) reduction;
- community investment tax (CITR) relief;
- social investment tax (SITR) relief;
- relief for interest on a loan to purchase an annuity; and
- qualifying maintenance payments

Most of the details of computing entitlement to these reductions are beyond the coverage of this book but we will illustrate the first of these for you as one example you may come across. We also discuss VCTs, EIS/SEISs, CITR and SITR briefly. All others are handled in the tax computation in the same way.

Venture Capital Trusts

4.40 When taxpayers subscribe for newly issued shares in an HMRC approved Venture Capital Trust (VCT), a tax reduction of 30% of the amount invested is available. To be eligible the company will normally need to be less than 12 years old (for investments made after April 2015) and the taxpayer must keep the shares for at least five years to keep the tax savings. Dividends received from these shares are exempt from income tax, and if the taxpayer sells the shares, he or she won't have to pay capital gains tax (see Chapter 8).

Fiscal Fact

Around 4,000 companies raise capital via EISs and 30 via VCTs each year. Since the EIS tax relief scheme was launched in 1993/4 almost 33,000 companies have participated in the scheme raising almost £24 billion of funds between them. Since VCTs were introduced in 1995 they have raised just over £9 billion of funds and in 2020/21 they issued shares to the value of £668 million.

Enterprise Investment Schemes

4.41 This tax reduction of 30% of the amount invested is available when a taxpayer subscribes for newly issued shares in qualifying Enterprise Investment Scheme (EIS) companies. These are mainly smaller, unlisted companies but can include businesses up to 250 employees and assets of no more than £15 million before the investment and £16 million after. These limits rise to less than 500 employees, and assets of no more £20 million for businesses in knowledge intensive industries (i.e. businesses in industries such as science and engineering that rely on significant investment in research and development and innovation).

An annual limit to tax reductions under this scheme of £1million per investor applies from 6 April 2012. This limit rose to £2 million from April 2018 provided that any amounts over the £1 million previous limit is invested in one or more so called 'knowledge-intensive' companies. Unlike VCT investments, dividends from EIS shares are not exempt from income tax, although capital gains tax does not apply to the sale of the shares, so long as they are held for at least three years.

From 6 April 2012 a new Seed EIS (SEIS) became available to investors. This applies to new investments made into early stage companies (less than 25 employees and assets less than £200,000). For investments in such businesses tax reliefs of 50% will apply to investors with less than 30% stock in such business (including their directors). A cap of £100,000 per investor applies (unused amounts can be carried back one year). Shares acquired under this scheme are also exempt from capital gains tax – as for the main EIS.

Community Investment Schemes

4.42 Community Investment Tax Relief (CITR) was introduced in 2003 to encourage investments into Community Development Finance Institutions who on lend to SMEs based in disadvantaged communities. Tax relief of up to 25% of money invested is available, spread over 5 years. Maximum relief is available for investors who hold the investment for at least 5 years.

Social Investment Tax Relief

4.43 Budget 2014 introduced a new tax reducer – the social investment tax relief. From July 2014 (now at least until April 2023 after being extended in Budget 2021) individuals who subscribe to qualifying shares or who make qualifying debt investments in a social enterprise that meets the rules for the new tax reducer can get a 30% relief of the amount invested, subject to a maximum annual investment of £1 million. The investment must be held for 3 years to keep the relief given. The investor must have sufficient UK tax liability to offset the relief, although the investor does not have to be a UK resident. The relief can be carried back so it can be treated as having been made in the prior year if sufficient income exists in that year to offset it, but it cannot be carried forward. Therefore, if the taxpayer has not got enough UK tax liability to offset the payment made in the current or prior year then the excess relief is lost.

The social enterprises that can qualify for this investment relief on issuing their shares or receiving loans are carefully defined in the rules. They must have less than 500 employees, not be controlled by another company, must be a charity (or a so-called community interest company or benefit society) and not have more than £16 million in gross assets once the investment has been made. Each qualifying social enterprise can only raise a maximum of £290,000 this way and once they have this money it must be used within 28 months or their investors will lose their relief. It also matters that they are not substantially engaged in a number of restricted activities. These include banking, money-lending, property development, road transport and insurance.

 You can now attempt Quick Quiz questions 7&8 and Full questions 1 & 6.

National insurance contributions

4.44 We saw in Chapter 1 that national insurance was introduced in 1948, largely to provide for the National Health Service, state retirement pensions, unemployment and sickness benefit. Much of the UK's social security system continues to be paid for, albeit indirectly now, by these payments made by the working population and by their employers.

Initially national insurance was payable at a flat rate by both employees and employers. The intention was for the payment to represent an insurance payment rather than to tax people based on an ability to pay. Thus, the burden of the tax fell heaviest on the lowest paid, i.e. the tax was regressive.

In subsequent years the amount which each contributor had to pay increased as social security expenditure grew. By 1961 the flat rate contribution was seen to be too great a burden on the lowest paid and earnings-related contributions were introduced. By 1975 the entire national insurance contribution was earnings related. Although national insurance is now assessed on a percentage basis there is an upper limit above which employees only pay 2% extra national insurance instead of the full amount. This arrangement means that the tax is still regressive, i.e. taxpayers on low incomes can pay a greater percentage of their income in national insurance contributions than taxpayers on higher incomes.

Until 2000/01 neither employee nor employer national insurance contributions were payable on most benefits in kind (i.e. benefits received by an employee related to their employment but not paid in cash e.g. goods, use of a company car for private purposes and so on), making provisions of benefits in kind a relatively tax efficient form of remuneration. Now employers (but still not employees at present) are required to pay contributions (called Class 1A) on most benefits in kind they provide to their employees. For example, if an employee has a company car and/or fuel for private motoring the employer must pay Class 1A contributions, at 15.05% of the value of the car and fuel benefits. (We will consider how these values are calculated in Chapter 5.)

National insurance contributions are collected by HMRC (http://www.gov.uk/topic/personal-tax/national-insurance). The PAYE system is used to collect these payments from employees and employers, but direct payment to HMRC must be made by those who are self-employed, or others not in employment but making contributions.

A record is kept of an individual's national insurance contributions during their lifetime and gaps in contributions can lead to a reduction, or even loss, of benefits in some circumstances, so national insurance still has some characteristics of an insurance scheme. The compulsory nature of national insurance and its payment using earnings as its base, just like income tax, makes it feel, however, very much like a tax.

Unlike income tax, which is charged on a taxpayer's expected income for the year and collected as income is received under PAYE, national insurance contributions are calculated according to the employee's income for each payment period separately. Hence, if a taxpayer works for a number of months during the year and then has no income for the rest of the year, he or she may be able to reclaim some of the income tax already paid when working so that the correct amount is paid over the whole year, however, no repayment of national insurance contributions already made (if made correctly) is possible. UK income tax is termed a 'cumulative tax' system because unused allowances accumulate; national insurance is a 'non-cumulative tax' because payments are only due in periods when payment thresholds are exceeded, irrespective of other earnings in the year.

There are four main classes of national insurance contributions:

- Class 1 are paid by both employees, (called primary contributions), and employers, (called secondary contributions);
- Classes 2 and 4 are paid by the self-employed;
- Class 3 payments are made on a voluntary basis, by those who, while in work and earning money, would otherwise not pay enough contributions via other classes to entitle them to a state pension when they retire.

Various personal circumstances can affect contributions paid; for example, employers don't pay if you are under 21 (this was under 16 before April 2015) but employees have to if they are 16 or over. If you are in full time education between the ages of 16-18, you get credited these years as if you'd paid them. If you are a full-time child carer, and therefore don't work in paid employment, you can claim home responsibilities protection which reduces the number of years of contributions needed to get a full state pension.

Once employees are over national pensionable age they are not required to make further national insurance contributions. They will, however, have to pay the new Health and Social Care Levy as we will see below. The employer's contributions are still payable. The national pensionable age in the UK used to be 60 for women and 65 for men, but this is gradually being increased so that eligibility for pension will be later, and also the rules for men and women will be aligned so that eventually, the state pension age will be 68 for both.

The rates have changed this year due to the introduction of the new Health and Social Care Levy that added 1.25% to all rates to be paid by employees and employers on earnings after 1 April 2022. This will show as a new separate deduction on payslips after April 2023 but for this year will only appear as an increase in NIC rates paid.

Some of the thresholds at which payments apply also changed from 5 July 2022 as a result of the Spring Statement 2022. Note that only the levels after this point are shown below and used in examples in this text although if you are doing this computation for the period between April and July 2022 do watch out for different thresholds that applied between these dates.

National insurance contributions for the current year (from 5 July 2022) are as follows:

Class 1

Employee: Pay per week (per month/per annum)	
£242.00 (£1,048/£12,570) or less	
– employee primary threshold	0%
£242.01 – £967.00 (1,048 – £4,189/£12,570 – £50,270)	
– employee's primary threshold to upper earnings limit (UEL) main percentage	13.25%
Over £967 (£4,189/£50,270)	
– additional primary percentage	3.25%

Employer: Pay per week (per month/per annum)	
£175.00 (£758/£9,100) or less	
– employer primary threshold	0%
Over £175.00 (£758/£9,100)	15.05%

Note that increasing the annual threshold to £12,570 means that those earning less than this sum with pay neither personal income tax nor NICs from 5 July 2022 onwards.

4.45 From April 2014, an 'Employment Allowance' has been available to offset national insurance contribution liabilities (and from 2023/24 their Health and Social Care Levy liabilities) for small employers. This allowance is set at £5,000 from April 2022 (£4,000 since April 2020 and £3,000 before April 2020), which means many small businesses do not have to pay employer national insurance contributions or be liable for the new levy in practice. This doesn't affect employee payments, only those of their employers. Owner-directors are not able to claim this if they are the only employee of their company (and since April 2020 business are only eligible for this allowance if their national insurance bill is below £100,000 in the previous tax year).

Employers also do not have to pay NICs for anyone under the age of 21, or those on approved apprenticeship schemes up to the age of 25, provided their earnings are below the Upper Earnings Limit (if their earnings are above this then the normal 15.05% applies on this excess).

Fiscal Fact

The UK Government estimated that increasing the allowance threshold to £5,000 will affect 495,000 business and mean 30% of all business will benefit from this new threshold level. It will take out 50,000 business from having to pay any NICs of the new Levy on their employees. It is estimated that this allowance cost £2.4 billion in 2021/22 with 1.1 million business in 2020/21 claiming this allowance. [Sources: HMRC Spring Statement 2022: Business Support Factsheet - published 22 March 2022 and HMRC Non-structural reliefs cost estimates]

From April 2022 businesses then located in one of the eight new freeports will also be exempt from employer (secondary) national insurance contributions for 36 months for new employees who spend 60% or more of their time working at a freeport site and earn up to £25,000 per annum (per National Insurance Contribution Bill 2021).

Class 1 contributions are based on the employee's gross pay without deducting pension contributions.

Because directors may be able to influence the timing of their remuneration package, their Class 1 national insurance contributions are always calculated on an annual basis for directors. In previous years this equated to the same basis as the effective annual threshold for employees but for 2022/23 this is set at £11,908. It will revert to be the same again for all i.e. £12,570 in 2023/24.

Activity

Calculate the primary and secondary (before employment allowance and assuming all are >25 years old) Class 1 contributions of:

- Matthew, who earns £125 per week.
- Mark, who earns £285 per week.
- Luke who earns £500 per week.
- John, who is a company director, earns £400 per week, receives an annual bonus of £10,000 in the year.
- Paul, earns £1,020 a week.

In all cases assume that the thresholds applicable after 5 July 2022 apply for the whole year.

Feedback

Matthew

Matthew does not pay primary Class 1 contributions because his earnings are less than the primary threshold of £242. Similarly, his employer does not pay secondary Class 1 contributions because his earnings are below the secondary threshold of £175.

Mark

Mark pays ((£285 – £242) × 13.25%) = £5.69.
His employer pays ((£285 – £175) × 15.05%) = £16.55.

Luke

Luke pays ((£500 – £242) × 13.25%) = £34.18.
His employer pays ((£500 – £175) × 15.05%) = £48.91.

John

For company directors, the annual earnings threshold is £11,908.

John receives an annual income of £30,800 (£400 × 52 + don't forget to include his bonus that is also subject to NIC at £10,000) so is below the employee's UEL and he only pays annual primary Class 1 contributions of (£30,800 – £11,908) × 13.25% = £2,503.19.

His employer will pay (£30,800 – £9,100) × 15.05% = £3,265.85.

Paul

Paul's weekly salary exceeds the £967 per week UEL level so he will pay:

(£967 – £242) × 13.25% = £96.06
+ (£1,020 – £967) × 3.25% = £1.72
total = £97.78.
His employer will pay:
+ (£1,020 – £175) × 15.05% = £127.17.

If someone has more than one employment, they are liable to pay primary Class 1 contributions for each job, subject to a maximum annual contribution. This maximum contribution is based on formulae that considers how much was earned in each employment (i.e. to balance how much should be paid at the regular rate and how much at the extra 3.25% rate). Any overpayments made can be reclaimed at the end of the year. To avoid the need for repayment, a taxpayer can also claim for a deferral of payment on some of their contributions. Any extra due at the end of the year will then need to be settled directly with HMRC (usually via completing a tax return in the normal way).

Class 1A

4.46 Benefits in kind (non-cash rewards related to an employment or office) are usually not chargeable to Class 1 contributions for employees; however, they do create a Class 1A contribution for employers (not employees). The value used to determine how much the contribution will be is the same as calculated for the employment income benefit in kind on which the employee pays income tax. We will see how this is determined in the next chapter in more detail. Class 1A contributions are paid at the same rates by employers as normal Class 1 contributions (i.e. 15.05%).

Class 2

4.47 The self-employed pay national insurance contributions of £3.15 (£3.05 for 2021/22) per week for the current tax year provided their annual profits are at least £11,908 (£6,515 in 2021/22). This large increase is made up of a rise in the small profits threshold (£6,725 in 2022/23) to keep those who are self-employed in line with those who are employed such that none will pay NICs below annual levels of the same amount. A new 'low profits limit' therefore will now be used to determine when Class 2 NICs are due. This is set at £11,908 for this tax year. It will then become the same level as that for personal income tax personal allowances for employees (i.e. £12,570) from 2023/24. If annual profits are below this level, no contributions are required.

Class 2 contributions used to be paid directly to HMRC on a monthly or quarterly basis if due but from April 2015, Class 2 contributions are paid via the self-employed tax return (alongside Class 4 payments if also due) as part of a simplification plan for these contributions.

Note that the new Health and Social Care Levy does not apply to Class 2 NICs.

Class 3

4.48 Anyone can pay voluntary contributions of £15.85 per week (£15.40 in 2021/22) to maintain rights to some state benefits (particularly the state pension) that they might otherwise lose, for example, because their earnings are too low to pay other contributions.

The new Health and Social Care Levy also does not apply to this Class of NICs.

Class 4

4.49 In addition to Class 2 and maybe Class 3 contributions, the self-employed pay 10.25% (this was 9% for many years before 6 April 2022 but the Health and Social Care Levy of 1.25% must now be paid on this Class of NICs), of their profits between lower and upper limits, which are £11,908 (£9,568 in 2021/212) and £50,270 (unchanged from 2021/22) for this tax year.

As for employees, profits earned above the upper limit are subject to a further 3.25% charge (called the additional Class 4 percentage) made up of a 2% NIC rate and the 1.25% Health and Social Care Levy.

For Class 4 national insurance contribution purposes profits are the taxable profits under the trading income rules less trading losses and any interest or annual payments to do with the business but not already deducted in working out trading profit. Personal allowances are not taken into account for Class 4 contributions. The calculation for this amount due usually forms part of the tax return. Class 4 contributions are normally paid at the same time as the income tax on their business profits (and assessed as part of the tax return process). This normally means it is paid in two instalments (on 31 January in the tax year and on 31 July following it) with a third payment due the following 31 January if any balancing payment is due.

Activity

Simon, who is self-employed, has taxable income from his business of £20,000 for this tax year. Calculate his national insurance contributions for the tax year.

Andrew, who is also self-employed, has taxable business income of £62,000 for this tax year. Calculate his national insurance contributions for the tax year.

In both cases assume that the thresholds applicable after 5 July 2022 apply for the whole year.

Feedback

Simon

Simon will pay Class 2 NI contributions of £163.80 (£3.15×52) as his earnings are over the small earnings exception limit for the year, and Class 4 contributions of £829.43 (10.25% × (£20,000 – £11,908)). These will both be collected as part of his self-assessment payments.

Andrew

Andrew will also pay Class 2 contributions of £163.80. His Class 4 contributions will be £4,313.33 (10.25% × (£50,270 – £11,908) + 3.25% × (£62,000 – £50,270)).

Benefits received

4.50 A full basic pension is paid to individuals who, for at least 35 years of their deemed working life, have paid at least the equivalent of the lower earnings limit contribution for the whole year, or 52 Class 2 or Class 3 contributions.

Some credits for contributions are available however, if you are registered as unemployed, are receiving job seekers' allowance, are unable to work through incapacity or disability, are in receipt of a carer's allowance or if you receive maternity allowance. People between 16 and 18 will also automatically receive credits if they do not pay enough contributions but this is not the case for anyone in full time education over the age of 18 (i.e. if you are at University, you only get the years of contribution counted if you actually make national insurance payments to the minimal levels, the same as for everyone else).

Taxpayers making Class 1 national insurance contributions at the higher rate are eligible to receive job seekers' allowance and earnings related (i.e. second) state pension which Class 2 and 4 contributors are not eligible to receive.

Impact of national insurance contributions

4.51 National insurance contributions are levied on earned income in addition to income tax – but not on savings or dividend income. This provides a distortion in the tax system between earned income and savings or investment income. A taxpayer with taxable income of less than £50,000 will have an effective marginal rate of tax (including both income tax and national insurance contributions) of 33.25% on earned income but either 0%, 8.75% or 20% on unearned income (depending on whether it is dividend or savings income). This anomaly may encourage those who are shareholders of businesses in which they are also employees to draw relatively low salaries and to pay dividends in order to reduce national insurance contributions. This question is discussed more fully in Chapter 11, as it is a common tax planning strategy.

 You can now attempt Quick Quiz questions 9-12 and Full question 4

Basic income tax planning points for couples

4.52 If one married partner's marginal rate of tax is lower than the other's it is tax efficient to shift income from the higher rate payer to the lower rate payer as this will reduce their combined tax bill. There are broadly two ways of doing this.

First, investments held in the higher rate payer's name could be transferred to the lower rate payer. (No capital gains tax liability arises from a transfer between spouses as we will see in Chapter 8). These might include shares in a family business, in which case dividends on the shares would be taxed at the lower rate.

The second opportunity for shifting income from the high rate taxpayer to the low rate taxpayer is where one or both of the spouses are running a business. For example, it is possible to pay a wage to a spouse who also does work for the business e.g. deals with telephone calls and paperwork (although beware – this must be a fair wage for the work actually done or it may be challenged by HMRC). The alternative is to set up in business as a partnership in which case the other spouse can be allocated a share of the profits. A similar strategy can be adopted with adult children with low marginal rates of tax if they also help run the business. If a partnership is established then it is the responsibility of the partners to agree the profit-sharing ratio and HMRC will not challenge such an agreement. However, if a relative is employed by a sole trader, partnership or company then HMRC may wish to be satisfied that the payment is wholly and exclusively for the purpose of trade. In the case of *Copeman v Flood* (1941) a farmer employed his son and daughter as directors of the company and they each received a salary of £2,600. The son was aged 24 and had some business experience but the daughter was only 17 and unable to carry out the duties of a director. Both did undertake some duties for the company but it was held that the entire salary was not an expense incurred wholly and exclusively for business purposes. The Commissioners were asked to decide how much of the payments should be allowable based on the actual work carried out by the son and daughter. This established the principle still in operation now nearly 80 years later.

Couples may also wish to transfer part of either of their personal allowances (maximum £1,260) if these are not being fully used up by them as their income is below the personal allowance threshold. This is allowed from April 2015 as long as the person to whom they are transferring only pays tax at basic rate.

Further discussion of income tax planning can be found in Chapter 11.

Summary

This chapter has explained the income tax framework, which will enable you to apply the legislation discussed in later chapters.

In order to calculate an individual's tax liability it is necessary to undertake a number of steps:

1.   Identify and categorise each source of income for a taxpayer.

2. Use the income tax rules to determine the basis of assessment for each category of income.

3. Determine the income tax rules that are used to calculate the taxable income for each category of income.

4. Calculate the income that is assessable and determine any reliefs and allowances from that income that are allowed for tax purposes. This will enable you to calculate the taxable income from each category.

5. Now you can calculate the tax liability of a taxpayer.

You should now be able to review the example personal tax computation for Thomas we presented at the start of this chapter to check that you understand how the figure of Tax Payable has been reached.

Some possibilities for simple tax planning for families were also briefly discussed in this chapter.

You are now able to progress to the next three chapters, which build on the foundations that have been laid in this chapter to provide you with further details of how to perform personal tax computations. In turn they expand on the rules for taxing property income, income from employment and pensions, and income from self-employment (trading income).

Project areas and discussion questions

1. Until April 2005 the various categories of income tax were called Schedules, each of which had sub-sections to them called cases. These names have disappeared now for individuals as part of a process of re-writing the Income tax laws. Check out the role of the Tax Law Rewrite Committee who undertook this work. What was their motivation for doing this work?

2. The additional 2% extra NIC on earnings of employees over the UEL was controversial when it was introduced as it marked a move away from an upper cap on this charge/tax. Is this a fair way to raise extra money by the Government? Is it appropriate that the Health and Social Care Levy should also apply to this extra rate?

3. Does it make sense to continue to have a separate income tax charge and national insurance contributions payment requirement? Review the Office for Tax Simplification's work on this idea:

   https://assets.publishing.service.gov.uk/government/uploads/system/uploads/attachment_data/file/567491/OTS_report_web_final.pdf.

4. Should unearned income such as investment income also be subject to National Insurance contributions and Health and Social Care Levy charges?

5. Is it fair that Child Benefit is restricted for higher income earners? What complications arise because of this interaction between the benefits and tax systems?

6. Does having a separate unit of taxation (i.e. everyone pays their own tax liability rather than combining this into family tax bills as was the case before the 1990s) make this a fairer (more equitable) system for all? Are there losers from charging income tax this way?

Quick quiz

1 Deirdre has employment income of £36,700. What is her tax liability for the year?

2 Benson has pension income of £28,650 and savings income of £1,500. What is his tax liability?

3 Candice has saving income of £18,870 and received dividend income of £2,500. What is her net tax payable?

4 Angela has non-saving income of £23,850 for the year and pays a patent royalty of £200 (net). What is her tax liability?

5 Erica has pension income of £13,350 and savings income of £500 for the year. What is her net tax payable?

6 Geoffrey earns net income of £110,500 from a business and has no other income. He makes no charitable donations, personal pension contributions or pays any subscriptions. What is his net tax payable?

7 Dominic has earnings from employment of £21,215 and no other income. He makes a charitable donation of £500 under the Gift Aid scheme during the year. What is his net tax payable?

8 Hillary earns net income of £73,850 from a business and has no other income. During the year she subscribes £50,000 to an eligible Enterprise Investment Scheme. What is her net tax payable?

9 Frank has net trading income of £33,350 for the year and receives dividends of £3,000. What is his net tax payable? What national insurance contributions are due on this income? (You can assume the thresholds and rates after 5 July 2022 apply for the whole year)

10 Ivan is a sole trader and has taxable profits of £46,000 for the year ended 5 April 2023 with no other income. What is his NIC liability? (assuming thresholds and rates after 5 July 2022 apply for the whole year)

11 Josephine is an employee with a salary of £500 per week. What is her weekly NIC liability?

12 Kamran is an employee and is provided with a computer for his private use which is a benefit in kind and has a value of £400 for NIC purposes. What is the NIC liability in respect of the computer?

Questions

Question 1

Sam has the following income:

	£
Gross salary (PAYE deducted of £3,080)	27,570
Building society interest	2,000
Dividends (from UK company)	3,000
Qualifying charitable donation (gross)	880

Required: Calculate Sam's income tax payable for the tax year.

Question 2

Jasper received the following income for the year ended 5 April 2023:

	£
Salary (before PAYE)	68,150
PAYE deducted	15,000
Dividends	6,000
Bank interest	3,000

Required: Calculate Jasper's income tax payable for the tax year.

Question 3

Janet and Dave have lived together for two years. Janet earned £39,850 during 2022/23 on which she paid £6,500 via PAYE. She also received an annual bonus of £3,000 in August 2022 for the year ended on the previous 31 March. She received income of £5,375 in interest payments from a Building Society account in her own name. She also received £1,000 winnings from her premium bonds. Janet owns a cottage in North Yorkshire which she let from 1 November, 2022 at an annual rent of £8,000 payable quarterly in advance. Her allowable expenses on the property while it was rented were £1,000.

Dave earned a salary of £37,650 in the tax year 2022/23 from which his employer deducted £4,780 in PAYE. He also had investment income of £3,750 from a bank deposit account and received dividends of £9,760 from UK shares.

Required: Compute Janet and Dave's income tax payable for 2022/23.

Question 4

Calculate the national insurance contributions due by both the employee listed below, and their employer (assume the rates and thresholds for NICs that are applicable after 5 July 2022 apply for the whole year):

a) Peter earns £550 per week.

b) Alan earns £280 per week.

c) Kath's earnings in the year are as follows (all for the same employer and all earned evenly over the periods given).

Jan – April	£1,500 per month
May – Aug	nothing was earned
Sept	£350 only was earned
Oct – Dec	£1,200 per month

d) Chris is self-employed. His adjusted profits for tax purposes (i.e. his trading profit) for 2022/23 were £27,600.

(Answer can be found in the lecturers' section of the website.)

Question 5

Zach is employed and has the following income and expenses:

	£
Employment income	52,000
Building society interest	2,100
National Lottery win	5,000
Qualifying charitable donation (gross)	2,000

Required: If PAYE of £7,300 had been withheld by his employer in the year, calculate Zach's income tax payable for the year.

(Answer can be found in the lecturers' section of the website.)

Question 6 (based on an ICAS question)

Mr Byte runs a successful software design business. His taxable trading income for the year was £193,900. In addition, he received the following:

1. During 2022/23 Mr Byte's accounts were credited with this interest:

	£
Building society accounts	17,250
NS&I Easy access savings account	9,800
ISA accounts	4,150

2. Mr Byte received UK dividends of £40,200 from his investment portfolio and £15,200 from Venture Capital Trusts.

3. Mr Byte made monthly donations of £200 cash under the Gift Aid scheme.

Required: Calculate Mr Byte's income tax and national insurance contributions payable for the year.

(Answer can be found in the lecturers' section of the website.)

 Further test questions for this chapter to test your knowledge can be found in the student section of the website at:

http://www.fiscalpublications.com/lymerandoats/2022

Further reading and examples

Boden, R. (2021) Pensioned Off? Evaluating the UK's National Insurance Scheme, *Public Money and Management,* 41(8) 646-655.

Clegg, D. (2015), The Demise of Tax Credits, *The Political Quarterly,* 86(4), pp 493-499.

Combs, A. and R. Tutin (2022), *Taxation: incorporating the 2022 Finance Act,* Fiscal Publications: Malvern.

– use this book for many other examples to further develop and test your knowledge of this chapter's contents.

See https://www.fiscalpublications.com/combsandtutin/2022

National Audit Office (2020), *The management of tax expenditures.*

https://www.nao.org.uk/report/the-management-of-tax-expenditures/

A large question bank that can be used to test your knowledge of material introduced in this chapter -

Combs, A. (2022), *UK Income Tax Practice Questions (2nd edition 2022/23),* Fiscal Publications: Malvern.

– a large test bank of questions linked to the content of this chapter that will enable you to thoroughly test your knowledge of this work with exam-level questions. See

https://www.fiscalpublications.com/uk-income-tax-practice-questions/2022

5 Taxing employment and pension income

Introduction

5.1 In Chapter 4 you read about income tax components and you learnt that to calculate a taxpayer's income tax liability it is necessary to identify the tax rules under which each receipt is taxed. In Chapters 6 and 7 you will study the trading income component rules which are used to tax income from trades (businesses – including those who are self-employed), vocations and professions (i.e. collectively called trading income) as well as the property income rules.

In this chapter you will learn about the detail of another set of key income tax component rules – namely employment and pension income taxable under Income Tax (Earnings and Pension) Act, 2003 (ITEPA).

At the end of this chapter you will be able to:

- understand the tax treatment of employment income, including benefits in kind, and calculate an individual's taxable income from employment; and
- understand how to apply the rules which relate to pensions and pension contributions.

Tax on employment earnings

5.2 This chapter examines the tax rules relating to employees. Since employees form most of the UK's working population (about 86% in May 2022), the rules which apply to them are clearly very important.

Employment earnings are defined as including 'any gratuity or other profit or incidental benefit of any kind obtained by the employee if it is in money or money's worth' (ITEPA 2003, s62). This means that tax must be paid not only an employee's earnings (wages or salary) but also any bonuses an employee may receive, tips from customers if working in the kind of job where this occurs, and also any non-cash payments received (called *benefits in kind*).

Employment or self-employment

5.3 It is not always clear whether an individual taxpayer working in conjunction with someone else is in fact employed by them (working *for* them) or is self-employed (working *with* them). This distinction is important for tax purposes as it will determine whether the taxpayer is taxed using the trading or the employment income rules. The total tax the taxpayer will pay on their earnings will vary, sometimes significantly, based on how they are classified.

To determine this classification an important consideration is the contract that describes the working relationship. At the most basic level, if it is a contract *of* service, this indicates employment, and the taxpayer will be taxed under employment income rules as an employee. If it is a contract *for* services then this indicates a self-employed (contract) relationship and the taxpayer will be required to pay tax under trading income rules (we will look at these in Chapter 6). As the latter usually results in lower income tax and national insurance bills, taxpayers, and those that hire them, often try to achieve trading status if they can.

However, it isn't always this simple and an examination of the contract title alone is not sufficient. Its content will need to be examined to look for the real relationship that exists between the person doing the work and the person or business paying for it. For example, parts of the contract may indicate:

- who has control in the relationship;
- who provides the equipment;
- whether further work must be accepted by the taxpayer;
- whether the 'employer' must provide further work;
- who is responsible for providing other staff to help the taxpayer;
- who bears the financial risk involved in the contract;
- who benefits from efficient management of the contract; and
- whether the taxpayer can choose when to work on the contract.

This list is illustrative, not exhaustive, and to determine if this is really a contract of, or for, service, HMRC may be interested in other aspects of a contract in some circumstances. However, these are the key features most often used to make a judgement which type of contract it is and using these questions when examining any contract will therefore give you a pretty good idea of how to approach this classification task. If the taxpayer appears to be suitably in control of the relationship, providing their own equipment, hiring their own staff, bearing the risk of the contract but benefiting from managing it well, and so on, then the relationship is likely to be treated as a self-employed relationship. If the balance favours the grantor of the contract, then it is likely the taxpayer will be classified as an employee instead and taxed as such. In all cases the facts are used to determine which type of contract it is, irrespective of what those involved might prefer.

In Tomlinson v R&C Commrs (2017) UKFTT489, a double glazing salesman, was held to be self employed because he assumed considerable financial risk, being paid solely through commission on sales. In this case, the fact that both parties had for a long time viewed the salesman as self-employed was also influential. In *Professional Game Match Officials Ltd v R&C Commrs* (2020) UKUT 147, professional football referees were found to not be employees for the purposes of PAYE and NICs.

In recent years HMRC has examined more closely the range of occupations which are taxed under the employment income rules to try and ensure people are taxed correctly and don't try and avoid paying taxes they should be paying. For example, many individuals who work in television or in IT consulting in the past (to name just two) were able to operate their relationships with their 'employers' as if they were self-employed. In many more cases than used to be so they are now considered to be employees and therefore need to be taxed under employment income rules instead of trading income rules. In *Albatel Ltd v R&C Commrs* [2019] UKFTT195, Lorraine Kelly, the TV presenter, was found to have substantial control over her show and was not therefore considered to an employee of ITV. In contrast, in a similar case, Christa Ackroyd was found to be an employee because the BBC did have high enough levels of control in her case (*Christa Ackroyd Media Ltd v HMRC* [2019] UKUT 326.

The media and IT industries are not unique however. These principles are applied across all industries.

The taxation of so called 'personal service companies' has also been caught in this process. These are created when individuals set up companies with themselves as the only employee and with their 'employer' as their key client so as to benefit from being taxed as a company rather than as an employee. There are special rules dealing with personal service companies (called the IR35 rules), which we consider in Chapter 11.

Activity

While you are reading this chapter and undertaking the activities you might like to try and identify the reasons for HMRC's tactics in wishing to have more people taxed under employment income rules rather than taxed under trading income rules.

In Chapter 11 we will look more closely at the implications for a taxpayer's tax bill of the classification as being an employee or self-employed.

If you want to explore further the various factors HMRC will consider in determining employment versus self-employment status you can now use an Employment Status Indicator tool on HMRC's website (https://www.gov.uk/guidance/check-employment-status-for-tax). This tool asks you various questions, similar to those we have just been discussing, and then it will give you an indication of what the likely employment status is based on the facts you provide. This is a useful guide as to how HMRC are likely to view your situation (if you answer the questions truthfully!).

Basis of assessment

Employees

5.4 As we saw in Chapter 4, in general, employment earnings (including benefits in kind which are non-cash payments related to employment) are taxed on a receipts (i.e. cash) basis, that is, they are taxed in the tax year in which the date of the receipt falls. In contrast, pensions and some benefits, such as job-seekers allowance, are taxed on the accruals basis (although the Universal Credit now being rolled out across the country will not be taxable – the logic in so doing is that otherwise money is paid over and immediately then collected back!).

Fiscal Fact

Excluding all Universal Credit receipts from tax, despite several of the benefits it replaces being taxable currently, is expected to reduce tax receipts to the UK Government by approximately £30 million per annum. Around 300,000 individuals who are moving into Universal Credit during its roll out are estimated to have been paying tax previously on their benefits.

For all employees, other than directors, the date of receipt of employment income is deemed to be the earlier of the date on which payment is made and the date on which there is an entitlement to payment. This legislation is intended to prevent employees from transferring earnings, such as seeking to delay bonuses being paid, to a tax year in which their marginal rate of tax is lower.

Activity

When might a taxpayer's marginal rate of tax be likely to fall?

Feedback

There are several possible reasons for a fall in a taxpayer's marginal rate of tax. These are most likely to be related to hours they work, or to changing tax rate bands or allowances. Firstly, he or she might suffer a drop of income, or an increase in allowable deductions, which reduces his or her highest rate of tax by dropping then into a lower income tax band. This might happen if, for example, they change their terms of employment to a part-time basis.

Secondly, since 1979 there has been a downward trend in income tax rates (in fact, when the 50% rate was introduced in Budget 2010 it was one of the first increases to rates of personal income tax in many years – and this was itself then cut back to 45% from 6 April 2013, so it didn't last long). In years where rates fall, anyone in the bands where rates drop will benefit from a lower marginal rate of tax. This principle applied, for example, from April 2013 for anyone paying tax at 50% on any of their earnings. There was an incentive for these people to move income receipts into the 2013/14 year if they could, as they would then have saved 5% tax on their earnings over £150,000 when the top rate of tax fell to 45%. These rates don't change very often however.

The same principle applies if tax bands increase while the taxpayer's income doesn't change as much. If the taxpayer is on the bottom edge of a band, increases in that band starting point could move them into the lower band thus dropping their marginal rate of tax to that of the lower band. This would also occur if tax allowances increase for those whose income then falls within the new limits.

Directors

5.5 There are additional restrictions on the date of a receipt for tax purposes if the employee is a company director who may be able to influence when the payment is received. Directors' earnings are taxed in the tax year which contains the earliest of the following dates:

- the date of receipt as determined by the above rules for all employees;
- the date when the payment is charged in the company's accounting records;
- the end of the company's period of account in which the amount arose provided that it had been determined by then; or
- the date on which the amount is determined if it is after the end of the company's period of account.

Allowable expenses

5.6   After determining what income received by a taxpayer should be subject to income tax in a given tax year, the next key question is what allowable expenses can they claim against this income? Allowable expenses are the deductions that a taxpayer can subtract from their income to compute their employment income and therefore reduce the overall tax bill on that income.

There are two basic rules to determine if an expense is allowable:

1.   first, the employee must be obliged to incur and pay the expense as the holder of the employment. This means that it is the needs of the job itself that is important, not the preferences of the person doing the job. An expense will therefore only be deductible if every holder of the particular job would have to incur it. As such, it is said to be *necessary* for employment; and,

2.   second, only expenses which are also *wholly* and *exclusively* incurred in the performance of the duties of employment will be allowable deductions. 'Wholly and exclusively' means that if an expense has more than one purpose, e.g. is partly used for some private purpose, then the private part will not be deductible.

In practice, proving the first part (that it is necessary to do the job) is often difficult. Indeed, one judge in 1953 described the three part wholly, exclusively and necessarily requirement as 'notoriously rigid, narrow and restrictive', yet we still use it 70 years later.

Some trade unions and associations have negotiated special allowances on behalf of their members to help employees with overcoming this problem in practice. These are typically for specialist equipment, such as safety equipment, that is genuinely necessary to carry out their jobs. For example, if you are in the agricultural trade you can claim a fixed deduction of £100 annually for specialist clothing and upkeep of your tools. If you are in the food industry this is £60 or in healthcare, it varies with your job from £80 for laboratory staff or pharmacy workers to £185 for ambulance staff (a full list can be found in the HMRC manual:

https://www.gov.uk/hmrc-internal-manuals/employment-income-manual/eim32712

These deductions are, of course, only available to workers who have to buy specialist clothing or upkeep tools to do their jobs – they will not be available to other workers in these trades or if the employer provides these items to their employees. However, in other cases you may need to negotiate with HMRC if you wish to get deductions from your employment income.

Key to making this system work in practice is the substantial amount of case law that is used to identify expenditure which is an allowable deduction for the purposes of employment income computations. For example, in *Brown v Bullock* (1961) the employee, a bank manager, was required by his employers to join a London club. Even though a case could perhaps have been made that this expenditure was wholly and exclusively used for business (not private) purposes, his subscription was held not to be an allowable deduction because it was not considered to be necessary for the performance of his duties, despite his employer's wishes. Therefore, all three parts needed to be an allowance expense were not satisfied.

In *Lupton* v *Potts* (1969) a solicitor's articled clerk was not able to claim the costs of his examination fees because the expenditure was held not to be incurred wholly and exclusively in the performance of his duties.

In another case (*Fitzpatrick v CIR*, 1994), the House of Lords disallowed the cost of newspapers bought by journalists arguing that buying and reading the newspapers was preparation for work rather than part of the performance of their duties. There are many other examples of similar case law.

Despite the lack of a specific definition in law of what is allowable in all circumstances, some expenditure is specifically allowed by law as a deduction from employment earnings. This includes:

- contributions to an approved pension scheme;
- subscriptions to professional bodies and learned societies approved by HMRC, provided they are relevant to the duties of the employment;
- payments to charities under a payroll deduction scheme (as we discussed in section 4.45);
- expenses incurred in performing duties and reimbursed by the employer (within limits); and
- capital allowances on plant and machinery if owned by the employee – rather than, as is more usual, their employer (see Chapter 7).

In practice, an employer will usually pay for most of the expenses you incur as an employee that are 'wholly, exclusively and necessarily' for your job. An employer will usually reimburse these costs to the employee and deduct them as an allowable trading expense as part of their own income tax, or corporation tax computation (as we will see in Chapter 6). In this situation the employee will have to declare this reimbursement as income and then seek a deduction for expenses incurred. This prevents abuse of the expenses system through employers reimbursing employees more than actual expenditure incurred.

Fiscal Fact

The estimated cost to the UK Treasury of allowing professional subscriptions to be tax deductible is £160 million for 2021/22. Much more significant however, is the cost of making contributions to approved pension schemes tax deductible – estimated to be £22.5 billion for 2021/22 (Source: 'Estimated costs of non-structural reliefs' – HMRC website)

Following are further details of specific expenses that are not always allowed as deductions.

Travelling expenses

5.7 There are special rules dealing with travel expenses incurred by an employee. These will often be paid for by the employer and where this occurs, the amount of allowance or reimbursement is included as income for the employee and the actual cost of the journey will then be deductible. Travel expenses that are not reimbursed by the employer may be deductible to the employee.

There are two main issues to consider here. The first concerns the nature of the journey. The basic rule is that ordinary commuting (travel to and from your place of work) and private travel (unrelated to your work duties) does not qualify as an allowable deduction. The second concerns the amount of expense that can be allowed as a deduction. We will now look at these two issues in further detail.

Allowable journeys

5.8 It is important to be able to establish where you work (according to the tax rules) to know when you are travelling to get there (not deductible expenses) and when you are travelling 'for' work (usually deductible expenses).

Examples of travelling 'for' work that qualifies for relief include:
- From a permanent place of work to visit a client and back;
- Where the travel is a normal part of the employee's job, for example a service engineer who moves from place to place throughout the day; and
- Travel to a temporary workplace, such as a client's office, even if from home, but only so long as it is because of the nature of the job and not just for the employee's convenience.

A distinction is made between 'ordinary commuting' (which is not deductible) from other deductible travel. Ordinary commuting is defined as travel between home and a permanent place of work. So, travel to a temporary place of work will not be ordinary commuting and on the face of it will be eligible for relief.

This raises the question of what is a 'permanent place of work'. As a general rule, it will be somewhere where the employee attends regularly to perform the duties of the job. A temporary place of work on the other hand will be where an employee attends for only a limited amount of time.

However, to prevent abuse of the temporary place of work exemption, a rule is needed describing how long a place of work can be temporary for tax purposes before becoming considered a permanent place of work instead. If an employee is required to work to a significant extent at a place for a continuous period of more than 24 months, this place will be considered to be a permanent place of work. HMRC considers 'significant extent' to be at least 40% of the employee's time. So, if an employee spends at least 40% of his or her time at a particular place over a period of more than 24 months, there is no relief for the cost of the travel to and from that particular place as it then becomes part of ordinary commuting.

An employee may not have a normal place of work but may have a normal *area* in which they work. An example might be a district nurse who is required to cover a particular area but lives outside it. In this case the whole area would be considered to be the normal place of work and so costs of moving around in this area would not be deductible.

What if an employee doesn't have a permanent place of work? For example, 'site-based' employees have no fixed place of work but are required to perform duties at several sites by their employer. These are allowed to set the full costs of travelling to and from sites against their employment income. They can also obtain relief for subsistence expenses when staying at a site if that is required.

What if an employee has to incur additional expenses through no fault of their own? In one particular case, there is an exemption from tax – for payments made to employees if a strike or other industrial action disrupts public transport that the employee would usually use (e.g. a train strike). Payments made by the employer to cover additional costs for overnight accommodation or the provision of alternative transport are exempt. If the employee meets these additional costs without reimbursement from the employer, however, they cannot claim tax relief.

As you can see, this area of allowable expenses can be difficult to apply in practice. Attempt the following activity to see if you have grasped the basics.

Activity

Consider the following situations, drawn from HMRC Guidance on employee travel expenses. Will relief for the cost of travel be available?

(a) Dermot's employer sometimes requires him to attend his permanent workplace outside of normal hours, for example, on the weekend.

(b) Doris has worked for 5 years at her employer's head office in Warrington. She is sent by her employer to perform duties at a branch office in Wigan for 18 months.

(c) Ellery is employed as a financial adviser in Brighton. His employer sends him to an office in Bournemouth for one day a week over a 10 months period. He travels to Bournemouth directly from his home in Hastings.

Feedback

(a) No relief is available for Dermot because the journey is classified as 'ordinary commuting' i.e. between home and a permanent workplace, even though his employer requires him to be there after hours.

(b) Relief is available for the full cost of Doris' travel between home and the temporary workplace in Wigan (i.e. because her time there is less than 24 months).

(c) Ellery is entitled to relief for his travel to Bournemouth because he has gone there for a temporary purpose. He does not expect to spend more than 40% of his time there, nor does he expect to be going there for more than 24 months.

The amount of the relief

5.9 Having decided that a journey is eligible for tax relief by deducting the cost from the employee's employment income, the second task is to work out how much is deductible. As a general rule, the full cost of the travel will be deductible, regardless of the amount of allowance or reimbursement the employer pays. The cost of travel includes subsistence costs such as accommodation and meals that are attributable to the travel. It also includes car parking expenses, but not things like private phone calls, newspapers and laundry costs. An exception to this is when employees are required to stay away from home overnight on business. In this case, employers can pay for incidental overnight expenses up to a tax-free limit (currently £5 per night within the UK and £10 per night outside the UK).

Activity

Consider the following situations, also drawn from HMRC Guidance on employee travel expenses. How much will each employee be entitled to deduct?

(a) Mary has to travel on business. Her employer pays a travel allowance to cover the cost of a plane fare. Mary travels by train instead, which is cheaper.

(b) Mathew receives payment from his employer to cover the cost of a hotel, but instead decides to sleep in his car.

(c) Mercy has to travel on business and receives a travel allowance from her employer to cover the cost of a standard rail ticket. She decides to travel first class.

Feedback

(a) Mary is taxable on the full payment from her employer but can only claim relief for the cost of the train ticket.

(b) Mathew is taxable on the full amount received from his employer and cannot claim any relief because he hasn't incurred any expenses.

(c) Mercy is taxable on the full allowance from her employer, and relief is available for the cost of the first-class ticket, even though this is more than the amount paid for by the employer. It is the actual cost of the travel that is allowed as a deduction.

You might think that these rules are a bit complicated. HM Treasury agreed this might be the case and so they announced in Budget 2014 a review of travelling and subsistence expenses but the responses received indicated that the current rules are generally well understood. Budget 2016 therefore announced that no further action would be taken to amend the travel and subsistence rules at that time.

Using your own car

5.10 We have explored the general rules for allowing travelling expenses as tax deductions, but what happens when the employee uses his or her own car? The question of whether the cost of the journey qualifies as a deductible expense is the same, but there are special rules for working out the cost of the journey, which could be quite complicated. To make the process simpler, the government has set out some rates of tax free allowance so that the employer can pay an amount to the employee to cover the cost of using his or her own car without creating a tax liability. The maximum rates payable before a taxable benefit will arise are given in the table below. These are called 'approved mileage allowance payments' or AMAPs. If they are exceeded both income tax and national insurance contribution liabilities (Class 1) will be created. The miles given are for *business miles* driven in a year (i.e. any private miles paid for by an employer will always be a taxable benefit).

If the rate of allowance paid by an employer does not exceed these amounts, then no tax is due on these payments and neither are any national insurance contributions required.

Type of vehicle	Rate
Car or van	45p per mile on first 10,000 business miles in the year
	25p per mile on excess over 10,000 miles
Motorcycle	24p per mile
Cycle	20p per mile

Employees using their own cars who do not receive any mileage allowance payments from their employers, or who receive less than the prescribed levels, will be able to claim tax relief on the difference as an allowable deduction against their employment income.

A rate of up to 5p per mile can also be paid (tax free) to the driver of the car if they carry a fellow employee as a passenger, provided they are also travelling on business. This rate will apply for each passenger and in both private cars, as discussed here, but also for company cars used for business travel. From 6 April 2011 this 5p rule also applies to carrying volunteers when reclaiming from volunteer organisations. This allowance, however, cannot be reclaimed as a deduction if the employer does not pay the full amount – unlike the regular mileage rates.

Activity

Fred uses his own car when travelling for his employer. During the tax year he drove 8,600 business miles. How would Fred's tax computation be affected if his employer paid him the following rates for his business miles:

a) 30p per mile

b) 50p per mile.

c) 4p per mile for the 2,000 miles he drove with a fellow employee in his car.

Feedback

a) This payment is below the mileage allowance rate Fred is entitled to. He would receive £2,580 (30p × 8,600 miles) from his employer but could have been paid £3,870 (45p × 8,600 miles) before a taxable benefit arose. He is able to claim a deduction of the difference (£1,290) against his employment income.

b) This payment is above the mileage allowance rate and so a benefit in kind is created. Fred will have to add £430 ((50p × 8,600 miles) – £3,870) to his employment income and pay tax on this at his marginal rate of income tax.

c) This rate is below the tax-free sum allowed and therefore no benefit would arise. He would receive £80 therefore tax-free. He is not able to claim the extra 1p per mile, however, as a deduction against his income.

We consider the situation where the employer provides a car for the employee to use later in the chapter under the heading of Benefits in Kind.

Other allowable expenses

5.11   There are a number of expenses other than travelling and the specific items listed earlier that may be deductible if they meet the *wholly, exclusively and necessarily* requirement. We will look at some of the more commonly occurring expenses in this section.

Phone calls

The cost of business phone calls made using a private phone are deductible, but usually no line rental for that phone can be claimed unless it can be proven to be solely dedicated to work related use.

Work clothing

An employee cannot claim the cost of work clothes, unless they are specialist or protective. In *Hillyer v Leeke*, the High Court denied the taxpayer a deduction for clothing that was 'ordinary civilian clothing...of the sort that is also worn off-duty'. In a 2010 case, the BBC television news presenter Sian Williams attempted to claim the cost of clothing, laundry and hairdressing as a deduction. The Tribunal held that she was not entitled to the claim, even though her work meant that she had to appear well dressed and groomed. The clothing was considered to be 'ordinary civilian clothing'.

Working from home

If you work from home by choice, for your own convenience, then the costs will not be deductible. If you are required or allowed to work from home under flexible working arrangements agreed with your employer you will usually be able to claim a part of your additional domestic bills (e.g. heating, lighting, business calls etc.). These rules have been particularly important recently as many people have been required to work from home during the lockdown period related to Covid-19. They will allow, if applied correctly, many people to get some tax relief for at least some of any extra costs incurred (heating, lighting etc) when having to work from home, if these are not met by their employer. Further details on how this works in practice is provided in the exempt benefits in kind section below.

Education and Training

As a general rule, training is considered to be in addition to, rather than part of, the duties of employment and so is not deductible. In *HMRC v Banerjee* [2009] EWHC 62 (Ch) however, the High Court found that the cost of training courses paid for by Dr Banerjee was deductible. This was because it was a condition of her contract of employment with the NHS that she had to undertake continuous training which meant that in this case it was a part of the duties of the job.

There are a number of other examples of allowance expenses. A good place to review some others of these is on the Tax Guide for Students website – see: http://www.taxguideforstudents.org.uk/working/employed/employment-benefits-and-expenses/what-payments-and-benefits-are-non-taxable .
The full official list of the treatment of expenses from an employer's perspective is at: https://www.gov.uk/expenses-and-benefits-a-to-z

The area of allowable deductions from employment income is complex due to a lack of clear guidelines from legislation and case law. The 'necessary' rule causes many problems for employees seeking to claim tax deductions, often probably legitimately, for costs they incur in working for their employers but not fully reimbursed by them. Where many of these may be deductible if the employee was instead self-employed (the 'necessary' rule does not apply for self-employed deduction computations as we will explore further in Chapter 6, section 6.4), it seems a little unfair that they cannot claim the same costs just because their employment status is different. This rule is unlikely to change in the near future however, because of the substantial cost to the Government if it were to be more generous for employee claims for deductions.

You can now attempt Quick Quiz questions 1-3.

Benefits in kind

5.12 In addition to receiving a wage or salary, many employees receive other benefits because of their employment. These so-called *benefits in kind* may include things such as subsidised lunches, non-contributory pensions, private health care, sports facilities, childcare, company cars etc. There is an endless list of such benefits in practice, however, tax treatments for them all must be determined to create an equitable tax system. Any taxable benefit received as part of an employment must therefore be given a value that can be included in employment income calculations and either be exempted or be taxed accordingly.

When computing a taxpayer's employment income, the value of all taxable benefits must be added to their wages or salaries in the tax computation. You have already briefly met the issue of national insurance contributions, which must also be paid on benefits in kind, in Chapter 4, section 4.10. In this section we will consider the income tax issues.

Fiscal Fact

It is expected that 3.66 million individuals received approximately £8.25 billion of taxable value in benefits in kind between them for 2016/17. This resulted in a tax liability of £2.84 billion and national insurance contributions of £1.14 billion. Company car benefits made up 55% of the taxable value from benefits in kind in that year (£4.357 billion – producing an income tax liability of £1.55 billion and a national insurance contribution liability of £630 million), although private medical and dental insurance benefits had the largest number of recipients at 2.38 million (representing 65% of all benefit in kind recipients). [Source: HMRC Statistics Table T4.1]

A limited number of specific benefits in kind are exempt from taxation. For most benefits, the general rule is that employees are normally assessed on the *cash equivalent* of the benefit. However, this becomes the *marginal cost* if the benefit is provided to non-employees as well. For a limited number of benefits where there are specific rules to allow this, it is *actual cost of provision* that is used. We will look in more detail at each of these rules, and how they apply to specific benefits, in the sections below.

The cash equivalent is taken to be the amount that the benefit could be sold for once the employee has received it. This rule tends to operate in favour of the employee because benefits in kind may have either no resale value, for example, a travel season ticket, or a low resale value, such as the second-hand value of a suit or uniform.

Before considering the rules for determining the value of different types of benefit in kind for income tax purposes, we will first look at some forms of benefit that are specifically exempted.

Exempted benefits in kind

5.13 Not all benefits in kind are taxable. Some are specifically excluded from assessment to tax in the hands of all employees. This section explores some of the most common of these.

Sports facilities and cycling to work

5.14 In-house sports facilities for employees and their families do not have to be treated as a benefit in kind and are not therefore liable to tax. Similarly, employers can create schemes to encourage employees to cycle to work without creating benefits in kind. If they lend bikes, or cycling safety equipment, to employees, or allow them use of a bike from a pool of bikes that the employers own, these do not create specific benefits on the users.

Gifts

5.15 Employees are also not assessed on the benefit of any small gifts which are provided to them by third parties (i.e. not the employer) so long as the following conditions are met:

- the gift was not provided, or procured, by the employer or persons connected to the employer, (Note: a list of who are *connected persons* can be found in the Glossary); and
- the gift was not provided in recognition of services which have been, or are to be, performed.

If these conditions are met, the most an employee can receive tax-free by way of a gift from a single third party is £250 p.a.

Parties, functions and meals

5.16 Tax free benefits can also be received by employees for annual parties or functions provided by the employer. There is a limit of £150 per head for the exemption to apply. The figure of £150 is not an allowance; if the expenditure exceeds this amount then the full amount will be assessable, not just the excess over £150.

Meals which are provided in the employer's cafe for the staff generally are not an assessable benefit. A special rule provides that meals provided to employees on designated 'cycle to work' days are also exempt.

Long service awards

5.17 Employees are not assessable on non-cash long service awards provided that they have worked for the organisation for at least 20 years, have not received a similar award within the past ten years and the cost to the employer of the award is no more than £50 per year of service. If the award is made in cash, it is taxable.

Suggestions

5.18 Rewards for suggestions are usually taxable, but an exemption exists for awards provided there is a formal suggestions scheme which is open to all employees in a relevant group and all of the following conditions are met:

- the suggestion relates to activities which are outside the scope of the employee's normal duties;
- if the award is more than £25 it is only made after a decision has been taken to implement the suggestion;
- awards over £25 either do not exceed 50% of the expected net financial gain during the first year after implementation or do not exceed 10% of the expected net financial gain during the first five years after implementation; and
- awards over £25 are shared equitably between any employees making the suggestion.

If the award exceeds £5,000 the excess is always taxable.

Relocation costs

5.19 If an employee has to move their only, or main, residence for work reasons, and the new work location is more than a reasonable day's commute from the current residence, the costs of relocation paid for by the employer up to a maximum of £8,000 are not taxed as a benefit in kind. If expenses of more than £8,000 are paid, the employee will be assessed on the excess over £8,000 as a benefit in kind. Note that it is not necessary for a taxpayer to sell a house in order to qualify for this relief.

Child care

5.20 A nursery place at a workplace nursery (crèche) is not a taxable benefit. All other forms of childcare provision, including cash or vouchers, provided by the employer are generally taxable. Since 6 April, 2006, however, employees have been able to receive up to £55 per week (or £243 per month) free of tax and NICs for childcare so long as approved childcare providers are used. This scheme is only available however, where employers offer it and was closed in October 2018 (although you can keep using the scheme once in it until you change employers or take an unpaid career break of longer than a year).

New entrants have not been allowed to join this scheme since April 2011. A new scheme was announced in Budget 2013 that began operation in April 2017. It is called the Tax-free childcare scheme. An eligible working family will get 20p contributed to their childcare account for every 80p they contribute up to £2,000 per child per year (i.e. equivalent to getting the basic rate of 20% tax back). A family will be eligible if one (or if two, both) parents earn less than £100,000 a year each (i.e. £200,000 combined), at least one earns more than £120 a week or is self-employed or on maternity or paternity leave, and do not already receive child tax credit or universal credit. This voucher scheme is available to all eligible parents, whether part of the previous scheme or not. For those in the old scheme they can choose which scheme they wish to continue to use – they cannot use both. It is available for each child they care for up to the age of 12 (or 17 if the child is disabled). The new scheme does not involve employers directly.

Working at home

5.21 If an employer requires their employees to work from home, they are able to pay up to £6 per week (up from £4 per week before 6 April 2020), or £26 per month (£18 per month before 6 April 2020), tax free, towards the additional costs their employees incur (e.g. extra costs of gas, electricity and of business phone calls) although this can't be used to also cover costs that relate to combined work and private use (e.g. broadband access). These costs do not need to be supported by evidence, as is usually required for allowed tax deductions, as there is a concession from HMRC for up to these amounts to be paid tax-free. If amounts over £6 per week are paid, however, they can still be tax free if evidence is provided of actual incremental expenditure resulting from working at home. If sums of less than £6 per week are paid then you can't get personal tax relief for the difference however. The tax-free payments don't apply if employees simply choose to work from home rather than being required to by their employer.

These rules were widely used by good employers over the last two years given so many employees were required, if not furloughed or made redundant, to work from home during the Covid-19 related lockdowns.

Trivial benefits

5.22 In addition to the above, benefits in kind that cost the employer less than £50 per individual to provide. This excludes therefore small gifts, such as flowers for a retirement or illness, from potentially becoming a taxable charge (for income tax and for Class1A national insurance contributions) on the employee – although in reality many of these were exempted in practice before and as such this largely formalises a limit for this exemption.

If the recipient is an office holder in a business (e.g. a director) or is a close family member of one, a cap of £300 per individual applies for this exemption however.

Others

5.23 Several other benefits are commonly provided. These include:

- Free car parking space provided to employees is also a tax-free benefit, provided it is at, or near, the employee's place of work.
- Counselling or welfare services generally provided to employees are tax free.
- Goods sold at a discount to employees are tax free provided they are sold for at least a price that covers the costs incurred by the employer making the goods.
- Health screening and medical check-ups provided once a year.
- Costs of providing electricity for electric company cars and vans, including the cost of providing a charging point at the employee's home.
- No taxable benefit arises with benefits such as air miles or loyalty points that employees receive from employer's expenditure provided this is part of a publicly available scheme and not just given to them as an incentive, bonus etc.
- Broadband internet access is a tax-free benefit if provided by your employer for work purposes if there is no realistic way of distinguishing any specific private usage of this benefit. Note, however, the cost of a computer or tablet device to use this access is likely to be a chargeable benefit unless it is mostly for business use – as we will discuss further below.

Taxable benefits

5.24 This section reviews benefits in kind that all employees may be taxed on when they receive them.

General rule – cash equivalents

5.25 The general rule for benefits in kind received by employees is that if because of their employment, an employee or members of the employee's family or household, receive any benefits, they are to be treated as part of the earnings and are chargeable to income tax under the employment income rules. The amount to be taxed as the benefit is the cash equivalent of the benefit (i.e. an amount equal to the *cost* of the benefit) less any contribution made by the employee to those providing the benefit.

The cost for this purpose is not defined in the tax legislation, but in *Pepper* v *Hart* (1992) the House of Lords found that cost should mean the marginal cost to the provider (i.e. rather than other possible costs such as the average cost) in circumstances where the benefit is also available to the non-employees. In this case the benefit received was school education provided to children of the taxpayer. The taxpayer successfully argued the value of the benefit was only the marginal cost of providing for an extra child and not the full cost of that place. This will usually have the effect of substantially lowering the value of the benefit to be taxed. Of course, if it is not possible to directly attribute any costs to the provision of the benefit to the taxpayer then there will be no assessable benefit.

Vouchers

5.26 Any employee who receives cash vouchers, credit tokens or exchangeable vouchers as part of the reward for their employment will be assessable on the cost to the employer of providing the benefit.

Accommodation

5.27 If an employee is provided with accommodation by an employer, the employee will be assessed for tax on the *annual value* of the property less any contributions made by the employee to the employer for the accommodation. This rule does not apply if the accommodation provided is *job related*, as defined below, or only made available to them 'temporarily', defined as the same period of up to 24 months we saw for travel costs benefit in kind rules above.

The annual value to be used in this computation is taken to be the rent that "might reasonably be expected to be obtained on a letting of the accommodation from year to year". This amount assumes the employee pays all the taxes, rates, bills etc associated with living in the property, but the employer pays to maintain the property. In practice, however, the annual value is typically taken to be the rateable value of the property, if this value is known, or a value estimated by HMRC if the property does not have a rateable value. The rateable value is the value used to compute the 1970s rating valuation for that property (i.e. the old valuation system is used from before Council tax was introduced).

If the property is not owned by the employer but is simply rented by the employer for the employee, the employee will be assessed on the higher of the annual value and the actual rent paid by the employer.

If the accommodation either,

- cost over £75,000 when acquired, or
- if acquired more than six years before it was first provided to the employee, its market value on the date it was first provided to the employee was over £75,000,

then the accommodation is classified as "expensive" and a further benefit is charged to the employee. This is equal to the excess of the cost of providing the accommodation over £75,000 multiplied by the *official rate* of interest. The official rate is the interest rate given by the Treasury for various tax related charges – particularly loans. This rate varies periodically, but the latest rate can be found by looking at the 'Rates and Allowances' section on the HMRC website. For the purpose of this book, for simplicity, we will use 2.25%. The cost of providing the accommodation includes the costs of any improvements undertaken before the start of the tax year as well as the purchase price of the property. If the property is only available for part of the year, the benefit arising is reduced proportionately.

If the accommodation provided is *job related* then there is no assessable benefit in kind on the employee (although if the employee is a company director, then they may still incur a tax liability as the rules for directors can be more stringent). Accommodation is job related if either:

- the employee is required to live in the accommodation for the proper performance of their duties, for example a caretaker; or
- the employment is of the kind where it is customary to provide accommodation or the accommodation is provided to enable the better performance of the employee's duties, for example a clergyman, farm worker, pub manager or policeman; or
- the accommodation is provided for reasons of security.

HMRC have recently announced in relation to the Higher and Further Education Sector that it has established that because less than half of employees in the sector are provided with living accommodation, it can not be regarded as 'customary'. This new treatment is effective from 6 April 2019

If living accommodation is provided because of a person's employment, then alterations and additions to the accommodation which are of a structural nature, or repairs which would be required if the property were leased under the Landlord and Tenant Act 1985, are not assessable benefits.

Activity

George is provided with the use of a flat in Birmingham as part of his remuneration package for a new job. The flat cost George's employers £150,000 to buy and is brand new. George is a management consultant and the flat allows him to live in the city close to his office. George pays all the bills associated with the flat's running and makes a £200 per month contribution to his employer for the use of the flat. The flat has an annual value of £6,000. What is the accommodation benefit in kind assessable on George, assuming an official interest rate of 2%?

Feedback

George's use of the flat would not be considered job-related, it is just a benefit he receives that makes his job easier to perform, but it is not necessary to enable him to do his job (he could live elsewhere and still do the job as well). He will therefore have the value of this benefit added to his employment earnings when his tax bill is calculated. The value to be added is:

	£
Annual value of the property	6,000.00
Additional value	
(£150,000 – £75,000) @ 2%	1,500.00
Less George's contribution £200 × 12	(2,400.00)
Benefit in kind	5,100.00

Accommodation related expenses

5.28 Employees who are provided with living accommodation are assessed on the benefit of the accommodation. In addition, however, they are taxed on any other expenses which are paid by the employer which relate to the accommodation, for example, the cost of heating, lighting and of any repairs that are carried out at the employer's expense. They are also taxed on 20% a year of the cost of any furniture provided to them with the accommodation.

If the accommodation is job related, as we defined earlier in the chapter, a cap on these extras is applied – but some charge will still arise. The maximum assessment of the ancillary services is then set at 10% of the employee's net employment earnings. Net employment earning is the employment income assessment after any allowable expenses and pension contributions but excluding the cost of any ancillary services. If the accommodation is not job related, the taxpayer will be assessed on the full cost to the employer of providing any ancillary services.

A director can only claim to be living in job-related accommodation if, as well as meeting the conditions given above, he or she has an interest in less than 5% of the company and he or she is either a full-time working director or the company is non- profit-making or is a charity, unless the accommodation is provided as part of special security arrangements.

Activity

Alexandra has a house in Yeovil and normally lives there but she has been transferred to London for three years to establish a new branch of the company she works for. Her gross salary for the tax year is £27,000. She has been provided with a flat in Mayfair that has an annual rateable value of £1,000. In this tax year the company paid £5,000 in ancillary services. Alexandra made a contribution of £1,000 to these services. Determine Alexandra's employment income for the tax year.

Feedback

Employment income assessment: Alexandra

	£	£
Salary		27,000
Accommodation benefits:		
Annual value (not job related)	1,000	
Ancillary services – cost:	5,000	
Less employee's contribution	(1,000)	5,000
Employment income		32,000

Note that, had this accommodation been job-related, the annual value charge (£1,000) would not have been applied and the ancillary services total would have been capped at 10% of Alexandra's net employment earnings i.e. £2,700. Her revised assessment would therefore have then totalled £28,700 (i.e. £27,000 + (£2,700 – £1,000)).

Assets used by employees

5.29 If an asset is provided for the private use of an employee or a director then the assessable benefit is the annual value, which is the greater of:

- 20% of the market value of the asset when first provided as a benefit to an employee, and
- the rent or hire charges paid by the employer if the asset was rented or hired.

If the asset is only available to the employee for part of the year then this cost is pro-rated (reduced) for the proportion of the year they do have the use of it.

If ownership of the asset is transferred to the employee at any point a further assessable benefit may be due equivalent to the difference between the sum (if any) paid for the asset by the employee and the *higher of*:

- the current market value of the asset on the date transferred; or
- the market value of the asset when it was first provided to the employee less the total of the annual benefits assessed on the employee so far for the use of the asset.

Activity

On 6 April 2020, Edward's employer provided him with a computer for his private use which cost them £1,500 to buy for him. On 5 October 2022 Edward purchased this computer from his employer for its market value at that date of £500. What is the amount of Edward's assessable benefit for 2020/21, 2021/22 and 2022/23?

Feedback

For 2020/21 and 2021/22 Edward had use of this asset for the entirety of both years. His annual charge therefore was 20% x £1,500 = £300 per annum.

[Note – if the asset had been provided part way through the 2020/21 the first year's charge would have been adjusted to cover just the period it was available to him. For example, if it had been provided halfway through the year, the £300 for that year would have been halved to £150.]

For 2022/23 – a half year's charge will be due for the period 6 April to 5 October – i.e. £150.

The further assessable benefit is difference between £500 and the *higher of*:

1.   The current market value of the asset when transferred to Edward; or
2.   The market value when first provided, less assessable benefits to date.

1)   This is £nil as Edward paid the market value when the computer was transferred.

2)

	£
Market value when first provided	1,500
Less Assessable benefit (2.5 years×20%×£1,500)	(750)
	750
Less price paid by Edward	(500)
Benefit in kind	250

The benefit in kind Edward will have to add to his employment income in 2022/23 to be taxed therefore is £250. Adding the half year charge for the time before he acquired it personally (£150), this gives a total for the year of £400.

Cars

5.30   One of the most common benefits in kind, in terms of the number of employees receiving it, is the company car. All employees and directors are assessed on a benefit if they are provided with a company car.

Company cars became widespread during the 1970s for a number of reasons. The most important was probably the wages legislation in force at the time which attempted to limit increases in wages. Providing cars to some employees was a way of increasing the rewards to employees despite this legislation.

Providing company cars to employees was extremely tax efficient at the time. The employer could deduct the full cost of providing the car and the employee suffered relatively little tax on the benefit. At that time the provision of a company car also did not then lead to an increase in the national insurance contributions of either employees or employers.

During the 1980s and 1990s, successive Chancellors amended the rules for the taxation of company cars and over a number of years the tax on this benefit has increased very substantially. While there may still be some limited tax advantages for some employees that encourage the use of company cars, the benefits are lower now than in the past. Employers are now required to pay national insurance contributions on company cars (under Class 1A – as we saw in Chapter 4) although employees are still not currently required to pay national insurance contributions on this benefit.

Determining the company car benefit charge requires the following pieces of information to be available:

1. List price of the car when new;
2. Age of the car;
3. Vehicle's CO_2 rating;
4. Fuel/alternative fuel (e.g. electricity or hybrid) type;
5. Details of any accessories added;
6. Information on any contributions towards the cost of buying the car (called capital contributions) or any contributions made by the employee towards any private usage;
7. Any periods the car was not available to be used.

We can now review how the rules apply to determine each of these items and to then compute the overall company car benefit charge to be added to the employee's employment income figure when computing the total subject to income tax:

Fiscal Fact

Approximately 900,000 taxpayers were recipients of taxable benefits in kind for cars in 2017/18 creating a tax liability of £1.62 billion and national insurance contributions of £670 million. The average taxable value of car benefit received in that year amongst claimants was £5,390. [Source: HMRC Statistics Table T4.1]

1. List price

From 1994/95 all car benefits have been assessed on their list price, rather than actual cost paid by a purchaser. This was to prevent abuse of the benefits in kind system when car manufacturers quoted a higher retail price and then offered discounts. The list price is the inclusive price published by the manufacturer, importer of distributor of the car, for a single sale in the open market in the UK on the day of the car's first registration. It should include all standard accessories and any relevant taxes (VAT, any customs or excise duty or car tax if applicable) and delivery charges

2 – 4. Age, CO_2 rating and fuel type

The rules for calculating the benefit of using a company car are based on the CO_2 emissions of the car, rather than how it is used. These rules have been amended several times since they were first introduced (in April 2002) and have in fact changed four times in the last five years. The Government appears to be using these rules expressly to encourage more environmentally friendly cars to be used as company cars and so have been systematically making more polluting cars more expensive to use (we will talk more about the use of taxes to change people's behaviour in Chapter 14 and particularly about taxes used to effect environmental benefits in Chapter 13).

From 6 April 2020 further new rules have been rolling out for how the benefit charge is to be computed. After 6 April 2022 (i.e. for the 2022/23 tax year) the rules create two different scenarios that must be correctly chosen from to compute the relevant benefit charge –

1. for electric cars – both partially electric (i.e hybrid cars where their CO_2 emissions levels are at or below 50g/km) or fully electric (that can only be powered by electricity), and
2. for all other cars (including for hybrid electric cars with CO_2 emission levels of more than 50g/km).

The rates for 2022/23 are as follows:

1. Company car benefit charge for fully electric or hybrid cars with CO_2 <51g/km:

CO_2 g/km	Electric only mileage range	Taxable %
0		2
1 to 50	130 +	2
1 to 50	70 to 129	5
1 to 50	40 to 69	8
1 to 50	30 to 39	12
1 to 50	< 30	14

2. Company car benefit charge for petrol and diesel powered cars, or where the car is a hybrid electric vehicle with CO_2 emission levels >50g/km:

CO_2 g/km	Taxable % Petrol	Taxable % Diesel	CO_2 g/km	Taxable % Petrol	Taxable % Diesel	CO_2 g/km	Taxable % Petrol	Taxable % Diesel
0	2		85	22	26	130	31	35
1	14	18	90	23	27	135	32	36
51	15	19	95	24	28	140	33	37
55	16	20	100	25	29	145	34	37
60	17	21	105	26	30	150	35	37
65	18	22	110	27	31	155	36	37
70	19	23	115	28	32	160+	37	37
75	20	24	120	29	33			
80	21	25	125	30	34			

To use these tables, of course, you need to know the CO_2 emissions level of your company car. For all cars registered after 1 January, 1998 these can be found:

- on the cars registration document (V5)
- from the dealer
- in car magazines (for current models only usually)
- on the Vehicle Certification Agency (VCA) website at http://carfueldata.direct.gov.uk/

Once you have found the emission level of your car you look up the percentage rate in the applicable table above for the car you are assessing. The CO_2 level for that car is rounded *down* to find the correct percentage. This percentage is then multiplied by the list price of the car when it was new, to give you the annual benefit in kind that must be added to the car driver's employment income.

You will see from the table above that diesel-powered cars have a 4% supplement over petrol-powered cars up to a maximum charge of 37%. This supplement only applies to vehicles that are propelled solely by diesel (i.e. does not apply to hybrid vehicles after 6 April 2018). This supplement also does not apply if the diesel car is certified as meeting the Real Driving Emissions 2 (RDE2) EU standard created in 2017 (the car's documentation will state this).

Further, for diesel cars, the rates apply irrespective of registration date of the vehicle, however, for petrol cars registered before 1 January, 1998 these rates apply instead:

Engine Capacity	Rate
up to 1400 cc	15%
1401 – 2000cc	25%
over 2000cc	35%

5. Accessories

If the car is supplied with accessories that were not standard on the car when new then the cost of these must be added to list price of the car in this computation (unless the cost of the accessory is less than £100 in which case it can then be ignored). If the accessories are only made available for part of the year though, no reduction is allowed – the full year's charge is applied.

6. Contributions

If an employee makes a contribution towards the capital cost of the car, this is deducted from the list price for the purposes of this computation (i.e. affects each subsequent year's benefit computation for as long as the employee has use of that car). The maximum capital contribution that be used in this way however, is capped at £5,000 even if the actual contribution made by the employee was higher than this.

If an employee must make a contribution to the employer towards the running costs of the car (not including insurance costs) this is deducted from the annual benefit charge. Be careful however, as the payment will only count if made in the tax year in which the private usage occurred. If payment is made too late it will be applied against the next year's computation instead. Payments towards private fuel however are dealt with separately as we will see in the next section below.

7. Period of availability of car

The rates calculated by this system produce benefit in kind values for full tax years. If the company car is unavailable to the employee for part of the year these calculated rates are pro-rated proportionately for the part of the year the benefit is actually received. For example, if you only had a company car for 6 months of the tax year then only half of the annual benefit is taxable.

Unavailable times obviously include before and after the taxpayer is allowed to use the car, but also if the car is not available to be used while being repaired for at least 30 consecutive days during the year this period. (Note that no reduction is made if *you* are unable to drive the car, only if *the car* cannot be driven). [For an interesting case on this involving an antique dealer and a Ferrari, see the 2011 Tribunal case of *Michael Golding v HMRC* (TC01097)]

This system is designed to benefit people driving newer, lower emission cars. It is designed to achieve the opposite of the old system which benefited older, higher business mileage cars.

Fiscal Fact

According to a Revenue press release, the reform of company car tax in April 2002 has saved between 0.15 and 0.2 million tonnes of carbon, which is equivalent to around 0.5% of the CO_2 emissions from all road transport. These reforms continue to have an impact on CO_2 emissions levels of cars. In 2021 the average new car in the UK was emitting less than 119.7g/km of CO_2 according to a report produced by the Society of Motor Manufacturers and Traders (SMMT). This is the lowest average level ever recorded, in large part due to growing numbers of electric and hybrid vehicles forming the new car sales market. Today's new cars are 20% more efficient than the average car on the road. While diesel cars produce 15-20% less CO_2 emissions than petrol cars, they are now considered to be less environmentally friendly as they produce other harmful emissions.

Fuel benefit

5.31 If employees receive any fuel for private use as part of their company car package, they are taxed on the benefit of the fuel in addition to the car charge.

If employees make a contribution to the cost of the fuel used for private purposes, but do not reimburse the entire cost, the assessable benefit is not reduced. Hence, if they make a partial contribution it is more tax efficient if they contribute to the running costs of the car rather than to the cost of the fuel, as such a payment would reduce the overall benefit charge (see point 6 above).

What cost should be repaid to ensure that the private fuel is fully reimbursed to avoid this fuel benefit charge? HMRC helpfully publish guidance figures to help an employer ensure they collect enough reimbursement (called Advisory Fuel rates) – the actual cost of petrol charges therefore isn't used to compute this benefit. The current guidance (from 1 March 2022 – these are reviewed quarterly) for petrol and LPG cars is:

Engine size	Petrol	LPG
1400cc or less	14p	9p
1401cc to 2000cc	17p	11p
Over 2000cc	25p	16p

The corresponding rates for diesel cars are:

Engine size	Diesel
1600cc or less	13p
1601cc to 2000cc	16p
Over 2000cc	19p

Lower rates of repayment may be acceptable to HMRC however, so long as evidence of actual costs is then provided and accepted by them. (Note – these rates are reviewed four times a year currently so you should check them on the HMRC website to confirm the current rates – search for 'Advisory fuel rates').

For any reimbursement to count in preventing the fuel benefit falling due it must also be paid in the tax year (i.e. by the 5 April at the end of the tax year) or a short time after this date or the payment may not be counted as a 2006 case has illustrated (see *Impact Foiling Ltd v HMRC*, 2006).

Fiscal Fact

Budget 2008 stated that the number of company car drivers getting free fuel for private use has dropped by approximately 600,000 since 1997 to around 300,000, in part due to these various measures being introduced. In 2016/17 there were approximately 160,000 recipients of fuel benefit in kind creating £230 million in tax liabilities and £90 million in national insurance contributions. The average car fuel benefit tax liability paid in that year was £1,410 and NIC liability of £560 [Source: HMRC Table T4.1].

If the employee does not repay all the fuel costs related to private mileage, then an emissions-based charge has been used since 6 April 2003. To compute this charge, we use the same table on the previous page. Unlike car benefit itself (which multiplies the emissions level percentage by the car's new list price when it was new) the same relevant percentage is instead multiplied by a set monetary amount set for each tax year to go into the employee's tax computation. This amount is set at £25,300 for 2022/23 (£24,600 for 2021/22).

If an employee opts out of free fuel during the year, only the proportion (pro rata) of the annual charge will be assessable as a benefit. If the employee subsequently opts back in to receiving fuel paid for by the employer then they will have to pay the full annual charge – with no discount allowed for the opted-out period.

Activity

Sarah had the use of a 1400cc, petrol-engined (non-hybrid) company car throughout the tax year. The car has an emissions rate of 127g/km of carbon dioxide and had a list price of £14,000 new (no accessories are attached to the car). Sarah contributed £50 per month towards the running costs of the car and £30 per month towards part of her private fuel. Sarah drove 18,000 miles in the year of which 75% is business mileage. Determine the benefit assessable to Sarah if:

a) The car was first registered on 1 May 2022.

b) The car is instead a hybrid (petrol-electric) car with a CO_2 emissions level of 45g/km, which can drive 85 miles on a full electric charge (other facts unchanged as above).

Feedback

a)   The assessable benefit is therefore:

$$(£14,000 × 30\%) - (£50 × 12) = £3,600$$

As Sarah only makes a partial contribution towards her private fuel, a taxable benefit arises for this also. This will equate to £25,300 × 30% = £7,590. No reduction is given for her contribution towards her private fuel as it is not all paid back. Sarah's total benefit in kind cost related to her car is therefore £11,190 (£3,600 + £7,590). This should be added to her employment income for her tax computation.

It was very expensive for Sarah not to reimburse all her private fuel. If she had paid back the guidance price of 14p per private mile driven, she would have paid 14p × (25% × 18,000) = £630, or £52.50 per month. Not paying this extra £22.50 a month (£52.50-£30.00) therefore created a total of £6,960 (£7,590 - £630) as extra benefit which she could have avoided! She'd be better advised next year to pay back all her private fuel (unless she drives a lot more private miles).

b)   The table for hybrid cars producing emissions rates <51g/km should be used (Table 1 above), providing a charge rate of 5% (as her electric only mileage range is 85 miles). Her benefit charges therefore now would be:

- Car = (£14,000 x 5%) – (£50x12) = £100
- Fuel benefit = £25,300 x 5% = £1,265
  i.e. a combined total of £1,365.

As you can see from this example, there is a significant motivation under this new system to use hybrid cares with larger electric-powered mileage capabilities for company cars in future.

Activity

Jane has an 1800cc, diesel-engined company car which was first registered in 2019 when it had a list price of £24,000 and produces emissions of 93g/km of carbon dioxide. Fifty per cent of Jane's mileage was for business purposes and she makes no contributions towards the cost of the car or her private fuel. Her car has no accessories attached. Calculate Jane's car related benefits assessable in the tax year if:

a)   Jane has the use of the car for the whole year and drives a total of 4,800 miles during the year.

b)   Jane has the use of the car only from 5 October 2022 and she drives 4,800 miles between 5 October 2022 and 5 April 2023.

c)   She has the car for the whole year but has a satellite navigation system fitted as an accessory to the car (not standard) costing £250.

Feedback

(a) As for Sarah above, Jane's business miles and the age of her car is not relevant to the computation.

The assessable car benefit is £24,000 × 27% = £6,480.

Her fuel benefit for the year will be £25,300 × 27% =£6,831

(b) As she only had the car for six months her car benefit rate is halved to £3,240 (Note that this calculation should ideally be done to the nearest day). Jane's fuel benefit will also be halved to £3,415.50.

(c) The cost of the accessory must be added to the list price of the car in the computation as it is more than the £100 minimum that can be ignored, therefore the car benefit calculation will become a total of: £24,250 × 27% = £6,547.50 (the fuel charge is not affected).

Special rules for vans

5.32 For vans, as distinct from motor cars, special rules apply. If an employee is provided with a van in which they are allowed to do private motoring, he or she will be taxed on a flat rate charge of £3,600 for the year (£3,500 in 2021/22). Unlike for cars, he emissions levels, or how it is fuelled, does not affect this flat rate. As for other vehicles, this benefit cost is pro-rated if the van is only available to the employee for part of the year.

An additional charge of £688 for the year (£669 for 2021/22) will apply if the employee is also provided with private fuel for the van (unless all of this fuel for private use is reimbursed). Van benefit charges increase annually in line with inflation (CPI).

There are only two (legal) ways for employees who are drivers of company provided vans to avoid these rules. Firstly, if they prove they do no (or very few) private miles in the van. However, these claims are carefully examined to prevent abuse.

The other way to avoid any benefit in kind arising from private use is if the van provided produces 0g/km of emissions. As part of the UK Government's move towards NetZero, such vans have attracted a £0 van benefit rate since 2021/22 if there is any private usage. These rules being transitioned in over the last few years were aiming to lift this benefit closer to that of other cars. It is suggested this was necessary to reduce tax avoidance that was occurring where employees are provided with vehicles that can be classed as vans just to reduce the normal tax benefit charge on cars. However, this policy review appears to have determined this isn't needed after all and reinstated a significant incentive for new vans to be zero emissions.

Loans to employees

5.33 If an employee or director, or a member of their family, receives a loan which was obtained because of their employment and either no interest was paid on the loan for the year or the amount of interest paid on the loan in the year is less than interest at the *official rate* published by HMRC, then the employee will be assessed on the cash equivalent of the benefit of the loan. The cash equivalent is equal to the difference between the interest the employee has paid on the loan to the employer (if any) and the interest calculated at the official rate. However, a minimum level of loan applies before this charge is commenced. If the total amount of all loans the employee has received from the employer does not exceed £10,000 then no tax liability will arise (i.e. the benefit is therefore ignored for tax purposes). Once the loan or loans exceed the £10,000 threshold however, it is all liable for a taxable benefit calculation, not just the excess over this amount.

The amount of the loan for this benefit computation is normally taken to be the average of the balance at the beginning of the year and the balance at the end of the year, if the loan had been in existence throughout the year. Otherwise, the balance on the dates on which the loan was taken out and/or repaid is used instead. Only complete tax months in which the loan existed are taken into account (a tax month runs from the 6th of the month to the 5th of the following month). Under this circumstance the taxpayer can also make an election for interest at the official rate on the outstanding balance to be calculated on a daily basis if they want to, which is obviously more accurate, and therefore could lower their final tax bill.

If an employee receives a loan that comes under the 'qualifying loan' rules for tax deductibility (e.g. typically to buy necessary equipment to carry out their job as an employee – see section 4.32 above) then no benefit will arise. Loans at full commercial rates to employees where the employer is in the business of providing loans, also give rise to no taxable benefit.

Activity

Harry has loans from his employer that have been in existence all year:
a) An interest-free loan of £50,000 which Harry used to finance the purchase of his main residence.
b) A loan of £1,500 to buy an annual season ticket for rail travel at an interest rate of 1.5% pa.
c) A personal loan of £2,000 at an interest rate of 3.5% which Harry used to refit the bathroom in his home.
d) A loan of £1,800 at an interest-free rate to buy equipment he needs for his job.

Take the official rate of interest to be 2.0%. Determine the benefit assessable on Harry for the tax year.

Feedback

Loan d) is qualifying and therefore does not form part of any benefit calculations. The other loans can be totalled to calculate the benefit arising.

		£
a)	50,000 × (2% – 0%)	1,000.00
b)	1,500 × (2% – 1.5%)	7.50
c)	no benefit as rate exceeds official rate	–
		1,007.50

Other benefits

5.34 It is not possible here to list and explain all the detailed rules relating to the full range of possible benefits in kind as so many exist; however, a number of other specific benefits in kind are worth mentioning briefly because of their relative importance for large numbers of employees.

Mobile phones

No benefit arises from provision and use of a mobile phone even if private calls are allowed and paid for by the employer. This benefit is restricted to a single phone per employee, for their use only, to prevent possible exploitation of this benefit by the giving of multiple phones for use by an employee's family members, as well as the employee, on a tax-free basis. Any money paid by an employer to an employee for the use of their own phone must be declared as taxable as normal (and will be taxed if reimbursements are greater than the cost therefore).

Computers

A second benefit worth specific comment is the loan of a computer to an employee for their home (i.e. part business, part private) use. Somewhat controversially and unexpectedly the rules for this benefit were changed in the 2006 Budget, and an exemption that existed then for the first £500 of this benefit was withdrawn.

Since 6 April 2006 the computer benefit is valued at the full 20% of the cost of provision, just like other loaned assets, to represent the private use element. This extra tax cost is only avoidable under these new rules if it can be proven that there is no private use of the computer of any kind.

For all other loaned asset benefits (other than cars) a rate of 20% of the cost when new applies each year as we saw earlier.

Scholarships

Another special benefit you may come across is the provision of scholarships. We saw in Chapter 4 that scholarships paid to employees for their own education are exempt from tax. The situation is different, however, when the scholarship is for an employee's family members. If a scholarship of any kind is made available to the employee's family the employee is taxed on the actual cost of the scholarship, except when no more than 25% of the award is available because of the fact the recipient is a family member of an employee (i.e. at least 75% of the amount needs to be available to any applicant irrespective of any family ties to the giver of the scholarship).

Pension Advice

Finally, with effect from April 2017, if you are an employee you can receive up to £500 worth of pensions advice arranged via your employer without a benefit in kind being deemed to have occurred (the cost of any advice above this level is however, taxable).

Fiscal Fact

Private medical and dental insurance is the largest benefit in kind by number of recipients at 2.38 million in 2016/17. This benefit produced £670 million in tax liability and £260 million national insurance contributions in that year. [Source: HMRC Table T4.1]

Making Good

There was a tightening of the rules on making good what would otherwise become taxable benefits in kind enacted as part of the Finance Act (no. 2) 2017. A firm date of the 6 July following the tax year end (i.e. by 6 July 2023 for the 2022/23 tax year) is now the cut-off date by which making good must have occurred for payments that would otherwise be considered to be benefits-in-kind.

You can see from this section that there are a number of benefits in kind that either have a low value, or are exempt from income tax. This gives rise to some tax planning opportunities for employers and employees. We will consider these, including salary sacrifice arrangements, in more detail in Chapter 11.

A summary of the benefits in kind treatment detailed in this section, together with some further examples, can be found as a handout in the student section of the website.

You can now attempt Quick Quiz questions 4-10 and Full questions 2-6.

Termination payments

5.35 We saw in Chapter 4 that there are exemptions from income tax for certain types of payments received on termination of employment. When employment is terminated, the former employee may receive a number of types of payment for example, unpaid salary, damages, a payment in lieu of notice and compensation for loss of office. Some payments are fully taxable, some are fully exempt, and some are partly taxable, which can be confusing.

Fully taxable payments include unpaid salary, bonuses and payments made under a pre-existing contractual arrangement. Fully exempt payments include payments made where the employee has to give up work due to illness or injury, and statutory redundancy payments. Redundancy is where the employee has to leave employment because the job he or she was doing is no longer required.

Partly taxable payments arise due to a monetary limit on some termination payments, in particular those that are *ex gratia*, which means they are for gratuitous reasons and not a contractual entitlement. In this case only the first £30,000 is exempt. One complication that can arise is where the taxpayer receives a mix of payments e.g. statutory redundancy payment and also an ex gratia payment. In such cases, the £30,000 exemption is reduced by the amount of the statutory redundancy payment. From 6 April 2018, a reform to these rules came into force making taxable as earnings all contractual and non-contractual payments in lieu of working notice and requiring all employers to tax the equivalent of an employee's basic pay if notice was not worked. Since 6 April 2020, employer's National Insurance Contributions is due on termination payments in excess of the £30,000 threshold under these proposals.

The following activity illustrates these rules:

Activity

Oliver was made redundant on 31 August 2022 and received the following payments:

Statutory redundancy pay	£1,600
Discretionary payment for loss of employment	£42,000
Payment in lieu of notice	£4,300
Bonus under employment contract	£5,000
Holiday pay owing	£1,200

How much (if any) is taxable?

Feedback

Oliver's taxable redundancy payment is calculated as follows:	£
Statutory redundancy pay – exempt	nil
Discretionary payment – partly taxable	42,000
Payment in lieu of notice – fully taxable	4,300
Bonus – fully taxable	5,000
Holiday pay owing	1,200
Total before partial exemption	52,500
Partial exemption (£30,000 – £1,600)	(28,400)
Taxable amount	24,100

Pensions

5.36 There are a number of different methods for dealing with income tax on pensions used throughout the world. What makes pensions different from other forms of income receipt is the fact that they are earned over a long period of time. Governments have to make decisions about whether to allow tax concessions:

- to taxpayers for contributions they make to their pension fund;
- for the pension fund as it invests the contributions and earns income over the years; and finally,
- for the pension income itself when the taxpayer eventually withdraws from the fund.

The rationale for giving tax relief for pensions is to encourage taxpayers to provide for their own income in retirement, so they are not entirely dependent on state benefits. The UK adopts an 'EET' method, meaning that contributions to the fund receive tax relief (i.e. payments into a pension fund are exempt from income tax (E)), the pension fund is exempted from income tax on its earnings (E), but the pension received once the taxpayer starts to draw it is taxable (T).

In the UK, an individual can potentially derive a pension from two direct sources: state provided pension schemes, and a private pension (or more than one) provided by themselves and/or their employer.

The state pension schemes are funded from the Government's general funds, as discussed in Chapter 1. Entitlement to state pensions is determined in part by national insurance contributions made over your working life. Contributions to the state pension schemes via national insurance contributions have no specific income tax computation consequences, however, when state pensions are received on retiring, they are potentially taxable as part of a taxpayer's employment income. State pensions must therefore be added into the tax computations of anyone who receives them along with any other income when computing what, if any, income tax is payable (this is listed as 'pension income' and is treated like employment income in the tax computation). The current rate of payment for basic state pensions can be found in Appendix A.

Since April 2006 a new pension structure relates to all other pension funds created directly by taxpayers and/or their employers during their working lives. We briefly review below the options now available to taxpayers for providing their own pension incomes. In all cases however, for your tax computations the treatment is the same. If a taxpayer is in receipt of a pension, it must be added to their income tax computation as if it were an earned source of income. Non-cash benefits received as part of a pension are also taxable just like benefits received as part of employee incomes. The rules for taxing non-cash items are broadly the same as we reviewed in this chapter for benefits in kind.

Pension contributions are a tax efficient way of saving for retirement as the fact that pension contributions do not attract income tax makes them effectively tax deductible and what's more, deductible at the taxpayer's marginal tax rate. Therefore, higher (40%) or additional (45%) rate taxpayers get a better tax deduction per £1 paid into their pensions than do basic rate (20%) taxpayers. This tax deductibility is however, not allowed without limits, as we will see below.

A good source of further information about pensions is the Gov.uk website. For example, see:

https://www.gov.uk/browse/working/workplace-personal-pensions or
https://www.gov.uk/browse/working/state-pension

Current pension regime

5.37 Pension contributions have long been allowed as deductible expenditure from employment or trading income. This deduction has historically been allowed at the marginal rate of the taxpayer. This was introduced to encourage people to make at least some personal pension provision, rather than relying solely on state provision, by making contributions effectively made out of untaxed income. Tax relief under the new pension regime is usually given to the taxpayer in one of two ways depending how the pension scheme operates.

Contributing to a pension

5.38 First, for an employee contributing to a pension directly through their salary (e.g. as they participate in their employer's workplace pension scheme) their deduction will be taken out before PAYE is computed to ensure that they receive the full tax deduction they are entitled to at the correct marginal rate. This is referred to as a 'net pay arrangement'. In this circumstance you will not need to make any further adjustment to their tax computation.

Second, members may receive '*relief at source*' by making their contributions to a pension provider net of the basic rate of income tax. This is how self-employed taxpayers typically make contributions. A pension scheme member, for example, who wanted £100 added to their scheme, would pay only £80. The scheme administrator then claims basic rate tax applicable to that net sum paid (in this case £20) from HMRC and credits the member with having paid £100. If the member is a higher or additional rate taxpayer, they can get the extra higher or additional rate relief (i.e. a further 20% or 25%) on their self-assessment return by extending the basic rate band limit by the gross amount of the contribution (i.e. using the same process as for charitable donations, as shown in Section 4.38).

Activity

Bert earns £63,650 from his business in the tax year. He has no other taxable income. He makes a personal pension contribution in the tax year of £8,000 (net).

What is his tax liability for this tax year?

Feedback

Bert's tax liability will be:

	£
Trading income	63,650
Personal allowance	(12,570)
Taxable income	51,080

The grossed-up pension contribution Bert has paid (£8,000 x 100/80) will extend his basic rate tax band to £47,700 (i.e. £37,700 + £10,000).

47,700 @ 20%	9,540.00
3,380 @ 40%	1,352.00
Tax liability	10,892.00

Fiscal Fact

The cost to the Treasury of income tax relief for contributions to registered pension schemes is estimated to be £22.5 billion for 2021/22. This is the largest non-structural relief provided in the UK, underling how important the Government considers supporting pension provision in the UK. There are calls however, for a review of this sum as a significant percentage of this goes to the wealthier pension savers, given the extra benefits they accrue under the current system, either because they can afford to make larger contributions, or because if they are higher or additional rate taxpayers, the cost of these deductions falls due to higher tax relief levels they can claim. [Source: HMRC 'Estimated costs of non-structural tax reliefs']

Fund and contribution caps

5.39   Under the current rules while there is no limit on the size an individual's total pension funds can be, there is a life-time maximum limit on the total size of the pension funds on which tax relief can have been claimed. This is set at £1,073,100 for this tax year (no change from 2021/22 – although this level was a reduction from the £1.25 million in 2014/15). If your total pension funds rise above this sum, then a tax charge on the excess will need to be paid when the pension is taken (at 55% if you take any of the excess as a lump sum, or 25% if you take the excess as part of your pension).

In addition to the cap on the overall size of the pension fund that can be accumulated, there is an annual maximum cap on the amount you (and your employers if they also make contributions on your behalf) can contribute to your pension funds each year and claim tax relief on the contributions. This is set at £40,000 for 2022/23 (unchanged for the last seven years). This was much higher for 2010/11 at £255,000 but was dramatically cut by the Coalition Government that year and subsequently. If you wish, you are allowed to make contributions to your pension fund in excess of this sum (there is no maximum limit), however, you will be charged at your marginal income tax rate on your extra contributions so that they are no longer tax relieved (i.e. the excess effectively becomes like any other form of saving paid out of after tax income with no special tax treatment).

Drawing your pension

5.40   Once a taxpayer decides to start to draw their pension they are allowed to take up to 25% of the accumulated funds as a tax free lump sum to do with as they wish. Until April 2015 the remainder had to be invested in a product called an *annuity* – that provides a regular (usually monthly) payment to the taxpayer in return for the lump sum they invested.

From April 2015, more flexibility has been introduced to how these rules apply so that, for example, an annuity is now only one way to access these funds in future. You are also able now to draw from your capital held in your pension as you wish (for those in defined contribution pensions at least) and you pay tax only at your marginal rate of tax on the income (i.e. as you would if it was any other source of income).

The minimum age at which a taxpayer can take their pension is 55 (this will rise to 57 after 6 April 2028 under a new rule change brought in with Finance Act 2022), but they can delay this as long as they wish to enable their fund to continue to grow so as to maximise their tax free lump sum, annuity levels or the size of the pot from which they can withdraw capital flexibly.

Further, from April 2015, if a pension recipient dies before their 75th birthday, their nominated beneficiary can receive the funds remaining in their pension tax-free. If they die after becoming 75, the beneficiary will only pay tax on the remaining funds they receive at their own marginal rate of tax (or at 45% if funds are withdrawn as a lump sum).

 You can now attempt Full question 1

The Pension Credit

5.41 Additional pensions, like those detailed above, give recipients an additional source of income in retirement to supplement the basic state pension. As such they are an important part of an individual's financial planning, at least for those that can either afford to pay into them during their working life or have an employer who does it for them. However, a significant number of pensioners do not have these extra sources of income to rely on. A pension credit system is therefore in place to provide a minimum income for all pensioners if their other pension sources don't lift them to this level.

The Pension credit commenced in October 2003 and operates with similar aims to the Child Tax Credit and Working Tax Credit we discussed in Chapter 4. Its aim is to ensure no pensioner lives on less than £182.60 a week (£177.10 in 2021/22) or £278.70 a week as a couple (£270.30 in 2021/22). Direct credit payments are made to qualifying pensioners to ensure this is the case.

Summary

In this chapter we have focused on the taxation of income from employment and pensions. Since the majority of the UK workforce are employees it is an important area of the UK tax system. The general rule is that, unless specifically exempted, every benefit received from an employment is taxable, with just a very few deductions allowable. There are some tax planning opportunities for employers and employees. These particularly include the provision of some benefits in kind and planning for retirement.

You have encountered a number of different forms of tax relief in this chapter and the previous one, and may well be confused about how they all work. The following table should help clarify this for you.

Type of payment	how paid	how relief is given
Charges on income		
Patent royalties	net	Deduct gross amount paid (step 2) Add tax to tax liability
Copyright royalties	gross	Deduct gross amount paid (step 2)
Interest	gross	Deduct gross amount paid (step 2)
Gift aid donations		
Gift to charity	as if net	Don't deduct payment. Extend basic rate band by grossed up amount (higher and additional rate taxpayers)
Pensions		
Relief at source	net	Don't deduct payment Extend basic rate band by grossed up amount (higher and additional rate tax payers)
Net pay arrangement	gross	Paid before PAYE is calculated so relief is automatic, i.e. doesn't affect the tax computation. If the salary figure you're given in a question is before this has been deducted, deduct from gross salary.

Project areas

The taxation of income from employment provides a number of interesting areas to research. One such topic would be to undertake a comparison of the taxation of employment throughout the EU. Another interesting area is the question of the impacts and costs of altering benefits in kind, for example, extending the existing tax relief for workplace nurseries to all kinds of child-care costs.

A topical project would be an investigation into the provision of private versus company cars or of private fuel by employers. It would be interesting to find out how the role and use of company cars is changing in the UK as a result of the new rules introduced for fuel and for car benefit, or how many employers pay for their employees' private fuel and whether their decisions will change as a result of the Chancellor's measures.

Given the recent introduction of various radical changes to the pension regime in recent years, and further major changes in 2011, you could also look at how these differences have changed the nature of pension provision.

Discussion questions

1. Is it right to tax heavy users of vehicles more under the emissions-based rules when they need to use their cars for work?

2. Is it right to impose the extra 'necessary' rule, not present for sole-traders, on employees for deductibility of expenses from their taxable income?

3. Is it appropriate that some benefits in kind should not be taxable? (e.g. mobile phones provided to employees).

4. What are the implications for individual taxpayers, employers, the Government and society as a whole of our current pension provision options? Is the reduced focus on state pensions appropriate for those who can and can't fund their own pensions? What are the implications of such frequent changes to the pension rules?

Quick quiz

1. Helena, who is not a director, receives a bonus from her employer of £5,000. She became entitled to payment on 31 March 2023 but agreed to delay receipt until 30 April 2023 because of cash flow problems being experienced by the employer. When will Helena's bonus be taxed?

2. Iain makes £125 worth of business calls on his (non-business dedicated) home telephone and pays line rental on this phone of £28 per quarter. How much of these costs could he deduct from his employment income if his employer doesn't reimburse him for these costs.

3. Julia receives a mileage allowance of 30p per mile and drives her car 3,000 business miles during the year. How much (if any) is chargeable as employment income?

4. Keith's employer supplies him with the use of a company house which cost £250,000 and has an annual value of £10,200. He makes no contribution towards the running costs, which cost his employer £2,500 for the year. How much (if any) is chargeable as employment income, assuming an official rate of 2%, and that the accommodation is not job related?

5. Lorna is provided on 6 April 2022 with a new diesel-engine company car with a list price of £27,000 that had no non-standard accessories fitted and an emission rating of 152g/km. Assuming she had access to this car for the whole year, and no contributions towards the capital or usage costs of the car were paid to her employer by Lorna, how much (if any) is chargeable as employment income?

6. Michael works for a Big 4 accounting firm. He joins the local golf club and uses the club to meet with clients. He pays for the subscription himself. Is Michael entitled to a tax deduction for this payment?

7. Nola works for a company that provides her, from 6 October 2022, with a computer for her family to use that cost £1,500. What is its value as a benefit in kind?

8. Pauline is provided with a bicycle by her employer on 6 April 2022 for her private use including traveling to work. The bicycle cost the employer £975 when new and was transferred to Pauline free of charge on 6 October 2022, when it was valued at £500. What is Pauline's taxable benefit in 2022/23?

9. Quentin starts a new job during the tax year and his new employer pays for his removal expenses of £3,500. What is his taxable benefit?

10. Ravi's employer provides him with free car parking close to the building where he works. If he had to pay for the parking, it would cost Ravi £700 p.a. What is his taxable benefit?

11. Sumo has earnings from a business of £85,500 for the tax year and no other income. She pays personal pension contributions of £7,200 (net). What is her income tax liability?

12. Tiffany has employment income of £30,850 (gross). Her contribution to her employer-provided pension scheme is £5,000 during the tax year. Her employer contributes £2,000. What is her income tax liability?

Questions

Question 1 (based on an ACCA question).

Serene Volley is employed as a sports journalist by Backhand plc, a newspaper publishing company. During the tax year 2022/23 she was paid a gross annual salary of £26,400. Income tax of £4,190 was deducted from this under PAYE.

Throughout the tax year 2022/23, Backhand plc provided Serene with a petrol-powered car that had a list price of £16,400 when first registered in January 2020 (no accessories have been added). The official CO_2 emission rate for the car is 123g/km. The company did not provide Serene with any fuel for private journeys. Serene contributed 5% of her gross salary of £26,400 into Backhand plc's HMRC registered pension scheme. In addition to her employment income, Serene received interest of £1,200 on the maturity of a savings certificate from the National Savings & Investments Bank during the tax year. This was the actual cash amount received.

Required: Calculate the income tax payable by Serene for the tax year 2022/23.

Question 2 (based on an ACCA question).

Kim White is employed as a sales person by Sharp-Suit plc, a clothing manufacturing company. During the tax year 2022/23 she was paid a gross annual salary of £21,600.

On 1 June 2022, Sharp-Suit plc provided Kim with an interest free loan of £18,750 so that she could purchase a new car. During the period from 1 June 2022 to 5 April 2023, Kim used her private car for business and private purposes. She received no reimbursement from Sharp-Suit for any of the expenditure incurred. Kim's mileage during this period included the following travel:

Normal daily travel between home and permanent workplace	3,400
Between permanent workplace and Sharp-Suit plc's customers	9,200
Between home and a temporary workplace for one month	1,300

During the tax year 2022/23, Kim paid interest of £140 (gross) on a personal loan taken out on 1 January 2023 to purchase a laptop computer for use in her employment with Sharp-Suit plc. Kim received building society interest totalling £750 during the year, which was the actual cash amount received.

Required: Calculate Kim's income tax liability for the tax year 2022/23 (before PAYE). Assume an official interest rate of 2%. You should ignore any capital allowance that Kim might be entitled to.

Question 3 (based on an ACCA question).

Domingo and Erigo Gomez are brothers. The following information is available for the tax year 2022/23:

Domingo Gomez
1. Domingo is aged 78
2. During the tax year he received a state pension of £6,082 and a private pension of £3,480.
3. In addition to his pension income, Domingo received building society interest of £18,160 and interest of £600 on the maturity of a savings certificate from the National Savings and Investments Bank during the tax year. These were the actual cash amounts received.
4. During the tax year Domingo made donations of £300 (gross) to local charities. They were not made under the gift aid scheme.

Erigo Gomez
1. Erigo is aged 66.
2. He is employed as a business journalist by Economical plc, a magazine publishing company. During the tax year Erigo was paid a gross annual salary of £36,000 (gross).
3. During the tax year, Erigo used his private car for business purposes. He drove 18,000 miles in the performance of his duties for Economical plc, for which the company paid an allowance of 20p per mile.
4. During June 2022, Economical plc paid £11,400 towards the cost of Erigo's relocation when he was required to move his place of employment. Erigo's previous main residence was 140 miles from his new place of employment with the company. The £11,400 covered the cost of disposing of Erigo's old property and of acquiring a new property.
5. Erigo contributed 6% of his gross salary of £36,000 into Economical's HMRC registered workplace pension scheme.
6. During the tax year, Erigo donated £100 (gross) per month to charity under the payroll deduction scheme.

Tax returns

For the tax year 2022/23, Domingo wants to file a paper self-assessment tax return and have HMRC prepare a self-assessment on his behalf. Erigo wants to file an online return.

Required:

(a) Calculate the respective income tax liabilities for the tax year 2021/22 of Domingo and Erigo.
(b) Advise Domingo and Erigo of the latest date by which their respective self-assessment tax returns for the tax year 2021/22 will have to be submitted given their stated filing preferences.
(c) Advise Domingo and Erigo as to how long they must retain their records used in preparing their respective tax returns for the tax year 2021/22, and the potential consequences of not retaining the records for the required period.

Question 4 (based on an ACCA question).

Edward King is trying to calculate his tax liability for the tax year 2022/23 and the following information is available:

1. Edward was born on 29 October 1951 and is employed by Stately Ltd as a marketing director. During the tax year 2022/23 he was paid director's remuneration of £179,000 (gross).

2. On 1 December 2022, Stately Ltd provided Edward with an interest-free loan of £87,000, which he used to purchase a holiday cottage.

3. Stately Ltd has provided Edward with a home entertainment system for his personal use since 6 April 2019. The home entertainment system had been purchased by Stately Ltd on 6 April 2019 for £5,200. The company gave the home entertainment system to Edward on 6 April 2022 for no charge, although its market value at that time was £2,200.

4. During the tax year 2022/23, Edward contributed 4% of his gross director's remuneration of £179,000 into Stately Ltd's HMRC registered workplace pension scheme. The company contributed a further 6% on his behalf.

5. During the tax year 2022/23, Edward donated £200 (gross) per month to charity under the payroll deduction scheme.

6. During the tax year 2022/23 Edward used his private motor car for business purposes. He drove 12,000 miles in the performance of his duties for Stately Ltd, for which the company paid an allowance of 35 pence per mile.

7. On 1 January 2023, Edward paid a professional subscription of £240 to the Guild of Marketing, an HMRC approved professional body.

8. For the tax year 2022/23, Stately Ltd deducted a total of £61,600 in PAYE from Edward's earnings.

Required: Calculate Edward King's tax liability for the tax year 2022/23. He has no other income or expenses for the year. Assume an official interest rate of 2%.

Question 5 (based on an ICAS TPS Tax Paper question).

Jon was working as a dentist in a long established local practice but was recently offered an exciting new job at a dental research company. He left the dental practice on 5 April 2022 and started his new job the following day. Details of Jon's new salary and benefits are given below, together with details of his other income.

Salary

Jon started his new job on 6 April 2022. His annual salary is £110,000 (gross). In addition, the company will make contributions to its approved pension scheme of 6% per annum, while Jon will make employee contributions of 5% per annum. Jon has advised you that monthly PAYE of £3,000 was deducted from his salary.

Benefits

- The company has provided Jon with a diesel BMW 1 Series company car. It has CO_2 emissions of 61g/km and its list price was £21,000 when first registered on 1 April 2022. Optional extras which Jon asked the company to add to the car totalled £800. Jon's local garage was offering the same car (with extras) at a cost of £20,500. The company have agreed to meet the cost of all of Jon's fuel (for both private and business use). The car was made available from 6 April 2022.

- Jon has been provided with a laptop, which he uses for both business and private purposes. He estimates that his private use will be approximately 50%. The laptop cost £950 when he was provided with it on 1 June 2022.

- Jon was provided with an iPhone which he uses principally for business. The rental is £45 per month and it cost £650. He has had use of the iPhone since the first day of his employment.

- Jon and his wife travelled to Paris for a weekend in the middle of November where Jon attended an introductory company conference. Other than attending the end of conference dinner, Jon's wife was free to shop and sightsee. Travel and expenses met by the company amounted to £850 each.

Other receipts

Jon received the following amounts in 2022/23:

	£
UK dividends	20,000
Bank interest	800
Interest on ISA account	1,500
Premium bond winnings (received in May 2022)	1,000

Required: Calculate the income tax payable by Jon for the tax year 2022/23.

(Note: answer available via lecturer's website)

Question 6 (based on an ACCA question).

Peter Chic is employed by Haute-Couture Ltd as a fashion designer. The following information is available for the tax year 2022/23:

1. During the tax year Peter was paid a gross annual salary of £45,600 by Haute-Couture Ltd. Income tax of £15,558 was deducted from this figure under PAYE.

2. In addition to his salary, Peter received two bonus payments from Haute-Couture Ltd during the tax year. The first bonus of £4,300 was paid on 30 April 2022 and was in respect of the year ended 31 December 2021. Peter became entitled to this bonus on 10 April 2022. The second of £3,600 was paid on 31 March 2023 and was in respect of the year ended 31 December 2022. Peter became entitled to this second bonus on 25 March 2023.

3. Throughout the tax year, Haute-Couture Ltd provided Peter with a diesel car which has a list price when new on 6 April 2021 of £22,500. The car cost Haute-Couture £21,200, and it has an official CO_2 emissions rate of 232g/km. Peter made a capital contribution of £2,000 towards the cost of the car when it was first provided to him. Haute-Couture Ltd also provided Peter with fuel for private journeys.

4. Haute-Couture Ltd has provided Peter with living accommodation since 1 January 2009. The company had purchased the property in 2007 for £160,000, and it was valued at £185,000 on 1 January 2022. Improvements costing £13,000 were made to the property during June 2015. The annual value of the property is £9,100.

5. Throughout the tax year Haute-Couture Ltd provided Peter with two mobile phones. The telephones had each cost £250 when purchased by the company in January 2022.

6. On 5 May 2022, Haute-Couture Ltd paid a health club membership fee of £510 for the benefit of Peter.

7. During June 2022, Peter spent five nights overseas on company business. Haute-Couture paid Peter a daily allowance of £10 to cover the cost of personal expenses such as telephone calls to his family.

8. During the whole of the 2022/23 tax year Peter was required to work from home due to Covid-19. The business did not however pay anything towards his extra costs incurred as a result of this. Peter estimates these costs to be approximately £5.50 per week.

Other information:

1. During the tax year Peter received building society interest of £2,200 and dividends of £800.

2. On 4 August 2022, Peter received a premium bond prize of £100.

3. During the tax year Peter made gift aid donations totalling £2,340 (net) to national charities.

Required: Calculate the income tax payable by Peter Chic for the tax year 2022/23. Assume the official rate of interest is 2%.

(Note: answer available via lecturer's website)

Further test questions for this chapter to test your knowledge can be found in the student section of the website at:

https://www.fiscalpublications.com/lymerandoats/2022

Further reading and examples

Combs, A., and R. Tutin (2022), *Taxation: Incorporating the 2022 Finance Act*, Fiscal Publications: Malvern.
  – use this book for many other examples to further develop and test your knowledge of this chapter's contents. See
  https://www.fiscalpublications.com/combsandtutin/2022

Combs, A. (2022), *UK Income Tax Practice Questions (2nd edition 2022/23)*, Fiscal Publications: Malvern.
  – a large test bank of questions linked to the content of this chapter that will enable you to thoroughly test your knowledge of this work with exam-level questions. See
    https://www.fiscalpublications.com/uk-income-tax-practice-questions/2022

Full guidance on the taxation of expenses and benefits in kind can be found in Tax Guide 480(2013) – see https://www.gov.uk/government/publications/480-expenses-and-benefits-a-tax-guide

6 Taxing trading and property income

Introduction

6.1   In this chapter and the next we will explore the taxation of unincorporated businesses, which are businesses that are not run as limited liability companies, focussing on taxation of sole traders (but the same rules apply for all unincorporated businesses). Unincorporated businesses are not treated as separate taxable entities for tax purposes. Rather, the *trading income* rules are used to determine the taxable income resulting from their business activities so that this can then be included in the business owner's tax computation alongside any other income categories they have to pay tax on for the tax year.

As *property income* is also calculated using similar rules to trading income, the final section of this chapter reviews this component of income.

At the end of this chapter you will be able to:

- state the badges of trade and use them to identify trading activities;
- identify income that is chargeable and expenses which are deductible under the trading income rules;
- convert accounting profits into trading profits for tax purposes; and
- compute property income and discuss the special property related tax schemes currently in operation.

Introduction to the trading income rules

6.2   In Chapter 4 we discussed how income taxed by direct assessment is assessed for tax purposes. Such income is taxed under one or other of the various tax component rules. The basis of assessment that applies, and other rules to determine how much tax will be due on the income, depends on which component the income is assessed under. We saw in Chapter 5 how income from your job is taxed under the *employment income* rules. Income from a trade or business and income from a vocation or profession are taxed under the *trading income* rules. There are some small differences in the way that the tax due is calculated for trade and vocation/professional incomes (we'll meet one later as an illustration), but for our purposes in this book we will treat them as being the same.

Although we focus on sole traders, many of the rules also apply to partnerships as the other form of unincorporated business structure.

We will not discuss the rules for partnership income tax in more detail in this book however you can find information and worked examples on our website.

Many of the trading and property income rules also apply to companies, with some modifications that we will discuss further in Chapter 9.

There are approximately 4.1 million people, or about 11.6% of the current working population (of approximately 35 million), who are sole-traders and therefore are taxed under the trading income rules (Source: ONS – Employment in the UK, March 2022). They are expected to have paid a total of approximately £38 billion in taxes in 2021/22 (Source: HMRC Receipts). While some trading taxpayers run large businesses, many are running relatively small undertakings, as sole traders or with a small number of employees.

Fiscal Fact

The Department for Business, Energy and Industrial Strategy (BEIS) reported in October 2021, that there were an estimated 5.6 million private sector enterprises in the UK at the start of 2021. This is a decrease of 389,600 businesses (6.4%) compared with 2020 but 2.1 million (or 60%) more than at the start of 2000 (although 75% of these businesses are non-employing businesses – i.e. they have no employees listed working for these businesses other than the self-employed owner and companies with one employee, the employee director). These businesses employed 27 million people and had an estimated combined turnover of £4.45 trillion. The same report said that almost 3.2 million (56%) of these businesses were sole traders, 37% (2 million) were (actively trading) companies and 7% (384,000) were partnerships. Taken together, small and medium sized enterprises count for 99.9% of all businesses by number. (Source: Business Population Estimates for the UK 2021 - Statistical Release October 2021)

This large number of businesses can be split into three groups for the purposes of determining how they must account for tax on their profits:

1. All larger businesses, sole traders and partners are assessed on the profits which arise in the business' accounting period that ends during the tax year being assessed. These businesses use generally accepted accounting principles where receipts and expenditure are matched to the period on an accruals basis (i.e. whether or not they had been received or paid). Adjustments are then made for any receipts or payments that relate to a

different period. For many businesses this remains the way which they account for their tax liabilities.

2. From 6 April 2013 smaller businesses have been able to opt to use cash accounting rules (the so called '*cash basis*') to compute their tax liability From April 2017 this has become the default approach for many individuals operating a property business. This option is available to businesses with a *turnover* below the current VAT registration threshold (£85,000) (or £150,000 if a property business) who are not benefiting from limited liability (as a company or partnership). We will review these rules in more detail in sections 6.6 and 6.46.

3. Rules now allow the very smallest of businesses (those with a turnover of less than £1,000) to not have to file tax returns for this income and not to have to pay any tax on it at all. We introduced this 'trading allowance' rule in section 4.26 that in effect means, where an entity that would normally be subject to tax on trading income has a turnover of less than £1,000, this can be completely covered by the new allowance and no tax is due. This excludes the very smallest of business from having to use either the cash basis or the accruals basis to compute their profits. It therefore excludes many who might not have thought themselves trading at all if just selling a few things they own on eBay from paying income tax on their trading incomes!

Most businesses continue to use an accruals-based accounting system (i.e. group 1 above) to determine their tax liability. This is therefore the system we will focus on in this chapter, but some details of the cash basis approach are also provided (see sections 6.6 and 6.46).

Before any taxable profit under the trading income rules can be calculated (i.e. if the business is in any of the groups above) it is necessary to demonstrate that trading is actually taking place. In this chapter we will review the principles referred to as the *badges of trade*, which are used to determine this. Once the existence of trading has been established, you will then need to undertake at least two steps to determine the trading income for a tax year. These are:

1. determine which of the trader's accounts will form the basis period for the tax year; and

2. adjust the accounting profits to derive the tax adjusted trading profits.

To fully determine the trading income for tax purposes you may need to establish the tax implications of any investment in capital assets, so we will look at those rules in the next chapter.

Once you have computed the tax adjusted trading profits, you can add this amount to the tax computation to determine the total income (or it can be ignored in this computation if the business falls under group 3 above). The Thomas Lester example at the beginning of Chapter 4 showed you how to do this. Look back to this illustration if you need to be reminded which number we are now working towards determining.

Identification of trading activities

6.3   The first thing for us to do is to consider when an activity is 'trading' and so is subject to trading income rules. The definition of 'trade' is quite wide and is defined to include 'any venture in the nature of trade' (ITA s989). This brings some isolated (single, or 'one-off') transactions within the concept of 'trade'.

For anyone who is not an employee, it is very important to determine whether money received in conjunction with carrying out an activity is trading income or not, as this could significantly affect how much tax is due.

Before 1965, if a receipt was found not to be trading income then it was likely to be a *capital gain* (meaning simply, selling something for more than its purchase price). At that time capital gains were not taxable and therefore obtaining receipts in this form was a tax-free source of increased wealth. Since 1965 however, most capital gains have been taxable in the UK (we will look at how these rules work in Chapter 8). The main capital gains tax rates for the last few years are either 10% (for a basic rate taxpayer) and 20% (for a higher or additional rate taxpayer). These rates are lower than the taxpayer's marginal rate of income tax and so there is still an advantage to having a receipt of money classed as a capital gain.

Because of these different potential tax rates, it is important to know whether trading is occurring, or some other type of activity (e.g. just a hobby or one-off activity), so that the correct method of taxing this activity is applied. For example, if you bought and sold a number of works of art or collectables (e.g. perhaps on EBay or via newspaper ads), at what point would this go from being a hobby or occasional pastime (on which you may have to pay capital gains tax if you sell anything for more than you bought it for, but not income tax) to being a 'trade' you are engaged in (which is then subject to income tax trading rules)?

For most of us hobbies cost money rather than make money; the tax system will not give us tax relief on any losses (e.g. costs) related to hobbies, however, relief is often available for costs/'losses' incurred when trading. Correct classification is therefore important for a variety of reasons.

Unhelpfully, the UK tax legislation does not give us a neat definition of what constitutes trading for tax purposes. We must therefore look to case law or other sources of tax principles, for guidance in determining whether trading is taking place that therefore may create a tax liability.

Often the decision whether trading is occurring or not is clear cut e.g. if the taxpayer is running a shop and selling goods to the public, they will very likely be considered to be trading for tax purposes. But, where doubt exists, and in the extreme where there is perhaps only a one-off transaction occurring, a mechanism is needed to confirm if activities (one-off and other) can be taxed as trading income. In 1955 a Royal Commission (Cmd 9474) reviewed the existing case law in this area, particularly on one-off transactions, and drew together the principles applied by the courts when considering cases of whether trading was occurring or not. These principles (six in total) have become known as the *'badges of trade'*.

None of the six badges offer a conclusive test of trading by themselves, although some are stronger indicators than others in practice. If trading is taking place it is likely that there will be evidence of this in more than one 'badge'. HMRC use these tests in deciding whether they agree with a claim made by a taxpayer to be trading, or not. If they disagree with the taxpayer's assessment, they may challenge this opinion and seek to tax them on that activity differently.

Badges of trade

6.4   The six badges of trade are as follows:

1   The subject matter of the transaction

6.5   If the property forming the subject matter of the transaction does not provide either direct income or enjoyment to the owner, it is likely that the transaction will be considered to be trading. It seems unlikely that articles which are normally the subject of trading will be treated as anything other than a trade. For example, in *Rutledge* v *IRC* (1929) while in Berlin on business the taxpayer bought one million rolls of toilet paper for £1,000 from a bankrupt German firm. The toilet rolls were sent to the UK and the taxpayer endeavoured to sell them. Eventually he found a buyer who bought the whole quantity for £12,000, earning him a considerable profit. The transaction was held to be 'in the nature of a trade' largely because of the quantity of the goods involved but also because of the nature of the goods, after all, one million toilet rolls are unlikely to be used by the taxpayer personally!. This case demonstrates that even a single transaction can sometimes be trading.

In contrast, in *IRC v Reinhold* (1953) the taxpayer had bought four houses within a two year period intending to sell them on. The Court of Session stated that 'heritable property is not an uncommon subject of investment' and so the taxpayer was not considered to be trading on this occasion.

In the case of *Marson v Morton* (1986) the taxpayer bought land intending to develop it, but in fact sold it on for a profit. The taxpayer was held not to be trading, confirming that land can be held for investment purposes even if it does not yield an income.

2 The frequency of similar transactions

6.6 Although a single transaction can be considered to be trading repeated transactions in the same subject matter is likely to be a stronger indicator that the taxpayer is trading.

In *Pickford v Quirke* (1927) the taxpayers formed a syndicate to buy and resell cotton mills. There were four such transactions over a period of time. The membership of the syndicate was not identical for each transaction. It was held that any one transaction would not have constituted trading but the four taken together did. In *Akhtar Ali v R&C Commrs* (2016) UKFTT 8, the taxpayer was a pharmacist who also bought and sold shares. He was held to be operating a trade, even though he was not successful and was not a sophisticated share trader.

3 The circumstances responsible for the realisation

6.7 There is a presumption that trading is not occurring if the property is disposed of to raise money for an unexpected event.

In the case of *The Hudson's Bay Company v Stevens* (1909) the taxpayer company had sold off a large quantity of land over several years which it had acquired in return for the surrender of its charter. The company was held not to be trading, the court offering the following explanation: 'The company are doing no more than an ordinary landowner does who is minded to sell from time to time as purchasers offer, portions suitable for building of an estate which has devolved upon him from his ancestors.'

4 Supplementary work on or in connection with the property realised

6.8 Trading is more likely to be taking place if either work is done on the property to make it more marketable, or an organisation is set up to sell it. The courts have decided that if there is an organised effort to obtain profit there is a source of taxable income but in the absence of such effort the presumption will be that trading is not taking place.

In *Cape Brandy Syndicate v IRC* (1927) a group of accountants bought 3,000 casks of Cape Brandy, blended it with French Brandy, re-casked it and sold it in lots over a period of 18 months. They were held to be trading because they did not simply buy an article which they thought was cheap and then resold it; the syndicate bought the brandy intending to modify its character so that it could be sold in smaller quantities. In *TA Hartland v R&C Commrs* [2014] UKFTT 1099, a builder bought a number of properties and demolished some and renovated others before advertising them for sale. He claimed to have used two of the properties as his principal residence. The First Tier Tribunal held that one of the properties had been purchased and reconstructed and sold in the course of a trade, and so the profit was taxable under the trading profit rules.

5 The motive for the transaction

6.9 There is some evidence of trading taking place if the objective of undertaking the transaction is to make a profit. However, even in the absence of a motive to make a profit it may still be concluded that trading is taking place. The subject matter of the transaction may be crucial.

In *Wisdom v Chamberlain* (1968) the taxpayer, a well-known comedian, bought silver bullion as a hedge against an anticipated devaluation of the pound. It was held that the taxpayer had undertaken an 'adventure in the nature of a trade' when he realised a profit three months later, because the transaction was entered into on a short-term basis with the sole intention of making a profit from the purchase and sale of a commodity.

However, in *Richard Murray v R&C Commrs* [2014] UKFTT388, the taxpayer engaged in racehorse training and breeding with the intention to make a profit, but rather made losses, in part due to the economic downturn. The Tribunal, however, held that the activities in this case were not trading as they were not undertaken on a commercial basis. This demonstrates that a profit motive alone is not enough to make an activity trading.

6 The length of ownership

6.10 The presumption in this badge of trade is that the shorter the period of ownership the more likely it is that trading is taking place. This is a weaker badge than some of the others, however, because the short period of ownership can often be explained by the taxpayer if they need to, perhaps for example, by demonstrating a need for cash at the time of the sale. Hence there are many exceptions to this as a universal rule.

In addition to these six main badges of trade, other factors might be considered by HMRC when deciding whether trading is taking place. There could perhaps include:

- the source of finance for the transaction;
- the circumstances surrounding the acquisition of the asset; and
- whether the subject matter of transaction is in any way related to trades and other activities carried on by the taxpayer.

To summarise this section, and to illustrate the practical difficulties courts have in deciding over the trading question, attempt the following activity:

Activity

Stirling Hamilton is a vintage motor car enthusiast. On 1 January, 2020 he took out a loan of £40,000 at a fixed rate of interest of 10%, and spent £30,000 on having a workshop built. This was completed on 31 March 2021, when a further £8,000 was spent on tools and equipment. On 6 April 2021, Stirling bought a dilapidated vintage motor car for £3,000, and proceeded to restore it at a cost of £7,000 in spare parts. The restoration was completed on 30 June, 2021. Unfortunately, Stirling was made redundant on 15 September 2021, and was forced to sell the motor car for £25,000. Not being able to find further employment, Stirling proceeded to buy three more dilapidated vintage motor cars on 15 October 2021 for £4,000 each. The restoration of these was completed on 28 February 2022 at a cost of £7,000 per motor car, and two of them were immediately sold for a total of £50,000.

On 31 March 2022 Stirling obtained employment elsewhere in the country, so he immediately sold the workshop for £25,000, and repaid the loan of £40,000. Stirling personally retained the tools and equipment, which were worth £4,500, and the unsold vintage motor car which was valued at £25,000.

You are required to:

(a) Briefly discuss the criteria which would be used by the courts in deciding whether Stirling will be treated as carrying on a 'trade' for his vintage motor car activities; and

(b) Explain whether or not you would consider Stirling to be carrying on an adventure in the nature of a trade.

Feedback

To answer this part of the question you need to discuss the six badges of trade.

The acquisition and disposal of the first car, taken in isolation, is unlikely to be deemed to be trading because:

- Vintage cars are often owned and restored by individuals in order to derive enjoyment and/or as investments.
- The length of ownership after the restoration work is completed does not suggest trading is taking place.
- The circumstances surrounding the sale of the car suggests that the disposal was a forced sale rather than trading.

However, the loan taken out to build and equip the workshop and help to finance the acquisition of the car might be taken to be a sign that trading is taking place. The acquisition and disposal of the next three cars is likely to be treated as an adventure in the nature of a trade because:

- Stirling devoted the whole of his time to the activity.
- There were three acquisitions and disposals.
- Two of the cars were sold as soon as their restoration was completed.

If, as seems likely, Stirling Hamilton is deemed to be trading we now need to determine whether the first transaction will be deemed to be trading as a result of the later transactions. To decide this we need to refer to case law again. In the case mentioned above of *Pickford* v *Quirke* (1927) the taxpayer bought a mill and sold all the assets. This would normally be treated as a capital transaction but the taxpayer carried on to asset strip a total of four mills. The courts decided that the taxpayer was trading and that the three later transactions could be considered when deciding whether the first transaction was trading.

In the case of *Leach* v *Pogson* (1962) the taxpayer set up 30 driving schools which were then sold. Again, the courts decided that the 29 later transactions could be considered when deciding whether the first transaction was trading and hence the taxpayers were trading.

Finally, in the case of *Taylor* v *Good* (1974) the taxpayer bought a country estate, intending to live in the house. His wife refused to live in the house and so he instead obtained planning permission to build 90 houses on the land. He then sold the property to a property developer having owned the property for about four years. The courts decided that the transactions undertaken to enable the taxpayer to sell the property at a profit were not enough for the first transaction, the acquisition of the property, to be considered trading.

On balance it seems likely that Stirling will be taken to be trading on all his transactions. Do you agree? You might like to think about what arguments Stirling could offer against this decision if he challenged it in court.

Adjustment of profits

6.11 Now that you can identify trading activities you need to be able to calculate the taxable trading income that arises from any trading transactions.

Taxable trading income is made up of the difference between trading receipts and allowable expenses during a period of assessment. As we noted earlier, this computation can be undertaken in one of three ways for businesses:

1. using generally accepted accounting principles (an *accrual basis*). HMRC refer to this as 'traditional' accounting;
2. using a *cash basis* (small businesses only);
3. applying the *trading allowance* so that any trading income is not taxable (the very smallest of businesses).

We review the first of these options, the accruals basis, in sections 6.12 to 6.39, and provide an example to illustrate how this is applied in practice in section 6.40.

We will review the cash basis option in more detail in section 6.41. The cash basis is used by relatively few, mainly new or very small, businesses. In section 6.42 we look more closely at the basis of assessment for trading activities.

The accruals basis

6.12 The normal approach to the adjustment of profits for tax purposes, starts with the net profit for accounting purposes i.e. using accruals based accounting. Under this approach, accounting profit includes all receipts that relate to the relevant period, whether actually received in the period itself or not. From this accrued income is then deducted all relevant expenses. These will include all those relating to the period you are computing the profit for, whether actually paid or not within the period itself.

The tax rules then require a number of adjustments to convert the accounting profit to a tax adjusted profit. To do this, you will need to:

- determine which accounting period will form the basis of assessment for trading income for the tax year; and
- identify taxable income and allowable expenditure for the basis period.

In the remainder of this section we will first briefly summarise the rules for recognising receipts and allowable expenditure for tax purposes. Then we will explore specific trading receipts that form part of the trading income in more detail. Finally, we will consider what expenses are allowable in determining trading income.

We will now look more closely at the calculation of trading income to illustrate how these general rules are applied in practice.

Recognition of income - Trading receipts

6.13 A receipt is a trading receipt if it is a payment for services or goods supplied by the taxpayer. But how do we determine when a trading receipt has been received, and how much should be recorded in our tax computation? There are a number of rules and principles we must apply in practice to answer this question to ensure we don't either under or over report the amount (so we don't under- or over-pay tax). These include, for example:

1. The receipt must be income and not capital;
2. Voluntary payments received are not trading receipts; and
3. Goods taken from the business for private purposes must be valued at market price and not cost.

We will now examine each of these principles in more detail:

1   Income versus capital receipts

6.14   As a general rule, to be taxable as trading income, a receipt must be income related and not related to the non-current assets of the business (also referred to as its 'capital'). Receipts related to capital assets (i.e. the proceeds from selling a capital asset) are instead generally taxed under the capital gains tax rules (see Chapter 8). The distinction has proved difficult to draw in practice and several tests have been developed over a long period of time to help get this right. The most straightforward is to determine if the receipt relates to an asset that is part of the businesses' non-current assets (therefore likely to be a capital receipt) or to the current assets of the business (therefore likely to be an income receipt). While this might on the surface seem a fairly straight forward rule, it isn't always easy to determine if an asset is inventory or a non-current (capital) asset as it can depend on the type of business. You will have looked at this distinction if you have studied accountancy and will have seen how difficult this can be to determine.

The courts have devised a broad test, called the '*trees and fruit*' test, which can be applied to help resolve this issue in practice. Here the analogy is that the tree is the enduring part (considered to be the capital), producing the fruit, which is the recurring product (considered to be the income).

One characteristic of income receipts is that they are often recurring, compared to capital receipts that are often (but not always) one-off items. So how often a taxpayer receives a particular kind of payment may be a clue as to whether it is income or capital for tax purposes.

To decide whether a receipt is income or capital, we also need to think about what it is paid for and how it relates to the taxpayer's particular activities. Case law gives us several examples and some general principles that can be used to help make this decision.

For example, what if an amount is received in return for a taxpayer restricting his or her activities in some way (e.g. agreeing not to trade in a particular area)? If the receipt is to compensate the taxpayer for not being able to use a business asset at all, sometimes referred to as 'sterilisation' of the asset, then it will probably be a capital receipt. However, if it is to substitute for a receipt that would have been a trading receipt, then it is more likely to be treated as income.

In *Higgs v Olivier* (1952), Sir Lawrence Olivier received £15,000 from the makers of the film Henry V, in which he starred, in return for an agreement not to act in another film for 18 months. This payment was separate from the fee he was paid for starring in the film. The Court of Appeal held that the payment was for a substantial restriction of his income earning activities, and so was not a trading receipt. If a restriction is not substantial, or only short term, it may be classified as an income receipt.

More recently, in *J Lints v R&C Commrs* [2012] UKFTT 491, a solicitor was paid compensation for possible disruption to his business while the Edinburgh tramway was being built. The tribunal agreed with HMRC that the sum was a trading receipt because it effectively replaced business turnover.

In *Glenboig Union Fireclay Co Ltd v IR Commrs* (1922) the company leased some fireclay fields and the seam ran underneath a railway track. The railway company paid a large sum of money to stop the company from working the fireclay seam, and the House of Lords held that this was a capital receipt. It was considered to be a payment for the sterilisation of an asset of the business.

In *Burmah Steamships Co Ltd v IRC* (1930), the company bought a ship that needed extensive repairs before it was seaworthy. The repairer took longer than agreed to finish the repairs and so paid compensation to the company, calculated by reference to the profits lost during the delay. This was held to be income because the compensation filled a 'hole' in the taxpayer's profit.

Some other areas where the distinction between capital and income arise are:

- Compensation for cancellation of commercial contracts or connections. Where the compensation relates to contracts which are relatively small compared to the overall size of the business activities, they will usually be income in nature and form part of the trading profits. Receipts which are compensation for contracts which are large compared to the size of the business, on the other hand, are generally considered to be capital.
- Appropriations of unclaimed deposits and advances.
- Receipts from the sale of information. This receipt is covered by statute, unlike the two above which have been decided by means of case law. Provided that the vendor continues to trade after the sale, the receipt will be treated as a trading receipt.
- A trade debt which has been deducted as a trading expense and is subsequently cancelled is treated as a trade receipt.

Sometimes a payment can be divided into both capital and income parts for tax purposes. This is what happened, for example, in the case of *London and Thames Haven Oil Wharves v Attwooll* (1967) where £100,000 compensation was paid after a tanker crashed into a jetty, causing serious damage. The sum was split into a capital sum, which was intended to be used to rebuild the jetty, and an income receipt, which was compensation to the jetty owners for loss of income due to the accident. The income part alone would qualify as a trading receipt.

2 Voluntary payments

6.15 Payments made on a voluntary basis for some personal quality of the taxpayer are not generally trading receipts. In *Murray v Goodhews* (1976), the brewing company, Watneys, made *ex gratia* (voluntary) lump sum payments to landlords of public houses when they terminated tied tenancies, partly as an acknowledgement of the good relationship they had with their tenant and partly to preserve their good name. These sums were held not to be trading receipts in the hands of the landlords since the amounts of the payments had no connection with the profits earned nor was it linked with future trading relations between Watneys and the taxpayer.

However, in *McGowan v Brown and Cousins* (1977), the taxpayer, an estate agent, received a lower than usual fee for acquiring property for a company in the expectation that he would be retained to deal with letting the property. The company owning the property later paid the taxpayer £2,500 as compensation when they retained another agent instead to deal with the lettings. The payment was held to be a trading receipt this time despite the lack of a legal obligation to pay it.

HMRC (BIM15035) provides an example of a payment that is outside of income tax: a greengrocer witnesses a car breakdown, helps the passengers to their destination and repairs their car. In return, he or she receives an unsought payment for the assistance. The payment is unsolicited and made in recognition of personal qualities and so is outside of income tax altogether.

3   Goods taken for private purposes

6.16 For tax computation purposes goods disposed of, other than in the ordinary course of business, must be accounted for at market value as a trading receipt. In *Sharkey v Wernher* (1956) the taxpayer who ran a stud farm as a business also raced horses as a hobby. She transferred five horses from her stud farm to her racing stables and recorded the cost of breeding the horses as a receipt of the stud farm. The Revenue argued that the market value of the horses should be entered in the accounts rather than cost, and the courts agreed. The rule derived from this case applies to all goods taken by owners for their own use, as well as goods they give to others for non-business purposes. Finance Act 2008 enshrined this rule in statute. Beware, as this is usually different to the way such adjustments are made in accounting (where cost is used not market value). We will illustrate this principle for you later with an example when we discuss common adjustments needed to convert accounting profits to tax profits.

This rule can also apply if goods are sold at less than their market value. However, provided that the disposal can be shown to have been made for genuine commercial reasons (e.g. as the result of a sale or special offer) the rule in *Sharkey v Wernher* does not apply. Additionally, the rule applies to traders only. It does not apply to professional persons (i.e. it does not apply in relation to intangible goods or services). In *Mason v Innes* (1967) the novelist Hammond Innes gave the manuscript of *The Doomed Oasis* to his father. The writer had deducted allowable travelling expenses, which had been incurred while researching the book, from his income. The Revenue wanted to assess the writer on the market value of the script. Lord Denning said:

> "Suppose an artist paints a picture of his mother and gives it to her. He does not receive a penny for it. Is he to pay tax on the value of it? It is unthinkable. Suppose he paints a picture, which he does not like when he has finished it and destroys it. Is he liable to pay tax on the value of it? Clearly not. These instances therefore show that that *Sharkey* v *Wernher* does not apply to professional men."

This latter example is one of the main differences between business and professional income categories. Other examples are beyond the scope of an introductory tax course.

Deductible expenses

6.17   Having looked at the income element in determining a trader's taxable income we should now consider the allowable expenses that can be deducted from this income. For expenditure to be an allowable deduction for tax purposes it must satisfy three criteria:

1. it must be incurred *wholly and exclusively* for the purposes of the trade;
2. it must be a *revenue* item, not a *capital* expense (unless specifically allowed for in the legislation); and
3. it must not be specifically disallowed by statute.

We will now examine each of these concepts in more detail before discussing how a simplified expenses scheme can be used by some businesses who wish to account for their allowable costs in a different way:

1   Wholly and exclusively

6.18   Only expenditure that is *wholly and exclusively* incurred for the purposes of the trade or business will be deductible to determine taxable trading income. This concept is similar to the one we met in section 5.2 when discussing employment income, except there the requirement was for expenses to be wholly, exclusively and *necessarily* for the purposes of employment. For a self-employed taxpayer there is no need, however, to prove an expense they incur is necessary to perform their income earning activities. As long as the wholly and exclusively aspects are met then an expense can be allowable. This means more expenses may be allowable for self-employed taxpayers than for employees.

There are two situations where a business is likely to fall foul of the wholly and exclusively requirement. The first is when the payment is not directly related to the business activities, which is tested using what is called the *remoteness test*. The second is where the expenses have a more than one purpose, tested using the *duality test*.

The remoteness test

6.19   This test considers whether the expense is closely enough related to the day to day running of the business, or whether it really relates to an activity outside of the business. This means you can't just put any expense through your business accounts and get a tax deduction for it just because the business paid for it.

For example, consider whether subscriptions and donations are deductible or not. Subscriptions to trade associations will generally be deductible as it is usually easy to see the benefits that arise to the business from membership of a trade association, and it is closely related to the running of the business. Subscriptions and donations to political parties on the other hand are likely to be disallowed, as they are usually remote from the business activities of most businesses. It is therefore difficult to create a case to demonstrate how they can relate to business operations directly.

In one case, however, a donation to a political party was held to be allowable where this link to business operations was considered to have been adequately made (i.e. payment was not considered to be remote). This was the case of *Morgan v Tate and Lyle Ltd* (1954) where a donation to the Conservative Party was allowed as a business expense because it was made in order to resist the nationalisation of the sugar industry proposed by the Labour Party, which would have led to the cessation of the business.

Donations to charity will generally not be deductible as they are considered to be remote from the business activities. However, where the donations are only small and are to local charities, they are often allowable as a deduction in practice.

In applying the remoteness test you also need to consider in what capacity the proprietor has incurred the expense. In a 1906 case, *Strong & Co of Romsey Ltd v Woodifield*, a guest at a hotel was injured when a chimney fell, and the company paid an amount of damages to the guest as compensation. These were considered to be paid by the company in its capacity as an owner of property, and not in the context of the business operations and so were not allowed as a business deduction. Similarly, a misappropriation, or theft, of profits by the owner or a director of the business will be considered to be outside of the business activities and not deductible (e.g. see *Curtis v J & G Oldfield* (1933)). On the other hand, if the theft is by a member of staff, the loss will usually be an allowable deduction.

The duality test

6.20 If an expense has a dual purpose, for example, the sole trader gets some private, as well as business related, benefit from the expense, then the duality test will operate to deny deductibility of the expense. In *Caillebotte v Quinn* (1975) the taxpayer, a self-employed carpenter, claimed the difference between the cost of eating at home (at 10p a meal) and the cost of eating in a café (at 40p - it was before 1975 remember!) for those days when he was working away from home. It was held that the expenditure was disallowable because he ate to live as well as to work and so the expenditure was 'tainted' by the private purpose. In *Parsons v R&C Commrs* [2010] UKFTT 110, however, the taxpayer, who was a stunt performer for film and TV, was allowed to deduct various medical and dental costs.

There have been a number of other cases dealing with this rule, such as *Mallalieu v Drummond* (1983), a barrister tried to deduct the cost of the clothes she wore in court. The House of Lords said that in addition to a business purpose, there were other purposes, namely to provide 'warmth and decency' which meant that the expense had a dual purpose and was not deductible.

Sometimes when it is not possible to split an expense into a business and a personal element directly, it may be possible to split the payment up using an acceptable allocation formula and allow the business portion as a deductible expense. A common example of this situation that occurs for a large number of self-employed taxpayers are expenses relating to a car which is used for both business and pleasure. The proportion of business miles compared to total miles can usually be used to determine the proportion of expenses such as servicing, insurance and petrol which are allowable deductions.

In a case heard by the tax tribunal, *Interfish v HMRC* [2012] UKFTT 599], a successful seafood supplier based in Plymouth donated over £1m to the local rugby club. The taxpayer argued that the donation benefited the business, but the tribunal held that it wasn't wholly and exclusively for the purposes of the trade. It had the dual purpose of improving the rugby club's financial position as well as improving the taxpayer's business. If Interfish had been able to separate part of the payment as advertising, for example having the logo on players' shirts, it would probably have been able to deduct that component. This decision of the First Tier Tribunal was upheld by the Upper Tribunal in August 2013.

Other examples of this occur for taxpayers who undertake all or part of their business from their home. Part of the cost of running their house is deductible from their trading profits as long as they can justify that these shared costs are allocated to the business correctly or (from April 2013) the fixed rate deductions are used (see Chapter 5 for these details).

2 Revenue not capital expenditure

6.21 The second question we need to consider in determining if an expense is deductible is whether it is a revenue or capital expense. As we discussed above, there is a need to distinguish between revenue and capital receipts, as generally only revenue receipts are part of trading income for tax computations. Equally revenue expenses are normally deductible from trading profits whereas capital expenses have to be dealt with differently - using the capital allowances rules (we'll discuss these rules in Chapter 7). These principles will sound familiar to those of you who have studied accounting where what goes directly into the income statement, or what needs to go into the balance sheet, is considered on a very similar basis.

The distinction between *revenue* and *capital* expenditure for tax deductibility has developed over the years, largely from case law, which tries to be consistent in its treatment of revenue income and expenditure. The tests that are used to determine whether a receipt is capital or revenue, as we discussed above, are generally also used to test whether expenses are of a capital or revenue nature. These rules largely follow normal accounting principles, however, there is not always a clear cut distinction and some cases appear to be at odds with these tests. For example, in the case of *Lawson v Johnson Matthey plc* (1992) a payment of £50 million was made as part of a deal with the Bank of England in order to save the banking subsidiary from a threat of insolvency. Despite the size and one off nature of the payment it was allowed as revenue expenditure.

The question of how often a payment is made can play a part in deciding whether it is capital or revenue in nature. As we saw with receipts, capital payments are often one-off, single payments, whereas revenue payments are often recurring. One of the tests the courts have established is the *enduring benefit test*, where we ask 'does the expense bring into existence something that has enduring benefit for the trade?' If so, it is probably capital and therefore not deductible.

In *Tucker v Granada Motorway Services Ltd* (1979), the rent payable by the taxpayer company under a lease agreement was calculated based on the previous year's takings, which included an amount of tobacco duty. By paying a lump sum to the lessor, the company was able to have the formula changed to take out the tobacco duty and so in the future the rent paid under the lease would be lower. The House of Lords held that this was a capital payment, because it created an enduring benefit, i.e. future reduced rent payments.

To help explain these rules in more detail, and to show you how these rules work in practice, let us review some commonly encountered items for which the revenue/capital distinction is important:

Self education expenses

6.22 Expenditure on a training course for the proprietor of a business which is intended to provide new expertise, knowledge or skills brings into existence an intangible asset which has enduring benefit for the business and is therefore really of a capital nature. On the other hand, if the training course is to update expertise, knowledge or skills already possessed by the proprietor it will normally be regarded as revenue expenditure.

Repairs and improvements

6.23 Amounts spent on repairs to an asset will generally be allowable for tax purposes but amounts spent on improvements will not be deductible. As a general rule, repair means restoring an asset to its original condition, whereas an improvement means making the asset bigger or better in some way, therefore changing its character. Given the frequency of these kinds of payments occurring in business, this distinction is very important to understand. Normal accounting principles are used as guidance when differentiating between repair and improvement expenditure and case law has been used to decide marginal cases.

Two types of expenditure cause particular difficulties. The first is expenditure which is incurred to renovate assets soon after they were acquired. When a taxpayer buys an asset, the purchase price is, of course, a capital expense. What if the asset needs to be repaired soon after purchase? There is an argument that if the asset was purchased for a low price because it needed to be repaired, then the cost of those repairs is also a capital expense, because it is effectively an additional purchase cost. In *Law Shipping Co* Ltd v *IRC* (1924) a ship, which was built in 1906, was bought in December 1919 for £97,000. The ship was ready to sail with freight that was booked for transport at the time of the purchase. The required periodic survey of the ship (for sea-worthiness etc.) was then considerably overdue and an exemption from the survey had to be obtained. The ship was granted a Lloyd's Certificate for a single voyage to enable it to be taken into dock to undergo its survey. The purchaser had to spend £51,558 on repairs.

It was agreed that the expense of keeping a ship, which is employed in trade, in proper repair is normally an expense 'necessary for the purpose of trade' (i.e. a revenue expense), even if it is deferred. In fact, had the previous owners undertaken the repairs, they would have been able to set the costs against their income for tax purposes. However, the accumulation of repairs required extended partly over a period during which the ship was used, not in the purchaser's trade, but the seller's. A ship which is dilapidated is worth less than a ship which has been well maintained and is in good condition. Its condition at the time of the sale was reflected in the price paid. The value of the ship was presumably increased by the repairs and hence some of their cost should be treated as capital expenditure since they increased the value of a capital asset.

It was held that most of the expenditure was incurred because of the poor state of repair of the vessel when it was bought and this amount was disallowed as a capital expense, but £12,000 of the total expenditure was allowed for post-acquisition repairs.

In a contrasting case of *Odeon Associated Theatres Ltd* v *Jones* (1972) a cinema had been bought which was in a fairly dilapidated condition after the Second World War. The cinema was used for a number of years by its new owners before it was refurbished. In this case all of the refurbishment expenditure was allowed despite the poor condition of the cinema when it was bought.

There are two essential differences between the two cases which led to the differing conclusions. First, when the cinema was bought, the purchase price was not reduced to reflect the condition of the property which was both usable and used immediately after purchase. In the *Law Shipping* case, however, the purchase price did reflect the condition of the ship which was not seaworthy immediately after purchase. Second, the Court of Appeal decided that the costs of refurbishment for the cinema were deductible expenses in accordance with accounting principles (i.e. would go directly to the income statement, not to the balance sheet) and therefore tax principles should not deviate from the normal accounting rules unless there was strong reason to – which they argued was not so in this case.

The second area which has depended on case law for clarification concerns the question of *repair or replacement*. That is, has an asset been repaired or effectively replaced following the expenditure? The cost of replacing part of an asset will generally be deductible as a revenue expense, but if it is the whole of the asset that has been replaced, it will generally be considered capital expenditure and therefore not be deductible.

To illustrate these situations, we can use the example of the case of *Samuel Jones & Co (Devondale) Ltd* v *CIR* (1951) where expenditure on a new chimney to replace the existing one was allowable because the chimney was held to be a subsidiary part of the factory. In a second case, *Brown v Burnley Football and Athletic Co Ltd* (1980), the football club replaced a wooden spectators' stand with a concrete structure which also provided additional accommodation. The expenditure was disallowed because the entire stand was replaced, which was held not to be part of a larger asset, but a distinct and separate part of the club.

Professional fees and charges
6.24 In some cases you will need to look behind the expenses to see what they relate to in order to classify them as revenue or capital. This is the case with professional fees and charges. Where they relate to capital assets or non-trading

items, they will not be deductible. Use the following activity to see how these rules can be applied.

Activity

For each of the following legal and professional charges decide whether they are allowable deductions for the purposes of computing trading income:

1   Charges incurred when obtaining a long (more than 50 years) lease.
2   Charges for trade debt collection.
3   Charges incurred with respect to an action for breach of contract.

Feedback

The first charge would be disallowed because it relates to a non-revenue item. The second charge would be allowable and the third charge would be allowable provided that the contract itself has the quality of revenue and not capital.

However, while this rule works most of the time, it is not always possible to classify all legal and professional charges using this rule alone. Some further exploration of the actual purpose of the expenditure may be needed to determine if it can, or cannot, be deducted for tax purposes. For example, the normal fees for preparing accounts and agreeing tax liabilities are allowable while legal fees incurred during tax appeals are not deductible, regardless of the outcome of the appeal. However, accountancy expenses incurred due to a HMRC investigation will be allowable provided that taxable profits for earlier years are not increased and that an increase, if any, made to the taxable profits of the year under review does not lead to interest charges or penalties.

Costs of obtaining finance

6.25 In relation to loans, interest on qualifying loans for partners or employees is treated as a tax relief, and dealt with in the personal tax computation (as we saw in Chapter 4). However, for the self-employed, interest on other types of business loans such as overdrafts, credit cards and hire purchase agreements will be allowable as revenue expenses (i.e. fully deductible in the year it is accrued) so long as they meet the 'wholly and exclusively' rule. If there is any private use of the assets purchased with the loan then this part of the interest paid is not tax deductible. Note, however, that interest paid on overdue tax is not an allowable expense for those who are self-employed (for what should be obvious reasons!). [These are however, deductible for companies who can in fact claim a non-trading loan relationship expense for this as we will see in Chapter 9, section 9.7]

The incidental costs of obtaining finance for the business could be considered to be capital expenses on the basis that they are one-off expenses. A special rule, however, provides that if the interest paid on the loan is tax deductible, then the incidental costs of obtaining the loan will also be deductible. This includes fees, commission, advertising and printing but does not include any stamp duty costs.

Registration of Patents
6.26 A patent is an item of intellectual property that is an asset of the business. It would be reasonable therefore to classify the cost of registering a patent as a capital expense, however the legislation specifically allows for this cost to be deductible.

Staff secondments
6.27 A secondment is the temporary transfer of a worker to another position or employment. Where staff of the business are seconded to work for another organisation, but the business continues to pay their wages, it is arguable that the wages are no longer paid wholly and exclusively for business purposes. By special provision, where the secondment is to a charity or to an educational institution, the business can continue to claim the salary of the seconded employee as a tax deduction.

Lease premiums
6.28 If a taxpayer leases premises he or she may be required to pay a premium when the lease is granted as well as periodical rent. Because it is a one-off payment related to the acquisition of a right to use whatever is being leased, a lease premium is really capital in nature. However, a special provision allows for the premium to be claimed as a deduction. The lessee can claim the amount on which the landlord is assessable under property income for the premium paid; spread over the term of the lease agreement.

Activity

The lessee of business premises pays a premium of £36,000 on the grant of a 25 year lease. How much, if any, can be claimed as a deduction under the trading income rules?

Feedback

For the landlord, under the property income rules (see later in this chapter) the assessment will be the amount of the premium reduced by 2% for each year of the lease except the first. Therefore 48% (24 × 2%) of the premium is not taxable and the remaining 52% is taxable. The property income assessment is therefore 52% of £36,000 or £18,720.

The tenant can claim a deduction for that amount spread over the lifetime of the lease, i.e. £18,720 ÷ 25 or £748.80 each year.

3   Specifically disallowed items

6.29   The final of our three criteria for deductibility of expenses in trading income tax computations is whether the expenses are specifically disallowed by legislation. There are a number of items which would appear to be deductible for trading income purposes using the first two rules we outlined at the start of this section (namely incurred wholly and exclusively for the purpose of trade and not of a capital nature) but are specifically excluded from being deductible by legislation. The following are some of the more commonly encountered cases in this category:

Fines and penalties

6.30   Any payments made which are held to be contrary to public policy, such as fines or penalties, are disallowable. However, in practice, deductions for parking fines incurred by employees parking the employer's cars during the course of their employer's business are usually allowed, although such fines incurred by directors and proprietors are never allowed.

In the 2012 McLaren case (*McLaren Racing Ltd v Revenue and Customs UKFTT 601*), the Formula One racing team was fined £32m for breaching the FIA International Sporting Code. The first tier tax tribunal held that the penalty was deductible because McLaren were obliged to pay it under its contractual terms. This case may be appealed by HMRC because it undermines the principle that it is in the public interest not to allow a tax deduction where there has been a breach of non-statutory regulations. With effect from 1 April 2002, deductions also cannot be claimed for any payments, such as bribes, made overseas that would be a criminal payment if made in the UK.

Entertainment

6.31   Most expenditure on hospitality and entertainment is disallowed. This includes entertaining customers and clients whether they are UK based or overseas. The main exception is the entertainment of genuine employees of the business. This expense, as with most expenses relating to employees, is fully deductible. You will recall from section 5.16, however, that where an employee is entitled to attend an annual Christmas party or similar, the value of which is more than £150 a person, a benefit in kind will arise to the employee. The full cost of the function will still be deductible to the employer however much they spend per employee.

Gifts

6.32 Gifts to charities are given special treatment in the personal income tax computation outside of the trading income calculation. Businesses may, however make gifts to other categories of people, including customers and employees. As a general rule, gifts to customers are disallowed unless they cost less than £50, contain a conspicuous advertisement for the business and are not food, drink or tobacco. Gifts to employees are allowable deductions for the business, but may be a taxable benefit in kind for the employee, as we saw in Chapter 5.

Expensive car leases or hire charges

6.33 The cost of hiring or leasing plant and equipment for business purposes is generally deductible. The on-going lease rental payments are of a revenue nature, not a capital expense which their outright purchase would be.

For lease agreements longer than 45 days there is an exception to this general rule in the case of cars. For leased cars with CO_2 emissions of more than 50g/km (was 110g/km until 6 April 21) a flat 15% disallowance applies, i.e., only 85% of the lease payments are deductible.

Where the car is a low-emission vehicle (i.e. now defined has having CO_2 emissions of less than 50g/km), this special rule does not apply and the full amount of the lease expense is deductible irrespective of the cost and length of the lease arrangement.

Redundancy payments

6.34 Where payments are made to staff who are made redundant, they will be deductible so long as it can be shown that they are wholly and exclusively for the purposes of the trade. If the payments are made by a business that is ceasing to trade, however, there is a restriction on the amount that can be claimed as a tax deduction. The limit is the statutory amount plus three times this statutory amount for each employee (i.e. a total of four times whatever that employee's statutory redundancy pay entitlement is).

Pre-trading expenses

6.35 Expenditure can only be a deductible expense from trading income if it is incurred on or after the date on which the business commences to trade. However, expenses incurred in the seven years prior to this date will be treated as a loss which arises on the date of commencement provided they relate directly to the new business. The reason for treating it this way relates to the way in which the basis period rules work for commencing businesses.

Appropriations of profit

6.36 Where a sole trader makes drawings from the business profits (this typically may include paying themselves an income from the business' assets), this is an appropriation and is not deductible. As such, any drawings must be included in the taxable profit calculation.

Provisions

6.37 Another item that is not deductible is a provision for accounting purposes. For tax purposes, to be deductible an expense must be reasonably certain to arise. Where for accounting purposes an adjustment is made to profit in the interests of prudence, for example a provision for doubtful debts, this will not be deductible. In the case of adjustments to debtors, for tax purposes, only debts written off or which are reasonably estimated to be bad will be deductible.

A further example of an unacceptable provision is depreciation for accounting purposes. Where depreciation is included in the accounts, it cannot be claimed as a tax deduction. As depreciation is related to apportioning the costs of capital assets over time and may be subject to abuse (at least in theory) to affect reported tax profits, the tax system has its own regime for calculating allowable costs related to the purchase of certain capital assets (called capital allowances) which we will examine more closely in the next chapter.

A question of timing

6.38 The timing of expenses deductions usually follows the accounting rules, i.e. expenses are deducted for tax purposes in the year in which they accrue (not when they are paid). There are two main exceptions to this general rule. One is for payments to employees. A special rule says that if a business deducts payments to employees on an accrued basis, but then the actual payment is not made until more than 9 months after the end of the accounting period, then the deduction is disallowed and deferred to the following year.

Another variation is for pension contributions made by a business for its employees. Where contributions are made to registered pension schemes, they are deductible in the period in which they are paid, which is different to the accounting treatment.

Simplified Expenses Scheme

6.39 In addition to changes to introduce the cash basis scheme in 2013/14, the Government also introduced a *simplified expenses scheme*. This scheme can be used by business that are sole-traders and by business partnerships or limited liability partnerships (as long as they have no companies as partners). It is not available to limited companies.

This scheme creates the possibility to use more flat rate expense deductions i.e. a fixed amount can be deducted irrespective of what was actually paid out. For example, if you are eligible to use the cash basis, any business mileage expenses can be computed on a flat rate basis that mirrors the rates we discussed for company car mileage rates in section 5.10 i.e. 45p/mile for the first 10,000 business miles driven annually and then 25p/mile for any further miles. Similarly, 24p a mile can be claimed for using a motorbike.

Some restrictions do apply to these rules for business mileage however. If the business is already in operation and claims capital allowances for the vehicle currently (see Chapter 7) then switching to the cash basis does not allow you to use the flat rate scheme for deductions for this vehicle. You will have to continue to use actual expenses incurred for this vehicle for the duration of the time you own it.

Businesses can also opt for certain other expenses to be deductible at a flat rate. For example:

- *Use of your home to work from* – the fixed rate deduction will be based on the number of hours your home is used for work purposes each month as follows:
    - 25-50 hours/month   £10
    - 51-100 hours/month   £18
    - 101+ hours/month   £26

    Note – that no deduction under this scheme can be claimed if you work less than 25 hours a month at home)

- *Premises used for business and as a home* – for example, if you run a guest house it may be expected that you will live in part of the property and let out other parts. In this situation you will be allowed a fixed rate deduction based on the number of occupants you have each month;
    - 1 occupant   £350/month
    - 2 occupants   £500/month
    - 3 or more occupants   £650/month.

In either case, these are optional flat rate deductions if the taxpayer wishes to use them, regardless of whether the cash basis scheme is used. Alternatively, they can opt to deduct the allowable part of any actual expenditure incurred – as usual.

It can reasonably be expected that other flat rate deductions will be introduced in future years if this scheme proves popular and workable, although some years have now passed since these were introduced and there is no sign of any development of this scheme currently.

Calculating tax adjusted trading profit

6.40 You can now identify taxable revenues and allowable deductions for trading income purposes using the accruals basis. To determine tax adjusted trading profit, rather than start a whole new calculation from scratch, we instead start with the net accounting profit. This is then adjusted to take into account those items where the tax treatment of items is different to the accounting treatment. Because the final figure we are calculating is the trading income, adjustments also need to be made to remove items that are dealt with under different categories for tax purposes, but form part of the accounting profit for the business, for example, savings or property income. Remember these have their own separate rules in a taxpayer's tax computation. In undertaking this computation for exam questions, or in practice, you may find it helpful to use this pro forma to undertake the adjustment of profits to the trading income (Note: figures are for illustration only):

Computation of the trading income assessment:

	£	£
Net profit per accounts		20,000
Add:		
Expenditure in the accounts which is not		
deductible for tax purposes	3,000	
Income which is taxable but		
not directly credited to the P & L account	1,000	4,000
		24,000
Less:		
Income in the accounts which is not taxable	2,000	
Expenditure not in the accounts which		
is deductible for tax purposes	3,000	(5,000)
Tax Adjusted Trading income		19,000

To see how this is useful in practice, examine the following activity.

Activity

Monica has been in business for a number of years. Her income statement for the year to 31 August, 2022 is as follows:

	Note	£	£
Sales			100,000
Less: Cost of sales			(40,000)
Gross profit			60,000
Add:			
Bank interest		500	
Profit from sale of plant		300	
Rental income		1,000	1,800
			61,800
Less:			
Rent and rates		3,000	
Insurance		1,000	
Heating, lighting and power		1,500	
Repairs and renewals	(a)	1,500	
Telephone	(b)	400	
Motor expenses	(c)	500	
Bad debts	(d)	200	
Wages and salaries	(e)	20,000	
Legal fees	(f)	300	
Sundry expenses		1,000	
Interest on a credit card		100	
Depreciation		3,000	(32,500)
Net Profit			29,300

Notes:
(a) This figure includes £1,000 spent on furnishing a new showroom and £200 redecorating the reception area.
(b) 30% of the telephone cost relate to private use.
(c) 20% of the motor expenses relate to private use.
(d) Bad debts is made up of £120 trade debt written off and £80 increase in the general provision for bad debts.
(e) This figure includes drawings of £8,000.
(f) The legal fees related to the purchase of plant and machinery.

Required: Determine the tax adjusted trading profit using the accrual basis for the year ended 31 August, 2022.

Feedback

	£	£
Net profit per the accounts		29,300
Add: Disallowed expenditure		
Drawings	8,000	
Capital expenditure	1,000	
Telephone 400 × 30%	120	
Motor expenses 500 × 20%	100	
General provision for bad debts	80	
Legal fees	300	
Depreciation	3,000	12,600
		41,900
Less: Non-trading income		
Rental income	1,000	
Bank interest	500	
Profit from sales of plant	300	(1,800)
Tax adjusted profit		40,100

Notes:

- Drawings are not allowable as they represent an appropriation of profit by the proprietor.
- The £1,000 spent on furnishing the new showroom is capital expenditure. This may qualify for capital allowances which we will discuss in the next chapter. Note that the cost of redecoration, which has to be done periodically, is of a revenue nature, so no adjustment is necessary for that expense.
- Private expenditure must be excluded under the wholly and exclusively rule (e.g. for telephone and car expenses).
- General provisions are not allowable for tax purposes.
- To decide whether legal fees are deductible, you must consider what they relate to. Here it is for purchase of plant and machinery, a capital transaction, and so the legal fees are also considered to be capital and disallowable.
- Accounting depreciation is not deductible for tax purposes (capital allowances related to these assets will potentially be claimable instead as we will see in the next chapter).
- Rental income is taxed as property income and so must be excluded from the trading income computation. It will appear in a separate part of Monica's overall tax computation.
- Bank interest is taxed as savings income and so must also be excluded here. Again, it is instead listed separately in Monica's overall tax computation.
- Profit on sale of plant is a capital receipt and must be excluded. There may be capital gains tax liability on this item, see Chapter 8 for details of how this could be calculated and taxed.

To draw together all the points made in this section outlining the normal rules for computing trading income, we will use another activity. You are advised to work through this long example carefully so that you can be sure you understand how the principles we have discussed are translated into a trading profit adjustment and how these are placed into a simple tax computation.

Activity

Roger Riviere is a self-employed wholesale clothing distributor who commenced trading on 1 July, 1999. His summarised accounts for the year ended 30 June, 2022 are:

			£	£
Sales		(1)		400,000
	Opening inventory	(2)	40,000	
	Purchases		224,000	
			264,000	
	Closing inventory	(2)	(32,000)	232,000
Gross profit				168,000
	Wages and national insurance	(3)	52,605	
	Rent and business rates		31,140	
	Repairs and renewals	(4)	3,490	
	Miscellaneous expenses	(5)	665	
	Taxation (Roger's income tax)		15,590	
	Bad debts	(6)	820	
	Legal expenses	(7)	1,060	
	Depreciation		570	
	Loss on sale of office furniture		60	
	Transport costs		4,250	
	Interest	(8)	990	
	Motor car running expenses			
	(Roger's car)	(9)	2,000	
	Lighting and heating		1,250	
	Sundry expenses (all allowable)		710	
	Relocation expenditure	(10)	2,400	117,600
Net profit				50,400

Notes to accounts:

1. Sales include £500 reimbursed by Roger's family for clothing taken from stock. This reimbursement represented cost price.

2. Inventory: The basis of both opening and closing inventory valuations was 'lower of cost or market value' less a contingency reserve of 50%.

3. Wages: Included in wages are Roger's drawings of £50 per week, his national insurance contributions of £320 for the year and wages and national insurance contributions in respect of his wife totalling £11,750. His wife worked full-time in the business as a secretary.

4. Repairs and renewals: The charge includes £3,000 for fitting protective covers over the factory windows and doors to prevent burglary.

5. Miscellaneous expenses:

	£	£
Theft of money by employee	65	
Political donation to Green Party	100	
Gifts of 100 'Riviere' calendars	500	665

6. Bad debts:

	£	£
Trade debt written off		720
Loan to former employee written off		250
Provision for bad debts (2% of accounts receivables)	450	
Less: Opening provision	(600)	(150)
		820

7. Legal expenses:

	£
Defending action in respect of alleged faulty goods	330
Costs in connection with lease of new larger premises	250
Successful appeal against previous year's income tax assessment	200
Defending Roger in connection with speeding offence	190
Debt collection	90
	(1,060)

8. Interest:

	£	£
Bank overdraft interest (business account)	860	
Interest on overdue tax	130	990

9. Motor car running expenses. One-third of Roger's mileage is private. Included in the charge is £65 for a speeding fine incurred by Roger whilst delivering goods to a customer.

10. Relocation expenditure. The expenditure was incurred in transferring the business to new and larger premises.

The following information is also provided:

1. Capital allowances for the year to 30 June, 2022 are £480 (in Chapter 7 we will show you how to undertake the computation to produce these numbers).

2. Roger was born on 8 April, 1969 and, due to his rapid aging, decided to increase his pension pot by £13,500 by making a 'relief at source' pension contribution.

3. Roger has no other sources of income.

You are required:

a) To prepare a profit adjustment in respect of the accounting period to 30 June, 2022 showing the tax adjusted profit.

b) To calculate the Class 4 national insurance contributions payable for 2022/23 (using the data provided and assuming rates and thresholds appliable from 6 July 2022 apply for the whole period)

c) To prepare an estimate for Roger of the income tax payable for 2022/23 and to advise him when the tax will become due for payment.

Feedback

(a) Profit adjustment statement year ended 30 June, 2022

	£	£
Net profit per accounts		50,400
Add:		
(1) Sales: Goods for own use (see working 1 below)	334	
(3) Wages: Roger's drawings (appropriation)	2,600	
Roger's NIC (private)	320	
(4) Capital cost of fitting covers	3,000	
(5) Miscellaneous:		
Political donation (not wholly and exclusively)	100	
Taxation (private)	15,590	
(6) Loan to former employee (not business)	250	
(7) Legal expenses:		
Lease of new and larger premises (capital)	250	
Cost in connection tax appeal (private)	200	
Defending re: speeding offence (private)	190	
Depreciation	570	
Loss on sale of office furniture (capital)	60	
(8) Interest: on overdue tax (private)	130	
(9) Motor car running expenses:		
Fine (not deductible)	65	
1/3 of remaining expenses (private)	645	
(10) Re-location expenditure (capital)	2,400	26,704
Less:		
Capital allowances	480	
(Chapter 7 will discuss this item further)		
(2) Inventory adjustment for contingency (working 2)	8,000	
(6) Reduction in general bad debt provision	150	(8,630)
Tax adjusted trading profit		68,474

(b) Class 4 National insurance contributions

10.25% x (£50,270 – £11,908) + 3.25% x (68,474 – 50,270) = £4,523.73

(c) Computation of income tax liability 2022/23

	Non-savings £	Total £
Income:		
Trading income		
(adjusted profits)	68,474	68,474
Total Income	68,474	68,474
Less Personal Allowances	(12,570)	(12,570)
Total Taxable Income	55,904	55,904

Roger has made pension contributions of £13,500. This is the gross amount of the payment. As we saw in section 5.3, basic tax relief for the pension payment is obtained by Roger making the payment net of income tax at the basic rate. That is, he will pay only £10,800 (£13,500 × 80%). Higher rate relief is given by extending his basic rate band by the gross amount of the premium, £13,500. Roger's basic rate band is therefore increased to £51,200 (£37,700 + £13,500).

Tax Due:

		£
Non savings income	51,200 @ 20%	10,240.00
	4,704 @ 40%	1,881.60
Tax Liability		12,121.60

Workings

1. Goods taken for Roger's own use must be included at market value. They have been reimbursed at cost, so we need to increase Roger's profit by the tax profit associated with goods costing £500:

	£
Sales £500 × 399,500/239,500	834
Less cost of sales	(500)
Profit	334

The sales price of the goods for Roger's own use is arrived at by multiplying the cost of those goods (£500) by Roger's gross sales figure (£400,000) less the cost of those goods taken for Roger's own use (£500) divided by the restated cost of sales (£240,000 – see working 2 below) again without the reimbursed goods' cost (£500) i.e. £239,500.

2. The valuation of inventory for tax purposes is on the basis of 'lower of cost or market value'. Therefore the cost of goods sold by Roger for tax purposes is:

Opening inventory	80,000
Plus purchases	224,000
	304,000
Less closing inventory	(64,000)
Cost of goods sold	240,000

Roger has only deducted cost of goods sold of £232,000 in his profit and loss account – a further deduction of £8,000 is required.

The Cash Basis Scheme

6.41 Having examined the normal method for determining trading income in sections 6.12 to 6.39, we can now turn to the second of the methods listed at the start of section 6.11. The cash basis is an alternative allowable way of determining the taxable trading income for some businesses. Under this basis, trading income is simply determined using business cash received in the year (of whatever type and in whatever form payment is received, including payments in kind) and deducting business expenses that have actually been paid during the period (irrespective of the tax or accounting years to which they actually relate).

This scheme for small business started in 2013/14. The Government stated at the time that they were introducing this because they believed it was a simpler way to do tax accounting for the smallest businesses, decreasing their tax compliance costs, and better reflecting in their tax computations the way in which they run their businesses already (i.e. on a cash basis). Given its simplicity, it is therefore most likely to be used by new start-up businesses.

To be eligible to use the cash basis turnover must be less than £150,000 for 2022/23 (unchanged from 2021/22). If you are an individual who is in receipt of Universal Credit, however, this threshold is £300,000. For businesses below the threshold, the cash basis scheme is optional. You can choose to use accrual accounting if you wish to.

If your business receipts exceed the threshold, you will be required to start using the accruals basis rules from the following tax year onwards (unless your receipts fall back below the relevant limit in the following year). You can also opt to switch out of the cash based system at any point should you so wish. In either case there are transition rules that must then be applied (see the HMRC website for guidance on these if you need them as they are beyond the scope of this book).

Fiscal Fact

In 2019, the Institute for Fiscal Studies reported (using data from 2015/16) that business owners were the fastest growing part of the UK labour force, growing 25% compared to employee numbers rising only 15% (4.9 million people operating through self-employment compared with 3.9 million in 2000/01). They also reported that business owners were disproportionately male (70%) and on average older than employees. They also showed that combining business and employment activity is common – one quarter of those who are self-employed also report at least some employment income. However, on average their income is fairly low at a mean annual taxable income of £21,000. It is also a risky activity as 20% of newly set up sole traders are not trading after their first year, 60% cease by year 5 and 80% after 12 years. [Source: Institute for Fiscal Studies (2019), 'Who are business owners and what are they doing?']

The cash basis rules apply for all business that an individual runs either as a sole-trader or in partnership. That is, if the taxpayer runs more than one business, then the cash receipts in the year for all the businesses are added together in checking if they all can use the cash basis. This will prevent taxpayers artificially splitting up their businesses to stay under the thresholds.

A cap exists for the deductibility of loan interest under this scheme. You can only claim up to £500 a year as a deduction for interest on borrowing to fund your business. If the interest expense is more than £500, it may be better not to use the cash basis scheme as you could lose some of your tax deductible interest.

Bad debts (actual or provisions for) are not deductible under the cash basis. Income from sales is recorded when received and so no adjustment for bad debts will be needed.

Not all business ventures are eligible for this scheme, even if their business receipts come below the threshold levels. Specifically excluded business types include the following examples:

- Companies and Limited liability partnerships (LLPs);
- Businesses that have claimed research and development allowances (see Chapter 7); and,
- Businesses that are involved in the mineral extraction trade.

The cash basis scheme does not affect the decisions about your tax year. This can still be determined as best suits business needs, as we will see in section 6.7.

Basis of assessment

6.42   Income tax is calculated for individuals for tax years (6 April to following 5 April). These are called 'Assessment Years'. For employed people it is easy to assign their income to these periods to calculate their income tax liability as most employees are paid on a weekly, or monthly, basis – so we can just add up their payslips for the twelve month period (or use their P60 issued annually by their employer if they have this). For self-employed people paying tax on trading income however, this is not quite so straightforward because their income is based on their accounts, as we have just seen in the previous section. Accounts are produced in periods usually, but not always, of twelve months in length. These accounting periods may start and finish at different point during the year to the tax year, as suits the business. To perform tax computations for self-employed people we therefore need rules for how to allocate their trading income to tax years. In this section we will discuss how these rules operate in the UK at present.

As described in section 4.5, the normal basis of assessment for unincorporated businesses is the *current year* basis. If a sole trader or partnership uses an annual accounting date that is not 5 April, the accounting period ended in the tax year will normally form the basis period for the tax year. This basis of assessment is changing for unincorporated businesses from 2023/24 but the rules for 2022/23 are as explained below.

To ensure you understand these rules, try the following activity:

Activity

For each of the following annual accounting dates state the tax year for which they will form the basis period.
- a)   30 June, 2022
- b)   31 August, 2021
- c)   30 November, 2022
- d)   31 January, 2022
- e)   31 March, 2023
- f)   30 April, 2023.

Feedback

The tax years for which these accounts form the basis period are:
- (a)   2022/23
- (b)   2021/22
- (c)   2022/23

(d) 2021/22

(e) 2022/23

(f) 2023/24

There are some circumstances in which the normal basis of assessment cannot be applied. These usually fall in the opening and closing years of a business trading or when the business decides to change its accounting date. Further explanations and worked examples for these extra rules can be found on the website.

Loss relief

6.43 What happens then, if the allowable expenses of a trading business exceed the revenue for tax purposes? In such a case, there are a number of possible ways of relieving the tax loss. These differ depending on the basis used to compute the trading loss for the year. If the cash basis is used the loss can be carried forward to the following year to offset trading income for that year, or subsequent years. If the accruals basis is used, in addition to the option to carry losses forward, the loss can be also offset against other categories of income that the taxpayer has during the year (sideways relief). Alternatively, the loss can be carried back to previous years to be offset against the general income of that year. The accruals basis therefore gives extra options for loss relief over the cash basis. We will look more closely at these rules in section 7.24 onwards.

You can now attempt Quick Quiz questions 1-7 and Full questions 1-4.

Property income

6.44 Having examined how tax adjusted trading profit is computed, the final income component we will examine is *property income*. Most income from land and property located in the UK is taxed under the property income rules. This includes rents, lease premiums (if the lease is for not more than 50 years), income from rights of way or sporting rights over land or income from letting of fixed caravans or permanently moored house boats. The exceptions to this rule are hotels and guest houses as these are treated as trading income (use the rules therefore contained in the earlier parts of this chapter).

Taxable income from UK property is pooled (i.e. added together) to create one net profit or loss from all property belonging to a taxpayer. This profit or loss is calculated in the same way as trading income is computed (i.e. as discussed previously) – on either the accruals basis or, if eligible, the cash basis. Receiving money from UK property is referred to as running a 'property business'.

Income from most property (apart from furnished holiday lettings) is treated as 'unearned' income in a taxpayer's income tax computation, not 'earned' income (i.e. not considered to be trading income). A key implication of this is that it cannot be used as a source of income to count towards deductible pension contributions, nor can this type of property usually gain from business asset rates for rollover relief when calculating capital gains tax on property sales. The rules for furnished holiday lettings are different – these can count for pension contributions and for business asset rates of rollover relief etc. We will examine these specific differences later in this section.

The basis of assessment for property income is the income for the tax year, most often computed using the accruals basis. However, for very small, simple businesses, for example where income is only received from one property, and the taxpayer is trading below the VAT threshold, the cash basis can be applied.

Normal rules

6.45 Under the normal property business rules, we include the total income from land and property in the UK, regardless of the source, less total allowable expenses – i.e. to follow the same principles as we outlined above for trading income. Examples of allowable expenses include:

- expenses incurred wholly and exclusively for the purpose of the business such as repairs, insurance, advertising, legal costs, etc.;
- capital allowances for plant and machinery which enable taxpayers to carry on their business (unless the property is a dwelling where no capital allowances are available – see Chapter 7 for more on this);
- capital allowances for landlords of residential property on loft and cavity wall insulation up to a value of £1,500; and
- rent paid by the property business to another landlord (e.g. when rental income results from sub-letting).

If the rental comes from a fully furnished residential dwelling (of any kind other than holiday lettings – see below), the cost of replacing furnishings, appliances and kitchenware is allowed as a deduction. The replacement must be like for like, or nearest modern equivalent and relief is also given for any costs incurred in disposing of the asset being replaced. The deduction is reduced by any amounts received on disposal of the old item.

Unlike normal trading businesses (see Chapter 7), these are the only capital expenditure deductions allowed for property businesses.

This activity illustrates how property income can be assessed in practice:

Activity

Andrew has a furnished house which is let for £4,800 per annum payable monthly in advance. Andrew incurred the following expenditure in the tax year.

		£
June 2022	Replacement of doors and windows with double glazed units.	1,500
July 2022	Annual insurance premium runs from 1 August to 31 July (last year's premium was £600)	900
November 2022	Redecoration	500
June 2023	Repairs to boiler – the work was undertaken and completed in January 2023	200

Andrew's tenant left in May 2022 without paying the rent due for May. Andrew was unable to recover the debt, but he let the house to new tenants from 1 July 2022. Determine Andrew's property business profit for 2022/23.

Feedback

	£	£
Rent accrued (£400 × 11)		4,400
Less allowable expenses:		
Doors and windows replacement	1,500	
Insurance (4/12 × £600 + 8/12 × £900)	800	
Redecoration	500	
Repairs to boiler	200	
Bad debt – May 2022 rent	400	
	(3,400)	
Property business profit		1,000

Cash basis

6.46 Alternatively, when eligible (e.g. if total turnover from the property business was less than £150,000, the business is not run by a limited company or limited liability partnership but only be an individual – or where jointly owned, for that part only that is owned by an individual), the property owner will usually be presumed to use the cash basis for computing their property income for the tax year unless they specifically make an election to be assessed under the accruals basis rules. Where no election is made the same rules will then apply as were described above for trading income, i.e. the property income total to be subject to taxation will be determined by using the income received from the property (or properties if more than one owned by the business) in the year from which actual expenses paid in the period (including costs that would be classified as capital outlays in the accruals basis rules) will be deducted. This implies that no capital allowances will apply.

Where a property business owner has more than one property in their portfolio they can opt to use different basis for different properties if they so wish (i.e. some could be assessed under the cash basis and some under the accruals basis).

The cap of £500 for allowable loan interest deductions that applies when using the cash basis for trading income computations does not apply when using the cash basis for property income computations. Instead, the rules applying for determining the allowable deductions for the costs of the financing of the property (or properties) are outlined in the next section.

Activity

If Andrew (as in the activity above) used the cash basis, what would his property business profit be for 2022/23?

Feedback

	£	£
Rent received (£400 × 10)		4,000
Less allowable expenses:		
Doors and windows replacement	1,500	
Insurance	900	
Redecoration	500	(2,900)
Property business profit		1,100

Notes:

1. Rent received is now just recognised for 10 months as the total amount received in the tax year (as no payments were received in May and June 2022). The tenth payment is received at the start of April 2023 which, whilst is primarily for rent for the period that falls into 2023/24 (i.e. the period after 6 April 2023), is actually received in the 2022/23 tax year and so must be counted as income for that year under the cash basis. In the accruals basis case above, the tenth payment would be treated as a pre-payment for April 2023 that would need to be partly allocated to 2022/23 and partly to 2023/24. As bad debts do not apply under the cash basis, the eleventh payment under the accrual system, (then deducted as an expense determined as bad) is not relevant under the cash basis.

2. Each expense that occurred in the year is included (i.e. doors and window replacements, redecoration and the actual insurance premium payment made – in full, not adjusted for accrual or pre-payment). The repairs to the boiler will not be included as, despite this work occurring during the year,

it is not actually paid for until June 2023 and so will be a deduction in 2023/24, not this tax year.

In this case, Andrew is better off not electing to use the cash basis, but the position may be different in future years.

Finance costs

6.47 Before 6 April 2017 landlords of residential property could fully deduct the cost of financing any loans they took out related to a property they were letting (e.g. the cost of interest they paid in the year on a mortgage taken out to buy the property). However, now only basic rate (20%) tax can be reclaimed on these particular costs as a tax reduction at the end of this period (as the Government wanted to reduce the attractiveness of buy-to-let investments). This means instead of the full cost being deducted against the income as an allowable expense of doing business, once the tax due is computed, an adjustment will be made to provide basic rate tax relief only.

The tax reduction is 20% of the lower of:

- The finance costs not deducted from rental income in the tax year;
- Property business profits after using any brought forward losses; and
- Adjusted total income, after losses and reliefs (but excluding savings and dividend income) that exceeds the personal allowance.

Between 2017/18 and 2020/21 there was a transition arrangement where part of the financing costs was deductible and part was applied as a reduction. The relevant percentages are as follows:

Tax year	% of finance costs deductible	% of basic rate tax reduction
2017/18	75%	25%
2018/19	50%	50%
2019/20	25%	75%
2020/21	0%	100%

To illustrate using Andrew's case above – if Andrew had purchased the house with a mortgage on which he paid £700 in interest in the year to 6 April 2017 this would have all been an allowable expense in computing his tax due from the property letting for 2016/17. Since 2017/18, he hasn't be able to claim the whole £700 as a deduction. In 2019/20, the third year of the transition period, only 25% of this (i.e. £175) could be claimed as an allowable expense. The remaining 75% of this interest (£525) would have been applied as a tax reduction at the basic rate of tax (20%) at the end of his income tax computation. Assuming Andrew is a higher rate taxpayer, and using the accruals computation as an example (although the same process applies if he is using the cash basis), his revised property business profit for 2019/20 would have become,:

	£
Property business profit (per computation above)	1,000
Finance Costs deduction:	
Mortgage interest (£700 x 25%)	(175)
Property business profit	825
Tax @ 40%	330.00
Finance costs reduction:	
(£700 x 75%) x 20%	(105.00)
Income tax due on the property business	225.00

Under these transition rules, in Andrew's case he would therefore have paid £105 (£225 – £120 (i.e. £1,000 – £700 @40%) in extra tax in the year compared to the previous rules.

In 2020/21 this transition period was completed and the finance costs deduction part of the property income computation has now disappeared completely so the partial deduction will no longer apply for 2021/22 and subsequent years. A tax reducer at a rate of 20% is now all that is available on finance costs. Continuing Andrew's example, this year his deduction (using the above data again for 2022/23) would be:

	£
Property business profit (per computation above)	1,000
Finance Costs deduction:	
Mortgage interest (£700 x 0%)	(0)
Property business profit	1,000
Tax @ 40%	400.00
Finance costs reduction:	
(£700 x 100%) x 20%	(140.00)
Income tax due on the property business	260.00

In Andrew's case, this will mean he would have paid £140 (£260 – £120) extra tax compared to the previous (pre transition) rules, or another way to say this, Andrew is now only getting 20% tax relief rather than his marginal tax rate of 40% (£700 x 40%-20%).

Do note that the new finance costs reduction computation should be applied at the same stage in Andrew's personal income tax computation as other tax reducers, i.e. at Step 6 of the computation (see section 4.2 for a reminder of the steps if necessary).

One further complication of these new rules is that if this computation creates a tax refund (e.g. as finance and other costs exceed income in the year) then the reduction allowed is capped and any further reduction that would have otherwise been allowed from these new finance costs rules is carried forward as extra allowable finance costs for use in the following year.

Examples of how the tax reduction may be limited if it creates a tax refund can be found on the gov.uk website if required at: https://www.gov.uk/guidance/changes-to-tax-relief-for-residential-landlords-how-its-worked-out-including-case-studies

Loss relief

6.48 Unlike trading losses, options to relieve property income losses are the same irrespective of basis used for the tax computation. Losses arising under property income rules can only be carried forward and set against the first available property income profits in the future. If a loss arises across all a taxpayer's property business, the assessment for that year will then be nil. If a loss arises for one part of the property business only it will be netted against any gains in other parts first however, as part of the pooling of property income.

Where a difference does occur between the cash and accruals basis computations however, is where the loss results from the use of capital allowances, as this can occur when using the accruals basis. These losses can be applied sideways (against other current non-property income). Where it is to be used as a relief against general income in this way, it is included in the tax computation at step 2. If the cash basis is used, carrying forward of losses will be the only option allowed.

An illustration of the property income loss rules can be found on the website. This demonstrates how they work in practice.

Furnished holiday lettings

6.49 A special tax position exists for furnished holiday lettings (including both houses and caravans). Income from this kind of property is assessed under property income rules, however, the regulations which apply to trading income are used to determine the taxable income as this income is normally treated as "earned income" unlike other property income (which you will recall we said at the start of this section is treated as unearned income). This means if you wish to, you can use the accruals basis system. If you don't opt for the cash basis, normal capital allowances can be claimed (i.e. instead of the renewals basis as for other dwellings), capital gains tax relief for the disposal of business assets (i.e. business asset disposal relief and rollover relief, which are explained in Chapter 8) is available and loss relief can be claimed under the regulations which apply to losses incurred by traders (see Chapter 7).

If the cash basis is used, then the usual rules will apply i.e. all trading receipts received in the year will form the basis of the income to be reported with only expenses paid in the year (of whatever kind) being deductible.

Because these profits are treated as earned income the taxpayer can also provide for retirement by making contributions to a pension fund that include this income in their computation (see the section in this Chapter 5 for more detail on pensions). However, no Class 4 national insurance contributions are due on this income source as Class 4 only applies to income assessed under trading income.

Note that the basis period rules for property income rather than trading income still apply to income from furnished holiday lettings despite this special treatment (i.e. you use the tax year).

To be eligible for this advantageous treatment the accommodation must be let commercially with the aim of making a profit. Also, these rules must apply:

1. *The availability condition:* the property must be available for letting to the public for at least 210 days in the tax year.

2. *The letting condition:* the property must have actually been let for at least 105 of those days.

3. *Pattern of occupation condition:* For at least 155 days (including the 105 days from rule 2) the property must not normally be occupied by the same tenant for more than 31 days.

In addition, if the taxpayer owns more than one property, each of which satisfies the 210 day rule, they will all be deemed to satisfy the 105 day rule providing their average number of days let is at least 105.

Also, if a property meets the 'actually let' threshold for any one year, the owner can elect for it to be treated as having also met this criteria for the following two years (called the 'period of grace') providing certain conditions are met. This may be useful if these criteria are periodically missed (e.g. while under refurbishment).

Activity

Leonard owned four furnished houses in a village in the Yorkshire Dales which are let as holiday homes. None of the houses are normally let to the same tenant for more than 31 consecutive days. The numbers of days for which each house was available for letting and actually let in this tax year were:

House	Days available	Days let
1	250	115
2	290	87
3	200	180
4	365	100

Determine Leonard's potential averaging claims.

Feedback

House 3 does not satisfy the 210 day availability rule and so cannot be included in an averaging claim even though it is let for more than 105 days, so meets the letting condition. If no averaging claim is made, only house 1 qualifies as furnished holiday accommodation.

Possible averaging claim	Average days let
House 1 and 2	101.0
House 1 and 4	107.5
House 2 and 4	92.5
House 1, 2 and 4	100.7

Averaging house 1 and 4 is beneficial because the average number of days let is more than 105. No other averaging claim would succeed.

The 'rent a room' scheme

6.50 If an individual lets one or more furnished rooms in his or her main residence then rents received up to a limit of £7,500 in 2022/23 are exempt from tax under property income. If another individual is also receiving rent from letting accommodation in the same property (for example, as joint owner) the limit of £7,500 will be halved. If the total receipts are in excess of £7,500 (£3,750 if halved) then the taxpayer has a choice as to how they are taxed. Either the excess receipts over £7,500 (£3,750) is taxed in full (i.e. no deductions are allowed) or they can choose to be taxed on a normal trading computation principle (i.e. the gross rents received minus any allowable deductions, such as heating costs is taxed instead – although note that for capital expenditure deductions, such as for the furniture for the room, normal capital allowances are not available as this is in a dwelling house, instead the replacement basis rules would be applied for these expense. If the cash basis is used, only actual expenditure in the year will be deductible. The taxpayer has the choice of which of these two calculations should determine their taxable income in this case.

Any income arising from the 'rent-a-room' scheme is normally likely to be treated as part of property income in the taxpayers' tax computation. If a trade is being carried out however, (e.g. if meals or cleaning/laundry services are also provided in addition to just the charge for the use of a room itself) then this income can probably be added to trading income totals.

This allowance cannot be claimed in addition to the £1,000 property income allowance (as described in section 4.37). The property owner must decide which of this allowance or this relief to claim.

Fiscal Fact

The estimated cost to the UK Government of allowing the rent-a-room scheme for 2021/22 is £210 million. (Source: HMRC Estimated costs of non-structural tax reliefs)

Premiums on leases

6.51 We saw in our discussion of trading expenses that when a lease is granted the lessee may have to pay a premium to the lessor. A premium is a lump sum payment at the commencement of the lease and is different to the regular lease or rental payments made throughout the course of the lease. In fact, some leases are structured so that the lessor receives very little rent for the duration of the lease but has to depend on the lease premium for income from the property. This situation is most typically found in commercial (e.g. office space) leases.

If the lease term is more than 50 years (termed a *long lease*) then the premium is taxable as a capital gain rather than an income. If the lease is for 50 years or less (a *short lease*) income tax is paid on the value of the premium less 2% of the premium for each complete year of the lease after the first. Written as a formula the assessable amount of the lease premium therefore equals:

$$P - (P \times (L - 1) \times 2\%)$$

where P is the premium on the lease and L is the length of the lease.

Activity

Amanda granted a 21-year lease on a property on 1 January, 2023 for an initial premium of £30,000 and an annual rent of £6,000 payable monthly in advance. Determine Amanda's property income for 2022/23 and 2023/24 using the accruals basis.

Feedback

In 2022/23 the assessment on the premium of the lease is £18,000 (£30,000 – (£30,000 × (21 – 1) × 2%)). The rent due in 2022/23 is £1,500 (£6,000 × 3/12). Hence the total property income for 2022/23 is £19,500 (£18,000 + £1,500). In 2023/24 the property income will be £6,000. The remaining £12,000 of the lease premium will fall to be taxed under the capital gains tax rules (see Chapter 8). It is an interesting example of how the law takes a capital receipt and turns part of it into an income equivalent receipt to be taxed under income tax, and leaves the balance to be dealt with as a capital gain under the capital gains tax rules.

We saw earlier that if the property is used for business purposes, the lessee on a short lease can claim a tax deduction against their trading profits of the annual equivalent of the amount of premium they paid and on which the landlord is liable to pay tax in each year of the lease. In the activity above, Amanda's tenant would therefore be able to claim a deduction of £18,000÷21 = £857 in each year of the life of the lease.

Note that the above rules on premiums only apply on the granting of the lease (i.e. from landlord to lessee) not if it is subsequently assigned (i.e. transferred from one lessee to another lessee).

In some cases, a premium may actually be paid by the landlord to the lessee (rather than the lessee to the landlord) perhaps as an inducement to the lessee to take on the lease. This occurs most commonly in commercial leasing. This type of premium is usually called a *reverse premium*. When a reverse premium is paid the landlord can usually either treat the payment made as an enhancement expenditure against their capital gains tax bill when they sell the property (see Chapter 8 for details of how this works in practice), or as an allowable business expense if they are a property developer or dealer. Of course, the lessee must declare the receipt of the premium as income on which they will have to pay tax (under trading income if the property rented is used for this business, or under property income if it is not for commercial use).

You can now attempt Quick Quiz questions 8-9 and Full questions 5-6.

Summary

This chapter looks trading and property income. It outlines how to distinguish between a trading activity and an activity that is carried out as a non-trading activity, maybe as a hobby. It outlines how the 'Badges of Trade' are used in practice for this assessment given we have no legal definition for trading. As accounting profit for the business is the foundation for trading income computations, it then focuses on how to adjust the accounting figures to arrive at the tax computation using either the traditional 'accruals basis' or the new simpler income tax 'cash basis' scheme introduced in April 2013 for some small businesses. This involves manipulation of both receipts and expenses from the accounts. A detailed worked example was then provided to illustrate these principles in practice.

The question of what happens when a trading activity results in a loss was outlined but this will be considered in more detail in Chapter 7.

Property income is discussed illustrating the specific rules used for computing this component of income, particular focusing on how income from furnished holiday letting property can be taxed differently to income from other dwellings. The special rules for the 'rent-a-room' scheme and for lease premiums were also outlined.

Project areas

This chapter provides a rich source of material for projects including:

- the impact of taxation on reported profit.
- the differences between trading and non-trading activities in practice
- the classification of expenses into revenue and capital items
- the use of different recognition bases for reporting profits
- the advantages of income from furnished holiday lettings being considered to be trading income. Does it just give special tax breaks to rich people with second homes distorting local housing in some areas of the UK?

Quick quiz

(Assume all the following relate to activities that are trading and the accruals basis is used unless otherwise stated)

1. Matthew charges £800 to his profit and loss account for bad and doubtful debts. This figure consists of £300 trade debts written off, £150 staff loan written off, £100 increase in specific provision and £250 increase in general provision. What amount (if any) is to be added back in the course of adjusting profits for tax purpose?

2. How would Matthew's (from Q1) assessment change if he opted to use the cash basis for this tax year?

3. Nola leases a car for use in her business, which costs £25,000 when new, for £4,200 per annum. What tax deduction will Nola be able to claim?

4. Orlando spends £500 on 100 T-shirts, printed with his business logo, to give to his customers, and spends £200 per head on a Christmas party for his 5 staff. How much (if any) of this expenditure is deductible?

5. Pauline takes goods costing £90 from her business stock for her own personal use. She normally sells such items for £115. What adjustment is required to her net profit for tax purposes if she pays nothing for the goods and records the £90 as a cost of sale?

6. Quentin pays a lease premium of £10,000 for the 15 year lease of his business premises. How much of this (if any) can he deduct?

7. Rachel incurs legal fees for her business of £500 being £30 for debt collection, £270 for the acquisition of new business premises and £200 for registration of a patent. How much (if any) can she deduct?

8. As a personal landlord Gerald owns a second house which he lets to a tenant for a rent payable monthly in advance. The annual rent of £8,400 was increased to £8,600 on 6 October, 2021. How much is assessable as Gerald's property income?

9. Heather receives a lease premium of £48,000 in respect of a 40 year lease. How much (if any) is chargeable as property income?

Questions

Question 1 (based on a CIMA question).

The following events occurred and were reflected in the profit and loss account of Mr Jones' self-employed business for the year ended 31 March, 2023.

Debits

(a) Expenditure of £8,500 was incurred on the reconstruction of a roof on a second-hand warehouse which was recently purchased. This had been damaged in a fire some months before Jones acquired it.

(b) During the year a director was convicted of embezzlement and the amount of the loss, as established in court, was £18,000.

(c) Due to a contraction of the trade, a works manager was made redundant. His statutory redundancy entitlement was £12,000 and the total gratuitous lump sum paid to him (including the £12,000) was £38,000.

(d) For the whole of the year, one of the senior managers was seconded to work full-time for a national charity. Her annual salary, included in the salaries charged in the profit and loss account, was £24,000.

(e) Costs of £24,000 were incurred in constructing a crèche to be used for employees' children. Administration costs include £8,000 in respect of the running costs of the crèche incurred during the year.

Credits

(f) £24,000 was received from an insurance company in respect of damage caused to a processing plant as a result of a fork-lift truck colliding with it. The cost of repairing the plant was £18,000 and this was credited against the repairs account. The additional £6,000 was an agreed sum paid for loss of profits while the plant was unusable and this was credited to the profit and loss account.

(g) A gain of £30,000 arose on the sale of selected investments. No details of the original cost or disposal price are given at this stage.

(h) Mr Jones has included in his sales figure for the year, sales amounting to £50,000 to X Ltd, a company in which he has an interest. These sales have been heavily discounted and, if they had been made at the normal retail price, would have been sold for £80,000.

Required: Indicate, giving full reasons and quoting case law where appropriate, how each of the above items would be dealt with in arriving at the tax adjusted trading profit figure for the year if Mr Jones is using the accruals basis.

You must state in your answer whether each item would be added to or subtracted from the profit shown by the profit and loss account (which is not given) or left unadjusted.

Question 2 (based on an ACCA question).

Sam is self-employed running a retail clothing shop. His income statement for the year ended 5 April 2023 is as follows:

	£	£
Gross profit		140,300
Depreciation	7,600	
Motor expenses [1]	8,800	
Patent royalties [2]	700	
Professional fees [3]	1,860	
Other expenses [4]	71,340	
		(90,300)
		50,000

Notes:

1. During the year ended 5 April 2023 Sam drove a total of 25,000 miles, of which 5,000 miles were driven when he visited his suppliers in Europe. The balance of the mileage is 25% for private journeys and 75% for business journeys in the UK.
2. During the year ended 5 April 2023 Sam paid patent royalties of £700 (gross) in respect of specialised technology that he uses when altering clothes for customers.
3. The figure for professional fees consists of £1,050 for legal fees in connection with an action brought against a supplier for breach of contract and £810 for accountancy. Included in the figure for accountancy is £320 in respect of personal capital gains tax advice for the tax year 2021/22.
4. The figure for other expense of £71,340 includes £560 for gifts to customers of food hampers costing £35 each and £420 for gifts to customers of pens carrying an advertisement for the clothing shop costing £60 each.
5. Sam uses one of the eight rooms in his private residence as an office when he works at home. The total running costs of the house for the year ended 5 April 2023 were £5,120. This cost is not included in the income statement's expenses of £90,300.
6. Sam uses his private telephone to make business telephone calls. The total cost of the private telephone for the year ended 5 April 2023 was £1,600 and 25% of this related to business telephone calls. The cost of the private telephone is not included in the income statement expenses of £90,300.

7. During the year ended 5 April 2023 Sam took goods out of the clothing shop for his personal use without paying for them and no entry has been made in the accounts to record this. The goods cost £820 and had a selling price of £1,480.

8. Sam is entitled to claim capital allowances of £ 6,100.

Required: Compute Sam's tax adjusted profits for the year ended 5 April 2023.

Question 3 (based on an ICAS TPS Tax Paper question).

Ben Roberts was employed for many years as a design engineer until he was made redundant on 5 June 2021. After a period out of work, Ben started his own design consultancy, BR Associates, on 1 February 2022. Ben wishes to draw up accounts to 31 January 2023 and has kept a cash book record of his receipts and payments as follows:

	Cash payments	Cash receipts
	£	£
Sales income received from customers [1]		75,000
Materials [2]	29,429	
Rent paid [3]	11,000	
Wages for Ben Roberts	12,000	
Machinery purchased	4,122	
Entertaining [5]	2,103	
New computer purchased	1,855	
Heat and light	1,123	
Travel and subsistence [6]	1,426	
Repairs [7]	1,250	
Interest paid	964	
Clothing [8]	680	
Motor expenses [4]	636	
		(66,588)
Surplus		8,412

Notes:

1. Accounts receivable at 31 January 2023 amounted to £2,900; the sales value of work done but not invoiced at this point came to £1,300.

2. The only accrued expense at 31 January 2023 was interest of £74. All materials are used up in the period.

3. Ben signed a 15-year lease on 1 March 2022. He pays rent of £1,000 each month in advance.

4. Ben's car is used two-thirds for business purposes. Ben wishes to use actual costs for this tax computation and not make use of optional fixed rate expenses.

5. Entertaining comprises £986 for entertaining UK customers and £1,117 in respect of potential overseas customers.

6. All travel was to clients and no overnight stays were involved. Subsistence includes £246 lunch costs while travelling undertaking his business activity, of which £158 relates to the extra cost of buying lunch over and above what Ben spends normally.

7. This relates to repairs which were necessary before the machinery purchased in the period could be used.

8. This relates to the cost of two new suits used only for work.

9. Ben is entitled to tax capital allowances of £6,830 for the year.

Required: Compute Ben's tax adjusted profits;
   a)   on an accruals basis;
   b)   on a cash basis.

You may ignore the VAT implications of the business. All costs were incurred within the tax year, and were paid in the tax year, unless otherwise indicated.

Question 4

Vincent's profit and loss account for the year to 31 August, 2022 was as follows:

	£		£
General expenses(1)	114,000	Gross trading profit	295,000
Repairs and renewals(2)	20,000	Bad debts recovered	
Legal and accounting charges(3)	1,200	(previously written off)	400
Subscriptions and donations(4)	3,000	Commissions received(5)	800
Manager's remuneration	40,000	Bank interest	1,000
Salaries and wages to staff	38,000		
Depreciation	20,000		
Rent and rates	1,500		
Net profit	59,500		
	297,200		297,200

Notes

(1) General expenses include the following:

	£
Travelling expenses of staff	1,000
Entertaining suppliers	600

(2) Repairs and renewals include the following:

Redecorating existing premises	300
Renovations to new premises to remedy wear and tear of previous owner (the premises were usable before these renovations)	500

(3) Legal and accounting charges are made up as follows:

Debt collection service	200
Staff service agreements	50
Tax consultant's fees for special advice	730
Audit and accountancy	220
	1,200

(4) Subscriptions and donations include the following

Donation to a political party	700
Staff Canteen facilities – running costs	500

(5) The commissions received were not incidental to trade

(6) Capital allowances for tax purposes for the year — 4,000

(7) No payment to Vincent is included in the Manager's remuneration or Salaries and Wages to staff

Required: Compute Vincent's tax adjusted profits and, assuming he has no other income or deductions, calculate the income tax and national insurance contributions payable (in the latter case, assume rates and thresholds applicable after 5 July 2022 apply for the whole year) .

(*Note: answer available via lecturer's website*)

Question 5 (based on an ACCA question)

Edmond Brick owns four properties which are let out. The following information relates to the tax year 2022/23:

Property one: This is a freehold house (purchased outright) that is let out furnished. The property was let throughout the tax year 2022/23 at a monthly rent of £575, payable in advance. During the tax year 2022/23, Edmond paid council tax of £1,200 and insurance of £340 in respect of this property. He brought no new capital items in this tax year.

Property two: This is a freehold house that is let out unfurnished. The property was purchased on 6 March 2022, and it was empty until 30 June 2022. It was then let from 1 July 2022 to 31 January 2023 at a monthly rent of £710 payable in advance. On 31 January 2023, the tenant left owing three months' rent that Edmond was unable to recover. The property was not re-let before 5 April 2023. During the tax year Edmond paid insurance of £290 for this property and spent £670 on advertising for tenants. He also paid loan interest (i.e. financing costs) of £500 in respect of a mortgage that was taken out to purchase this property.

Property three: This is a leasehold office building that is let out unfurnished. Edmond pays an annual rent of £6,800 for this property, but did not pay a premium when he acquired it. On 6 April 2023 the property was let to a sub-tenant, with Edmond receiving a premium of £15,000 for the grant of a five year lease. He also received the annual rent of £4,600 which was payable in advance. During the tax year 2022/23, Edmond paid insurance of £360 in respect of this property.

Furnished room: During the tax year 2022/23, Edmond rented out one furnished room of his main residence. During the year he received rent of £5,040, and incurred allowable expenditure of £1,140 in respect of the room. Edmond always computes the taxable income for the furnished room on the most favourable basis.

Required: Calculate Edmond's property business profit in respect of the three properties and the furnished room for the tax year 2022/23;

    a)   using the accruals basis;

    b)   using the cash basis.

(Note: answer available via lecturer's website)

Question 6 (based on an ACCA question)

Richard Tryer was born on 22 June 1971. He is employed by Prog plc as a computer programmer and is also self-employed as a website designer. Richard has tried to prepare his own income tax computation for the tax year 2022/23, but he has found it more difficult than expected. Although the sections which Richard has completed are correct, there are a significant number of omissions. The omissions are marked as outstanding (O/S). The partly completed income tax computation is as follows:

Richard Tryer – Income tax computation (2022/23)

	£	£
Trading profit 1 (note 1)		O/S
Employment income		
Salary	41,000	
Car benefit 2 (note 2)	O/S	
Fuel benefit 2 (note 2)	O/S	
Living accommodation 3 (note 3)	O/S	
		O/S
Property business profit (note 4)		O/S
Building society interest		1,260
Dividends		1,800
		O/S
Personal allowance		(12,500)
Taxable income		O/S

Note 1 – Trading profit

Richard commenced self-employment on 1 January 2022. He had a tax adjusted trading profit of £11,592 for the year ended 31 December 2022.

Note 2 – Car and fuel benefits

Throughout the tax year 2022/23, Prog plc provided Richard with a petrol-powered car which has a list price of £17,900. The car cost Prog plc £17,200 when bought on 1 January 2021, and it has a CO_2 emission rate of 93g/km. During the tax year 2022/23, Richard made contributions of £1,200 to Prog plc for the use of the car.

During the period 1 July 2022 to 5 April 2023, Prog plc also provided Richard with fuel for private journeys (before this he paid in full for fuel for private use). Richard did not make any contributions towards the cost of the fuel.

Note 3 – Living accommodation

Throughout the tax year 2022/23, Prog plc provided Richard with living accommodation. The property has been rented by Prog plc since 6 April 2022 at a cost of £1,100 per month. On 6 April 2022, the market value of the property was £122,000, and it has an annual value of £8,600.

On 6 April 2022, Prog plc purchased furniture for the property at a cost of £12,100. The company pays for the running costs relating to the property, and for the tax year 2022/23 these amounted to £3,700.

Note 4 – Property business profit

Richard owns a freehold shop which is let out unfurnished. The shop was purchased on 1 October 2022, and during October 2022 Richard spent £8,400 replacing the building's roof. The shop was not usable until this work was carried out, and this fact was represented by a reduced purchase price. During November 2022, Richard spent £800 on advertising the property for rent.

On 1 December 2022, the property was let to a tenant, with Richard receiving a premium of £12,000 for the grant of a 30-year lease. The monthly rent is £830 payable in advance, and during the period 1 December 2022 to 5 April 2023 Richard received five rental payments.

Due to a fire, £8,600 was spent on repairs to the shop during February 2023. Only £8,200 of this was paid for by Richard's property insurance.

Richard paid insurance of £480 in respect of the property. This was paid on 1 October 2022 and is for the year ended 30 September 2023.

Required: Given that PAYE of £9,130.00 has been deducted by Prog plc, calculate the income tax payable by Richard Tryer for the tax year 2022/23.

(Note: answer available via lecturer's website)

Further test questions can be found in the student section of the website at: **https://www.fiscalpublications.com/lymerandoats/2022**

Further reading and examples

Combs, A. and Tutin, R.(2022), *Taxation: incorporating the 2022 Finance Act*, Fiscal Publications: Malvern.
- use this book for many other examples to further develop and test your knowledge of this chapter's contents. See
https://www.fiscalpublications.com/combsandtutin/2022

Combs, A. (2022), *UK Income Tax Practice Questions (2nd edition 2022/23)*, Fiscal Publications: Malvern.
- a large test bank of questions linked to the content of this chapter that will enable you to thoroughly test your knowledge of this work with exam-level questions. See
https://www.fiscalpublications.com/uk-income-tax-practice-questions/2022

7 Capital allowances and trading losses

Introduction

7.1 This chapter continues the subject discussed in Chapter 6 – the taxation of unincorporated businesses. Here we consider the tax treatment of capital (i.e. non-current) assets under the capital allowances rules. Although we focus in this chapter on examples related to unincorporated businesses, you need to be aware that in fact these rules also apply for employees and companies that are eligible for capital allowances. The rules on capital allowances in this chapter do not apply if a business chooses to use the cash basis as discussed in Chapter 6.

At the end of this chapter we also consider the special tax rules that apply when an unincorporated business makes a loss.

At the end of this chapter you will be able to:

- identify plant and machinery that qualify for capital allowances;
- undertake capital allowance computations for plant, machinery, integral features and structures and buildings;
- apply the capital allowance rules for patents; and
- use the special tax rules that deal with the offset of trading losses for unincorporated businesses.

Overview of capital allowances

7.2 You will remember from the previous chapter that (as a general rule) neither actual capital expenditure (i.e. spending on non-current assets) nor depreciation are allowable deductions for income tax computations when using the accruals basis. Tax relief for capital expenditure, however, is given by means of *capital allowances*. This ensures consistent treatment of capital assets for tax purposes, rather than allowing the multiple possible treatments that would occur if accounting depreciation policies were used in tax computations. It also allows for special tax treatment of particular assets, asset groups or types of company as Government policy may require. We will see how the current special treatments are applied later in this chapter.

The bulk of the current legislation relating to capital allowances is contained in the Capital Allowances Act 2001 (CAA 2001), as modified by subsequent Finance Acts.

Capital allowances are available to individuals carrying on a qualifying activity, which includes trades, professions, vocations, ordinary property business (and also includes being an employee) as well as to companies. They are available for certain, but not all, capital assets. Just because you depreciate the asset for the accounting profit computation does not automatically mean you will also qualify for a comparable capital allowance for tax purposes.

Capital allowances allowed as a deduction each year are a fixed percentage of the value of the capital asset, or *pool* (collection) of assets, in question. They are usually given on a *reducing balance* basis and are called *writing down allowances* (WDA). Capital allowances are available on the date the payment is made for qualifying assets and ownership is transferred.

For expenditure on capital assets to be eligible for capital allowances they must fall into one of these categories:

- plant and machinery;
- integral features;
- non-residential structures and buildings;
- patents; and
- agricultural buildings and works.

The first three categories are the most common and so we will concentrate on these in this chapter. The rules for patents will be commented upon briefly at the end of this chapter. Since April 2019, a new allowance called the Structures and Buildings Allowance (SBA), has been available for industrial buildings (such as factories or workshops). However, land does not, and never has, qualified for any capital allowances.

Plant, machinery and integral features

7.3   To calculate capital allowances for plant and machinery and integral features, we need to go through a number of steps to decide:

1. whether the capital asset qualifies for capital allowances in the first place;
2. if so, which pool the asset belongs to and the relevant rate of capital allowance;
3. whether the Annual Investment Allowance applies;
4. whether the asset requires some special treatment; and
5. whether any disposals need to be dealt with.

Before we look at the details of each of these steps, we will first demonstrate how a capital allowance computation is performed.

Capital allowances pro forma

7.4   This is what a capital allowance computation will look like for a straightforward case. It is particularly important when doing these computations that you deal with things in a logical order. If you know the way to lay out a capital allowances computation you will be able to calculate the capital allowances for a business with relative ease. Therefore we advise you to use it wherever you do a capital allowance calculation to remind you of the necessary stages of the computation, and the order in which they should be applied.

Capital allowances on the main pool (we will explain what this is in section 7.9) for plant and machinery (numbers given are just for illustration).

	£	Main Pool £	Allowances £
Balance brought forward		130,000	
Additions qualifying for AIA:			
Plant	20,000		
AIA	(20,000)		20,000
Excess additions over AIA cap		0	
Disposals		(40,000)	
		90,000	
Writing down allowance (90,000 × 18%)		(16,200)	16,200
Written down value c/f		73,800	
Allowances for the accounting period			36,200

The 'allowances' column at the end is the one in which we record the amounts that will be allowed as a deduction in the computation of the tax adjusted trading profit for the business (or other qualifying activity). The columns to the left of the total 'Allowances' column show the way in which these deductions are computed.

Fiscal Fact

The estimated cost to the government of providing capital allowances under income tax was £20.5 billion for 2021/22 and under corporation tax was almost £99 billion for 2018/19. In the latter case this is a quarter higher than it was in 2013/14 when it was £80.3 billion. Over 2.13 million people and business claimed capital allowances in 2019/20 against their income tax liabilities. (Source: HMRC Corporation Tax Statistics - May 2021 and 'Structural relief cost estimates' - December 2021)

Take careful note of the order in which adjustments are made to the value of the capital allowance pool in the above pro forma. This order is important to ensure you calculate the correct writing down allowances each year. We will now consider each of the steps in turn so that you can see how the capital allowance computation is constructed.

Step 1: Does the asset qualify?

7.5　The first step is to decide whether the capital asset purchased by a business qualifies for any capital allowances or not. Like previous legislation on capital allowances, the CAA 2001 does not define plant and machinery and so it is necessary to look to case law for guidance. There has been a considerable amount of case law on this subject. One of the most important is *Yarmouth* v *France* (1887) in which the status of a horse was questioned. Lindley LJ concluded:

> "There is no definition of plant in the Act but in its original sense, it includes whatever apparatus is used by a businessman for carrying on his business, not his stock-in-trade which he buys or makes for sale; but all goods and chattels, fixed or moveable, live or dead, which he keeps for permanent employment in his business."

The *Yarmouth* v *France* decision therefore excludes trading stock from the meaning of 'plant' and implies that business premises are also excluded.

A number of subsequent cases have refined this definition somewhat. In *Wimpy International Ltd* v *Warland* (1988) three types of asset were excluded from the definition of plant and machinery:

- assets which are not used for carrying on the business;
- assets with a useful life of less than two years; and
- assets which form part of the setting in which the business was carried on, as opposed to assets actively used in the business.

As this judgment is actually the cumulative result of a number of earlier cases, it would be useful for us to review some of the more interesting ones. Understanding these rules is important as not having a proportion of capital expenditure allowed as a tax deduction has significant cost implications for businesses.

The last requirement is referred to as the '*function v setting*' test and has been the subject of a considerable number of cases, as it can be a difficult test to apply in practice. In *CIR* v *Barclay Curle & Co* (1969) the costs of building a dry dock, which is used for repair and maintenance work on ships, was held to be expenditure on plant and machinery because the dock played an active part in the operation of the company's trade as a ship builder. In *Cooke v Beach Station Caravans Ltd* (1974) the costs of excavating and installing a swimming pool were held to be expenditure on plant and machinery because the swimming pool performed a function, that of 'giving buoyancy and enjoyment to the swimmers' using the caravan park.

In *Benson v Yard Arm Club* (1978) a ship which was being used as a floating restaurant was held to be ineligible for capital allowances because it failed the functional test. It played a passive role as the setting for the restaurant business, rather than an active role. However, in another restaurant case, *CIR v Scottish and Newcastle Breweries Ltd* (1982) it was held that light fittings, decor and murals performed the function of creating an atmosphere and so were plant. In contrast, in *Wimpy International Ltd v Warland* (1988) a raised floor was held not to be plant as it was considered setting, despite the argument made that it was there to make the restaurant attractive to customers.

Another case, *Cheshire Cavity Storage* (2019) UKFTT 498 concerned costs associated with making caverns for available for storing gas. The taxpayer argued that the cavities had a plant-like function, but the tribunal found that their main function was storing gas, and so they were not plant. In a further recent case, *Stephen May v HMRC* (2019) the First-Tier Tax Tribunal held that a farm's silo that was used for temporary storage was plant, although HMRC tried to argue that it was a building.

The extent to which assets can be described as plant and machinery is highlighted in *Munby v Furlong* (1977) when a barrister successfully argued that his law library was plant because it was the apparatus used for carrying out his profession.

In the case of *Brown v Burnley Football and Athletic Co Ltd* (1980) expenditure on a new football stand was held not to be plant because it did not perform an active function in the business, just provided the setting. You will remember from the last chapter that *Burnley Football and Athletic Co Ltd* had also failed to claim the expenditure as a repair because the entire stand was replaced. Today, however, such expenditure would in fact be allowed under the special provisions currently in force, as below.

The following is automatically deemed to be plant and machinery by statute – expenditure:

- on equipment in order to comply with fire regulations for a building occupied by the trader;
- on thermal insulation in a building (excluding dwelling-houses);
- in order to comply with statutory safety requirements for sports grounds;
- on computer software;

- on alterations to buildings connected to the installation of plant and machinery; and
- on personal security equipment.

In order to claim capital allowances, a person carrying on a trade must incur capital expenditure on machinery or plant at least partly for the purposes of the trade (it doesn't have to be wholly), and the machinery or plant must belong to him or her.

Integral features

7.6 One of the problem areas for deciding what qualifies as plant and machinery is items that are attached to buildings. Some such items do qualify for capital allowances and are called *integral features*. This consists of the following items which are integral to a building:

- An electrical system (including a lighting system);
- A cold water system;
- A space or water heating system, a powered system of ventilation, air cooling or air purification, and any floor or ceiling that is part of such a system;
- A lift, escalator or moving walkway; or
- External solar shading.

The category does not just include newly acquired items; it also extends to replacements of these items where the whole or the majority (more than 50%) is replaced within a 12 month period.

Eligible costs will include demolition costs to prepare for building and all construction costs, but do not include costs for planning permission or the costs of obtaining land or the right to use land. Allowances can start to be claimed once the building is brought into use.

The building constructed does not need to be in the UK, it can be anywhere in the world as long as it is used by the person claiming the relief and the profits of this activity are chargeable to tax in the UK.

Subsequent work on an eligible building is also eligible for additional allowances – but this must be computed as a separate allowance related to the new costs incurred.

Once we have decided whether a new capital asset qualifies for capital allowances by being plant and machinery or integral features the next step is to decide how much the capital allowance will be.

Step 2: Pooling and rates

7.7   If businesses were required to calculate capital allowances for each and every asset separately, the compliance costs would be very high. In order to reduce these costs, and keep the system relatively simple, the Government allows taxpayers to 'pool' certain categories of assets and perform a single calculation based on the aggregate value of the pool. There are two pools, a *'main pool'* and a *'special rate pool'*. There are also some special rules for items that are not put into either of these pools and are treated separately for their capital allowances computation. We will consider how we deal with these as part of step 4.

For both the main and special rate pools, capital allowances are calculated on a reducing balance basis. This means that the starting point in any year's computation is the balance brought forward from the previous year. Before calculating the annual writing down allowance, however, we first must add to the balance brought forward the value of any new items acquired in the year, and subtract the value of any disposals that occurred during the year.

Writing down allowance is not apportioned for the part of the period that the asset has been owned – it is either allowed for the whole period or not at all. This is also in the interest of simplicity, and means that new items qualify for writing down allowances for the full year even if not owned for the whole year, and items disposed of don't qualify for any writing down allowance in the year of disposal even if owned for part of the year. This is an important difference from the way depreciation may be computed for accounting profit calculations where part year ownership may be taken into account.

Main pool

7.8   The main pool consists of all of a taxpayer's plant and machinery other than special rate pool assets (see below) or items that have to be treated separately (which we consider later in step 4). The current capital allowance rate for items in the main pool is 18%. This rates has not changed since 6 April 2012 (1 April 2012 for companies).

Special rate pool

7.9   The special rate pool attracts a lower rate of 6% writing down allowance (it was 8% between April 2012 and April 2019), which means the cost of these assets are spread over a longer period of time than items that qualify for the main pool.

Where a business has an accounting period that spans the introduction of such a rate change, a *'hybrid rate'* may have to be calculated, based on the number of days in each period to determine the relevant maximum percentage that can be used. For example, for a year ending 31 December 2019, this was 6.5% (computed on the basis of 3/12 x 8% for the period 1 January 2019 to 30 March 2019 + 9/12 x 6% for the period 1 April 2019 to 31 December 2019). However, as the writing down allowance rate has not changed since 2020/21, no hybrid rate is needed for the last three years' computations.

There are four categories of asset that qualify for the special rate pool;
- long life assets,
- integral features (see section 7.6 above),
- thermal insulation and
- 'high' CO_2 emission cars – this currently includes all cars emitting 50g/km or more, (before April 2021 this was set at CO_2 emissions levels at or above 110g/km) will be included in this category. We talk more about cars and capital allowances in section 7.13).

Long-life assets are those items of plant and machinery purchased since 26 November 1996 that have a useful life of 25 years or more when new. However, requiring allocation of long-life assets to the special rate pool only applies to businesses spending more than £100,000 per annum on such assets. Also, some assets are never treated as long-life assets including:

- machinery or plant in a building used wholly or mainly as (or for purposes ancillary to) a dwelling-house, retail shop, showroom, hotel or office,
- cars (including hire cars) and taxis, and
- sea-going ships and railway assets bought before the end of 2010.

Where businesses do not spend more than £100,000 a year on long-life capital assets, these assets are instead dealt with as part of the main pool, and not put into the special rate pool.

Basis periods

7.10 While capital allowances can be claimed for a full year even if we don't own the assets for a full year (see section 7.7 above), the rates of writing down allowance (18% for the main pool and 6% for the special rate pool), assume that we are dealing with a normal 12 month accounting period. However, if the taxpayer's business has an accounting period that is not 12 months in length then the relevant rate needs to be reduced (or expanded) pro-rata to the length of the accounting period. For example, an 18 month accounting period will result in 27% (18% × 1.5) worth of allowances for the main pool, or 9% (6% x 1.5) for the special rate pool.

Step 3: Annual Investment Allowance

7.11 In this next step for computing the correct capital allowances for a business we need to consider whether a newly acquired capital asset qualifies for the *annual investment allowance* (AIA). This allowance is designed to stimulate investment in new capital assets by accelerating the rate of deduction of cost that can be claimed (i.e. so the cost can be used to reduce tax due by a business more quickly).

The AIA allows businesses (of any size) to claim an allowance of 100% of the eligible expenditure incurred on plant and machinery and integral features (but does not include purchases of some assets, particularly cars and of course land) up to a given cap. For expenditure occurring between 1 January 2019 and 31 March 2023 this cap is set at £1,000,000 per annum. From 1 April 2023 the AIA cap will drop to £200,000 (the same rate applicable before this temporary increase on 1 January 2019).

The following Activities illustrate what we know from steps 1,2 and 3 so far:

Activity

Mulder, a small sole trader, prepares accounts to 31 December annually. His main pool of unrelieved expenditure on plant and machinery brought forward on 1 January 2022 was £20,000. During the year ended 31 December 2022, the following transactions took place:

			£
31 August 2022	Bought	Plant	20,000
31 December 2022	Bought	Plant	14,000

Calculate Mulder's allowable capital allowances for the year ended 31 December 2022.

Feedback

To perform this calculation there is a series of questions we need to ask:

1. Do the new additions belong in the main pool? Yes, they are neither long life assets nor special rate assets.

2. Do the new additions qualify for AIA? We can assume they do unless told otherwise.

		Main Pool	Allowances
	£	£	£
Written down value b/f		20,000	
Additions qualifying for AIA:			
Plant (£20,000 + £14,000)	34,000		
AIA (max)	(1,000,000)		34,000
Balance to main pool		0	
		20,000	

WDA 18%	(3,600)	3,600
Written down value c/f	16,400	
Total allowances for year		37,600

In this example, the new plant and machinery purchased in the chargeable period (1 January 2022 to 31 December 2022) does not exceed £1,000,000 so it can be fully covered by the AIA deduction available throughout this period. Had this not been the case the excess over £1,000,000 is simply added to the main pool and increases the sum available for the 18% WDV for that period and subsequently. See the Activity below to illustrate this.

Activity

During the year ended 31 December 2022, Mulder (from activity above) instead undertook the following transactions:

			£
31 August 2022	Bought	Plant	1,400,000
31 December 2022	Bought	Plant	150,000

Calculate the revised allowable capital allowances for Mulder for the year ended 31 December 2022.

Feedback

	£	Main Pool £	Allowances £
Written down value b/f		20,000	
Additions qualifying for AIA:			
Plant (£1,400,000+£150,000)	1,550,000		
AIA (max)	(1,000,000)		1,000,000
Balance to main pool		550,000	
		570,000	
WDA 18%		(102,600)	102,600
Written down value c/f		467,400	
Total allowances for year			1,102,600

If the item had been special rate expenditure, such as an integral feature, then the AIA limit should usually be applied to the special rate pool first (usually shown as an additional column alongside the Main Pool column so these assets can be separately tracked given a different writing down allowance rate must be applied – i.e. 6% not 18%). This is because these items get capital allowances at a slower rate than for main pool items so this gives more cashflow advantage to the taxpayer (this is allowed as it is the tax payers choice to what these are applied and in what order). See the following Activity that illustrates this for you.

Activity

During the year ended 31 December 2022, Mulder (from activities above) instead undertook the following transactions:

			£
31 August 2022	Bought	Integral features	1,400,000
31 December 2022	Bought	Plant	150,000

Calculate the revised allowable capital allowances for Mulder for the year ended 31 December 2022 (assume he had no special rate brought forward assets).

Feedback

£	Main Pool £	Sp Pool £	Allowances £
Written down value b/f	20,000	0	
Additions qualifying for AIA:			
Integral features		1,400,000	
AIA (max)		(1,000,000)	1,000,000
Plant (no AIA left to apply to this)	150,000		
Balance to pools		400,000	
Balance	170,000	400,000	
WDA 18%	(30,600)		30,600
WDA 6%		(24,000)	24,000
Written down value c/f	139,400	376,000	
Total allowances for year			1,054,600

Fiscal Fact

The estimated cost to the Government of AIA was £2.3 billion for 2021/22 (Source: HMRC – Estimated costs of non-structural tax reliefs – December 2021).

The AIA cap is currently £1,000,000 for new eligible assets acquired from 1 January 2019 to 31 March 2023, but previously this was:

£200,000   between 1 January 2016 and 31 December 2018

£500,000   between 1 April 2014 and 31 December 2015.

£250,000   between 1 January 2013 and 30 March 2014.

AIA is therefore a good example of a government policy that is flexible, i.e. easy to change, but that creates uncertainty because constant change creates uncertainty for business. As noted above, from 1 April 2023, the AIA cap reverts to £200,000 – unless the Government extends this higher level again (as it has more than once recently).

If a business has a chargeable period that spans the dates when the AIA rate changes, a transitional amount has to be calculated for the respective periods either side of the date the rate changes based on the number of months falling before and after the date of the change. This then becomes the maximum AIA that is allowed in that period. The following activity shows how this transitional amount is computed:

Activity

What would be the maximum AIA that a business with a chargeable period from 1 January 2023 to 31 December 2023 could claim (i.e. covering the date when the AIA rate is currently expected to revert back after the £1 million period)?

Feedback

The relevant AIA limits applicable to this business are therefore:
1. £1,000,000 from 1 January 2019 to 31 March 2023
2. £200,000 from 1 April 2023 to 31 December 2023

The business would therefore be able to claim:
(a) the proportion of the year to which a limit of £1,000,000 applied i.e. from 1 January 2023 to 31 March 2023 =
   $3/12 \times £1,000,000 = £250,000$
(b) the proportion of the year to which a limit of £200,000 applies i.e. from 1 April 2023 to 31 December 2023 =
   $9/12 \times £200,000 = £150,000$
i.e. their maximum AIA claim could be £400,000 (£250,000 + £150,000)

This computation must be done to determine the relevant AIA cap each time the AIA rate changes within the accounting period being assessed. There are some further transitional rules (e.g. to help reduce possible tax avoidance) that apply when the AIA rate changes, but these are beyond the scope of the book.

The AIA can only be given for the chargeable period in which the expenditure is incurred, so any unused allowance (i.e. if a business spends less than the AIA limit for the period) can't be carried forward and can't be transferred to another business. The allowance can't be claimed in the period when the qualifying activity ceases, and is not available for cars. Apart from these restrictions, businesses have a choice about how to apply the allowance to best effect, so as to maximise their capital allowance claim.

Step 4: Special treatment

7.12 Having looked at the rules that define what can be eligible for different capital allowances (step 1), apply to main and special rate pool items (step 2) and where the AIA might apply (step 3), we now consider some categories of capital asset that require special treatment as step 4. First, the special case of cars (which don't get AIA as discussed in 7.11 above), then items that qualify for first year capital allowances, which gives immediate write off (100% allowance) in the year of acquisition (i.e. before AIA is considered). We finally consider some categories of capital asset that need to be treated separately, i.e. not included in either the main or special rate pools.

Cars

7.13 The capital allowance system has always treated cars differently from other plant and equipment and the rules for cars were changed with effect from 6 April 2009 (1 April 2009 for companies).

For cars purchased after 6 April 2009 (1 April 2009 for companies), there are three possible treatments depending on the level of CO_2 emissions:

	> 6 Apr 21	6 Apr 18 – 5 Apr 21	< 6 Apr 18	WDA	Applicable pool
Low	0g/km	1-50g/km	1-75g/km	100%	N/A
Medium	1-50g/km	51-110g/km	76-130g/km	18%	Main Pool
High	>50g/km	>110g/km	>130g/km	6%*	Special Pool

* this rate was 8% if the car was purchased before 6 April 2019.

For example, in 2021/22 and 2022/23 only new cars bought producing no emissions can get 100% writing down allowance whereas before 2021/22 it could be any car producing emissions up to 50g/km.

A new car purchased on 1 July 2022 that produced emissions levels of 40g/km is therefore a medium emissions car in this tax year and would be eligible for 18% writing down allowances in 2022/23 as part of the main pool. However, the same car would have been eligible for 100% writing down allowance had it been bought on 1 January 2021 as part of a tax computation for the 2020/21 tax year.

Similarly, a new car brought on 1 October 2022 with emissions levels of 60g/km is classified as a high emissions car this year so only 6% writing down allowances could be claimable in 2022/23 as part of the special pool. Had this same car been brought on 1 October 2017 it would a low emissions car and could have given its owner 100% writing down allowances in that year of purchase (i.e. 2017/18)

As CO_2 emissions ratings are used to determine what annual capital allowances rates will apply, these rules are a deliberate attempt to encourage use of more environmentally friendly cars by businesses.

The following activity illustrates the use of the capital allowances rules for cars.

Activity

Luxury Travel, a business offering premium taxi services to customers to 'arrive in style' at airports, buys a car for one of its employees, Diane. The car costs a total of £30,000. A deposit of £5,000 was paid on 1 November 2018 and the balance of £25,000 when the car was delivered on 31 January 2019. The car's CO₂ emissions were 145g/km. No private usage of Diane's car occurs. Luxury Travel's accounting date is 31 December and had a special rate pool balance of £125,000 on 1 January 2018. Illustrate the maximum capital allowances that Luxury Travel could claim for the car for each year from 2018/19 to 2022/23 (assuming that no further acquisitions or disposals were made by Luxury Travel in these years).

Feedback

Based on the CO_2 emissions of more than 110g/km (as the applicable threshold when the car was purchased), the car would have been allocated to the special rate pool. It will therefore qualify for 8% capital allowances until April 2019 and then 6% thereafter. The deposit payment will fall into the 2018/19 tax year (as falls before Luxury's 31 December 2018 accounting year end). The final payment will fall into the following tax year (i.e. 2019/20).

	Special Rate Pool £	Allowances £
WDV b/f at 1 Jan 2018	125,000	
y/e 31 December 2018		
Acquisition	5,000	
	130,000	
WDA (@8%)	(10,400)	10,400
WDV c/f	119,600	
y/e 31 December 2019		
Acquisition	25,000	
	144,600	
WDA (@6.5%[1])	(9,399)	9,399
WDV c/f	135,201	

y/e 31 December 2020		
WDA (@6%)	(8,112)	8,112
WDV c/f	127,089	
y/e 31 December 2021		
WDA (@6%)	(7,625)	7,625
WDV c/f	119,464	
y/e 31 December 2022		
WDA (@6%)	(7,167)	7,167
WDV c/f	112,297	

[1] A hybrid rate must be used in 2019/20 as the applicable WDA fell to 6% from April 2019. This is computed by simply allocating the applicable WDA to the relevant period pro-rata ie as Luxury Travel operate a 1 January – 31 December year, their hybrid rate will be:

1 January 2019 – 31 March 2019 = 3/12 x 8% = 2%
1 April 2019 – 31 December 2019 = 9/12 x 6% = 4.5%
Therefore the hybrid rate is 6.5%

First year allowances (FYA)

7.14 In the 2000 Budget, and updated subsequently, the government introduced a number of enhanced capital allowances for certain 'green' capital items where the rate of allowance was 100%. This so called 'enhanced' capital allowance (ECA) applied in a computation before the AIA cap and so 100% was given for these assets even if the AIA cap was exceeded. The 100% ECA was available to all businesses, small, medium and large but in effect therefore only benefited businesses that spent more than their AIA cap in any given year.

It was announced in Budget 2018 that most of these allowances were to cease to be available from April 2020. The money saved by the Government is supporting a new Industrial Energy Transformation Fund (see details of this new fund at: https://www.gov.uk/guidance/industrial-energy-transformation-fund).

ECAs continued to be available to companies (but not individual sole-traders) for plant and machinery purchases if they were located in one of the various designated *enterprise zones* that had been created in 2011 and 2012. These are available until 31 March 2023.

While a variety of (relatively) environmentally friendly versions of products qualified for the 100% ECAs before 2020/21 (including energy saving plant and equipment, water conservation equipment, and energy efficient hand dryers), the only assets that now apply for this special treatment after April 2020 are the installation of electric vehicle charging points and gas refuelling stations.

Low emission cars used to qualify for ECAs, but from April 2020 the relief is categorised as a 100% first year allowance (FYA). The effect is the same as the old ECAs, i.e. 100% of the eligible cost is deducted in the first year as an incentive to try and get businesses to buy these types of vehicles in preference to other (more polluting) choices. Relief is only applicable for new cars registered after 6 April, 2014 and that are either fully electric (i.e. can't run on any other fuel) or emit 0g/km of carbon dioxide otherwise (this limit was 50g/km until 6 April 2021). (Note – purchases of second-hand low emission cars aren't eligible for this treatment – they must go into the main pool when acquired even if their emissions levels would have made them eligible when new for this enhanced treatment for their initial purchaser)

These 100% first year allowances will be available until April 2025 and the same 100% FYA rule also applies to new zero-emission goods vehicles (i.e. vans) and equipment purchased for gas refuelling stations.

Fiscal Fact

The estimated extra revenue that may be received by the Government as a result of scrapping many of the Enhanced Capital Allowances (subject to the impact of behaviour changes businesses undertake as a result of this policy change) will be £315 million from its point of being announced in October 2018 (Source: HMRC – Policy Paper: Capital Allowances: Ending enhanced allowances for energy and water efficient plant and machinery, published 29 October 2018).

Capital allowances and losses

Capital allowances are a deduction in the tax computation. This means that they are only really useful as an investment incentive if you are required to pay tax. But what if the business has a loss? With effect from 1 April 2008, this situation was partly addressed as companies in loss situations that are entitled to enhanced capital allowances are able to convert them to cash refunds of up to 19% of their expenditure incurred up to a maximum of £250,000 (or the total of their annual PAYE and NIC liabilities – whichever is the greater). From 1 April 2018, the 19% rate has been replaced by a rate equivalent to $2/3^{rds}$ of the corporation tax chargeable on the profits of the qualifying activity, or the average of the rates, if there is more than one rate for the chargeable period.

According to the Government when this was first introduced, this provides a cash flow benefit to loss making companies that invest in environmentally friendly products and technologies. Note that this special cash refund only applies to companies and not to sole traders, which some commentators feel is unfair and may lead to some businesses incorporating just for tax purposes.

The following activity illustrates the use of AIA and enhanced capital allowances (ECAs):

Activity

Philip, who runs a small printing business, buys a computer and software costing £2,500 on 1 May, 2022. He purchased a car (hybrid electric-petrol engine – CO, emissions of 86g/km) for £5,500 on 19 June, 2022 and installed an electric charging point to charge up this car on 25 June, 2022 for £1,600. His normal accounting year runs to 30 June and the brought forward written down value of his main pool at 1 July, 2021 was £15,000. No other purchases or sales of assets occurred in the year. Calculate the capital allowances available to Philip for the year ended 30 June, 2022.

Feedback

	£	Main Pool £	Allowances £
Written down value b/f		15,000	
Additions qualifying for ECA:			
Electric charging point	1,600		
ECA (100%)	(1,600)	–	1,600
Additions qualifying for AIA:			
Plant	2,500		
AIA	(2,500)		2,500
Additions not qualifying for ECA or AIA:			
Car	5,500		
Balance to main pool		5,500	
Writing down allowance:			
WDA 18%		(3,690)	3,690
Written down value c/f		16,810	
Allowances for tax year			7,790

Philip can receive 100% ECA on the electric charging point. He can also claim his expenditure on the computer as a deduction under the AIA rules, meaning he gets all the eligible tax allowances for these two purchases immediately – helping his cash flow. The car, however, won't qualify for 100% FYA, nor AIA, as its emission levels are too high and so this will need to be added instead to the main pool.

Note that it is important to list ECAs and FYAs separately to AIAs available assets as these are entitled to a 100% allowance rate even if the taxpayer uses up all their AIA in any given year - even though in Philip's case this make no difference to his eligible claims in this particular year.

Recap

7.15 At this point, we can now create an order of priority for the different allowances we have considered so far for when you acquire assets for your business as follows:

1. ECAs and FYAs are top priority so your first question must be - does the new asset qualify for 100% ECA/FYA or as a low emission car?

2. Then consider the AIA - do the other new assets qualify for AIA? If so, up to £1,000,000 (£200,000 if buying the assets after 1 April 2023) becomes fully deductible in addition to any ECA/FYA items.

3. Finally, what is left, i.e. the assets that don't qualify for ECA/FYA or AIA; or AIA expenditure in excess of the relevant cap, will be placed in either the main pool or the special rate pool and receive a 18% or 6% writing down allowance respectively.

Separately pooled assets

7.16 To determine the correct capital allowances some plant and machinery need to be treated separately rather than being placed into either the main or special rate pools. In this section we will review these situations. These include assets with some private use, leased assets, and short life assets.

Private use of assets

7.17 As we saw in the earlier discussion of cars, if plant and machinery is only partly used for the purpose of trade (e.g. the owner also gets some private benefit from their ownership) the capital allowances and charges described above are multiplied by the fraction A÷B, where A is the proportion of the time during which the asset was used for the purpose of trade while B is the total period of ownership. Because of the need to apply this fraction for each asset with any element of private usage, a separate capital allowances computation must be carried out for each asset. This means you should create a separate column in your proforma for assets with any private usage. Only the business use part of the total capital allowances can be claimed.

Activity

Jane bought a car for use in her car hire business for £30,000 on 9ᵗʰ August 2018. The car has CO₂ emissions of 220g/km. She uses the vehicle 25% for private purposes and has a 31 December year end. What are the maximum capital allowances she could claim for the years from 2018/19 to 2022/23.

Feedback

As the car has CO_2 emissions of more than 110g/km (the applicable limit when it was purchased) it would normally need to be allocated to the special rate pool as before, however, as it also has private usage, it will instead need its own pool – with WDA being applied at the same rate as for the special rate pool to which it otherwise would belong.

	Diane's car (25% private) £	Allowances £
y/e 31 December 2018		
Acquisition cost	30,000	
WDA (@ 8%)	(2,400) x 75%	1,800
WDV c/f	27,600	
y/e 31 December 2019		
WDA (@ 6.5%[1])	(1,794) x 75%	1,345
WDV c/f	25,806	
y/e 31 December 2020		
WDA (@ 6%)	(1,548) x 75%	1,161
WDV c/f	24,258	
y/e 31 December 2021		
WDA (@ 6%)	(1,455) x 75%	1,091
WDV c/f	22,803	
y/e 31 December 2022		
WDA (@ 6%)	(1,368) x 75%	1,026
WDV c/f	21,435	

[1] As the applicable WDA rate changed in April 2019, 3 months into Jane's accounting period, her hybrid rate will be (3/12 x 8%) + (9/12 x 6%) = 6.5%

Note that, even though only 75% of the allowances computed are claimed each year (£1,800, £1,345, £1,161, £1,091 and £1,026 respectively), it is the full WDA that is deducted to work out the asset's WDV – not just the 75%.

This rule for separately pooling items with private usage applies to all asset types, not just cars (although for companies the rules differ, see Chapter 9).

Leased assets

7.18 Assets which are owned by the business but leased to other people are not pooled with the other assets owned by the business. Instead, they are aggregated in a separate pool (i.e. they also get their own 'leased assets' column in the computation but not separate columns for each leased asset). The same WDA rate will apply however.

Short-life assets

7.19 The taxpayer may elect for certain machinery and plant to be treated as a short-life asset and given its own pool (a process referred to as 'de-pooling') in order for the balancing allowance to be computed when the asset is disposed of. This is a useful concession as it means the full allowances for the asset can be claimed sooner rather than the taxpayer only receiving 18% of it, on a reducing balance, each year as part of the main pool of plant and machinery for the remainder of the life of the business (Note, that this option is not available for special rate pool items).

The election to treat a purchased capital asset as a short life asset must be made not more than two years after the end of the chargeable period, or its basis period, in which the capital expenditure was incurred and once made is irrevocable. However, if the asset is not disposed of in a chargeable period ending on or before the eighth anniversary of the end of the chargeable period in which the cost of the asset was first recorded, then the tax written down value of the asset is transferred into the general pool at the beginning of the next chargeable period. From then on it will receive the normal treatment for other capital assets and the advantage of gaining a balancing allowance (if applicable) early is lost.

The legislation identifies a number of assets which cannot be treated as short-life assets, these are:

- ships;
- cars; and
- machinery or plant provided for leasing.

An example can be found on the website to illustrate the operation of the short life asset rules.

Step 5: Disposals

7.20 When assets are disposed of, we may need to calculate a balancing adjustment to charge extra to the tax computation or reduce the tax computation if too large/little an allowance has been taken in prior years. This will happen in the year in which a trade ceases, or when an item that has been kept out of the main or special rate pools is sold. The process is similar to the calculation of profit or loss on disposal for accounting purposes, and is to ensure the correct changes have been made to the records over the life of the asset.

Note that any disposals should be dealt with before calculating the current year's writing down allowance. This means that no writing down allowance is allowed in the year of disposal.

When performing this balancing adjustment computation we compare the disposal proceeds (or original cost if this is a lower sum, to ensure we never take out more from the pool than we originally put in) with the written down value of this asset in the tax accounts at the start of that year.

If the written down value exceeds the disposal value (or original cost if lower), then a balancing allowance equal to the whole of the excess can be claimed. This allowance is effectively an additional capital allowance claim to reflect allowable value deductions for tax purposes related to this asset, not previously claimed.

If the disposal value exceeds the written down value, then the opposite occurs i.e. a balancing charge equal to the excess will be levied on the taxpayer. This can be thought of as a 'negative capital allowance' and is effectively added to the trading profit for that year.

In the case of pooled assets, a balancing charge will arise if the disposal value is more than the balance in the pool. A balancing allowance, however, will not be allowed until such time as the qualifying activity itself ends (for example, when the trade ceases to operate). This is the reason for using the 'short life asset' option that we discussed earlier. If a taxpayer thinks that he or she will sell an asset within eight years and make a loss (balancing allowance), then by de-pooling the asset, the balancing allowance can be claimed in the year of disposal.

Activity

Catherine retired on 31 December, 2022 after trading for many years. The opening tax written down value of her capital allowances pool was £10,000 and of a short life asset (acquired in 2017 and used solely for the purposes of the business) was £4,500. The plant and machinery in the main pool had originally cost £12,000. Catherine sold the plant and machinery for £16,000 and the short life asset for £3,000 when she retired. Calculate the capital allowances and charges for 2022/23.

Feedback

Remember, short life assets have their own column, therefore, the capital allowances computation is:

	Main Pool £	Short life asset £	Allowances £
WDV b/f	10,000	4,500	
Disposal proceeds/cost	(12,000)	(3,000)	
	(2,000)	1,500	
Balancing allowance		(1,500)	1,500
Balancing charge	2,000		(2,000)
Net capital allowances			(500)

Although the plant in the main pool was sold for £16,000, it had originally only cost £12,000 so this is the figure we use as the disposal value to work out the balancing adjustment.

Small pools

7.21 Small pools of unrelieved expenditure can be written off where the balance brought forward is less than or equal to £1,000. This applies to both the main pool and special rate pool, but not to single asset pools such as short life assets. It is not compulsory to write off all of any small pools, and the taxpayer can choose how much, if any, to be written off each year.

Waiving rights to capital allowances

7.22 All or part of the capital allowance entitlement for any given year can be waived by the taxpayer (other than for SBAs as outlined below). This means a taxpayer can make a choice each year whether or not to claim any of their capital allowance deduction. Any amount waived has the effect of increasing the balance of qualifying expenditure which is eligible for capital allowances in future years.

Clearly it is usually in the interest of the business to claim tax relief as quickly as possible, but this may not always be the case, for example, if the business makes a loss that year. Rather than adding to this loss, the business may decide to carry forward their capital allowances by not including the deductions they could claim in this year's computation. Instead, the value of the pool will remain the same and so their claim is effectively deferred to offset against profit in later years.

A business might also waive the capital allowance on these occasions:

- if taxable profits would be reduced to such an extent that it would not be possible for the taxpayer to use all of his or her personal allowances
- if the taxpayer believed that his or her marginal rate of tax would increase significantly in future years and so the deduction will be more valuable to them in the future.

Structures and Buildings Allowances (SBA)

7.23 Capital allowances for non-residential buildings had previously been available under the Industrial Buildings Allowance (or IBA) regime, but this ceased in April 2011 and for some years no capital allowances were available for such buildings. A replacement was however, recommended by the Office for Tax Simplification in a report published in June 2018.

In October 2018 the Chancellor announced that the Government was to introduce a new allowance for non-residential structures and buildings. Relief is now provided for all eligible construction costs for non-residential property contracted on or after 29 October 2018. This allowance is called Structural Buildings Allowance (or SBA) and is more widely available than the previous IBAs regime, although at a lower rate of depreciation. This rate is 3% – i.e. spreading the allowable cost for eligible structures and buildings over $33\frac{1}{3}$ years (this has increased from 2%, which was the rate in place between the introduction of SBAs to 1 April 2020 for companies and 6 April 2020 for non-company businesses).

The aim of the relief is to encourage construction of new structures and buildings. These include offices, retail and wholesale premises, walls, bridges, tunnels, factories and warehouses. Only new building, or conversion costs of existing premises that creates new commercial property, is eligible for this allowance. This relief is not available for creating work-spaces within domestic property such as home offices, nor is it available against the costs of non-commercial parts of any otherwise commercial building development (e.g. for the costs of building a flat over a shop). The allowance for integral features (described in section 7.6 above) continues to apply to those. The SBA is therefore only available for capital costs that are not otherwise covered by the integral features (or any other) allowance.

Fiscal Fact

The estimated cost to the government of providing the extra 1% SBA is just over £1 billion over the term of this current parliament (i.e. to 2024/25). (Source: Overview of Tax Legislation and Rates - Budget 2020, 11 March 2020, HMRC)

7.24 The SBA rules provide for a rate of allowance for these assets of 3% per year on a straight-line basis. This means equal annual allowances can be claimed for $33\frac{1}{3}$ years.

Qualifying SBA additions are not pooled, instead each applicable allowance must be claimed for separately. Furthermore, if subsequent work is performed on eligible buildings then these allowances must be claimed separately from the allowance for the building to which they relate, even though this means they will then be claimed beyond the $33\frac{1}{3}$ year period for the building to which they relate.

If a business's accounting period is less than a year, the 3% allowance is pro-rated for the shortened period. If an asset ceases to be used for a qualifying activity then the relief can be claimed for a further period of up to two years and after this no further allowance can be claimed unless it returns to eligible use again. However, if the building is demolished and not replaced, then the owner can continue to claim the allowances for the remainder of term the building would have otherwise been allowed to be claimed for.

Unlike other allowances, under SBA rules no balancing charges or allowances can be claimed when ownership or use of the eligible buildings passes hands. Instead, the 'seller' simply ceases to claim the allowance from the point of sale, and the 'buyer' becomes eligible to pick up the remainder of the period of allowance still available.

Activity

On the 1 January 2022, Amer Consulting Services (ACS), a sole-trader, commissions the construction of a new office building from a developer at a total cost of £3 million. £250,000 of this cost relates to the purchase of the land on which the building is constructed. The building is brought into use at the start of the ACS's next accounting year, on 1 January 2023.

    a.   What will be the normal annual SBA available to the business? How long can ACS claim this for?

    b.   How will the allowances available be affected if ACS sells the building on 1 July 2025 to Sacranie Housing Services (who wish to use the office for a qualifying activity and also have a December accounting period)?

    c.   If Sacranie Housing Services make alterations to the building (that qualify for SBA and cost £350,000) before moving in on 1 January 2026 how will this affect the SBA they can claim?

Feedback

    a.   SBAs are at the rate of 3% of the eligible cost of construction, excluding the cost of land (i.e. £2.75 million (£3 million – £250,000). The allowances ACS can claim for the accounting period ended 31 December 2023 are:

($2.75 million x 3%) = £82,500 per annum (from 1 January 2023).

The business can claim this while the building is in commercial use for $33\frac{1}{3}$ years ie until 30 April 2056.

b.   If ACS sells the building on 1 July 2025 they will have claimed a full year of SBAs in each of the accounting periods ended 31 December 2023 and 2024, and would be eligible for half a year's SBA up to the date of disposal in accounting period ended 31 December 2025. So in total, ACS will have claimed SBAs £206,250 (£82,500+£82,500+£41,250) during the period it owned and used the building.

Sacranie Housing Services will take over the availability of the allowances from the point at which the building becomes theirs to use for a qualifying commercial activity, even though they do not move in for a further 6 months (they can normally take up to 2 years to do development work without loss of eligibility to the allowance). This means that they can claim £41,250 for the year ended 31 December 2025 and £82,500 a year thereafter, also for as long as they continue to use the building for a qualifying purpose, or until 30 April 2056.

c.   As Sacranie incurs further eligible expenditure on the building of £350,000 they can claim a further SBA related to the building, but this will need to be computed separately to the original building allowances. In this case the allowance will be £350,000 x 3% = £10,500 per annum. They can start to claim this allowance from the point at which they move back into the building – on 1 January 2026.

Where a year end is not 31 March (for companies) or 5 April (for non-company businesses) SBAs should be apportioned to apply 2% of the costs before 1 (or 6) April and 3% thereafter (this can be apportioned on a simple time basis). See the following Activity illustrates how this will work.

Activity

Jo, a sole trader, runs a metalcraft business and has outgrown her current premises. She decides to build a new workshop to relocate her business costing £100,000. All contracts for these works were entered into on 1 February 2019. The workshop was completed on 1 November 2019 and she started to use it on 1 December 2019. She prepares her accounts for each year ending on 31 December. What will be her SBA for 2020/21 to 2022/23?

Feedback

The construction of the new workshop had been contracted after the start date for SBA (29 October 2018) so qualifies for this allowance. It became eligible for SBA from 1 December 2019, the date Jo started to use it.

In Jo's chargeable year ending 31 December 2020 she can claim 2% a year for 3 months (from 1 January 2020 to 5 April 2020) and 3% a year for 9 months from 6 April 2020 to 31 December 2020.

3/12 x £100,000 x 2% = £500 +

9/12 x £100,000 x 3% = £2,250.

(Note – strictly this computation should be done on a daily basis – but we use months here to keep the computation simpler)

Her total allowance claim for SBA on this workshop for 2020/21 therefore is £2,750.

In Jo's chargeable years ending 31 December 2021 and 31 December 2022 she will be able to claim 3% for each full year as the applicable rate did not charge mid-year i.e. £100,000 x 3% = £3,000 each year.

Patents

7.25 If patent rights are purchased (i.e. rather than developed in-house) and used for trading purposes, a separate capital allowances pool is formed for all rights held on which writing down allowance of 25% per annum on a *reducing balance* basis is available for tax purposes, if the owner wishes to use them. These rules however, only apply to unincorporated business. For companies with expenditure on patent rights after 1 April, 2002, the write downs used in producing the accounts are now used (see the intangible assets description in section 9.17 for further details).

The rules for balancing allowances and charges are largely the same as for plant and machinery. If sale proceeds exceed the original cost the deduction from the pool is limited to the original cost, as for plant and machinery. One difference, however, is that the excess of proceeds over the original cost is taxed as miscellaneous income, and not as capital gains as plant and machinery are.

 You can now attempt Quick Quiz questions 1-8 and Full questions 1-4.

Trading losses

7.26 In this section we will briefly look at the special tax rules that apply for dealing with losses on trading activities. These differ if the cash basis is used to compute the trading loss as we will see later.

Calculating a tax loss is straight forward. If, after adjusting the profits for tax purposes (using either of the accrual or cash basis), the end result is a negative amount, i.e. the allowable expenditures exceed the taxable income, then you have a trading loss for tax purposes. Such a loss can be used to offset future tax bills or in some cases can be used to claim back tax paid in the recent past, with certain limitations. However, a loss can only be relieved once and the taxpayer may have to make a choice about how best to use the loss if using the accrual basis.

There are special rules for losses incurred in the early years of business, or at the end of the life of a business. In this chapter, we will only consider the position of an established, on-going business. In this case, the loss can be relieved by:

- Deducting it from general income, for the current year, the year before, or both years, or
- Carrying it forward to be offset against subsequent trade profits.

Deduction from general income

7.27 Where a taxpayer carries on a trade in the tax year and makes a loss in that year, he or she can claim a deduction for that loss against general income for that year as a tax relief (at step 2 of their income tax computation) instead of having to carry it forward against future profits. If there is still some loss left over after applying it against general income of the year, the remaining part can then be used to reclaim income tax paid in the previous tax year. This was extended to allow carry back for up to 3 years in Budget 2021 to aid with Covid-19 recovery for the trading years 2020/21 and 2021/22 – subject to a maximum loss of £2million. However, for accounting periods ending after 31 March 2022, the usual one year carry back rule applies again. This is done in practice by creating a deduction equivalent to the loss available to be carried back. This deduction can then be used to claim a repayment of tax previously paid or can be used to offset later year taxes (see an example of how this works in practice below) – the taxpayer has the choice.

Alternatively, the taxpayer can choose to first use the loss in the previous tax years and then, if there is still some left over, use it in the current year. This means that the taxpayer has to think about how much tax saving can be made from each course of action and can pick which option to use – usually opting for the one that creates the lowest overall tax bill across all periods.

There are some conditions that have to be met for this relief to apply. The main condition is that relief against general income is not available unless the trade is "commercial". This means that it is carried on during the year on a commercial basis and with a view to making a profit.

Losses have to be used to the full extent of the net income of the year to which they are applied. This can mean the loss of personal allowances for that year (as losses are deducted at step 2 of the personal income tax computation as we saw in Chapter 4 – before personal allowances are dealt with at step 3).

Carry forward

7.28   As an alternative to deduction from general income, a trading loss can be carried forward to be relieved against subsequent trade profits. However, this carry forward does have an important restriction; the loss can only be offset against the profits of the same trade in later years, not against profits from a different trade.

Any loss that is not used up in the following tax year can then be carried forward to the next year, and so on indefinitely until it is all eventually used up.

There are several drawbacks to this form of relief:

- Once a taxpayer has decided to use this form of relief, there is no flexibility, and the first available profits have to be used to relieve the loss. If the taxpayer has little income from other sources, this could mean a loss of personal allowances in these future periods that would ordinarily reduce the income tax liabilities anyway.

- There is also a delay in receiving the relief, until the year of assessment for the year in which profits are next made. As well as having potentially serious cash flow implications, the relief may be worth less because the tax rate applied to the relief is the one in force when the relief is received, not when it was incurred.

- In addition, the law is strict about what exactly constitutes the 'same trade'. In *Gordon and Blair Ltd v IRC* (1962), losses incurred from the trade of brewing could not be carried forward and relieved against profits from bottling. Whether the same trade is being carried on is a question of degree and so the facts of each case must be considered carefully. Hence there is an element of risk in choosing to receive relief in this way.

This is the default way HMRC will apply losses if the taxpayer does not tell them that they wish to do something different.

The Cash Basis

7.29 If the taxpayer is using the cash basis, it is not possible to use relief against general income, and the only way losses can be relieved is through the carry forward method.

Limit on Reliefs

7.30 There is a cap, or limit, on the amount of reliefs that taxpayers can claim. With effect from 6 April 2013 the limit is set at the greater of £50,000 or 25% of income. Income for this purpose is total income liable for income tax, adjusted for pension contributions and charitable donations.

If your course requires you to also know the other special cases of loss relief, additional material and examples can be found in the student section of the website at:

https://www.fiscalpublications.com/lymerandoats/2022

The rules for dealing with trading losses for companies are slightly different to these, which apply to sole traders. We will briefly examine the rules for corporation tax in section 9.22.

You can now attempt Quick Quiz question 9 and Full question 5.

Summary

This chapter continues our examination of the tax rules for unincorporated businesses. It looks at the capital allowance rules for capital assets. We examined what kind of plant and machinery qualifies for capital allowances and how they are calculated. We also discussed the new structures and buildings allowance and special cases of allowances for expenditure on patents. Finally, we briefly reviewed the basics of how trade losses can be handled for an ongoing business.

Project areas

This chapter provides some scope for projects including the:

- effectiveness of capital allowances as tools for accurately reflecting the real cost of using assets in businesses;
- question of whether increasing capital allowances leads to increased investment in plant and machinery (i.e do incentives, like the regularly changing AIA, or enhanced 100% FYAs, work to encourage investment);

- implications of having different accounting and tax treatments for capital assets and even between tax treatments when using the cash basis or accruals basis;
- reasons why cars are singled out for special capital allowance treatment.

Quick quiz

1. Samuel bought a motor car for use in his business on 1 September, 2022. The car cost £15,000 and has CO_2 emissions of 145 g/km. He draws up his accounts to 31 December each year. What is the capital allowance rate he can claim this year if the car is used solely for business purposes?

2. Theresa bought a motor car for use in her business on 1 September, 2022. The car cost £15,000 and is not electric, but has CO_2 emissions of 40 g/km. How much capital allowance can she claim?

3. Umut has a year end of 31 December for his business, which he has operated for several years. On 12 September 2022 he spent £1,450,000 on a machine for use in his business. The machine does not qualify for enhanced capital allowances and qualifies for the main rate pool. What is the capital allowances that he will be entitled to for the 2022/23 year?

4. Vivian buys a state of the art computer for her small business on 30 June, 2022 at a cost of £2,500. What capital allowance can she claim for the year ended 30 September 2022 (assuming the asset is used 100% for the business)? Should she treat it as a short life asset?

5. Walter sold a car for £3,000 which had a tax written down value of £8,000 at the start of the year. He used the car 75% for business purposes and had purchased it in October 2012. What adjustment is required to his capital allowance claim for the year?

6. Xanthe runs a clothing shop that she has operated for many years. At 1 April 2022, the written down value of her main pool was £15,000. In October 2022 plant and machinery that had originally cost £16,000 was sold for £14,200. What is the maximum amount of capital allowances that Xanthe can claim for the year ended 31 March 2023?

7. During the last part of 2021 Norma incurs £25,000 on conversion work to a shop she owns and operates a business from as a sole trader. £5,000 of this sum relates to integral features. Norma was able to use this building again after work was completed on 1 January 2022. What SBA can she claim for her year ended 30 November 2022?

8. Yolande started a new business on 1 October 2022 and prepared her first set of accounts for the period ending 31 December 2022. On 5 November 2022 Yolande purchased a new machine for £400,000, what is the

maximum capital allowance she can claim for the year ended 31 December 2022?

9. Zeus has been in business for many years and prepares his accounts to 31 March each year. In the year to 31 March 2022 Zeus made a taxable trading profit of £12,000 and in the year to 31 March 2023 he made a loss of £170,000. Zeus also has property business income of £250,000 in the year ended 31 March 2022, but no other income in the year ended 31 March 2023. What is the amount of loss that Zeus can set against his general income for the tax year ended 5 April 2023?

Questions

Question 1

Luke Skyrunner has a medium sized manufacturing business. The opening balance in his main pool of assets was £10,000. He has no special rate pool at the start of the year. All vehicles are used 100% for business purposes. During the year ended 30 June 2022, the following transactions occurred in relation to his fixed assets:

29 July, 2021	New van purchased for £4,000
25 October, 2021	New car (CO_2 emissions 0g/km) purchased for £6,000
15 February, 2022	Plant (bought on 1 August, 2001 for £8,000) was sold for £7,000
1 May, 2022	New plant purchased for £15,000
15 May, 2022	New car (CO_2 emissions 180g/km) purchased for £20,000
30 May, 2022	New lift installed in the warehouse for £8,000

Required: Calculate Luke's maximum entitlement to capital allowances for the year ended 30 June 2022.

Question 2 (based on an ACCA question)

Phil Fit, trading as 'Jogger' runs a business manufacturing running shoes. The following information is provided for the year ended 31 March 2023:

Depreciation of £12,340 has been deducted in arriving at the net accounting loss of £56,400. Phil Fit does not choose to use the cash basis.

On 1 April 2022, the tax written down values of plant and machinery was as follows (with no special rate pool):

Main pool	£21,600
Short life asset	£8,800

The following transactions took place during the year ended 31 March 2023:

20 July 2022	sold the short life asset	£11,700
31 July 2022	purchased Ford Focus car (CO_2 155 g/km)	£11,800
14 March 2023	sold a lorry	£8,600

The short life assets sold on 20 July 2022 for £11,700 originally cost £18,400. The lorry sold on 14 March 2023 for £8,600 originally cost £16,600.

Required: Calculate Phil's tax adjusted trading profit/loss for 'Jogger' for the year ended 31 March 2023.

Question 3 (based on an ICAS TPS Tax Paper question)

Stitched Up is an unincorporated business involved in the manufacture and sale of ladies' fashion that has a 30 June year end for accounting purposes. The tax written down values of the pools of expenditure at 1 July 2021 were:

Main pool	£59,400
Special rate pool	£14,200
Mercedes car (acquired 1 October 2017)	£26,300

The Mercedes car is used by Stitched Up's owner, Joe Brown, and it is estimated that he uses it approximately 50% for business. It has CO_2 emissions of 165g/km.

The following fixed assets were acquired by Stitched Up during the year:

	Acquired	Cost
New air conditioning system for factory	October 2021	£28,000
Installation of 3 electric car charging points (see below)	December 2021	£3,000
New industrial sewing machines (five machines)	January 2022	£15,000

A grant of £1,000 towards the cost of the electric charging points was received from the government. The gross cost of the electric charging points was £4,000.

The only fixed asset disposal by Stitched Up was the sale of five old sewing machines. They cost less than £6,000 each and were sold for £250 each.

On 1 January 2022, Stitched up started to use an extension to the factory that had been built over the previous year (contracts signed 10 January 2021) at a cost of £500,000. No integral features were part of this building.

Required: Calculate the capital allowances that Stitched Up is entitled to claim for 2022/23.

Question 4 (based on an ACCA question)

Harry Heavy runs a music publishing business. His operating profit for the year ended 31 December 2022 is £433,100. Deprecation of £12,880 has been deducted in arriving at this figure.

On 1 January 2022, Harry acquired a leasehold office building, paying a premium of £90,000 for the grant of a ten year lease. The office building was used for business purposes by Harry throughout the year ended 31 December 2022. Amortisation of leasehold property of £9,000 has been deducted in arriving at the operating profit.

On 1 January 2022, the tax written down values of Harry's qualifying assets were as follows:

Main pool (including car (1))	£14,100
Car (2)	£24,500
Special rate pool	£21,700

The following purchases and disposals of qualifying assets took place during the year ended 31 December 2022:

23 March 2022	Purchase of office equipment	£900
19 July 2022	Sold car (1)	(£14,600)
28 July 2022	Sold all special rate pool items	(£12,300)

Car (1) is used by one of Harry's employees and originally cost £19,200. Car (2) has CO_2 emissions of 185g/km. It is used by Harry and 30% of the mileage is for private journeys.

Required: Calculate Harry's tax adjusted trading profit for the year ended 31 December 2022.

(*Note: answer available on lecturers' website*)

Question 5 (based on an ACCA question)

Richard Desk has been a self-employed manufacturer of office furniture since 1993. His income for the last three years is as follows:

	2020/21	2021/22	2022/23
Trading profit/(loss)	14,800	(26,300)	8,600
Property income	nil	3,000	2,800
Bank interest	600	400	500

Required: Calculate Richard's taxable income for each year on the basis that he relieves the trading loss against general income in the previous year.

(*Note: answer available on lecturers' website*)

Further test questions for this chapter to test your knowledge can be found in the student section of the website at:

https:// www.fiscalpublications.com/lymerandoats/2021

Further reading and examples

Combs, A., & Tutin, R. (2022), *Taxation: incorporating the 2022 Finance Act,* Fiscal Publications: Malvern.
– use this book for many other examples to further develop and test your knowledge of this chapter's contents. See
https://www.fiscalpublications.com/combsandtutin/2022

Combs, A. (2022), *UK Income Tax Practice Questions (2nd edition 2022/23),* Fiscal Publications: Malvern.
– a large test bank of questions linked to the content of this chapter that will enable you to thoroughly test your knowledge of this work with exam-level questions. See
    https://www.fiscalpublications.com/uk-income-tax-practice-questions/2022

8 | Capital taxes

Introduction

8.1   Until capital gains tax (CGT) was introduced in 1965, capital receipts (such as sums received from selling privately owned, or non-current business, assets) were largely free of tax. This meant that increases in wealth resulting from growth in capital value, as opposed to receiving income, resulted in substantially less tax being paid. Some of the incentive to classify a receipt as capital rather than income was removed by the introduction and subsequent development of capital gains tax, although there are still differences between the operation of the income tax and capital gains tax systems, as you will see in this chapter.

During its life capital gains tax has undergone many changes as successive Chancellors have attempted to improve the tax or change its focus. CGT is charged on both individuals and companies, however, in recent years, this tax has become increasingly different for these two groups. For this reason, in this chapter we consider the basic principles and their application for individual taxpayers. We will examine how capital gains tax works for companies in Chapter 9, alongside corporation tax.

There are other forms of taxes on capital transactions in operation in the UK at present and in this chapter we will also briefly describe the operation of stamp duty, and inheritance tax.

After reading this chapter you will be able to:

- describe the introduction and development of CGT;
- calculate the capital gains tax liability which arises as a result of a range of transactions;
- describe the CGT reliefs available to taxpayers;
- briefly describe the application of stamp duty; and
- briefly describe the operation of inheritance tax.

Capital gains tax

8.2   We saw in Chapter 6 that one of the key concerns of the income tax system is to distinguish income receipts from capital receipts given that, as a general rule, capital receipts are not subject to income tax. A consequence of not taxing capital receipts, as happened in the UK before 1965, is that it creates a significant distortion in the tax system, i.e. an incentive for taxpayers to manipulate transactions so that they escape tax as capital receipts rather than attract tax as income, or revenue, receipts. Many tax systems therefore tax capital receipts to reduce these distortions, however, not always at the same rates, or using the same rules, as for income. Where differences exist there will continue to be an incentive towards capital receipts over income receipts where capital receipts attract lower tax, and vice versa if income is taxed more lightly. Most tax systems try to recognise, and do something about, this tax induced distortion.

The first modern attempt to tax capital gains in the UK was a short term capital gains tax introduced in 1962. The tax was replaced in 1965 by a full capital gains tax which was intended to tax 'profits' which were not subject to income tax.

Today capital gains tax accounts for only 2–3% of the revenue raised by direct taxation but, as the then Chancellor said at the time he introduced it, the tax was not primarily introduced to raise revenue for the Government but to 'provide a background of equity and fair play'. So, it has an importance beyond the amount it raises in tax revenue.

Fiscal Fact

In 2008/09 142,000 individual taxpayers paid capital gains tax of £7.8billion, however, for 2013/14 this sum dropped dramatically to £3.9billion from 211,000 taxpayers – a sign of the economic situation in the UK over that period. It had been down as low as £2.5bn for 2009/10 but the forecast for 2019/20 is an upward trend again to £9.97 billion and in 2018/19 (latest available figures) 276,000 individual taxpayers paid this tax. [Source: HMRC Tax Receipts Table 2.8 & Capital Gains Tax Statistics Table 1]

Look again at some of the legal cases in Chapter 6 which help to determine whether trading has occurred. Some of these pre-1965 cases may not be brought today because if the receipt is not a trading receipt it will now be considered under CGT, although maybe with different consequences as you will see later.

When CGT was introduced in the UK it was not intended to be retrospective so only gains which arose after 6 April, 1965 are liable to capital gains tax. You are unlikely to encounter assets owned before April 1965 in your course.

In 1988 the tax was rebased so that gains before March 1982 would no longer be liable to capital gains taxation. This is achieved by using the market value at 31 March 1982 as the cost of the asset.

Values of assets and the effects of inflation

8.3 Assets may increase in value over time for a number of reasons. For example, shares may become more valuable as the company's profits are accumulated year on year and if it is thought to have good prospects of continuing to earn profits in the future. You may also be able to sell assets for more than you paid for them, for example, if you buy 'collectables' that appreciate in value. However, one other factor that causes an increase in assets' value over time is inflation. While a gain may be made when selling an asset for more than it was bought for in absolute cash terms, you are only really better off if the cash value of that sale buys you more now than the original cash value of the cost.

The question of what to do with gains resulting from inflation is one that affects all countries that try to tax capital gains. The problem became particularly acute in the 1970s and 1980s when inflation was high, and is likely to return as UK's post Covid economy experiences increased inflation in the coming years.

When CGT was first introduced no relief was given for the effects of inflation. Broadly speaking tax was paid on the difference between the allowable costs of acquiring the asset and the disposal proceeds. In 1985 the law was amended to give full relief for inflation. The retail price index (RPI) was chosen as the inflation measure to be used for capital gains tax computations. The changes in the RPI between the date the asset was acquired and disposed of produced an *indexation allowance* that was used to reduce the total gain and remove the effect of inflation on the asset's value, but (from 1993) could not create a loss.

In 1998, in the interests of simplicity, the system of indexation allowances was replaced (for individuals only) by a fixed reduction based on the length of ownership of the asset, called *taper relief*. The rules meant that for individuals the taxable part of any chargeable gain diminished the longer the asset was owned. This was intended to encourage individuals to undertake long-term investment. Taper relief was also significantly more generous for business assets (i.e. assets used for business purposes) than non-business assets to encourage investment by entrepreneurs. For individuals, therefore, no indexation allowance is given for periods of ownership after April 1998.

In 2008, taper relief was abolished for individuals and replaced with a flat rate of tax at 18% for everyone. In 2010, a new rate of 28% was introduced for higher and additional rate income taxpayers. From 6 April 2016 these rates were reduced to 10% and 20% respectively. These rates are, however, lower than comparable income tax rates, perhaps providing some allowance for the impact of inflation. The justification for this new flat rate system (ironically perhaps) was to further simplify the system that the taper relief was supposed to have simplified.

We will examine how these rules work in practice for individual taxpayers, with examples, as we go through this chapter.

The charge to capital gains tax

8.4 A liability to capital gains tax arises when a *chargeable person* makes a *chargeable disposal* of *chargeable assets*. You need to be able to understand each of these terms and list exemptions to capital gains tax to understand how it works.

Chargeable person

8.5 A chargeable person may be:

- *An individual who is resident in the UK during the tax year in which the chargeable disposal occurs.* If the individual is resident in the UK, disposals anywhere in the world may give rise to a capital gains tax liability.
- *A partner in a business.* A partnership does not have a separate legal identity. When a partnership makes a chargeable disposal of partnership assets the partners are individually liable to tax in proportion to their share of the capital gain.

The legislation contains a list of exempt organisations that are not liable to CGT on asset disposals (but also therefore cannot claim any losses). These are:

- charities using gains for charitable purposes;
- approved superannuation (i.e. pension) funds;
- local authorities;
- registered friendly societies;
- approved scientific research associations; and
- authorised unit and investment trusts.

Although companies are also chargeable persons for CGT purposes, they don't pay a separate capital gains tax as individuals do. Instead, corporation tax is charged on total profits including chargeable (capital) gains. We will discuss the taxation of companies more fully in Chapter 9.

Chargeable disposal

8.6 The term *chargeable disposal* includes the sale or gift of all or any part of an asset. It also includes the loss or destruction of an asset, the appropriation of assets as trading stock and the receipt of a capital sum in return for the surrender of rights to assets. An example of this last case is the sale of rights which attach to shares when a company makes a rights issue. The chargeable disposal is deemed to take place when the title to the asset passes to its new owner.

A number of disposals are *exempt disposals* and do not give rise to a capital gains tax liability. These are:

- transfers of assets on death – the assets are instead deemed to be acquired by their new owners at their value at the date of death;
- transfers of assets to provide security for a loan or mortgage; and
- gifts of assets to charities and national heritage bodies.

Where an asset is damaged, and the taxpayer receives a capital sum as compensation (e.g. from an insurance pay-out), a special rule may apply. So long as the compensation is used to restore the asset (or most of it) the taxpayer can elect to have the compensation reduce the allowable cost of the asset instead of creating a chargeable disposal. This election can also be made if the capital sum is small (less than 5% of the value of the asset). Making such an election has the effect of delaying the capital gains tax payment until the restored asset is eventually disposed of.

Chargeable assets

8.7 All assets are *chargeable assets* unless they are specifically exempted from capital gains tax by law, or other regulation. Here is a list of some common exempt assets:

- motor vehicles (whatever their age);
- national savings certificates, premium bonds and SAYE deposits;
- foreign currency, provided it was for private use;
- decorations for valour (e.g. brave conduct medals) unless the chargeable person purchased them rather than being awarded them personally;
- damages (compensation) for personal or professional injury;
- life assurance policies when disposed of by the original owner;
- works of art or scientific collections given for national purposes are treated as being disposed of on a no gain/no loss basis;
- gilt-edged securities, for example Treasury loans and stocks;
- qualifying corporate bonds (debentures);
- the disposal of debts, other than debts on a security, by the original creditor;
- pension and annuity rights;
- betting and gambling winnings; and
- investments held in individual savings accounts (ISAs).

In addition, in certain circumstances tangible moveable property, also called *chattels*, are exempt from capital gains tax, as is an individual's principle private residence. We will consider both of these categories later in sections 8.19 and 8.26, as they are not always fully exempt.

If a taxpayer disposes of exempt assets no chargeable gain, or allowable loss, arises.

Activity

How should cryptoassets be treated for UK capital gains tax purposes?

Feedback

Cryptoassets are digital assets and include cryptocurrency such as Bitcoin and Ethereum, and non-fungible tokens (NFTs). The tax treatment of cryptoassets depends on the nature and use of the token in question. HMRC does not consider the buying and selling of assets to be the same as gambling. In most cases, individuals hold cryptoassets as a personal investment and so will be liable for capital gains tax when they are disposed of. If cryptoassets are received from an employer as a form of non-cash payment, they will be liable for income tax and national insurance on the best estimate of the value of the asset. If an employee later sells a cryptoasset received in this way, it may result in a chargeable gain for CGT purposes. For taxpayers who mine cryptoassets the question is whether the activity amounts to a trade. If the mining income does not meet the badges of trade (discussed in section 6.4 - 6.10), the pound value of tokens awarded will be taxable as miscellaneous income. If the individual keeps the awarded assets, they may have to pay CGT when they later dispose of them.

The basic computation

8.8   In this section we will first study the computation of the chargeable gain, or allowable loss. We will then illustrate how the calculation is applied in practice using a number of transactions.

The pro forma for calculating the chargeable gain or allowable loss is (numbers are for illustration only):

	£
Gross proceeds on disposal (or market value)	20,000
Less incidental costs of disposal	(1,000)
Net proceeds	19,000
Less allowable costs	(4,000)
Chargeable gain/(loss)	15,000

As you will see later, this calculation is performed for each disposal of a non-exempt capital asset; the results are then aggregated and an annual exemption applied (for individuals) to the total so that a certain amount of the total gain each year is tax free. For 2022/23 the annual exempt amount (AEA) is £12,300 (unchanged from 2021/22). The following activity provides an overview of the CGT computation. We will then explore each stage in further detail.

Activity

Ernie sold two chargeable assets on 1 July 2022 and had no other asset disposals during the tax year:

Asset 1: cost £5,000, sold for £15,000

Asset 2: cost £15,000, sold for £20,000.

What is the amount on which Ernie will pay capital gains tax?

Feedback

Capital gains tax is based on the aggregated net chargeable gains for the year, less the AEA. In Ernie's case, this will be:

Asset 1 (£15,000 – £5,000)	10,000
Asset 2 (£20,000 – £15,000)	5,000
Total	15,000
Less AEA	(12,300)
Amount subject to capital gains tax	2,700

We will now consider each of the elements of the capital gains tax computation in more detail.

Gross proceeds on disposal

8.9 In general, the proceeds received from an *arm's length* transaction are used when performing a capital gains tax computation. This is where the vendor and purchaser are not *connected* in any way that could affect the price agreed between them i.e. the price is one which two strangers might mutually agree. If the disposal is not 'a bargain at arm's length' the consideration used for the computation will be the market value of the asset at the point of the disposal, regardless of the value of any consideration actually given. The market value is also used if the consideration for the disposal cannot be valued for any reason.

Disposals to connected persons and gifts are assumed to be not at arm's length. Connected persons are generally:

- For an individual – his or her spouse, siblings, direct ancestors, lineal descendants (children) and their spouses. He or she is not, however, considered to be connected for tax purposes to lateral relatives such as uncles, aunts, nephews and nieces.

- Companies are connected to each other if they are under common control. A company is connected to a person if, either alone or with individuals connected to him or her, that person controls it.

Sometimes a taxpayer may try to reduce a CGT liability by disposing of assets piecemeal (ie piece by piece) to connected persons. Where this kind of disposal is made, the disposal proceeds for each transaction is taken to be an equivalent proportion of the value of the total of the assets transferred. Transactions in parts of an asset are generally considered to be linked if they occur within six years of each other.

For example, a majority shareholder of a company may pass their shares on to the next generation in a series of small gifts. If it were not for the above anti-avoidance legislation this might give a lower market value than if the shares were transferred in one single transaction.

There are strict rules for calculating the market value of some assets. When calculating the market value no reduction is made if several assets are sold at the same time. So if a large number of shares are disposed of to a connected person, then no account is taken of any reduction in the share price due to the size of the disposal.

Special rule for quoted securities

The market value of quoted securities is taken to be the lower of:

- The 'quarter-up': the lower of the two prices quoted in the Daily Official List plus a quarter of the difference between the two prices, and
- The 'mid price': half way between the highest and lowest prices at which bargains were recorded on the date of disposal excluding bargains at special prices.

Incidental costs of disposal

8.10   The incidental costs of disposal include fees, commission or remuneration for the professional services of a surveyor, valuer, auctioneer, accountant, legal adviser or agent as well as the cost of transfer or conveyance such as stamp duty. It also includes advertising to find a buyer. It does not, however, include any payment of interest or any cost that is allowed as part of a trading profit computation.

Allowable costs

8.11   Allowable costs include the following:

- The base cost of acquiring the asset – this will usually be the purchase price. However, there are several situations in which some other value will be used. For example, if the asset is inherited rather than bought, the market value at the date of death will be used as the allowable cost. There are other examples which we will consider later on.

- Any incidental costs of acquisition such as legal fees.
- Any capital expenditure incurred in enhancing the asset or establishing, preserving or defending title to, or a right over, the asset. For enhancement expenditure to be allowed the benefits of the expenditure must be reflected in the state or nature of the asset at the time of disposal. There are a number of specific exclusions from this category of allowable expenses. These are the costs of repairs, maintenance and insurance and any expenditure which is either an allowable deduction for income tax purposes or was met by public grants, such as home improvement loans.

Calculation of the capital gains tax liability

8.12 In this section we first discuss the basis of assessment for CGT, then the relevant rates of tax applicable and then briefly deal with losses and transfers of assets between husbands and wives where special rules apply.

Basis of assessment

8.13 For individuals, CGT is charged on the chargeable gains accruing during the year of assessment after the deduction of:

- allowable losses occurring during the year, and
- any allowable losses accruing from a previous year of assessment which have not already been allowed as a deduction from chargeable gains.

A year of assessment for an individual's capital gains tax runs from 6 April to the following 5 April, i.e. just like the income tax year. CGT is charged on a current year basis (i.e. what arises in the year of assessment). Any tax due is payable on the later of the 31 January following the year of assessment and 30 days after the issue of a notice of assessment from HMRC. Hence, for disposals made in the fiscal year 2022/23 the tax will be payable on 31 January, 2024. Since 6 April 2020 the rules for residential property disposals are different however. Any CGT on such disposals are due within 30 days of the disposal.

Rate of tax

8.14 An individual can realise capital gains up to the annual exempt amount (AEA) each year before any CGT liability arises. The AEA is like the personal allowance for income tax i.e. it works as a tax free threshold.

The rate of tax to be applied to net chargeable gains in excess of the AEA depends on the income tax band(s) the gain falls into. It is considered to be, in effect, the very top part of income for purposes of determining what CGT rate to pay.

This means you need to know what the individual's taxable income for income tax is for the tax year. The CGT rate is determined by using the income tax bands. If enough of the basic rate band (£37,500) remains after dealing with non-savings, savings and dividends for income tax to absorb all of the gain, the net capital gain is taxed at 10%. If the taxpayer is already paying income tax at the higher rate (i.e. taxable income is between £37,500 and £150,000) or additional rate (taxable income exceeds £150,000) then it is charged at a rate of 20%. If the taxpayer only paid basic rate tax on their income, but adding the capital gain to the taxpayer's taxable income takes them into the higher rate income tax band, then the part of the gain falling within the remainder of their basic rate band is taxed at 10%, and the rest is taxed at 20%.

Fiscal Fact

The Government estimated that cost to the Exchequer of reducing the rates of capital gains tax to 10% and 20% would be £735million per year by 2020/21. [Source: HM Treasury TIIN on Capital Gains Tax rate changes 16 March 2016]

The 10% and 20% rates, however, do not apply to all disposals of all assets. The sale of residential property (other than a principal private residence – see section 8.26) will be taxed at the old rates of 18%/28%. The same rules apply to land that was associated with a residential property at any time, including where the property has not yet been built (i.e. so called 'off-plan'). In effect there is now an 8% surcharge on the sales of residential property if subject to capital gains tax. The reason given for this in the associated TIIN was that the Government wanted this to motivate investments in companies, not in property.

Activity

Bianca's capital gains, on non-residential properties, after reliefs, are £13,000. What is her capital gains tax liability in 2022/23 if her taxable income, after deducting allowances and reliefs, is:

    a) £17,000
    b) £40,000
    c) £27,000

Feedback

In each case we need to compute what income tax band Bianca would be within once she added the capital gains to her income to determine the relevant rate of capital gains tax to apply.

a) £17,000 taxable income + £13,000 capital gain = £30,000. As this will all fall within the basic rate band for income tax in this tax year, her capital gain can all be taxed at 10%. Her capital gains tax liability will therefore be £1,300 (£13,000 x 10%).

b) £40,000 taxable income means she is a higher rate income taxpayer. All of her capital gains will therefore be taxed at 20%. Her capital gains tax liability will therefore be £2,600 (£13,000 x 20%).

c) £27,000 taxable income + £13,000 capital gain = £40,000. Therefore, part of the gain will be taxed at 10% and part at 20%. Her capital gains tax liability will therefore be:

(£37,500 – £27,000) x 10%	£1,050.00
£13,000 – (£37,500 – £27,000) x 20%	£500.00
	£1,550.00

These rules therefore mean two individuals with the same capital gain, perhaps even from selling the same asset bought on the same date, will pay different rates of CGT depending on taxable income for income tax purposes.

If the house was not her home, Bianca would have had to apply tax rates of 18% and 28%.

Capital losses

8.16   If a taxpayer incurs a capital loss in a year, the loss is first set against any gains for that year. If the taxpayer has an overall net loss for the tax year, ie total losses for the year exceed the total gains, the net loss is carried forward to future fiscal years.

Losses carried forward must be set against the first available gains in future years. In that year any losses for that year are deducted first before any prior year losses brought forward are deducted. However, the use of brought forward losses is restricted to preserve the AEA for that year. Any remaining amounts still not used are then carried forward to the subsequent year.

Allowable losses cannot be carried back except on death – they can only be carried forward.

We can illustrate these rules with the following example:

Activity

Ewan had the following capital gains and losses:

Year	Gain	Loss	AEA for year
	£	£	£
2020/21	4,000	9,000	12,000
2021/22	7,500	3,000	12,300
2022/23	12,600	nil	12,300

Calculate Ewan's net chargeable gain for each year.

Feedback

2020/21	£
Gain	4,000
Loss	(9,000)
Net loss	(5,000)

Ewan's AEA is wasted for this year and the loss of £5,000 is carried forward to the next year.

2021/22	£
Gain	7,500
Loss	(3,000)
Net current year gain	4,500
AEA	(12,300)
Net chargeable gain	nil

Ewan's AEA covers his net current year gain and he pays no capital gains tax in this year. The £5,000 loss carried forward from 2020/21 is carried forward again into 2022/23.

2022/23	£
Gain	12,600
Loss	nil
Net current year gain	12,600
Loss brought forward	(300)
AEA	(12,300)
net chargeable gain	nil

In 2022/23, Ewan has a net chargeable gain of £12,600. The AEA is £12,300. This means that Ewan only has to use £300 of his loss brought forward to make the chargeable gain equal to the AEA. He is then left with £4,700 of the loss to be carried forward into 2023/24.

Note that where a loss arises on the disposal of a chargeable asset to a connected person (using market value as the deemed proceeds), that loss can only be offset against gains on disposals to the same person.

 You can now attempt Quick Quiz questions 1-3.

Special capital gains tax rules

8.16 Now that you are able to calculate the basic CGT charge on a disposal there are some special situations which you need to be able to deal with. These are (1) transfers between husbands and wives and between civil partners, (2) part disposals, (3) chattels and wasting assets, and (4) negligible value claims.

Spouses and civil partners

8.17 CGT gets a little more complicated when it comes to its treatment of spouses and civil partners. For most purposes spouses and civil partners are treated as separate people. They each have the full AEA and each pays tax on their capital gains at either 10% (18%) or 20% (28%) depending on their marginal rate of income tax. As they are treated separately it is not possible for losses to be transferred from one spouse, or civil partner, to the other.

If an asset is jointly owned any chargeable gain, or allowable loss, on disposal to a third party must be split between the husband and wife, or civil partners based on their respective beneficial interest of each in the asset.

Disposals between a husband and wife, or civil partners, living together, however, are treated on a 'no gain or loss' basis. This is done by taking the net proceeds to be the amount that makes the chargeable gain nil, regardless of any consideration paid.

These rules give scope for tax planning. Assets can be transferred between spouses or civil partners before their final disposal to make the best use of the AEA or may enable gains to be taxed at 10 (18)% instead of 20 (28)% if transferred from a higher rate income tax partner to a basic or non-taxable partner. There are also opportunities to maximise the benefit to be obtained from capital losses. We will review tax planning in more detail in Chapter 11, however, to illustrate these ideas, work through the following example.

Activity

Richard and Judy are a married couple. In May 2009, Judy is a higher rate taxpayer who bought a chargeable asset for £10,000 (net of incidental costs of acquisition and on which no further capital expenditure was incurred and which is not residential property), which she gave to Richard in November 2019. Richard sold the asset for £30,000 in March 2023. Calculate the chargeable gain that arises when Richard sold the asset, assuming he had no other chargeable disposals during the year.

Feedback

The transfer from Judy to Richard in November 2019 will be on a no gain/no loss basis. This means Richard is treated as having acquired the asset at the same value as Judy did in May 2009 – i.e. £10,000.

Assuming Richard is a basic rate taxpayer with taxable income of £15,000, when Richard sold the asset:

	£
Proceeds	30,000
Less Deemed cost	(10,000)
Chargeable gain	20,000

Note: Richard has an AEA this year of £12,300. This may mean that this sale attracts CGT of (£20,000 – £12,300) x 10% ie £770.00. The 10% rate applies as the chargeable gain, when added to his taxable income, does not exceed the income tax basic rate band.

This transfer makes sense because Judy is a higher rate taxpayer and therefore would be liable to 20% CGT if she hadn't transferred the asset to Richard first.

Part disposals

8.18 A taxpayer may dispose of all or part of an asset, or a part share in an asset; for example, selling a one-third interest in a race horse. A part disposal may still be a chargeable disposal even if the rest of the asset is still owned by the seller.

A question then arises – how do we work out how much of the cost of the asset belongs to the part that has been disposed of? Suppose an individual buys a large plot of land and then sells a small part of it. It is possible that the large plot is worth more per acre than the part sold. If the taxpayer is simply allowed to apportion allowable costs by reference to the area sold, a lower chargeable gain will arise than if the cost was apportioned according to the market value of the part disposed of and the part retained. Perhaps understandably, the rules require that the allowable costs are allocated according to market values when part disposals are made.

To calculate the portion of the cost that is attributed to the part disposed of, multiply the allowable cost for the entire asset by:

$$\frac{A}{A+B}$$

where A is the value of the part disposed of and B is the market value of the remainder.

In a way this rule is an anti-avoidance measure. Sales of parts of assets will typically be worth less than the aggregate value of all of the parts of an asset sold together. As such, selling parts could produce a lower capital gains bill than selling the whole asset in one transaction.

Activity

Susan gave a third interest in a painting of her great-grandfather, which had been commissioned at a cost of £30,000 in April 1982, to her daughter for her 21st birthday in June 2022. The market value of the third disposed of was estimated to be £20,000. The market value of the remaining two-thirds of the painting was estimated to be £55,000. Calculate Susan's chargeable gain.

Feedback

The allowable cost using market value in June 2022 is:

$$\frac{£20,000}{£20,000 + £55,000} \times £30,000 = 8,000$$

	£
Proceeds (deemed to be market value)	20,000
Less allowable cost	(8,000)
Chargeable gain	12,000

There is a special rule which deals with the part disposal of small areas of land. Where there is a part disposal of land, it will not be treated as a disposal if the taxpayer elects, so long as two conditions apply:

- the total consideration for all disposals of land for the year is not more than £20,000; and
- the consideration for the transfer of this land is not more than one-fifth of the value of the total just before the transfer.

Here, the consideration for disposal is deducted from any allowable expenditure when computing the gain on disposal of the rest of the land.

This special rule can also be used where part of a holding of land is compulsorily acquired, for example by a local government authority, so long as the consideration is small in relation to the market value just before the transfer (in practice, less than 5%).

Chattels

8.19   Chattels are tangible and movable, property. Assets such as cars, paintings and horses are chattels. Securities (intangible) and land (not movable) are not chattels.

A relief is available for all chattels subject to CGT which have a relatively low value. If the proceeds of sale are £6,000 or less, no CGT liability will arise. This is true even if the asset was eligible for capital allowances. If the sale proceeds exceed £6,000 the chargeable gain is equal to the lower of:

- $5/3 \times$ (gross proceeds – £6,000); and
- the gain computed in the usual way.

It is not possible to give a benchmark of when it is no longer worth checking both calculations, and so for relatively low value chattels both calculations will have to be done to be sure which applies.

The following activity illustrates this.

Activity

Jack sold a valuable book in June 2022 for £6,600. He had bought the book for £100 in November 1984 in an antique shop. Calculate the chargeable gain.

Feedback

A book is a chattel, but as the proceeds are more than £6,000 it is not exempt, although the maximum gain calculation can be used to cap any gain.

	£
Proceeds	6,600
Less cost	(100)
Chargeable gain	6,500
$5/3 \times$ (£6,600 – £6,000)	£1,000

The chargeable gain is the lower of £6,500 and £1,000. Hence the chargeable gain will be £1,000.

If a chattel is sold for less than £6,000 any allowable loss is calculated as if the chattel had been sold for £6,000. This will have the effect of reducing or extinguishing the loss, but cannot create a gain.

Wasting chattels

A wasting asset is one with an estimated remaining useful life of 50 years or less. A horse, as an example, is a wasting asset but a painting will probably not be.

Determining whether a chattel is 'wasting' matters because different rules apply to *wasting chattels*. They are usually exempt from CGT. This at first sounds like a generous concession as it could exclude lots of assets from CGT. However, there are two special exceptions we must consider to this general rule. First, you will remember that cars are entirely exempt from CGT anyway. Second, any assets (including plant) used in a trade, profession or vocation that are eligible for capital allowances, are subject to CGT even if they are wasting chattels.

The CGT computation for plant and machinery that are eligible for capital allowances depends on whether a loss arises or not. Capital allowances are not deducted from cost in computing a capital gain. But if a loss arises, the allowable cost is reduced by the lower of the loss and the capital allowances, including any balancing allowance or charge given for the asset. (See the Oliver example below for an illustration of these rules related to fixed plant).

For plant and machinery that is moveable rather than fixed (i.e. it is a chattel), the usual chattel rules apply i.e. there is no chargeable gain if the sale proceeds are £6,000 or less. If the proceeds are more than £6,000, and a gain is made, the rules for all chattels apply as set out above.

Wasting assets other than chattels

8.20 It is possible to have assets that are not chattels, but are wasting because they have a limited life. Examples include intangible assets such as registered designs and copyrights with less than 50 years to run. In such cases the allowable cost is the full original cost of the asset written down over its useful life on a straight line basis.

Note that this rule does not apply to leases, which generally don't lose value evenly over their life. Special rules apply for leases to work out how much of their cost is deductible.

Activity

Stephen sold a registered design, a business asset with a 30 year life and a remaining life of 14 years, for £12,000 in March 2023, which had cost £10,000 in March 2006. Calculate the chargeable gain.

Feedback

The registered design is a wasting asset, and so the acquisition cost must be restricted to reflect the wasting of its value over time. Only the part of the acquisition cost that has not been written off at the time of the disposal will be allowed.

	£
Proceeds	12,000
Allowable cost	
10,000 × 14/30	(4,666)
Chargeable gain	7,334

Capital gains tax may be payable on fixed plant and machinery (i.e. not chattels as they are fixed) that is disposed of. Capital allowances are not deducted from the cost to compute the chargeable gain, because relief will be given under the capital allowance rules.

Activity

In January 2023 Oliver sold fixed, business, plant for £72,000. The plant had cost £25,000 to buy in August 2015. As part of the sale he incurred incidental costs of £2,000. Calculate the chargeable gain/loss. What difference would it make if the plant was sold for £22,000?

Feedback

Since the plant was sold for more than it originally cost, only the £25,000 will be deducted from the capital allowance pool balance (as we described in section 7.20). There is a capital gain of £72,000 – £25,000 – £2,000 = £45,000.

If the plant was sold for £22,000, part of the capital allowances would be recouped by the balancing charge in the capital allowance computation. However, £3,000 of the capital allowances would not be recouped because the sale price (£22,000) is less than the original cost (£25,000) and the CGT calculation would be:

	£
Proceeds	22,000
Incidental sale costs	(2,000)
Original cost	(25,000)
Capital allowances given	(3,000)
Allowable loss	(8,000)

Negligible value claims

8.21 If an asset becomes effectively worthless the taxpayer can make what is called a "negligible value" claim. This means the asset is deemed to be sold at its then market value and immediately re-acquired at the same value. This generates a capital loss which can be relieved in the normal way. The allowable cost on any later disposal then becomes the market value at the date of the negligible value claim, which could lead to a future CGT bill if the value of the asset increases later.

We have now considered the more common special CGT situations which you may come across. However, there are two more important categories of asset that you need to know something about. The first is quoted securities and the second is principal private residences.

Shares and securities

8.22 Special rules are needed for calculating the capital gains on the sale of shares and securities because a taxpayer may undertake many transactions in the same shares and securities and in these cases a *matching problem* may arise. For example, suppose a taxpayer acquires a number of ordinary shares in a company on several different dates. When a disposal occurs it will be necessary to calculate the allowable cost of the shares. As the shares are effectively identical, but will probably have been purchased at different prices, rules are needed to determine which shares are actually being sold. This is much the same problem as arises in the valuation of stock for accounting purposes and many of the same techniques offer possible solutions, for example, First-in, First-out (FIFO), Last-in, First-out (LIFO) and average cost. There are also circumstances when it may be difficult to identify the appropriate allowable costs, for example when rights and bonus issues are made. Since 1985, weighted average cost has been the method used to address these problems.

To work out the cost of shares disposed of, the shares are matched against acquisitions of shares in the same company and of the same class, in the order:

1. any shares acquired on the day of disposal;
2. any shares acquired in the 30 days after the disposal (on a FIFO basis); and finally
3. any shares in what is known as the 's104 pool', which means all shares acquired before the date of disposal.

Capital distributions

8.23 A capital distribution is a repayment of capital to the shareholder and is treated as a part disposal for CGT purposes. Provided it has a value of more than 5% of the value of the shares, then the part disposal rules in 8.18 will apply.

However, if the capital distribution is 5% or less than the value of shares, the distribution can be deducted from the allowable cost of the shares. This effectively defers any gain until a future disposal occurs.

Reorganisations

8.24 During a corporate reorganisation, new shares, and possibly debentures, are exchanged for the original shareholding. If the exchange is for only one class of shares, for example ordinary shares, there is no difficulty. The allowable cost of the original holding becomes the allowable cost of the new holding.

If, however, shares are exchanged for more than one class of shares or securities, such as ordinary shares and debentures, it is necessary to apportion the allowable cost of the original shares to the new holdings. If any of the new shares are quoted on the stock exchange, the allowable cost is split in proportion to their market values on the first day on which they are quoted after the reorganisation.

Takeovers and mergers

8.25 The way in which share exchanges which occur during a takeover or merger are valued is exactly as you might expect from reading the sections on reorganisations and capital distributions.

New shares and securities received in exchange for existing holdings do not lead to a CGT liability. Their allowable cost is derived from the allowable cost of the original holding as described in 8.24 above. If new capital is introduced it becomes an allowable cost. If part of the consideration is in the form of cash, a capital distribution is deemed to have taken place and the procedure described in the section on capital distributions (8.23) is followed.

Private residences and capital gains tax

8.26 An individual's only, or main, residence (termed their *principal private residence* or 'PPR'), including grounds of up to 5,000 square metres, is exempted from capital gains tax provided that he or she has occupied the whole of the residence throughout the period of ownership.

This means that homeowners are in a unique position to become highly geared, with loans of up to 100% (or even more in some cases) of the value of their house. This means that even a small increase in the value of houses could generate a tax-free increase in the value of the owner's equity. This has led to a sense of economic well-being among households who own their own homes when house prices rise. Imagine the impact of applying CGT to principal private residences. Increases in value would no longer be seen as beneficial to the same extent because of the large amount of tax which may be payable.

There is some pressure on the Government to remove this exemption, but this would be very unpopular with voters and therefore unlikely to change in the immediate future.

There are, however, some restrictions to this generous rule that you should be aware of. For example, a husband and wife, or civil partners, can claim only one principal private residence between them. If you own more than one property, and live in them both at any time, you must elect (i.e. tell HMRC in writing) which of them is your principal private residence. The sale of the other property will be subject to CGT under the rules explained below. This implies you can only have a single principal private residence at any one time. You must tell HMRC which is your principal private residence within two years of residing in the second or subsequent property.

Where the taxpayer has not occupied the residence throughout the period of ownership a CGT liability may arise. To calculate the proportion of the gain exempt from CGT multiply the total gain, calculated in the normal way, by:

$$\frac{\text{Period of deemed occupation since 31 March, 1982}}{\text{Total period of ownership since 31 March, 1982}}$$

(Remember that capital gains which arose prior to 31 March, 1982 are not taxable.)

Provided that the residence was the taxpayer's principal private residence at any time during their period of ownership, the final months of ownership are counted as a period of occupation, even if the taxpayer nominates another property to be their principal private residence during this period. This measure is designed to help taxpayers who have moved house and are trying to sell their old house and may otherwise be caught by the CGT rules. From 6 April 2020, this period is 9 months. It was originally 36 months, then from 2016 it was reduced to 18 months, except for people who are disabled or in long-term care.

Fiscal Fact

 The cost of tax revenues foregone to the Exchequer of exempting gains on PPRs is forecast to be a huge £30.2 billion for 2020/21 [Source: HMRC – Structural Relief costs estimates as at December 2021]

There are a number of other occasions when a period of absence can be treated as a period of deemed occupation provided that the property both before and after the period of absence (although not necessarily immediately before or immediately after) was occupied as the taxpayer's principal private residence. The periods of deemed occupation are not affected if the property is actually rented to tenants.

The periods of deemed occupation are:

- any periods of absence totalling up to three years;
- any periods during which the taxpayer was required to live abroad in order to fulfil employment duties; and
- any periods totalling up to four years during which the taxpayer was required to work elsewhere in the UK for employment purposes.

Strictly, therefore, each period of absence should be followed by a period of occupation. However, if a taxpayer's employment requires him or her to work in the UK immediately followed by a period of working abroad or vice versa, the periods will still be allowed as periods of deemed occupation.

To try and make these complicated rules somewhat clearer we will illustrate them with the following example.

Activity

John bought a house on 1 April, 1995 for £45,000. He lived in the house until 30 June, 1997 when he obtained work in another part of the country. The house was let until he returned on 1 April, 2001. On 1 May, 2006 he went to work abroad until 1 May, 2011 when he returned to the UK and moved into his friend's house. John's house was sold on 1 January, 2023 for £320,000. John incurred fees and costs of £5,000 relating to the sale.

Feedback

It is first necessary to calculate the proportions of exempt and chargeable months for the period of ownership since 1 April, 1995. The total period of ownership is 333 months (27 years 9 months from 1 April 1995 to 1 January 2023).

Period	Exempt months	Chargeable months
1/4/95–30/6/97 (occupied)	27	0
1/7/97–31/3/01 (working away (in UK) <4 years)	45	0
1/4/01–30/4/06 (occupied)	61	0
1/5/06–31/3/22 (see below)	0	191
1/4/22–1/1/23 (final 9 months)	9	0
	142	191

The period from 1 May, 2006 to 31 March, 2022 is not exempt because the absence was not followed by a period of owner occupation. Had John re-occupied the house after this period instead of moving in with his friend, even if only for a short time, the period from 1 May, 2006 to when he moved out would also have been exempted under the working away rules, and the normal principal private residence exemption.

Now the chargeable gain can be calculated:

	£
Gross proceeds	320,000
Incidental costs of disposal	(5,000)
Net proceeds	315,000
Less allowable cost	(45,000)
Gain	270,000
Private residence exemption:	
142/333 × 170,000	(72,492)
Chargeable gain	197,508

Remember, this chargeable gain will be taxed at either 18% or 28% depending on John's income tax band as this is the sale of a residential property for the periods when it was not his main home – i.e. the 8% surcharge applies.

Taxpayers living in job-related accommodation will be able to claim any residence which they own as a principal private residence provided that they intend to occupy it as their main residence in due course. (See 5.27 for a definition of job-related accommodation).

Lettings

8.27 If a lodger (someone who rents a room in a house) lives with a family, sharing living accommodation and eating with them, there is no liability to CGT when disposing of the residence because of this. Principal private residence exemption may extend to gains which relate to the period of letting where the owner occupies part of the property and part of the property is let.

The relief available is the lowest of:

- the gain accruing during the letting period;
- £40,000; and
- the total gain which is exempt under the principal private residence provisions. However, this relief cannot turn a gain into an allowable loss for CGT purposes.

Business use

8.28 If part of the residence is used wholly for business purposes, then any gain which is attributable to that part is taxable. This is an important point to bear in mind when deciding whether to claim that part of a residence is used for business purposes, perhaps an office or a workshop. In the short term it may be possible to set some expenses against income for income tax purposes but it may give rise to a substantial liability for capital gains tax purposes in the future if that use is claimed to be exclusively for business purposes.

 You can now attempt Quick Quiz questions 4 – 7 and Full Questions 1 & 2.

Reliefs from capital gains tax

8.29 At the start of this chapter we discussed how CGT is largely intended to help create a fairer tax system and to reduce the incentives to artificially create a capital receipt to reduce the tax payable on the transaction. However, there are a number of situations when relief is available to mitigate the impact of CGT.

In this section we will look at five types of relief. The first three, Business Asset relief, Incorporation Relief and Gift Relief, all provide for a deferral of the capital gains tax liability, that is they affect the timing of payment rather than the amount to be paid. The fourth relief, Business Asset Disposal Relief, actually reduces the amount of CGT payable as does the fifth, Investor's Relief.

We will now consider each of these reliefs in more detail, in turn.

Business Asset Rollover relief

8.30 Businesses often sell an asset intending to replace it. For example, a business may move to new premises; sell the existing land and buildings they own and purchase the new property. Rollover relief, which defers CGT due, may be available if the proceeds from a sale of business assets are invested in new business assets. You may consider this to be entirely reasonable since, although a liability to CGT has arisen because of the sale, the business is clearly no better off than they were just before they sold the property and may need the money raised from the sale to buy the new asset. The taxpayer has simply exchanged one asset for another.

Favourable tax treatment in this situation will encourage a business to reinvest their money into other businesses assets rather than to take it out of the economy. This is arguably good for an entrepreneurial society.

If the consideration received for the disposal of certain capital assets is used, by the taxpayer, to acquire other specified capital assets, then rollover relief is available. This will result in neither a gain nor a loss on disposal, but the allowable cost of the new asset is then reduced by the amount of the gain on the old asset. This way the new asset absorbs the gain from the old asset until it is disposed of later. Both the old and the new assets must be used solely for the purpose of trade and also must fall into one of the following classes (Note: it does not matter if they fall into different categories.):

Class 1: any land or building or part of a building used only for the purpose of trade and fixed plant or machinery which does not form part of a building (but fixed plant and machinery is subject to holdover relief rather than rollover – see below)

Class 2: ships, aircraft and hovercraft

Class 3: satellites, space stations and spacecraft

Class 4: goodwill

Class 5: milk quotas and potato quotas

Class 6: ewe and suckler cow premium quotas.

Class 7: fish quota

Class 8: Lloyds syndicate rights

Note that for Class 1 above, it can sometimes be difficult to decide whether plant and machinery is 'fixed'. Moveable items cannot usually be treated as 'fixed' plant and machinery for this purpose, but there have been some interesting cases on this question. It is one of the many areas of tax law that is the subject of considerable dispute.

In order to claim the relief, the new asset must be acquired between 12 months before and three years after the disposal of the old asset. It is not necessary for the old and new asset to be used in the same business, just that they belong to the same taxpayer.

If the total proceeds from the sale of the old asset are reinvested in the new asset, then full relief is given. However, if some of the proceeds are not reinvested then a chargeable gain equal to the lower of the chargeable gain before rollover relief and the amount which has not been reinvested will be subject to capital gains tax immediately.

Activity

Mike bought a ship in March 2007 for £500,000 and sold it for £1,000,000 in September 2017. He bought a factory in November 2017 for £850,000. Both assets are or were used in his trade. Determine any chargeable gain that arises on the sale of the ship assuming that rollover relief is claimed and compute the chargeable gain arising when Mike sells the factory in June 2022 for £1.5 million.

Feedback

Disposal of ship	£
Proceeds	1,000,000
Less allowable cost	(500,000)
Chargeable gain	500,000

Less amount not reinvested	
£1,000,000 – £850,000	(150,000)
Gain eligible to be rolled over	350,000

The chargeable gain is £150,000 as this is the amount not re-invested and is lower than the gain calculated (£500,000). This gain will be liable for capital gains tax in the 2017/18 year.

Base cost of the factory:	£
Cost	850,000
Less rolled over gain	(350,000)
Base cost of the factory	500,000

Disposal of factory June 2021	£
Proceeds	1,500,000
Less allowable cost	(500,000)
Chargeable gain (2022/23)	1,000,000

Holdover relief

8.31 Rollover relief cannot be claimed if the replacement asset is depreciable. This means either the asset is:

- Fixed plant and machinery; or
- If it is, or within the next 10 years will become, a wasting asset. Remember that a wasting asset has a life of 50 years or less and so this rule will apply to any replacement asset with a life of 60 years or less.

In these cases, rather than rollover relief, we use another form of relief called holdover relief.

Holdover relief is given by reducing the amount of the chargeable gain according to the amount reinvested as we did with rollover relief, but instead of using the gain to reduce the cost of the new asset until it is finally sold, the gain is instead 'held over' until it crystallises, at which time it becomes chargeable.

The held-over gain becomes a chargeable gain on the earlier of:

- the date on which the taxpayer disposes of the replacement asset;
- the date on which the replacement asset ceases to be used for the purposes of a trade carried on by the taxpayer; or
- ten years after the date of the acquisition of the replacement asset.

If, before the held-over gain crystallised, the replacement asset is itself replaced by an asset which is not a depreciating asset then some or all of the held-over gain can be transferred to the new asset.

Activity

May bought a workshop in February 2014 for £25,000 and ran a business making and selling soft furnishings. In July 2018 she sold the workshop for £40,000 and in August 2018 she bought fixed plant for £50,000 to use in the new premises she was renting. In January 2021 May bought a new workshop for £35,000 and in October 2022 she sold the fixed plant for £80,000. Determine May's chargeable gains on each of the transactions, assuming that holdover/rollover relief is claimed where appropriate.

Feedback

July 2018 disposal:	£
Proceeds	40,000
Less allowable costs	(25,000)
Chargeable gain	15,000

The entire proceeds of £40,000 can be considered to have been reinvested in plant within the time period allowed, and so the £15,000 gain can be held over and no chargeable gain arises from the first transaction.

January 2021 purchase:

When the new workshop (not a depreciating asset) was bought part of the held-over gain from the first workshop could be rolled over to the new workshop because this asset was still bought within 3 years of the original workshop disposal. Rolled-over gains can be held indefinitely as long as the new asset is owned and as such is a better place to have the gain attached to than the plant. May is probably better off moving as much of the held-over gain (£15,000) as she can onto the new workshop.

	£
Total gain held over	15,000
Less proceeds not reinvested	
40,000 – 35,000	(5,000)
Gain eligible to be rolled over	10,000

The base cost of the new workshop would be £25,000 (£35,000 – £10,000). The £5,000 not eligible to be rolled over can continue to be held over until the charge crystallises.

October 2022 disposal of plant:

	£
Proceeds	80,000
Less cost	(50,000)
Chargeable gain	30,000

The remaining held-over gain of £5,000 crystallises as a result of the disposal of the fixed plant and will be chargeable in 2022/23.

Incorporation relief

8.32   A form of rollover relief is also available where an unincorporated business and all its assets (other than cash) are transferred to a company in exchange for shares in that new company. This relief is referred to as incorporation relief. It is automatically applied although the taxpayer can elect for it not to apply, for example to use up allowances that may otherwise be lost. The election must be no later than the second anniversary of the 31 January following the tax year in which the transfer occurs.

The relief works by deducting any chargeable gains from the disposal of business assets from the value of the shares received and the company is treated as receiving the assets at their market value. The relief only applies if the business is transferred to the company as a going concern, ie an operating business.

Activity

Zigmund decides to incorporate the business he has operated for a number of years as a sole trader. He transfers the business to the company as a going concern, and there is a chargeable gain of £75,000 for the business assets transferred. The market value of the shares in the new company is £200,000. What is the effect of incorporation relief on this transaction?

Feedback

The gain on the business assets is rolled over by reducing the value of the shares, so that their cost becomes £125,000 (200,000 – 75,000). This means that when Zigmund later sells the shares, the gain will crystallise at that time.

If only part of the consideration given by the company for the business is in the form of shares, for example part of the price is paid in cash, then only a proportion of the chargeable gain can be rolled over in this way and deducted from the value of the shares, based on the market value of the shares compared to the total consideration for the transfer of the business.

Gift relief

8.33 If a taxpayer makes a chargeable disposal for less than the market value of the asset (e.g. as a gift) then, providing both the donor and the beneficiary make an election, and provided the asset qualifies (see below), some or all of the chargeable gain can be deferred and transferred to the beneficiary by means of gift relief. This enables assets to be passed from one generation to the next without a capital gains tax liability arising and hence the name gift relief.

Gift relief only applies to qualifying assets, which means:

- it is, or is an interest in, an asset used for the purposes of a trade, profession or vocation carried on by:
  - the transferor, or
  - his or her personal company, or
  - a member of a trading group of which the holding company is his or her personal company or
- it is shares or securities of a trading company, or of the holding company of a trading group, and either:
  - the shares are not listed on a recognised stock exchange, or
  - the trading or holding company is the transferor's personal company.

If this election is made, the donee (recipient) is deemed to acquire the asset at its market value less the gain which would otherwise have arisen. This is referred to as a held-over gain.

Activity

Joe runs an IT firm. In October 2022 Joe decides to gift to his daughter, Lorna, the goodwill in the business. This was valued at £150,000 in April 2001 when Joe bought the business and its market value in October 2022 was £450,000. Both parties elect to treat the gift under the gift relief rules. How much of the gain qualifies for gift relief, and what will be the base cost of the goodwill for Lorna after the relief is applied?

Feedback

First, the chargeable gain without any relief needs to be computed for Joe. This will be £300,000 (£450,000 − £150,000). If gift relief is claimed, Joe has no CGT liability to deal with at the point of the transfer and this sum reduces the allowable cost of the asset in Lorna's hands to £150,000 (£450,000 − £300,000). In effect, the gain is transferred to Lorna to pay tax on when she disposes of the goodwill in the future.

If the donee pays consideration in excess of the donor's allowable costs, the relief is restricted to the amount of the gain less the excess proceeds, ie the amount received. This is illustrated in the next activity.

Activity

Alan sold the goodwill of a small paper recycling business to his daughter Sarah on 30 May 2011. The goodwill had a market value of £300,000 but Alan sold it to Sarah for £100,000 and both claimed gift relief. Alan had bought the goodwill in May 2001 for £50,000. Sarah intends to sell the business in May 2023 and believes that she will be able to obtain a price of £400,000. Determine Alan's chargeable gain and advise Sarah on the amount of any chargeable gain if she sells as planned.

Feedback

	£
Alan	
Deemed proceeds	300,000
Less allowable cost	(50,000)
	250,000
Less gain held over	
£250,000 – (£100,000 – £50,000)	(200,000)
Chargeable gain	50,000
Sarah – if sold in May 2023	
Proceeds	400,000
Less allowable cost (£300,000 – £200,000)	(100,000)
Chargeable gain	300,000

Alan's chargeable gain is £50,000, while Sarah's chargeable gain will be £300,000 if she sells the business as planned.

If the taxpayer makes a disposal by way of a gift to a charity or for national purposes, or for a consideration which would give rise to an allowable loss, then the disposal and acquisition is treated as being made for a consideration that results in neither a gain nor a loss on the disposal. The recipient of the asset is deemed to have acquired the asset at the same time and for the same consideration as the donor of the gift.

A gift is for national purposes if it is made to the National Gallery, British Museum or National Trust or to a university, among others.

It should be noted that no gift relief is available for any transfers of shares or securities to a company by individuals or trustees.

If an individual gifts shares in a company to another person, however, an apportionment calculation must be done as only gains related to chargeable business assets are eligible for gift relief. Any sum represented by non-eligible assets (for gift relief), like investments held by the company whose shares are being gifted, become chargeable instead on the transferor.

Business asset disposal relief

8.34 This relief was originally called entrepreneurs' relief and was introduced to complement the CGT reforms introduced in 2008 (i.e. the abolition of taper relief for individuals, replaced by a flat 18% tax rate). It was introduced following public concern that the changes to the rate of CGT would be detrimental to people selling all or part of a business as a going concern, or on cessation of the business, particularly as many small business owners treat the increase in goodwill which they will realise on sale of their business as a form of retirement provision.

Where individuals involved in running a business dispose of all or part of that business and make a gain on the disposal, the first £1million of gains that qualify for the relief will be charged to capital gains tax at a simple, fixed rate of 10%,. Any excess gain over the £1million limit is taxed at normal CGT rates (i.e. likely to be 20%).

This lifetime limit has been changed several times since the relief was introduced; initially it was £1million until 5 April 2010, then £2million for disposals 6 April 2010 to 22 June 2010, £5million for the rest of 2010/11, £10 million from 1 April 2011 and has recently been reduced to £1million for disposals after 11 March 2020.

Because this is a lifetime limit, a taxpayer may be able to make several claims until this total is reached.

The relief also applies to gains which arise on the disposal of shares in a trading company, providing that the individual making the disposal has been an officer or employee of the company and owns at least 5% of the ordinary share capital of the company. From 6 April 2019 there is a minimum holding period of 24 months, up from 12 months before that time.

In 2015, a restriction was introduced for gains arising from the transfer of goodwill to a limited company that is related to the claimant. It does not apply if less than 5% of the shares and voting rights in the acquiring company were held by the individual disposing of the asset.

Activity

Bethan is a higher rate taxpayer who sold a business that she had run for 10 years. The chargeable gains are agreed to be £15,750,000. Bethan has not made an business asset disposal relief claim previously and has no other chargeable gains or losses for the year. What will be her capital gains tax liability?

Feedback

	£
Total chargeable gain	15,750,000
less Business Asset Disposal relief	(1,000,000)
less AEA	(12,300)
Chargeable gain	14,737,700
Tax @ 20%	2,947,540
Tax @ 10% on 1,000,000	100,000
Total tax	3,047,540

Without the benefit of Business Asset disposal relief, Bethan would have to pay £3,147,540 in CGT.

Investors' relief

8.35 In 2016 a new relief was introduced related to new shares issued to external investors (i.e. not employees or directors of the business) with new money (i.e. not recycling money already invested in the company) in unlisted trading companies or their holding companies. Where new shares are issued in such companies after 18 March 2016, held for at least three years from 6 April 2016, and held for three continuous years prior to the disposal, then the gain from the disposal of the shares qualify for 'investors' relief', which is an additional relief subject to a £10 million limit.

You can now attempt Quick Quiz questions 8 – 10 and Full questions 3 - 5.

Stamp duty

8.36 Stamp duty was introduced into the UK in 1694, and is therefore one of the oldest taxes still in existence in this country. Stamp duty is a tax on transactions, imposed when certain types of property changes hands. As such it can therefore be thought of as a capital tax in the same category of taxes as CGT.

Stamp duty was charged on a wide variety of documents when first introduced. These included insurance policies, documents in court proceedings, grants of honour, grants of probate (wills) and letters of administration.

Stamp duty is now administered in the UK by HMRC through various Stamp Duty offices that can be found throughout the UK.

Payment of stamp duty used to be denoted by affixing a stamp to the transfer document or receipt which is the subject of the duty. With the introduction of Stamp Duty Land Tax (SDLT) in 2003, conveyancing can be done electronically,. Stamp duty is calculated at either a flat rate or *ad valorem* i.e. varying according to the value of the transaction to which it relates.

Property transactions

8.37 The most common form of stamp duty now is SDLT on transfers of property (land and buildings), both residential and non-residential/commercial, and on share transactions. It is always payable by the purchaser in a transaction to which it applies.

Under the previous stamp duty regime, transactions were sometimes structured to avoid or reduce payment of stamp duty and the government was concerned that this was interfering with commercial decision making. A major 2003 reform of stamp duty on land and buildings closed a number of loopholes and reduced some distortions in the old system.

SDLT applies to all land transactions. This includes the purchase of freehold land as well as the acquisition of an existing lease. The only exemptions to this are the sales of school owned land and of zero carbon homes (on the first £500,000 of purchase price only in the latter case) from 2007.

Fiscal Fact

The estimated cost of exemption for first time buyers is £430m for 2020-21 (HMRC - Non-structural relief cost estimates, December 2021).

The act of entering into a contract to purchase land is not enough to be considered a land transaction (i.e. what is called an 'exchange' in house purchase terms) rather it is generally 'completion' or the point at which possession transfers that is important. As the date of completion normally occurs immediately before possession is allowed, this will normally be the date of the transaction for SDLT.

The rates of tax on transfers of property vary from 0% to 15%. The table below shows you how the property related stamp duty rates apply in the UK. For residential properties, prior to December 2014, as soon as the value of the property transferred crossed a boundary, all of the transaction was taxed at the higher rate, not just the excess over the lower band. This 'slab' system was modified in 2014 to a 'slice' system where the tax is paid on increasing portions of the value of the property. This move to a 'slice' system applies to non-residential property and land transactions from 2016.

Fiscal Fact

The change of the rules for SDLT on non-residential property and land to a 'slice' basis from a 'slab' basis in March 2016 was estimated to produce more than £1billion in tax revenue for the Government each year according to the Budget 2016 summary of impact assessments.

The rates of SDLT vary depending on whether the purchaser is a natural person (an individual) or a non-natural person such as a company (for simplicity we use the term 'company' in this section to cover all types of non-natural entities).

In a move that angered many landlords, Finance Act 2016 also introduced an 'additional property supplement' to SDLT on purchases of buy-to-let residential property (but not for non-residential property). A 3% surcharge applies for all such property purchases over the £40,000 minimum limit. Note that a 'multiple dwellings relief' is available so that the surcharge does not apply if more than six properties are purchased in the same transaction.

The rates can be found in Appendix A, and you will see that they range from 0% to 15% with differences between residential properties and non-residential properties. For residential properties, there is also a difference between buy to let properties that are rented out to tenants, and properties that are not buy to let. When calculating SDLT therefore, you need to be careful about the various categories of property to make sure you are using the correct rates.

Since 2017, special rules are in place for first time buyers so that there is no SDLT for properties valued at up to £300,000, then 5% up to £500,000. This only applies to properties purchased for the first-time buyers only (or main) residence, i.e. it does not apply to buy-to-let purchases.

Activity

(a) Rhona enters into a contract in January 2023 to buy a residential house for her to live in, not in a disadvantaged area, for £243,000. How much SDLT will she have to pay on completion?

(b) What if this sale falls through and instead Rhona buys a house for £252,000. How much SDLT will now be due on completion?

(c) What if the second property was instead bought as a buy-to-let rather than for her to live in?

(d) What would the difference be in (a) – (c) if Rhona was a first-time buyer?

Feedback

(a) The house is in the 2% band and so she will have to pay
(£243,000 - £125,000) × 2% = £2,360 in SDLT.

(b) The second house is in the 3% band she will have to pay:

(£250,000 - £125,000) x 2%	£2,500
(£252,000 - £250,000) x 5%	£100
Total	£2,600

(c) As this is a buy-to-let property the new additional rates apply to increase the SDLT for each band by 3% so she will have to pay:

(£125,000 - £40,000) x 3%	£2,550
(£250,000 - £125,000) x 5%	£6,250
(£252,000 - £250,000) x 8%	£160
Total	£8,960

(d) If Rhona is a first-time buyer there would be no SDLT if Rhona purchased House (a) or House (b) as they are below £300,000. There would be no first-time buyer SDLT reduction if Rhona purchased a buy-to-let property like House (c)

Special rules for companies

8.38   From 2014 SDLT is charged at 15% on residential dwellings costing more than £500,000 purchased by companies. Prior to this, the threshold for this 15% rate was £2million. There are exclusions from this special rate for property rental businesses, property developers and traders, properties that are made available to the public, dwellings occupied by employees and farmhouses.

This higher level of SDLT for companies buying expensive UK-based property is a direct attempt by the Government to reduce the avoidance of this tax by those buying property through overseas companies that otherwise escaped the need to pay this tax.

Leases

8.39   When a new residential property has a substantial annual rent, SDLT is payable on both the lease premium (if any) and the net present value of the rent payable over the life of the lease.

The SDLT on the lease premium is the same as for SDLT on residential property purchases. The SDLT for new residential leasehold properties is 0% up to £125,000 and 1% on the excess over £125,000.

Where the property is non-residential, for example shops, offices and agricultural land, the SDLT on the premium is the same as for a freehold purchase.

For new leases on non-residential property the SDLT on the net present value of the rent is 0% up to £150,000 and 1% on the excess up to rents with net present value of £5million. From 2016 a higher SDLT rate of 2% is charged for those with net present values exceeding £5million.

As with all SDLT, these measures do not apply in Scotland where a different tax (LBTT) applies to similar transactions under its devolved tax powers (see 8.40) and only applied in Wales until 2018 when it also introduced its own SDLT style rules.

Activity

Lewis is granted a 15 year lease over a warehouse building which is not in a disadvantaged area. He pays a premium of £50,000 and the net present value of the rent is £190,000. How much SDLT will he have to pay?

Feedback

	£
On the premium £50,000 × 1%	500
On the rental 1% × (190,000 – 150,000)	400
Total	900

Scottish Land and Buildings Transactions Tax

8.40   Following the devolution of taxing powers to the Scottish Parliament, from 1 April 2015, instead of SDLT a different tax, the land and buildings transaction tax (LBTT) applies to property in Scotland. This tax is similar to SDLT and applies to 'slices' of with slightly different rates, which you can find in Appendix A.

The tax is administered by Revenue Scotland, a new government body set up to administer all Scottish devolved taxes.

Welsh Land Transactions Tax

8.41 From 1 April 2018 stamp duty land tax no longer applies in Wales. Like Scotland, the devolved government has introduced a new tax, the land transactions tax (LTT). The tax is administered by the Welsh Revenue Authority (WRA). The tax is payable when buildings or land is purchased or leased, and is broadly consistent with SDLT. The rates of Welsh LTT are given in Appendix A.

Additional Property/Dwelling Supplement

8.42   From 1 April 2016 additional rates apply to all SDLT and LBTT rates where the purchase is related to an 'additional' residential property. This is called the 'additional property supplement' for SDLT and Welsh LTT and the 'additional dwelling supplement' for Scottish LBTT but the same 3% supplement rate applies to all the standard rates for each SDLT and LBTT property value 'slice' (see tables above).

Who pays these additional rates? Broadly this is:

(a)   Companies and funds (i.e. 'non-natural' persons) when buying residential properties for values more than £40,000 always pay the additional rates;

(b)   Individuals holding large property portfolios – when buying residential properties for values more than £40,000 will always pay the additional rates unless the new property is replacing their main residence, or does so within 36 months;

(c)   Other individuals – buying (or leasing) properties for more than £40,000 (and at least seven years if a lease) if at the end of the day on which the purchase/lease transaction occurs the person buying, their spouse or civil partners, or any minor child of the purchaser/lessor (under the age of 18) have ownership interests in more than one residential property.

Overseas properties, or properties held in other parts of the UK, are also included in this count of residential properties owned for determining if additional rate applies if those properties are valued more than £40,000.

The rule for individuals is relaxed, however, if the property being purchased or leased is to become their main residence. It does not matter how many other properties they own for this exemption to apply. Proving that a property is a main residence is based on matters of fact (where you are registered to vote, where your children go to school if you have children etc.), not on the basis of an election, unlike the CGT rules for property transactions (see Section 8.26). This will work by payment being made at the additional rate when the new property is acquired, but where evidence is subsequently presented to show that this new property has become the main residence, a rebate of the supplement amount paid will be made. The current residence must be sold within 36 months of the purchase of the new one for this rebate to be payable.

Purchases of furnished holiday lettings also fall within these new rules as with any buy-to-let properties. However, the Government believes 90% of residential property transactions will be unaffected by these new rules. However, other forms of property you can live in (for example, caravans, mobile homes, timeshares and house boats) are excluded from these rules entirely. Accommodation provided by an employer is also not included within these rules.

Further, where less than 50% of a property is inherited the recipient is eligible for a rebate of the supplement if sold within 36 months of their inheritance, where this is not the only residential property owned by the person inheriting. Where larger shares in a property are inherited, or where sales do not complete within 36 months irrespective of the shareholding, these will be caught by these new supplement rate rules and no rebate will be paid.

Annual Tax on Enveloped Dwellings

8.43 An annual tax was introduced from 1 April 2013, designed to provide a disincentive to holding expensive UK residential property through a company or other non-natural entity. Liability to ATED arises where a company has a 'single-dwelling interest' in a dwelling worth £2million as at 1 April 2012. This is a freestanding tax, and so is not superseded by the Scottish LBTT as SDLT is.

A 'dwelling' includes the garden or grounds that go with the dwelling buildings. Where a company holds an interest in more than one dwelling, the interest is apportioned for ATED purposes and each interest in a single dwelling is treated as a separate chargeable interest, there is no aggregation.

ATED is chargeable for any day when the value of the single dwelling interest exceeds the threshold, unless any of the reliefs apply.

The flat rate of tax currently ranges from £3,700 to £237,400 depending on the value of the property and you can find the rates in Appendix A.

Prior to 1 April 2016, only properties valued at more than £1million were liable for ATED. From that date, a new lower rate was added. Properties worth between £500,000 and £1million are now charged at £3,700.

An ATED return and payment are due by 30 April, i.e. for the ATED period 1 April 2022 to 31 March 2023, both the return and payment are due by 30 April 2023.

If residential property which has been subject to ATED is disposed of, some or all the capital gains will be 'ATED related'. A special tax return is required for ATED related capital gains which is separate from the usual capital gains tax return. The general CGT rule that liability only arises if a person is a UK tax resident, does not apply for ATED related gains. CGT is charged under these rules on ATED related gains at 28% (i.e. they are not reduced by the 2016 changes to capital gains tax rates).

The ATED related CGT charge takes into account the ATED bands that apply for 2015 and 2016. Properties within the £1million to £2million bracket were rebased to 6 April 2015, and those within the £500,000 to £1million band were rebased to 6 April 2016.

Share transactions

8.44 The other main area to which UK Stamp Duty is applied is transactions in shares. When shares are purchased using a stock transfer form, stamp duty is payable at 0.5%, rounded up to the nearest £5 above.

Transactions with a purchase price of less than £1,000 are exempt from stamp duty, with effect from April 2008.

When you buy shares through a stockbroker, it will usually be a paperless (electronic) transaction. In this situation, Stamp Duty Reserve Tax (SDRT) is paid at a flat rate of 0.5% of the amount paid for the shares.

From 28 April 2014, stamp duty is no longer chargeable on transactions in eligible securities on London Stock Exchange's AIM or High Growth Segment.

Administration

8.45 Payment of stamp duty on share transactions is made by taking, or sending, the documents to be stamped to a Stamp Duty office. These offices can be found in various UK cities. Documents that need stamping should be presented to one of these offices within 30 days of the transaction occurring. If you are late making this presentation for payment you have to pay charges and interest as a penalty. The maximum penalty is an amount equivalent to the duty, or £300, whichever is less. This becomes a minimum of £300 if your presentation for payment is more than a year late. Interest is charged on overdue payments at normal official rates in addition to this penalty.

For property transactions, a self assessment system is now in operation that requires the purchaser to send HMRC a return notifying them of the completion of a taxable transaction within 30 days of the effective date of the transaction. The tax due should accompany this notification. Failure to submit a return and/or pay the tax due results in similar interest and penalty charges or legal proceedings that are linked with the self assessment procedures for other taxes, such as income tax.

Inheritance tax

8.46 Inheritance tax in its current form was introduced in 1986. A tax on the transfer of property on death has, however, been part of the UK tax landscape in some form or another since the eighteenth century. Like CGT and stamp duty it is a further example of a capital tax in operation in the UK at present as it related to capital transfers (i.e. to inheritances in this case).

An inheritance tax liability will arise when a chargeable person makes a transfer of value of chargeable property. Let's consider these terms further:

- *Chargeable person.* Inheritance tax only applies to individuals and not to companies. All individuals are potentially liable for inheritance tax, for UK domiciled persons on all chargeable property wherever it is located, and for non-UK domiciled persons on UK-situated property only. (See Chapter 12 for an explanation of the concept of domicile for tax purposes). There is an exemption for those who die while on active military service and emergency service and humanitarian aid workers killed in the course of duty.

- *Chargeable property.* All property is potentially chargeable to inheritance tax, although there are some exemptions or exclusions which we will consider briefly below - see the website chapter for full details.

- *Transfer of value.* The key trigger for inheritance tax to arise is a transfer of value between its current 'owner' and the person or entity to whom it is being given. This does not always just arise on an individual's death however. A transfer of value is essentially a gift of an asset by a chargeable person which results in a decrease in the value of that person's estate (total net worth). Usually the decrease in value we consider for inheritance tax purposes will be the open market value of the property at the time of its transfer. Some transfers, or dispositions, are not caught by the inheritance tax net however, including genuine commercial activities and those that are allowable expenses for income tax or corporation tax purposes. Also excluded are dispositions for the maintenance of the transferor's family.

Lifetime transfers

8.47 There are three types of transfer made during the lifetime of an individual:

- *Exempt transfers:* These include certain gifts, for example, between spouses or to charities, small gifts (you can give up to £250 as single gifts to as many people as you want in the year with no IHT implications) and those within the annual exemption, currently £3,000 per annum. You can also make gifts out of any 'excess income' (i.e. income you may receive in a year that is over and above reasonable costs incurred in living normally). No inheritance tax is payable on any of these gifts either during the transferor's lifetime or on death. Unused parts of the annual £3,000 exemption can be carried forward one year (only) so that the maximum annual exemption based gift can be as much as £6,000 if nothing was given in the previous year.

- *Potentially exempt transfers* (PETs): These are gifts to another individual or certain types of trust. No inheritance tax is payable during the lifetime of the transferor, however, some tax will be payable if he or she dies within seven years of the transfer.

- *Chargeable Lifetime Transfers* (CLTs): These are mainly gifts to discretionary trusts. Here lifetime inheritance tax is payable at a rate of 20%, and if the transferor dies within seven years of the transfer, another 20% becomes payable to bring the rate up to the full inheritance tax rate of 40%.

Payment of inheritance tax on lifetime transfers depends on when the transfer is made. For transfers made after 5 April and before 1 October in any year, payment is required by 30 April of the following year. Where the transfer is made after 30 September and before 6 April in any year, payment is required within six months of the end of the month in which the transfer is made.

Inheritance tax payable on death

8.48 When an individual dies, inheritance tax is calculated at the rate then applicable, currently 40%, subject to a nil rate band of £325,000 for the current tax year (unchanged from 2011/12). The nil rate band is applied first against lifetime transfers, i.e. CLTs and PETs which were made in the preceding seven years. Any remaining nil rate band after lifetime transfers have been considered then reduces the value of the total estate left at the point of death. The remainder of the estate after all the nil-rate band has been used up is taxed at 40%.

Since 2012, a reduction in this rate to 36% can be applied if 10% or more of the estate is left to charity.

Inheritance tax payable on death transfers is due six months after the end of the month in which the death occurs.

Married couples and civil partners are allowed to share their nil-rate bands so that any unused sums from these bands on the first partner's death can be added to the surviving partner's nil-rate band for when they die.

When a residence forms part of the estate passed on death to direct descendants (i.e. to children, grandchildren etc.) – a so called 'family home allowance' of £175,000 is available. As this extra nil-rate threshold is potentially available to both partners in a couple if the family home is owned between them, and worth more than £350,000 (i.e. 2 × £175,000), this will raise the overall combined inheritance nil-rate threshold they could get on the second death to £1million (i.e. £325,000 + £175,000 for each of the two partners). Properties worth more than £2million when sold however, will be subjected to a claw-back of this extra family home allowance, at the rate of £1 for every £2 the home is sold for over the £2million limit, back to the standard £325,000 limit.

Fiscal Fact

Despite the fact the published rate of inheritance tax is 40%, HMRC estimates that only 6% of value bequeathed in the UK is taxable due to the use of tax planning and the effect of the threshold; 94% of all estate value therefore is not subject to IHT. The estimated number of taxpaying estates in 2021/22 is 37,000, paying in total £5.2 billion in IHT in cash and other assets. [Source: HMRC Receipts & Number of taxpayers and registered traders]

Business and agricultural property relief

8.49 Special relief applies to agricultural (farmland) and business property so that they do not have to be sold in order to pay any inheritance tax due on transfer of an on-going business. Property which qualifies for business property relief includes unincorporated businesses and shares in unquoted companies, so long as they have been owned for at least two years prior to the transfer.

See the website for a supplementary chapter on Inheritance Tax that provides more detail on how this part of the UK tax system works, including worked examples.

Tax planning

8.50 CGT is a tax which is amenable to tax planning because the timing of events is often within the control of the taxpayer. Tax planning is also an important issue because it is possible to incur a significant CGT liability if good advice is not taken.

Consider the disposal of a company on retirement – the taxpayer can sell either the shares of the company or the business's assets and wind the company up. If the assets are sold, a capital gains tax liability will accrue to the company. When the company is then liquidated the taxpayer will incur a second capital gains tax liability on the gain received on the shares. If instead the shares are sold directly, then only the gain on the shares will be taxable.

However, for a number of reasons the purchaser may prefer to buy the assets than the shares. If the company is sold the purchaser also acquires the liabilities and obligations of the company whereas acquiring the assets is more straightforward.

These factors, often together with many more, will become part of the negotiations which are entered into before the business is sold.

In general, capital disposals should be made as early as possible in the fiscal year in order to delay the payment of tax as much as possible to allow inflation to reduce the impact of the tax charge. An individual or married couple should try to fully utilise their annual exemption limit(s) each year since, if it is not used in the year, it cannot be carried forward.

If at all possible losses should not be wasted by being set against current gains which would otherwise have benefited from the annual exemption limit.

It is important to obtain good tax advice before making a large disposal so that any exemptions and reliefs available can be claimed.

Summary

Capital taxes, including CGT, stamp duty and inheritance tax, are generally levied for reasons of equity and to reduce tax avoidance.

CGT was introduced in 1965. In the early years there were many changes in the legislation which were needed to correct fundamental flaws in the original legislation. One of the most important subsequent developments was the introduction of the indexation allowance. Of course, this significantly reduced the amount of tax which was collected by the Government but it might be argued that it made the tax 'fairer'- which seems to be one of the most important motivating characteristics of CGT. Now that the indexation allowance and taper relief have gone, the question of whether the tax is still fair must be raised again particularly as the amount collected from these taxes is now rising year on year.

Taxpayers, both individuals and companies, pay tax on their chargeable gains. However, there is considerable scope for tax planning as the taxpayer can often choose the date on which to make the disposal. There are a number of reliefs which are available to taxpayers including relief on a principal private residence, rollover relief, holdover relief, incorporation relief and gift relief. Remember also that gains on assets held in pension funds and individual savings accounts are not subject to income tax or capital gains tax. These reliefs, together with the annual exemption limit, enable most individuals to avoid any liability to capital gains tax.

Stamp duty is imposed on documents which evidence certain transfers of property. New rules for computation of SDLT on residential property transactions were introduced in December 2014 to move the system from a 'slab' basis to a 'slice' basis which many advocated was long overdue to reduce the impact of tax on transaction levels, Non-residential property was also changed to this system from March 2016. With effect from April 2015, the Land and Buildings Transactions Tax applies instead of SDLT to properties in Scotland, and from April 2018, the Land Transaction Tax applies in Wales.

Finally inheritance tax, which only applies to individuals, taxes the value of estates on the death of individuals, and sometimes also transfers of property during a taxpayer's lifetime.

Project areas

There is great increased scope for dissertations on the subject of CGT. A survey of holders of chargeable assets, especially chargeable business assets, to determine if it affects their decision to hold or sell might be interesting. A comparison of the taxation of capital gains in more than one country is likely to be interesting. The question of whether capital gains tax is a fair tax is also worth asking.

In the area of stamp duty you might like to consider what the impact of this tax is on the housing and share markets. What has been the impact of recent changes to a 'slice' based system on property transaction markets for example? Will the new additional property rates have an impact on buy-to-let and second home ownership markets?

For IHT, how has the significant increase in personal wealth of homeowners over the last 20 years or so affected the role of IHT as part of the tax system? Is this taxation of principal private residences by the back door?

Discussion topics

1. It is sometimes possible for individuals to arrange their affairs in order to have receipts taxed as income rather than a capital gain and vice versa. For example, directors planning to sell a family company could either pay themselves high salaries taxable under ITEPA 2003 or take relatively low salaries thus increasing the funds retained in the business, leading to a higher value for their shares when the company is sold. List the taxation consequences of making this decision and discuss the circumstances in which income may be preferable to capital gains.

2. What impact does stamp duty have on capital transactions, if any?

3. Is inheritance tax an unfair tax in that it taxes people on the results of their life-time's hard work when they die?

Quick quiz

1. Andrew bought a fixed asset (not exempt from capital gains tax) for use in his business in June 2001 for £1,700 and sold it in May 2022 for £5,000. Compute the chargeable gain.

2. In August 2015, Barbara bought a second-hand hearse at an auction for £4,000 which she then sold to the Atherstone Vintage Car Museum for £7,000 in May 2022. What are the CGT consequences?

3. Ian has a chargeable gain for the tax year 2022/23 of £24,800 and a capital loss of £12,200. He also has unused capital losses of £7,100 brought forward from the tax year 2021/22. What amount of capital loss can Ian carry forward to the tax year 2023/24?

4. Charlie bought a valuable modern impressionist painting for £3,400 in May 2003. He sold it in February 2023 for £5,500. What are the CGT consequences?

5. In August 2022 Davina sold part of her trading business and realised a gain of £450,000 before business asset disposal relief. She has not previously made any claims for business asset disposal relief and has no other capital gains or losses for the year. If she claims business asset disposal relief, how much CGT will be payable?

6. Eddie was given a chargeable asset (not a chattel) in August 2000 with a market value of £7,000. In June 2022 he was successful in claiming that the asset had a negligible value of only £50. What allowable loss (if any) will Eddie be entitled to?

7. Felicity sold one quarter of a parcel of land in May 2022 for £200,000. She had originally bought the land in May 2002 for £500,000 and the remainder was valued at £860,000 immediately after the part disposal. Assuming Felicity is a higher rate taxpayer and has no other gains for the year, what is her CGT liability?

8. Gregory sold an asset that qualifies for rollover relief in August 2022, making a chargeable gain. When must he acquire a replacement asset in order to qualify for the relief?

9. Helen incorporated her business in May 2022 and received 1,000 £1 ordinary shares in the company plus £20,000 in cash. At the time of incorporation, the business was valued at £100,000, and the agreed chargeable gain on the assets transferred was £50,000. On what amount will Helen be liable to capital gains tax as a result of the incorporation assuming she does not elect for incorporation relief not to apply?

10. Julia is in business as a sole trader and sold a freehold warehouse for £184,000 in May 2022 resulting in a chargeable gain of £38,600. She purchased a replacement freehold warehouse the same month for £143,000. Both warehouses are used for business purposes and Julia wants to claim rollover relief. What will be the base cost of the replacement warehouse for capital gains tax purposes?

Questions

Question 1 (based on an ICAS TPS Tax Paper question).

Ben disposed of the following assets in January 2023:

1. An antique table which cost £25,000 in April 2001 was sold at auction for £35,000 before commission of 10%.
2. A holiday cottage which was transferred to his brother for £35,000 when its market value was £45,000. It had cost £47,500 in May 2003 and the costs of conveyance (paid for by Ben) were £1,100.
3. One acre of a four-acre plot of land acquired in April 1988 for £24,000. This was sold for £13,000 at which point the remaining acreage was worth £15,000. Expenses of sale were £500.
4. 100 shares in Ryft plc held within his ISA. These cost £1,800 and were sold for £2,000 before commission of £50.
5. 1,200 shares in PK plc bought in January 1999 for £6,000. Ben realised £8,500 from this sale. The price dropped significantly in the days after Ben sold and he decided to reinvest the proceeds back into PK plc one week later. He managed to buy 1,600 shares with his proceeds of £8,500.

Required: Calculate Ben's capital gains tax liability for 2022/23, assuming he made no other disposals during the year and is a higher rate taxpayer.

Question 2 (based on an ACCA question).

David and Angela Brook are a married couple. They disposed of the following assets during the tax year 2022/23:

Jointly owned property:

(a) On 29 July 2022, David and Angela sold a classic Ferrari car for £34,400. The car had been purchased on 17 January 2014 for £27,200.

(b) On 30 September 2022, David and Angela sold a house for £381,900. The house had been purchased on 1 October 1997 for £86,000. David and Angela occupied the house as their main residence from the date of purchase until 31 March 2001. The house was then unoccupied between 1 April 2001 and 31 December 2004 due to Angela being required by her employer to work elsewhere in the UK. From 1 January 2005 until 31 December 2016, David and Angela again occupied the house as their main residence. The house was then unoccupied until it was sold on 30 September 2022.

David Brook

(a) On 18 April 2022, David sold an antique table for £5,600. The antique table had been purchased on 27 May 2009 for £3,200.

(b) On 5 May 2022, David transferred his entire shareholding of 20,000 £1 ordinary shares in Bend Ltd, an unquoted trading company, to Angela. On that date, the shares were valued at £64,000. David's shareholding had been purchased on 21 June 2009 for £48,000.

(c) On 14 February 2023, David made a gift of 15,000 ordinary shares in Galatico plc to his son. On that date, the shares were quoted on the stock exchange at £2.90 - £3.10. David had originally purchased 8,000 shares in Galatico plc on 15 June 2015 for £17,600, and he purchased a further 12,000 shares on 24 August 2015 for £21,600. David's total shareholding was less than 1% of Galatico' plc's issued share capital.

Angela Brook

(a) On 5 May 2022, Angela sold an antique cabinet for £7,200. The antique cabinet had been purchased on 14 June 2009 for £3,700.

(b) On 7 July 2022, Angela sold 15,000 of the 20,000 ordinary shares in Bend Ltd that had been transferred to her from David. The sale proceeds were £62,400.

Angela has taxable income of £40,000 for the tax year 2022/23. David does not have any taxable income.

Required: Compute David and Angela's respective capital gains tax liabilities for the tax year 2022/23, and state the due date for payment.

Hint: See section 8.9 to find out how to calculate the gain on Galatico Shares.)

Question 3   (based on an ACCA question).

Wilson Biazma disposed of the following assets during the tax year 2022/23:

(a) On 21 April 2022 Wilson sold a freehold office building for £246,000. The office building had been purchased on 3 January 1999 for £104,000. Wilson has made a claim to rollover the gain on the office building against the replacement cost of a new freehold office building that was purchased on 14 January 2022 for £136,000. Both office buildings have always been used entirely for business purposes in a wholesale business run by Wilson as a sole trader.

(b) On 26 May 2022 Wilson incorporated a retail business that he had run as a sole trader since 1 June 2009. The market value of the business on 26 May 2022 was £200,000. All of the business assets were transferred to a new limited company, with the consideration consisting of 140,000 £1 ordinary shares valued at £140,000 and £60,000 in cash. The only chargeable asset of the business was goodwill and this was valued at £120,000 on 26 May 2022. The goodwill has a nil cost. Wilson took full advantage of the available incorporation relief.

(c) On 17 August 2022 Wilson made a gift of his entire shareholding of 10,000 £1 ordinary shares (a 100% holding) in Gandua Ltd, an unquoted trading company, to his daughter. The market value of the shares on that date was £220,000. The shares had been purchased on 8 January 2011 for £112,000. On 17 August 2022 the market value of Gandua Ltd's chargeable assets was £180,000, of which £150,000 was in respect of chargeable business assets. Wilson and his daughter have elected to hold over the gain on this gift of a business asset.

(d) On 3 October 2022 an antique vase owned by Wilson was destroyed in a fire. The antique vase had been purchased on 7 November 2010 for £49,000. Wilson received insurance proceeds of £68,000 on 20 December 2022 and on 22 December 2022 he paid £69,500 for a replacement antique vase. Wilson has made a claim to defer the gain arising from the receipt of the insurance proceeds.

(e) On 9 March 2023 Wilson sold 10 acres of land for £85,000. He had originally purchased twenty acres of land on 29 June 2003 for £120,000. The market value of the unsold ten acres of land as at 9 March 2023 was £65,000. The land has never been used for business purposes.

Required: Calculate Wilson's chargeable gains for the tax year 2022/23, clearly identifying the effects of the reliefs claimed in respect of disposals (a) to (d).

Question 4   (based on an ACCA question)

Alice Lim disposed of the following assets during 2022/23:

(a) On 24 June 2022, Alice sold a freehold office building for £152,000. The office building had been purchased on 2 March 2013 for £134,000. Prior to this on 15 April 2012 Alice had sold a freehold warehouse for £149,000. The warehouse had been purchased on 20 November 2004 for £93,000. Alice made a claim to roll over the gain arising on the disposal of the warehouse against the cost of the office building. Both the office building and the warehouse were used entirely for business purposes in a manufacturing business run by Alice as a sole trader.

(b) On 9 January 2023 Alice sold 50,000 £1 ordinary shares in Alilim Ltd, an unlisted trading company, for £275,000. Alilim Ltd had been formed on 17 October 2012 in order to incorporate a retail business that Alice had run as a sole trader since 18 May 2005. She is an employee of, and active in, Alilim Ltd. The market value of the retail business on 17 October 2012 was £300,000. All of the business assets were transferred to Alilim Ltd. The consideration consisted of 200,000 £1 ordinary shares valued at £200,000, and £100,000 in cash. The transfer of the business assets resulted in total chargeable gains of £120,000. This figure is before taking account of any rollover relief that was available on incorporation.

(c) On 27 February 2023 Alice sold 40,000 £1 ordinary shares (a 40% shareholding) in Family Ltd, an unlisted trading company for £230,000. Alice had acquired the shares on 21 March 2013 when she purchased them from her mother for £120,000. Alice's mother had originally purchased the shares on 19 December 2004 for £128,000. Alice and her mother elected to hold over the gain arising on 21 March 2013 as a gift of a business asset. The market value of the shares on that date was £168,000. Alice has never been employed by Family Ltd.

Required: Calculate Alice's capital gains tax liability for 2022/23, given that her taxable income for income tax purposes is £30,000.

(*Note: answer available on the lecturer's website*)

Question 5 (based on an ACCA question).

Mick Stone disposed of the following assets during the year ended 5 April 2023:

(a) On 19 May 2022, Mick sold a freehold warehouse for £522,000. The warehouse was purchased on 6 August 2006 for £258,000, and was extended at a cost of £63,000 in November 2009. In January 2012, the floor of the warehouse was damaged by flooding and had to be replaced at a cost of £76,000. The warehouse was sold because it was surplus to the business's requirements as a result of Mick purchasing a newly built warehouse during 2017. Both warehouses have always been used for business purposes in a wholesale business run by Mick as a sole trader.

(b) On 12 August 2022, Mick sold an acre of land for £81,700. He had originally purchased five acres of land on 19 May 2003 for £167,400. The market value of the unsold four acres of land as at 12 August 2022 was £268,000. The land had never been used for business purposes.

(c) On 24 September 2022, Mick sold 700,000 £1 ordinary shares in Rolling Ltd, an unquoted trading company, for £3,675,000. He had originally purchased 500,000 shares in Rolling Ltd on 2 June 2010 for £960,000. On 1 December 2015, Rolling Ltd made a 3 for 2 bonus issue. Mick has been a director of Rolling Ltd since 1 January 2010.

(d) On 19 January 2023, Mick made a gift of his entire holding of 24,000 £1 ordinary shares in Sugar plc, a quoted investment company, to his son Keith. On that date the shares were quoted on the Stock Exchange at £6.98 - £7.10, with recorded bargains of £6.85, £6.90, £7.00 and £7.05. The shares had been purchased on 8 May 2013 for £76,800. Mick's shareholding was less than 1% of Sugar plc's issued share capital, and he has never been an employee or director.

Required:

1. Assuming no reliefs are available, calculate the chargeable gain arising from each of Mick Stone's asset disposals during the tax year 2022/23. You are not required to calculate the taxable gains or the amount of tax payable.

2. State which CGT reliefs might be available to Mick Stone in respect of each of his disposals during the year ended 5 April 2023, and what further information you would require in order to establish if the reliefs are actually available and to establish any restrictions as regards the amount of relief.

(Note: answer available on the lecturer's website)

Further test questions for this chapter to test your knowledge can be found in the student section of the website at:

https:// www.fiscalpublications.com/lymerandoats/2022

Further reading and examples

Chamberlain, E (2016) A review of agricultural property relief and business property relief, *British Tax Review* 2016, 5, 509 – 519. (Inheritance tax: policy reform options)

Combs, A. (2022), *UK Corporation tax, Capital Gains Tax and VAT Practice Questions (2nd edition 2022/23)*, Fiscal Publications: Malvern.
– a large test bank of questions linked to the content of this chapter that will enable you to thoroughly test your knowledge of this work with exam-level questions. See
https://www.fiscalpublications.com/uk-ct-cgt-vat-practice-questions/2022

Combs, A. & Tutin, R (2022), *Taxation: incorporating the 2022 Finance Act*, Fiscal Publications: Malvern.
– use this book for many other examples to further develop and test your knowledge of this chapter's contents. See
https://www.fiscalpublications.com/combsandtutin/2022

9 Corporation tax

Introduction

9.1 Corporation tax is charged on the profits of companies. Until 1965 companies were taxed under the income tax rules. In 1965 a reform of the tax system led to the introduction of corporation tax as a separate tax. As you will learn in this chapter, there are similarities between the way in which companies' profits are taxed under corporation tax rules and the taxation of sole traders and partnerships profits under income tax rules. There are, however, some important differences between corporation tax and income tax that you need to be aware of.

At the end of this chapter you will be able to:
- describe the imputation system of taxation;
- state the basis of assessment of tax for companies;
- determine the taxable total profits;
- calculate a company's corporation tax liability; and
- determine the date on which the corporation tax is due

Further details of other, more complicated, aspects of corporation tax can be found on the website, specifically tax implications of corporate losses and company groups.

The liability to corporation tax

9.2 For corporation tax purposes a company is defined as being either a body corporate or an unincorporated association. The definition of a company extends to organisations such as clubs and political associations which are therefore subject to corporation tax. The definition excludes partnerships, however, which are subject to income tax.

UK resident companies are liable to corporation tax on their total world-wide profits arising in an accounting period regardless of whether the profits are remitted to the UK or not. However, dividends received by a UK resident company from other companies are generally not liable to further corporation tax in the hands of the recipient. How to determine the residence of a company for tax purposes is further considered in Chapter 12.

The capital gains of a company are not subject to a separate capital gains tax. Instead, capital gains are chargeable to corporation tax along with other income and profits.

Historical overview

9.3 Before looking at the UK system of corporation tax more closely, we need to think about what companies are and the reasons why governments tax them. Companies are separate legal entities. Their operations are managed by directors, but they are owned by shareholders. Companies undertake activities to make profit, which can then either be retained for reinvestment within the company, increasing the value of shares, or distributed as dividends to shareholders. Company profits can be thought of then as passing through two layers; they are earned by the company itself, but then they are passed on to shareholders, who ultimately may have a right to the profits earned, either as capital gains as the value of their shares rise, or in dividends. So the question arises – should we tax companies on their profits? Most governments do so, and so corporation tax is a cost to the company in earning its profits. However, there is also a second question – should we tax shareholders on their dividends and capital gains as well? Some governments do and some don't.

When corporation tax was first introduced in the UK in 1965 the *classical system* was used. Under the classical system the relationship between a company and its shareholders is ignored for tax computations. A company pays tax on its profits without reference to its dividend policy and its shareholders pay tax on their dividends received without any relief for the tax already paid by the company on those profits. This is a simple system but does lead to profits being over taxed; in the hands of the company and then again in the hands of the shareholders.

Fiscal Fact

In 1973-74 it is estimated that 175,000 companies paid corporation tax, by 2018/19 the number had reached 1,534,000. [Source: HMRC Statistics – Numbers of taxpayers and registered traders April 2021]

In 1973 the problem of over taxation of distributed profits led the Government to switch to an *imputation system* so that shareholders were given a tax credit for some of the corporation tax which had been paid by the company. The tax credit was used to offset at least some of the shareholder's liability to income tax. This was the system in operation in the UK until 6 April 2016. The primary advantage of the imputation system of company taxation over the classical system is that the over taxation on distributed profits is reduced.

For many years the dividend tax credit was set at a rate of 10%. Taxpayers received a tax credit equal to 1/10th of any gross dividend from a UK company. Gross dividends received by basic rate taxpayers, that is the dividend actually received together with the related tax credit, were subject to income tax at a rate of 10%. This meant that non-taxpayers and basic rate taxpayers had no further tax to pay. Higher rate tax payers had an effective 25% tax rate on dividends and additional rate taxpayers had an effective tax rate of 30.56%. Individual non-taxpayers were not able to reclaim the tax credit under this system if it was more than their total income tax payable, which might seem unfair.

From 6 April 2016 this system changed. As we saw in Chapter 4, shareholders are now given a tax-free 'dividend allowance' of £2,000 (£5,000 before 6 April 2018) only dividends above that level are subject to tax – at the special rates of income tax for dividends of 8.75%, 33.75% or 39.35% (depending on which tax band the dividends fall into as a top slice of their income). The reduction of the dividend allowance in 2018 from £5,000 to £2,000 meant that more people who rely on dividend income, such as retirees, have to fill in tax returns and pay tax.

The current system is simpler, but in effect there is still over taxation of corporate profits. The system for taxation of corporate profits in the UK effectively remains a partial imputation system.

As we discussed in Chapter 8, the rules for paying tax on capital gains made when selling shares has not changed; so when companies retain profits, the increase in share value that results may be chargeable to capital gains tax when shares are sold.

Calculation of the corporation tax payable

9.4   Companies are taxed on the full amount of the profits or gains or income arising in the accounting period for a company (whether or not received in or transmitted to the UK), after any deductions authorised by the Corporation Tax Acts. There are a number of key differences between how the rules are applied to sole traders to calculate income tax on their profits and to companies to calculate corporation tax on their profits and capital gains In this section we will examine the key similarities and differences.

To calculate corporation tax payable you need to undertake a number of steps.

1.   Determine the accounting period which is to be assessed.
2.   Adjust accounting profits for tax purposes and allocate income and allowable expenditure to the correct period.
3.   Calculate the taxable total profits.
4.   Ascertain the rate at which corporation tax will be charged.

In the first section of this chapter we will review each of these stages in order.

1. Determining the accounting period

9.5   Look for the similarities and differences between the basis of assessment for companies and unincorporated businesses when reading this section.

Corporation tax is assessed and charged for any accounting period of a company on the full amount of the profits arising in the period, whether or not received in or transmitted to the UK, minus allowable deductions. An accounting period of a company starts, for corporation tax purposes, whenever:

- the company comes within the charge to corporation tax; usually on commencing to trade as a company; or
- immediately after the end of the previous accounting period, if the company is still within the charge to corporation tax.

An accounting period of a company ends, for the purposes of corporation tax, on the earliest of the following:

- 12 months after the beginning of the accounting period;
- an accounting date of the company or, if there is a period for which the company does not make up accounts, the end of that period;
- the company starting or ceasing to trade;
- the commencement of a winding up;
- the date on which the company ceases to be UK resident; or
- the date on which it ceases to be liable to corporation tax.

Be careful that you do not confuse accounting periods for tax purposes (called 'accounting periods') with the company's reporting period for financial accounting purposes (called 'periods of account'). Whilst these two are often the same (usually 12 months long and ending on the same day) this is not always the case. The key rule to remember is a company's accounting period for tax purposes cannot be more than 12 months long. If the period of account (for reporting purposes) is longer than 12 months (e.g. perhaps when a company moves its year-end date) then the period of account must be split up into more than one accounting period for the tax calculations. If the accounting period is less than 12 months then it becomes its own chargeable period. This is one of the important differences between sole traders and companies. Sole traders can have tax periods longer than 12 months as we discussed in Chapter 6.

Activity

Apply the above rules to determine the accounting periods for tax when a company changes its year end from 31 December to 31 March by having a 15-month period of accounts starting on 1 January, 2022.

Feedback

For this company, 1 January, 2022 is the start of an accounting period because it is immediately after the end of the previous accounting period (i.e. 31 December 2021). Since it must end at the latest 12 months after it starts, the first accounting period must run from 1 January, 2022 to 31 December, 2022. The second accounting period must commence as soon as the first one finishes and so it begins on 1 January, 2023. It ends at the end of the period of account i.e. 31 March, 2023. This company will therefore have two accounting periods covering the 15 month period of account; one for the first 12 months and the other for the final 3 months.

2. Allocating profits to accounting periods

9.6   Income and expenses of a company are normally allocated to the accounting period in which they accrue however, the fact that companies can't have an accounting period of more than 12 months may cause complications. For example, in the activity above a 15-month period of account was split into two accounting periods for tax purposes, the first one 12 months long and the second one three months long. If this happens we must then split the income and expenses of the company between the two periods in the following ways:

- Trading profits and miscellaneous income before capital allowances is *apportioned* on a time basis. In our example 12/15ths would be included in the first accounting period while the remaining 3/15ths would be included in the second. This won't necessarily reflect exactly when any particular income is earned.
- Capital allowances, including balancing allowances and charges, are calculated for each accounting period by computing figures based on actual expenditure or disposals. Do not forget that writing down allowance percentages need to be reduced for short accounting periods as they are normally cited on a per annum basis e.g. 18% per annum for main pool plant and machinery. Also note that for companies, although a short period of account will result in an adjustment to the capital allowances available, there are never any reductions in capital allowances for private use of assets owned by the company, because a company is an artificial legal entity and can't have 'private' expenses. Instead any private use by employees or directors of the company may be charged on the user as a benefit in kind under employment income rules.
- Property business income is treated like trading income and time apportioned.
- Bank interest (and income from other non-trading loan relationships e.g. building society interest) are allocated on an accruals basis.

- Other income is usually allocated on an actual basis to the period to which it relates.
- Qualifying charitable donations are allocated to the period in which they are paid.
- Chargeable gains are allocated to the period in which they are realised.

Activity

Cherry Ltd. makes up accounts for the 18 months to 31 March, 2023. The company's results for the period of account are:

	£
Trading profit before capital allowances	300,000
Bank interest (gross) accrued:	
31/3/22	1,200
30/9/22	1,000
31/3/23	1,100
Chargeable gains on disposal of assets:	
31/12/21	5,000
6/6/22	3,000
31/12/22	7,000
Qualifying charitable donations:	
31/12/21	15,000
31/12/22	20,000

Calculate the taxable total profits for each accounting period within the period of account.

Feedback

The period of account will be split into two accounting periods, the 12 months to 30 September, 2022 and the 6 months to 31 March, 2023. The chargeable profits are:

	12 months to 30/9/22	6 months to 31/3/23
Trading profits		
12/18 × 300,000	200,000	
6/18 × 300,000		100,000
Bank interest received	2,200	1,100
Chargeable gains	8,000	7,000
	210,200	108,100
Less charitable donations	(15,000)	(20,000)
	195,200	88,100

Now you need to be able to adjust the company's trading profits for tax purposes. As for income tax, the easiest way of calculating the trading profits is to follow the proforma given here. (Note – the numbers are used in the proforma to make it easier to follow – they do not relate to the previous example.)

Adjustment of trading profits for the accounting period ended 31 December 2022.

	£000	£000
Net profits per accounts		3,270
Add expenditure disallowed		530
		3,800
Less: Income not assessable	120	
Expenditure not included in the accounts which is an allowable deduction	180	
Capital allowances	500	
		(800)
Tax Adjusted trading profits		3,000

Most of the rules you are already familiar with for sole traders, from Chapters 6 and 7, also apply to companies. These include the rules relating to capital receipts and expenditure, as well as prohibitions on certain deductions such as entertainment expenses. In the next section we will consider one particular area where companies are treated differently to sole traders. There are several more that we will consider later in the chapter.

Loan relationships

9.7 Individuals account for income and expenses, and gains and losses on loans using a combination of the income tax rules (for interest accrued and payable) and the capital gains tax rules (for any capital gain or loss when the loan is disposed of). Different rules apply to companies for loan relationships i.e. any relationship that involves borrowing or lending money.

Where a company borrows or lends money for the purposes of its trading activities, it is referred to as a *trading loan relationship*. Examples of trading loan relationships are bank overdrafts, loans to buy business premises or plant and machinery, and debentures. (Note: you will not usually see a company *receive* income under a trading loan relationship unless they are in the business of making loans). Trading loan relationships are included in the trading profit computation.

Income, expenses, gains and losses from *non-trading loan relationships*, i.e. those which are not related to the company's trading activities, are dealt with as a separate category, outside of the trading profit computation, as we will see later.

Income and other amounts receivable in this category usually relates to interest from bank and building society accounts and other interest receivable that is not related to the trading activity. This income is assessed on an *accruals basis*.

Any amounts receivable or payable under non-trading loan relationships must be aggregated. If the net figure is positive (debits are less than credits) then the total becomes the non-trading loan relationship income for the company and is included in the company's taxable profit figure for the year. If a net deficit exists then it can either be set against other income for the same accounting period, carried back against any surpluses on non-trading loan relationships in the last twelve months or carried forward to set against future non-trading profits (i.e. future taxable total profits less trading profit). This process applies not just to interest, but also to other gains and losses for loan relationships, for example when a loan is written off.

An important point to note is that for all loan relationships, trade and non-trade, profits and losses (referred to as credits and debits respectively) are treated as income for companies, i.e. the capital/revenue distinction, which we discussed in Chapter 6, does not apply. This is another important difference between sole traders and companies for tax purposes.

3. Taxable Total Profits

9.8   Now that the trading profit has been computed and allocated to the correct accounting period for the tax computation we can calculate the rest of the taxable total profits of the company. This computation is the equivalent of calculating taxable income for sole traders i.e. it is the aggregation of income from various sources minus any charges.

We will use a proforma (with example numbers) to illustrate how to do this:

Taxable total profits for the accounting period ended 30 September, 2022

	£000
Trading profit	3,000
Non-trading loan relationship	1,500
Property income	500
Miscellaneous income	300
Chargeable gains	700
Total profits	6,000
Less qualifying charitable donation	(1,000)
Taxable total profits	5,000

It is important to note that dividends received by a UK company from other companies are excluded from the tax computation, because they are not subject to further corporation tax in the hands of the receiving company.

We explored how to determine trading profit earlier in the chapter but you need to know a little more about some of the other items in the proforma before you are ready to calculate the taxable total profits for specific companies.

Non-trading loan relationships

9.9   Non trading loan relationships are treated as a separate category for the corporation tax computation. The reason they are treated separately is that there are different rules for how losses are dealt with for trading and non-trading loan relationships. We look at losses in section 9.22 below.

Property income

9.10   Income from land and buildings owned by companies is taxed regardless of whether the property is located in the UK or not. As for individuals, property income includes rents due, income from holiday lettings and furnished lettings, premiums on short leases, ground rents and payments for sporting rights.

Property income is calculated using all the same trading profit rules that you are familiar with. Because this is in line with normal accounting principles, no tax adjustments will generally be necessary. Capital allowances will also be deducted to determine the property income.

Interest payable by a company on a loan related to rental property, however is dealt with under the loan relationship rules, and so it is not an allowable property expense.

Charitable donations

9.11   The special treatment of charitable gifts for individual taxpayers i.e. the extension of the basic rate band (see section 4.45), does not apply to companies. For companies, qualifying gifts to charities and community amateur sports clubs (CASCs) are deductible under 'charitable donations relief' provisions introduced in Corporation Tax Act 2010. They are paid gross by the company (so no grossing up is required) and, unlike gifts from individuals, no further tax is reclaimable by the charity from the Government. The amount is deductible for the company making the donation when calculating its taxable profits, i.e. outside of the trading profit computation.

An exception is donations to local charities which are small in amount and are made wholly and exclusively for the purpose of the trade which are allowable deductions from trading profits. An example might be a gift to an employees' welfare organisation. Of course, there is no possibility of a double deduction, it must be used as one or the other and treated correctly in the tax computation.

The amount that is added back in the adjustment of trading profits computation is equal to the amount included in the profit and loss account. This figure will usually be determined using the accruals basis rather than the cash paid basis. The amount allowed in the calculation of taxable trading profits however is the cash actually paid. Hence the two figures may not be the same.

Companies and income tax

9.12   Where a payment is made net of tax, for example a patent royalty to an individual or partnership, the company must account to HMRC for the tax they have withheld. This is a separate calculation to the corporation tax computation. The income tax withheld is netted against any income tax that is withheld from the company as recipient and the difference is paid/reclaimed. Companies are required to submit quarterly returns to HMRC to reconcile any income tax on items received and paid. Income tax will only need to be deducted from patent royalties and interest where either the payer or recipient is not a UK company, for example a partnership.

The following activity illustrates the key points from above.

Activity

Bournemouth Ltd had the following results for the year ended 31 March, 2023

	£000	£000
Gross profit on trading		1,200
Investment income (a)	300	
Profit on sale of land (b)	200	500
		1,700
Less:		
Depreciation	100	
Directors' emoluments	250	
Qualifying charitable donation	30	
Audit and accountancy fees	45	
Legal costs (c)	20	
Salaries	100	
Premium on lease written off (d)	25	
Miscellaneous expenses	30	(600)
Net profit for year		1,100

Notes:

(a) Investment income:	£000
Dividends from UK companies (gross)	200
Loan interest from UK company (gross- non-trading loans)	100

(b) Profit on sale of land:

The profit on the sale of land relates to a plot of vacant land no
longer required by the company. The chargeable gain is   150

(c) Legal costs:

Costs re debt collection	5
Costs re issue of shares	12
Costs re renegotiations of directors' service agreements	3

(d) Lease premium

The lease premium written off relates to a lease entered into at
the beginning of the accounting period for a warehouse for a
period of 17 years. The premium paid was   25

(e) Capital allowances have been calculated as   50

Required: calculate the tax adjusted trading profits.

Feedback

First you needed to calculate the trading profit:

Trading profit	£000	£000
Net profit per accounts		1,100
Add: Depreciation	100	
Charitable donation (deducted from TTP)	30	
Legal costs (not allowable as capital)	12	
Lease premium written off (W1)	25	167
		1,267
Less: Investment income (loan relationship)	100	
Investment income (dividends)	200	
Profit on sale of investments	200	
Capital allowances	50	
Lease premium (W1)	1	(551)
Adjusted trading profit		716

Working 1

The amount of the lease premium assessable on the landlord under the
property income rules is:

£25,000 – [£25,000 × (17 – 1) × 2%] = £17,000.

The amount which is allowable for the lessee in the accounting period ended
31 March, 2023 is therefore £17,000 ÷ 17 = £1,000.

Now you can calculate the taxable total profits.

	£
Trading profit	716,000
Non-trading Loan relationship	100,000
Chargeable gains	150,000
	966,000
Less charitable donation	(30,000)
Taxable total profits	936,000

You will notice the treatment of the lease premium is the same as for individuals as we saw in Chapter 6.7.

4. The rate of corporation tax payable

9.13   Having learnt the basics of the first three stages of calculating corporation tax, we now need to work through the actual computation of the tax liability.

The rate of corporation tax is set for *financial years*. A financial year (FY) runs from 1 April to the following 31 March i.e. the financial year 2022 (or FY 2022) runs from 1 April, 2022 to 31 March, 2023. The rate of corporation tax for a financial year is set after the year has started, in the annual Finance Act. Hence the rate for the financial year 2022 is set in the Finance Act 2022.

There is only one flat rate of corporation tax, 19% (the same as for 2021/22), that applies to the taxable total profits. Changes are due to take place in 2023, which will be discussed in section 9.28 There is no equivalent to the personal allowance or annual exempt amount, and corporation tax must be paid from the first £1 of taxable total profit.

At present this rate is set for the whole of the UK. However, legislation has been passed to allow Northern Ireland to set a different rate of corporate tax to the rest of the country. This is to enable them to compete with the currently lower rate of corporation tax (12.5%) in the Republic of Ireland.

Fiscal Fact

In 2022/23 corporation tax is forecast to raise £48.8 billion, 5.5% of total tax receipts

You can now attempt Quick Quiz questions 1-4 and Full questions 1 & 3.

Other special rules for companies

In this section we will look at some more areas where companies are treated differently from individuals, in particular capital allowances super deductions, research and development expenditure, intangibles, creative industry relief and the patent box regime.

Super deduction

9.14 In addition to the new capital allowances available to all businesses and discussed in Chapter 7, two (temporary) new capital allowance deductions especially for companies have been introduced and are usable from 1 April 2021 until the end of March 2023. These new deductions are designed to boost capital investment between 1 April 2021 and when the new corporation tax rate of 25% is introduced on 1 April 2023.

There are two forms of new deduction:

- a 130% main rate first year capital allowance – a so called a 'super deduction', and
- a 50% first year allowance for special rate expenditure.

The new allowances do not replace the AIA, but are additional allowances that can be claimed.

Unlike AIA, there is no limit or cap on the sums that can be claimed at these super deduction rates.

Main rate super deduction
The main rate super deduction allows companies to claim 130% capital allowances on qualifying plant and machinery that would normally go into the main (18%) rate pool. The new rate does not apply to second hand or used assets, cars or plant and machinery for leasing.

When an asset for which the 130% super deduction is claimed is sold, the balancing charge will be taxable at that point, rather than being taken to the main pool. In addition, the disposal value for capital allowances is deemed to be the disposal receipt multiplied by a factor of 1.3, assuming the full super deduction rate is applicable. However, in the final year of operation of the new allowance, the year ended 31 March 2023, the rate of allowance may be a hybrid rate if the company's accounting period end straddles this date, in which case the disposal value uplift will be less than 1.3.

There are anti avoidance measures in place to prevent, for example, pre 31 March 2021 contracts being cancelled then put in place again after 31 March 2021 to get the allowance. If an asset will qualify as a short life asset, it may be beneficial not to claim the 130% super deduction; it should not be automatically assumed that the super deduction is the best option for a company.

Activity

Intrepid Ltd incurs £2m of expenditure on 1 December 2022 on plant that qualifies for the main rate super deduction. How much saving in corporation tax will the super deduction generate?

Feedback

As the company has spent £2m, it can deduct 130% of this when computing its TTP i.e. £2.6m. At the current corporation tax rate of 19%, this means the corporation tax saving will be £494,000. Had this super deduction not been available, it would have allocated £1m to AIA and the rest would have gone into the main pool receiving 18% capital allowances i.e. the allowance deductions from its TTP would have been at most £1.18m [£1m + (£1m x18%)] (assuming no other purchases used up any of the AIA available) so then its corporate tax saving would only be at most £224,200.

Special rate FYA

The temporary special rate pool deduction provides companies relief in the form of a 50% first year allowance. It applies to any plant and machinery that would normally qualify for the special (6%) rate pool (including integral features and long life assets). As with the main rate super deduction, any balancing charge goes directly into TTP and is calculated for this purpose using half of the disposal value. The remaining balancing allowance will be deducted from the special rate pool as usual.

Research and development expenditure

9.15   Companies are entitled to tax relief for research and development (R&D) expenditure. There are currently two systems in operation, one for small and medium sized companies (SMEs) that has been in operation since April 2000 and one for large companies which was introduced in 2013.

The SME R&D relief rules were first introduced in April 2000 for SMEs (we look at the system for large companies below at 9.16). The credits are only available to companies and not to sole traders and partnerships so the rules are another example of how the UK tax system treats companies differently from other forms of business. There is no lower limit to R&D spend in the year to qualify for the credits.

Research and development is defined by reference to Department for Business, Energy and Industrial Strategy guidelines which, at its most basic, implies the project concerned must be aiming to extend overall knowledge or capability in a field of science or technology, for example, creating a new process or product. R&D will not however, be eligible for relief if it is just increasing that business' level of knowledge or expertise with knowledge already available elsewhere.

Valid expenses include non-capital expenditure which directly relates to R&D activity, such as staff costs and consumables, expenditure on software development and any power, fuel or water expenditure directly related to the R&D activity.

The SME R&D relief system works by allowing SMEs to deduct 230% of valid expenditure in their tax computation i.e. a 100% normal deduction for the allowable R&D costs plus a further 130% deduction.

Activity

Ardvark Ltd has a turnover of £56,000 and allowable expenditure (other than R&D) of £16,000 for the year ended 31 March 2023. During the year, the company incurs £20,000 of qualifying R&D expenditure. What is the corporation tax liability for the year?

Feedback

	£
Turnover	56,000
Allowable expenditure	(16,000)
R&D expenditure	(20,000)
Enhanced R&D deduction	
130% x £20,000	(26,000)
TTP	0
Net corporation tax	0

What happens then, when a company is making a loss and therefore can't benefit from the enhanced tax deduction? In that case, it may be eligible for a special payment from the government of £14.50 for every £100 of actual R&D expenses. If SMEs claim a cash payment in this way, they then lose the special 230% deduction. From 1 April 2021, there is a cap on the repayable credit of £20,000 plus three times the company's relevant expenditure on workers.

In addition to R&D tax credits related to non-capital expenditure items, there is a separate 100% capital allowance for R&D capital expenditure such as the purchase of new buildings or machinery.

Research and development expenditure credit

9.16   A different system called research and development expenditure credit (RDEC) was introduced for R&D expenditure incurred on or after 1 April 2013. SMEs have a choice as to whether to use the old 130% deduction rule (i.e. 100% expense deduction for the cost incurred plus a further 30% deduction) or the RDEC credit rules. From 1 April 2016, RDEC is compulsory for large companies.

   With effect from 1 April 2020 the rate of RDEC increased to 13%.

   RDEC is designed to increase the visibility of R&D credits and also provide a cash flow for large companies that do not have a corporation tax liability.

   The credit is first offset against the company's corporation tax liability for the current year. Any remaining credit is then limited to the amount of PAYE and NIC liabilities related to the staffing costs for qualifying R&D expenditure. This restricted amount can be offset against other HMRC liabilities such as VAT, but only after being converted to a 'repayable amount', by treating it as being net of tax. Finally, if there is any excess remaining, it will be repayable to the company, so long as the company is a going concern. This activity shows how RDEC works.

Fiscal Fact

The cost to the Government of providing SME research and development credits is estimated to be £5,200 million for 2020/21. [Source: HMRC Structural relief cost estimates - December 2021]

Activity

Einstein Ltd has a turnover of £105m and allowable expenditure (other than R&D) of £1.5m for the year ended 31 March 2023. During the year, the company incurs £1m of qualifying R&D expenditure. Show how the RDEC affects Einstein Ltd's corporation tax liability.

Feedback

	(£'000s)
Turnover	105,000
R&D expenditure	(1,000)
RDEC @ 13%	130
Other expenditure	(1,500)
Profit	102,370
TTP	102,370
Tax @ 19%	19,450.30
RDEC	(130.00)
Net corporation tax	19,320.30

Creative Industries Reliefs

9.17 The UK Government has for some time been encouraging creative industries using the corporation tax system. There are a number of corporation tax reliefs under this heading, which all work by increasing the amount of allowable expenditure.

Qualifying companies are those directly involved in the production and development of certain films, high end television programmes, animation programmes or video games. To qualify for creative industries tax relief, the films etc must pass a 'cultural test', ie be a British production.

There are currently eight creative industries reliefs available as follows:

- Film tax relief
- Animation tax relief
- High-end television tax relief
- Video games tax relief
- Theatre tax relief
- Orchestra tax relief
- Museums and galleries exhibition tax relief.

You can find details of the reliefs or credits available to qualifying companies on the HMRC website at https://www.gov.uk/corporation-tax-creative-industry-tax-reliefs.

Intangibles

9.18 Intangibles include intellectual property such as patents, trademarks and copyright, as well as goodwill. Goodwill that only appears in the consolidated accounts and not in the individual company's accounts does not come under these rules, however, because the UK corporation tax system does not recognise groups of companies as a general rule (although see later at 9.22 in relation to losses).

Companies can claim tax relief for any amortisation or impairment claimed in the accounts for intangible assets. Alternatively, they can use a fixed rate of 4% per annum if the accounting treatment is not considered appropriate to use (e.g. where the asset is not amortised in the accounts or is amortised over a very long period). The company must justify why this will be the case to HMRC. Capital allowances for patent rights or know-how are not available to companies if acquired on or after 1 April, 2002.

If a company sells an intangible asset which was created or acquired after 1 April, 2002, any loss will be deductible from the total trading income and any profit will be taxable. In this way, the new rules remove the capital/income divide for these types of assets in a similar way to the loan relationship rules. If a profit arises but the proceeds are reinvested in a new intangible asset, the difference between the original cost and the disposal proceeds can be rolled over into the cost of the new intangible. This rollover rule applies to all intangibles, not just those acquired after 1 April, 2002, and for companies it supersedes the rollover capital gains tax rules we saw in Chapter 8.30.

Amortisation relief is available for acquired goodwill and other intangibles. since 1 April 2019. This recognises that businesses are often valued at a premium over the fair value of their assets, a problem particularly relevant for technology and pharmaceutical companies. Companies that acquire intangibles such as goodwill, customer information and customer relationships, which were previously excluded from the intangibles regime, can amortise the cost at 6.5% per annum.

Patent box regime

9.19 Under the patent box regime, companies can elect for profits from the development and exploitation of patents to be taxed at the rate of 10%. The rules only apply to companies that make profit from exploiting patented inventions.

The income to which the special tax rate will apply includes income from:
- selling patented products;
- licensing out patent rights;
- selling patent rights.

The aim of the Patent Box regime is to provide companies with an incentive to keep existing patents in the UK and also develop new and innovative patented products.

The regime provides for a deduction from taxable total profits that equates to a 10% tax rate for qualifying income. The deduction is calculated using the following formula:

$RP \times FY\% \times ((MR - IPR) \div MR)$

Where: RP is the profits of a company's trade relevant to Patent Box;
FY% is the appropriate percentage for each financial year;
MR is the main rate of corporation tax; and
IPR is the reduced rate of 10%.

Activity

Innovate Ltd is a UK resident company with no associated companies. In the year ending 31 March 2023, Innovate has tax adjusted trading profits of £10,000 all of which qualified for the Patent Box. Calculate Innovate Ltd's UK corporation tax liability for the year.

Feedback

Profit	£10,000
Patent Box Deduction:	
(10,000 ((19 – 10) ÷ 19))	(4,737)
Taxable Total Profits	5,263
Tax payable £5,263 @ 19%	£999.97

This is a very simplified example because it is unlikely that all of a company's profit would qualify for the Patent Box and there are some rules for calculating the profits that can benefit from the Patent Box. This is done in three stages:

1.   Identify profits attributable to income from exploiting patented inventions (relevant IP income).

2.   Remove an amount called 'routine profit', which takes into account that a business would probably earn a profit even if it didn't have access to patented technology or IP.

3.   Remove the profit associated with intangible assets, e.g. brands. This is because the Patent Box regime doesn't apply to other forms of IP.

The profits qualifying for the reduced rate of corporation tax are determined by reference to the company's direct engagement in R&D.

Close Companies

9.20 Close companies are those that are closely held, i.e. the shares are held by only a small number of people, often related as in family companies. There are concerns that these companies could be used for tax avoidance, and so a special set of rules applies to them. For tax purposes a close company is one that is controlled by five or fewer shareholders or any number of shareholding directors, who are referred to as 'participators'. When deciding whether this control test is met, it is not only the direct interests of the shareholders that is taken into account but also their 'associates', which are direct relatives or business partners.

There are two consequences of being classified as a close company. The first is an additional tax charge of 32.5% that must be paid when a close company makes a loan to one of its participators. The purposes of this rule is to make sure some tax is paid when profits are extracted from the company other than as a dividend. For non-large companies, the penalty tax must be paid nine months and one day after the end of the accounting period. For large companies, quarterly payments must be made. If the loan is repaid before the due date for payment of corporation tax, then the penalty tax will not be imposed. If it is repaid in full or in part, or if the company writes the loan off, the company may reclaim the penalty tax from HMRC. This is because the writing off of a loan is treated as a dividend in the hands of the participator.

The second consequence of being a close company is that benefits given to participators and their associates that are not taxable as earnings, are treated as distributions. This means the company cannot deduct the cost of the benefit and its value is treated as a dividend in the hands of the participator or associate.

 You can now attempt Quick Quiz questions 5-8.

Chargeable gains for companies

9.21 Companies are not liable to capital gains tax as a separate tax, but their chargeable gains and allowable losses are subject to corporation tax at the current rate of corporation tax.

Many of the CGT rules that we examined in Chapter 8 for individuals also apply to companies. There are a few exceptions you should be aware of, however. For example, unlike individuals, companies do not have an AEA to set against their chargeable gains, and they are also compensated for changes due to inflation using an indexation allowance rather than reduced rates of tax.

From 1 April 2020 only 50% of brought-forward capital losses are available. This ties in with the non-capital loss restrictions which are explained later in section 9.22.

The pro forma for calculating the chargeable gain or allowable loss is (numbers included only for illustration purposes):

	£
Gross proceeds on disposal (or market value)	12,000
Less incidental cost of disposal	(2,000)
Net proceeds	10,000
Less allowable costs	(2,500)
Unindexed gain/(loss)	7,500
Less indexation allowance	(1,000)
Indexed gain/(unindexed loss)	6,500

The indexation allowance is designed to compensate for the inflation component of the increases in the value of the asset so that companies only pay tax on the real gains they make – not those solely due to inflation. It does this by using the percentage increase in the retail price index from the month in which the asset was acquired until the month in which the disposal took place. The indexation allowance is applied to all items of allowable costs (except incidental costs of disposal as these are already at current value).

If the asset being sold was acquired before 31 March 1982, two calculations are required, one based on the original cost and the other on the value as at 31 March 1982, and the higher value is used to calculate the indexation allowance. Companies can elect to always use 31 March 1982 values. In 2017, indexation was frozen as you will see below.

The indexation factor for companies is:

$$\text{RPI for month of disposal* } - \text{ RPI for month of acquisition}$$

RPI for the month of acquisition

* Note that the indexation allowance for the disposal of assets on or after 1 January 2018 is calculated using the December 2017 RPI figure.

The retail price index figure for the appropriate months can be found in the RPI table in the rates and allowances section in Appendix A.

The indexation factor should be stated as a decimal correct to *three decimal places*. It is important you round to three decimal place or your answers will be wrong – it is not more accurate to use more decimal places in this case.

Be careful in use of indexation allowance as it cannot create or increase a loss for the chargeable gains computation. At best it will reduce the gain to zero.

The following activities will illustrate how to compute indexation allowances for chargeable gains computations for companies:

Activity

Calculate the relevant indexation allowance for an asset purchased in June 1989 and sold in April 2022.

Feedback

a)   Using the RPI tables in the Appendix A, the indexation allowance will be:

$$\frac{278.1 - 115.4}{115.4} = 1.410$$

(Don't forget to use the December 2017 indexation factor in place of the actual disposal date and to round the indexation factor to three decimal places)

The indexation allowance is equal to the indexation factor multiplied by the allowable cost. Each element of the allowable cost has a separate indexation calculation as the expense may have been incurred at different times. For example, if there is enhancement expenditure this also is indexed but from the date of the expenditure on the enhancement, not from the date of the original acquisition of the asset of course.

Activity

Cream Ltd sold land and buildings for £200,000 in April 2022. The property cost £50,000 when bought in December 1991. Cream Ltd spent £30,000 extending the building in June 1996. Calculate the chargeable gain on the property.

Feedback

	£	£
Proceeds		200,000
Less allowable costs		
Cost	50,000	
Enhancement expenditure	30,000	(80,000)
Unindexed gain		120,000
Indexation allowance		
$\dfrac{278.1 - 135.7}{135.7}$		
$1.049 \times 50,000$	52,450	
$\dfrac{278.1 - 153.0}{153.0}$		
$0.818 \times 30,000$	24,540	(76,990)
Indexed gain		43,010

Other aspects of taxation of chargeable gains for companies

9.22 The treatment of the disposal of chattels, part disposals and negligible value claims is the same for companies as it is for individuals, subject only to the differences set out above. However, the principal private residence relief, gift relief and business asset disposal relief, are not available to companies.

Rollover relief and holdover relief is available to companies, but not for intangible assets (e.g. goodwill and the various quotas we listed in Chapter 8.9). As we saw earlier, a different form of rollover relief is available on disposal of intangible assets where the proceeds are reinvested in new intangibles. The company has the right to choose which set of rules to apply if the assets were owned on 1 April, 2002.

Companies can also benefit from a substantial shareholdings exemption that provides that a gain on a disposal of shares by a company will not normally be a chargeable gain so long as certain conditions are met. 'Substantial' here means at least 10% of the ordinary shares and entitlement to at least 10% of the assets on a winding up. The shares must have been held for at least 12 months in the six years prior to disposal. The exemption only applies to sales of shares in a trading company (or holding company of a trading group), sold by a trading company itself or a member of a trading group.

Companies also need special rules for determining the cost of quoted securities, in much the same way as we saw for individuals. The rules for companies are slightly different however, and you will need to see the website for an explanation and worked examples.

Relief for losses

9.23 As with individual taxpayers, companies are entitled to relief for trading and property business losses. The rules are slightly different for companies, however, and companies are also entitled to loss relief for non-trading loan relationship deficits (which don't arise for individuals).

The rules for loss relief for companies were changed with effect from 1 April 2017. Therefore there are two periods with different treatment i.e. pre and post April 2017, but for our purposes we will only consider the post April 2017 rules.

Trading losses

9.24 If there is a loss after adjusting trading results, then that loss can be deducted from total profits before deducting qualifying charitable donations of the same period (and the previous 3 years). A current year claim must be made first, but then any remaining loss can be carried back to the previous 12 month periods.

In response to the impact of Covid-19, this "carry back" relief was temporarily extended and losses could be carried back an additional 2 years earlier from relevant accounting periods ending in the period 1 April 2020 to 31 March 2022. This extended relief was capped at £2,000,000 of losses for all relevant accounting periods ending in the period 1 April 2020 to 31 March 2021 and a separate cap of £2,000,000 applied for all relevant accounting periods ending in the period 1 April 2021 to 31 March 2022, with groups will be subject to a group cap of £2,000,000 for each relevant period.

Although the company cannot restrict loss relief it is claiming, it can however choose not to claim the loss in the current and prior period(s), and may chose instead to carry the loss forward to future periods. A loss carried forward can be claimed against total profits, and when carried forward in this way, does not have to reduce total profits to nil i.e. it is possible to preserve qualifying charitable donations. Note, the loss can only be offset against total profits of a later period if the company is carrying on the same trade.

With effect from 1 April 2017, the amount of a company's annual profits that can be relieved by losses brought forward is limited to 50% of the company's TTP in excess of £5million. The £5million needs to be pro-rated for accounting periods which less than 12 months long. This means that large companies with profits over £5m will still pay some corporation tax despite having brought forward losses available.

Activity

Zoot Suit Ltd had the following results over a number of years:
y/e 31 March 2020 trading loss of £10m and chargeable gains of £1m
y/e 31 March 2021 trading profit of £8m and property business profit of £3m
y/e 31 March 2022 trading profit of £3m and qualifying charitable donations of £1m.
How will the trading losses be relieved?

Feedback

The 2019/20 loss can be offset against total profits up to the maximum of £10m, in this case the total profits are £1m. The remaining £9m can be carried forward.

In 2020/21, Zoot Suit Ltd will be able to claim maximum relief of £5m plus 50% x ((£8m+£3m) – 5m) = £3m i.e. £8m in total. This TTP in the year of £3m and £1m loss to be carried forward to 2021/22.

In 2021/22, Zoot Suit Ltd will be able to claim relief for the remaining £1m of losses, leaving enough total profit to absorb the qualifying charitable donations in that year resulting in net taxable profit of £1m.

A company that makes a trading loss therefore has to make a decision about whether to use the loss in the current period, carry the loss back to the previous 3 years or carry it forward to later periods. A number of things have to be considered. Carry back to the previous 12 months has the advantage of generating an immediate repayment i.e. it has a cash flow advantage. This is therefore often what business will prefer to do. The respective rates of corporation tax in each of the years is relevant, as is the possibility that qualifying charitable donations may be lost.

Non Trading losses

9.24   Loss relief is also available for non-trading losses. A property business loss can be offset first against total profits of the current period. Any amount not used can be carried forward to future periods so long as the property business continues in those periods.

Non trading loan relationship deficits can be offset against total profits in the current year, or against non trading loan relationship income in the previous year. The company can choose how much to claim, if any, and any part not claimed in the current or prior period can be carried forward for offset against total profits in future periods.

Company groups

9.25   While companies may operate alone, it is not unusual to find groups of companies, consisting of a parent company and subsidiary companies. The UK tax system does not allow for consolidation of group profits as is done for accounting purposes. Instead, as we have seen, each separate company is responsible for its own tax liability even if part of a group. There are, however, some special rules that recognise group relationships and allow for certain reliefs between group members.

There are three forms of group relationship:

- Related companies (51% groups) – are used to allocate shared thresholds between groups, eg AIA, instalment payments;
- Loss groups (75% groups and consortia) – allow group members to transfer losses to other group members; and
- Capital gains groups – allow capital assets to be deemed to have been transferred to other group members, so that they carry the capital loss.

 If you cover company groups in your course, please see the separate chapter online that will lead you through these special rules.

Payment of corporation tax

9.26 In the UK, companies are required to use a system of *self-assessment* for their corporation tax computation. A company is required to perform its own tax computation and pay over the tax due according to this computation on the correct dates. HMRC have up to one year from the date the return is due to be filed (or at least a year after the return is filed if filed later) to query the calculations. If they do not query the computation within this time then the year is completed.

Companies are also required to maintain full records of all the information they use to produce their tax computation for 6 years beyond the end of the period of assessment. Companies failing to be able to produce records if asked to by HMRC in this period could be prosecuted.

Large companies are required to nominate a 'senior accounting officer' who will be required to certify each year that the tax accounting arrangements for the company are appropriate. If he or she fails to comply with this new rule, a personal fine of up to £5,000 could be imposed.

Payment dates

9.27 Companies with taxable profits of up to £1.5million mostly pay their corporation tax liability 9 months and one day after their accounting period end. For example, a company with a 31 December year end will be required to pay corporation tax on the following 1 October. However, for large companies there is a requirement for quarterly instalments of their corporation tax liability to spread their payments throughout the tax year.

Companies that have augmented profits of (TTP + non-group UK dividends) more than £1.5m required to pay a percentage of the total tax liability in four equal payments. The actual quarterly dates on which payments should be made are calculated using the rule: the first payment is due on the 14th day of the 7th month of the accounting period, then in three further equal payments at quarterly intervals.

Activity

Calculate the corporate tax payment dates for a large company with a 12 month accounting period ending 31 December 2022.

Feedback

The due dates will be:

1st instalment	14 July 2022
2nd instalment	14 October 2022
3rd instalment	14 January 2023
Final instalment	14 April 2023

You should note that the final instalment is not due until 3 months and 14 days after the accounting period ends. This enables the company to ensure all their records have been completed for the accounting period so that a full determination of the tax due is possible.

From 1 April 2019, very large corporations with augmented profits in excess of £20 million are required to pay in the 3rd, 6th, 9th and 12th months.

Where accounting periods exist of less than 12 months, then fewer than four payments will be made. The final instalment will always be due 3 months and 14 days after the end of the accounting period. Earlier instalments are only due if the due dates of the usual gaps (six months and 13 days then 3 monthly intervals) fall before the due date for the final instalment.

This means:

Accounting period length	Instalments due
less than 3 months	final
3–6 months	first + final
6–9 months	first, second + final
9–12 months	all four instalments

Activity

Calculate the instalment dates due for a large company with an accounting period of 1 January 2022 to 31 July 2022.

Feedback

First instalment	14 July 2022 (14th day of 7th month)
Second instalment	14 October 2022 (3 months after 14 July)
Third instalment	not due (would be due 3 months after 14 October 2022 which would fall after final instalment)
Final instalment	14 November 2022 (3 months and 14 days after the end of the accounting period)

Where a company has an accounting period of less than 12 months the amounts of tax due at each instalment should be calculated using the formula:

$$\frac{3 \times \text{CTL}}{n}$$

where:

- CTL is the amount of the company's total tax liability for the accounting period due for payment by instalments
- n is the number of months in the accounting period.

Where a company has reasonable grounds for believing that its total tax liability at the end of the year will be less than the total amounts that will be paid based on amounts currently being paid in instalments, then the company can adjust subsequent payments to reflect the correct liability (or make a claim for a repayment if they have already paid too much).

In working out whether a company is 'small' or 'large' for the purposes of paying corporation tax, by reference to the taxable profits, we need to take into account any 51% group companies, which means companies where more than 50% of its ordinary shares is beneficially owned by another company. Company A is a related 51% group company of company B if:

1. A is a 51% subsidiary of B
2. B is a 51% subsidiary of A
3. A and B are 51% subsidiaries of the same company.

If a company has 51% group companies, the £1.5million threshold for deciding whether instalment payments are required is divided by the number of associated companies. For a company with 4 related 51% group companies, the threshold becomes £1.5m/5 or £300,000. If any of these companies has taxable profits in excess of £300,000, it will be required to pay by instalments.

 You can now attempt Quick Quiz questions 9-12 and Full questions 2 & 4-6.

Corporation tax reform

9.28 In March 2016 a 'Business Tax Roadmap' was released by HM Treasury. This makes suggestions for further changes to all business taxes, particularly those paid by corporations. Some of these changes have been outlined above, such as changed rules for the carrying forward of corporate losses. Several other changes in relation to international issues will be explored in Chapter 12.

The Office for Tax Simplification published a report in July 2017 which makes recommendations for simplifying corporation tax, particularly for small companies, including closer alignment between tax rules and accounting rules. Much of the focus for corporation tax in more recent years has been on corporate tax avoidance, and in particular by multinational companies. This has overshadowed attempts to simplify the current system, which remains very complex and constantly changing.

The UK was on target for a phased reduction in the corporation tax rate to a minimum of 17% when the Covid-19 pandemic created a need to reassess tax policy. As a result of this reassessment, the corporation tax rate will now be increased from 19% to 25% from 1 April 2023. This delay in implementation of the new rate will allow companies time to prepare, but will mean that the Government will not see the increased revenue until 2023/24.

Concern about the impact of a 25% rate on small companies has also led the Government to reintroduce the small profits rate for companies, also from 1 April 2023, allowing them to continue to be taxed at 19%. This will reinstate the system that used to apply prior to 2015, where a transitional rate band is introduced to smooth the transition from 19% to 25%.

Basic tax planning of UK resident companies

9.29 Companies which are family owned and managed may have some flexibility when remunerating their owner/managers. Paying dividends or providing benefits in kind rather than high salaries may reduce the total national insurance contributions which must be paid. For example, when employees make contributions to a pension scheme the contributions are allowable deductions for tax purposes but not for national insurance contributions. However, if the contributions are made by the employer, then they are fully deductible for tax purposes and do not give rise to a liability to either employee or employer national insurance contributions. Hence it may be tax efficient for small companies to operate non-contributory pension schemes.

The new super deduction for capital allowances need careful consideration. It should not be assumed that it will automatically be beneficial for the company and some long term planning is required to manage the transition to the 25% corporate tax rate in 2023.

Further discussion of tax planning related to companies can be found in Chapter 11.

Summary

This chapter has provided you with the skills needed to calculate the corporation tax liability of companies which are resident in the UK.

To calculate a company's tax liability it is necessary to undertake a number of steps:

- identify each source of income for a company;

- determine the category of income which is used to calculate the taxable income for each source of income;

- using the current year basis (which applies to the income and expenditure of companies) to calculate the income that is assessable and determine any deductions from that income which are allowable for tax purposes; and

- determine details of any charges on income which are paid by the company.

This will enable you to calculate the corporation tax liability.

You have been able to compare and contrast the taxation of companies with the taxation of individuals. You might like to list the similarities and differences and decide if the differences between the two are sufficient for one business medium to be preferred to the other. However, it is important to remember that tax is just one aspect of the environment in which businesses operate. Other considerations are at least as important, for example the benefit of limited liability and the ability to raise extra finance. We will look at this more in Chapter 11.

Discussion topics

1. What are the key differences between the application of trading profit rules for sole traders and for companies? Must these differences exist?

2. Is it fair that dividends paid by companies attract special treatment via a lower rate of tax compared to other forms of income?

3. Why are tax years and financial years different?

4. Why are special rules needed for describing how loan relationships, research and development costs and intangibles costs should be allocated to accounting periods for tax computations?

5. Should large companies have to pay their corporate tax bills so much earlier than smaller companies?

6. What are the pros and cons of using profits calculated using International Financial Reporting Standards as a basis for corporation tax?

7. Is it fair that the smallest company now pays the same rate of corporation tax as the very largest?

8. Why do companies in the creative industries appear to get special tax treatment? Is this fair on companies in other sectors?

Quick quiz

1. Grotius Ltd prepares accounts for the sixteen months to 31 December 2022. What are its accounting periods for corporation tax purposes?

2. Helvetius Ltd receives dividends from a UK company of £132,000. How will they be treated for corporation tax purposes?

3. Justinian Ltd licences a partnership to use its patent and accrues patent royalties of £3,900 (net) for the year. How will this be treated for corporation tax purposes?

4. Magician Ltd's accounts for the year ended 31 December 2022 show the following accrued income received and interest paid:

Bank interest receivable	£7,000
Interest payable on loan to purchase a rental property	£5,650
Interest payable on overdue corporation tax	£1,200
Interest on loan to purchase plant used in the trade	£3,600

    What is the amount taxable as a non-trading loan relationship?

5. New Money Ltd is a small company. It spends £11,000 on hiring temporary staff to carry out scientific research in connection with its business activities. What effect will this expenditure have on the company's corporation tax liability?

6. Isocrates Ltd acquired a patent during the year ended 30 June 2022 and charged amortisation in its accounts at the rate of 3%. How will it be treated for corporation tax purposes?

7. Quay Ltd, a small close company, made a loan of £30,000 to a shareholder in July 2021. The company's accounting period ends on 31 July each year. The loan was not repaid and penalty tax of £9,750 was paid to HMRC. In July 2022, the shareholder repaid £15,000 of the loan. How much of the penalty tax can be recovered and when?

8. Ranch Ltd is a close company and provides a new car for one of its participators, Billy. Billy is neither a director nor employee of Ranch Ltd. As a benefit in kind for income tax, the value of the car would be £2,750. What are the tax consequences for Ranch Ltd and for Billy?

9. Perigrine Ltd sold an asset for £14,600 in August 2022 that had been originally purchased in February 2003 for £5,000. What is the amount of the indexed gain on the sale of the asset?

10. Origami Ltd has trading profit of £7m and investment income of £4m for the year ended 30 June 2022. The company has a loss brought forward from the year ended 30 June 2021 of £10m. What is the maximum amount of loss that can be set off in the year ended 30 June 2022?

11. Time Ltd has the following shareholding:

Usual Ltd	40%
Verity Ltd	60%
Wallace Ltd	80%

Which companies are related for the purposes of determining the limit for paying by instalments?

12. Lycophron Ltd has a corporation tax liability of £650,000 and has an accounting period of 5 months to 31 May 2022. When will its instalments of corporation tax be due?

Questions

Question 1

Ultimate Upholsterers Ltd is a UK resident company which manufactures leather upholstered chairs. It has been trading for many years. The company's results for the year ended 31 March 2023 are summarised as follows.

	£
Trading profits*	375,000
Dividend from UK company (received 29 May 2022)	18,000
Gross (non-trading) loan interest receivable	12,000
Gross (non-trading) debenture interest payable	10,000
Profit on sale of land	37,000
Writing down allowances on plant and machinery	49,000

* As adjusted for taxation, but before capital allowances and adjustment for the lease premium on the factory (see below).

The company operates from a factory that was first occupied by Ultimate Upholsterers Ltd on 1 October 2002, under the terms of a 25-year lease which was acquired for a premium of £50,000. The land had been purchased in December 1984 for £10,000 and sold in February 2023 for £47,410.

Required: Calculate the corporation tax payable for the year ended 31 March 2023.

Question 2

ABC Ltd (a company with one related associate company) has augmented profit of £1.2million and a corporate tax liability of £228,000 for FY22.

Required: Calculate the due dates for instalments of corporation tax ABC Ltd will have to pay and the amounts due on each of these dates if:

(a) The company has a 12 month accounting period to 31 October 2022;
(b) The company produces accounts for 8 months to 30 June 2022 instead (assume the amount of the tax liability is not affected for the purpose of this question).

Question 3

Pendulum Ltd is a medium sized UK company that owns a gymnasium and leisure facility in Stafford. The company has been trading for several years. During the year ended 31 March 2023, the company's accounts revealed the following:

	£		£
Depreciation	43,150	Trading profit	262,772
Directors' fees (1)	37,840	Building society interest accrued	759
Patent royalty payable (2)	3,500	Debenture interest accrued	1,200
Qualifying charitable donation	5,000		
Entertaining customers	730		
Salary and wages	16,500		
Non trading loan interest payable (3)	700		
Rent of business premises	3,000		
Audit fee	1,320		
Trading expenses (4)	25,328		
Net profit before taxation	127,663		
	264,731		264,731

(1) Directors' fees were all paid within 9 months of the year end.
(2) The patent royalty is payable to a UK company.
(3) £100 of the £700 non-trading loan interest payable was accrued as at 31 March 2023.
(4) The trading expenses include the following items:

	£
Legal expenses in respect of the following:	
The non trading loan	500
Staff service agreements	90
Gifts to customers:	
6 bottles of malt whisky	280
1,000 diaries bearing the company's name	1,250
Redecoration of café area	3,200

(5) The written down value of plant and machinery on 1 April 2022 was £263,504. On 1 August 2022 the company sold some plant for £9,400 which had originally cost £11,000. On 31 January 2023 plant costing £10,500 was acquired. On the same day, a low emission car costing £13,000 was purchased for the use of the marketing director of the company, who used the vehicle 50% for private purposes.

Required: Compute Pendulum Ltd's trading profits, taxable total profits, and corporation tax payable for the accounting period 31 March 2023. State when the tax will be payable.

Question 4

(a) Burgundy Ltd bought an office block to use in its business in August 1992. In April 2022 the company sold the building for £300,000, resulting in an indexed chargeable gain of £125,400, and at the same time bought another office block to use in its business.

Assuming that Burgundy claims rollover relief calculate the chargeable gain arising on the disposal of the office block if the replacement block costs:
- (a)   £380,000
- (b)   £280,000
- (c)   £120,000.

(b) Navy Ltd sold a warehouse used exclusively for business purposes for £200,000 in November 2014 realising an indexed chargeable gain of £50,000. The company bought fixed plant for £240,000 in November 2014. The company elects to hold-over the gain on the warehouse against the fixed plant.

How will the held-over gain be treated (assuming current tax rules apply) if:
- (a)   Navy Ltd sells the fixed plant in January 2023
- (b)   Navy Ltd sells the fixed plant in April 2025
- (c)   Navy Ltd bought another warehouse for business use in December 2014 and elected to transfer the held-over gain on the fixed plant to the new warehouse which cost £220,000
- (d)   The new warehouse in part (c) cost £185,000.

(Note: answer available via lecturer's website)

Question 5 (based on an ACCA question)

Retro Ltd's summarised statement of profit or loss for the year ended 31 March 2023 is as follows:

	Notes	£	£
Gross profit			127,100
Operating expenses:			
Depreciation		27,240	
Gifts and donations	1	2,300	
Impairment loss	2	1,600	
Leasing costs	3	4,400	
Other expenses	4	205,160	
			(240,700)
Finance costs:			
Interest payable	5		(6,400)
Loss before taxation			(120,000)

Notes:

1. Gifts and donations are as follows:

	£
Gifts to employees (food hampers costing £60 each)	720
Gifts to customers	
(calendars costing £8 each and displaying Retro's name)	480
Political donations	420
Qualifying charitable donations	680
	2,300

2. On 31 March 2023, Retro Ltd wrote off an impairment loss of £1,600 relating to a trade debt. This was in respect of an invoice which had been due for payment on 10 November 2022.

3. The leasing costs of £4,400 are in respect of a motor car lease which commenced on 1 April 2022. The leased motor car has CO_2 emissions of 145 grams per kilometre.

4. The figure of £205,160 for other expenses includes a fine of £5,100 for a breach of health and safety regulations, and legal fees of £4,860 in connection with the defence of Retro Ltd's internet domain name, the remaining expenses are all fully allowable.

5. The interest payable is in respect of the company's 5% loan notes which were repaid on 31 July 2022. Interest of £9,600 was paid on 31 July 2022, and an accrual of £3,200 had been provided for at 1 April 2022. The loan notes were issued to finance the company's trading activities.

Additional information:

On 1 April 2022, the tax written down value of the plant and machinery main pool was £39,300. The following vehicles were purchased during the year ended 31 March 2023:

	Date of purchase	Cost	CO_2 emissions
Motor car (1)	8 June 2022	14,700	44 g/km
Delivery van	3 August 2022	28,300	162 g/km
Motor car (2)	19 October 2022	12,400	0 g/km

Retro Ltd commenced trading on 1 September 2020. The company's results for its two previous periods of trading are as follows:

	y/e 31/8/21	p/e 31/3/22
Tax adjusted trading profit	56,600	47,900
Bank interest receivable	1,300	0
Qualifying charitable donations paid	(540)	(330)

Retro Ltd is expected to return to profitability in the year ended 31 March 2024 and continue to be profitable in subsequent years.

> *Required:*
> 1. Calculate Retro Ltd's adjusted trading loss for the year ended 31 March 2023;
> 2. Assuming Retro Ltd claims relief for its trading loss as early as possible, calculate the company's taxable total profits for the year ended 31 August 2021 and the seven month period ended 31 March 2022.
> 3. Identify the amount of unrelieved trading loss which Retro will have at 31 March 2023, and state how this can be relieved.
> (Note: answer available on lecturer's website)

Question 6 (based on an ACCA question)

Gastron Ltd, a UK resident company, is a luxury food manufacturer. The company's summarised income statement for the year ended 31 March 2023 is as follows:

	Notes	£	£
Gross profit			876,500
Operating expenses:			
Depreciation		85,660	
Amortisation of leasehold property	1	6,000	
Gifts and donations	2	2,700	
Professional fees	3	18,800	
Other expenses	4	230,240	(343,400)
Operating profit			533,100
Income from investments:			
Income from property	5	20,600	
Bank interest	6	12,400	
Dividends	7	54,000	87,000
Profit from sale of fixed assets:			
Disposal of shares	8		80,700
			700,800
Interest payable	9		(60,800)
Profit before taxation			640,000

Notes:
1. Leasehold property: on 1 April 2022, Gastron acquired a leasehold office building, paying a premium of £60,000 for the grant of a new ten-year lease. The office building was used for business purposes by Gastron Ltd throughout the year ended 31 March 2023.

2. Gifts and donations were as follows:
Gifts to customers (pens displaying Gastron's name, £60 each) 1,200
Gifts to customers (bottles of alcohol costing £25 each)   1,100
Donation to local charity (Gastron Ltd received free advertising
in the charity's magazine)   400
    2,700

3. Professional fees are as follows:
Legal fees in connection with the renewal of a 45 year property lease in respect of a warehouse   3,600
Legal fees for the issue of debentures (see note 9)   15,200

4. Other expenses: the figure for other expenses includes £1,300 for entertaining suppliers and £900 for entertaining employees.

5. Income from property: Gastron Ltd lets out the whole of an unfurnished freehold office building that is surplus to requirements. The building was let from 1 April 2022 to 31 December 2022 at a monthly rent of £1,800, payable in advance. On 31 December 2022, the tenant left owing two month's rent which Gastron Ltd was unable to recover.

During January 2023, the company spent £3,700 redecorating the property. The building was re-let from 1 February 2023 at a monthly rent of £1,950, on which date the tenant paid six month's rent in advance.

6. Bank interest received: the bank interest was received on 31 March 2023. The bank deposits are held for non-trading purposes.

7. Dividends received: during the year ended 31 March 2023 Gastron Ltd received dividends of £36,000 from Tasteless plc, an unconnected UK company and dividends of £18,000 from Culinary Ltd, a 100% UK subsidiary. Both figures are the actual cash amounts received.

8. Profit on disposal of shares: The profit on disposal of shares is in respect of a 1% shareholding that was sold on 14 October 2022. The disposal resulted in a chargeable gain of £74,800. This figure is after taking account of indexation.

9. Interest payable: this is in respect of the company's 5% debenture loan stock that was issued on 1 April 2022. The proceeds of the issue were used to finance the company's trading activities. Interest of £30,400 was paid on 30 September 2022 and again on 31 March 2023.

10. Plant and machinery: on 1 April 2022, the tax written down values of plant and machinery were as follows:
Main pool   16,700
Special rate pool   18,400

These transactions took place during the year ended 31 March 2022:

		£
19 May 2022	purchased equipment	12,792
12 July 2022	purchased car (1)	9,800
11 August 2022	purchased car (2)	16,200
5 October 2022	purchased lorry	17,200
5 March 2023	sold equipment	(3,300)

Motor car (1), purchased on 12 July 2022 for £9,800, has a CO_2 emission rating of 135g/km. Motor car (2), purchased on 11 August 2022 for £16,200 is a low emission car (CO_2 emission rate of 0g/km). The equipment sold on 5 March 2023 for £3,300 was originally purchased in 2005 for £8,900.

Required: Calculate Gastron Ltd's corporation tax payable for the year ended 31 March 2023 and state the due date for payment.
(Note: answer available on lecturer's website)

Further test questions for this chapter to test your knowledge can be found in the student section of the website at:

http://www.fiscalpublications.com/lymerandoats/2022

Further reading and examples

Combs, A. (2022), *UK Corporation Tax, Capital Gains Tax and VAT Practice Questions (2nd edition 2022/23)*, Fiscal Publications: Malvern.
   – a large test bank of questions linked to the content of this chapter that will enable you to thoroughly test your knowledge of this work with exam-level questions. See
      https://www.fiscalpublications.com/uk-ct-cgt-vat-practice-questions/2022

Combs, A., Tutin, R. & Rowes, P. (2022), *Taxation: incorporating the 2022 Finance Act*, Fiscal Publications: Malvern.
   – use this book for many other examples to further develop and test your knowledge of this chapter's contents. See
      https://www.fiscalpublications.com/combsandtutin/2022

Evans, C., Hasseldine, J., Lymer, A., Ricketts, R. & Sandford, C. (2017), *Comparative Taxation: Why tax systems differ*, Fiscal Publications: Malvern.
 – further details on the principles of how and why corporates are taxed and comparisons of how this is achieved in different countries.

James, S. & Nobes, C. (2018), *Economics of Taxation: 18th edition*, Fiscal Publications: Malvern.
   – useful additional perspective on the role and design of corporation taxation in the UK.

For more information about how different systems of corporation tax work to reduce the double taxation of dividends, see Oats, L (2002) "Taxing Companies and Their Shareholders" in *The International Tax System*, Lymer & Hasseldine eds, Springer.

10 Value Added Tax

Introduction

10.1 Value Added Tax (VAT) has become an increasingly important source of income for the government since it was introduced in 1973. It is the third highest tax revenue source after income tax and national insurance contributions.

At the end of this chapter you will be able to:

- state the broad principles of the UK's VAT system;
- state the criteria for compulsory registration and deregistration for VAT and explain the advantages and disadvantages of registration;
- identify taxable supplies and calculate a trader's VAT payable/repayable;
- list which goods are standard rated, zero rated and exempt from VAT and explain the differences in their treatment;
- describe the main characteristics of the administration of VAT including various special schemes that currently exist in the UK;
- state the VAT consequences of importing and exporting goods and services; and
- describe the system for administering VAT which operates within the EU.

Background

10.2 VAT was introduced in April 1973 partly as a consequence of the UK joining the European Economic Community (now the European Union). It replaced purchase tax and introduced three classifications into which all goods and services are allocated – zero rated, exempt and standard rated. Sales and purchases of goods and services (from UK or overseas traders) are taxed according to their classification into one of these categories.

When VAT was first introduced it was a relatively simple tax, however it has increased in complexity and can now be a difficult tax to apply in practice. It has become a specialist area of tax compliance and planning.

The legal basis for VAT is contained in the Value Added Tax Act (VATA 1994) and subsequent Finance Acts. VAT is managed by HMRC.

Principles of VAT

10.3 VAT is an *indirect tax* and is the UK's primary *consumption* or *expenditure tax*. VAT is borne by the final consumer, although it is charged whenever a *taxable person* makes a *taxable supply* of goods or services in the course of business at each stage in a supply chain for any taxable supply. It is a tax on turnover, not on income or profit.

Before giving more detail of how VAT operates in practice, let's review what we mean by the terms taxable persons and taxable supplies.

A taxable person

10.4 A person is a taxable person, referred to as a trader, for the purposes of VAT while he or she is registered under the Value Added Tax Act 1994. As we see below, a trader is required by law to register for VAT once their annual turnover of a taxable supply reaches a registration threshold that is set each year in the budget. For this tax year it is set at £85,000, unchanged from the previous two years and to be maintained at this level until March 2024. However, any trader making a taxable supply can register for VAT even if their turnover for the year is less than the threshold.

A taxable person can be an individual or partnership, company, club, association or charity.

A taxable supply

10.5 A taxable supply includes all forms of business supply made in return for consideration (i.e. for money or payment in kind) unless it is explicitly exempted from VAT by law or regulation. For example, in addition to the normal sales activities a business may engage in, the following transfers are all taxable supplies:

- Any transfer of a whole asset is a supply of goods. The transfer of any share of an asset is a supply of services.
- The supply of any form of power, heat, refrigeration or ventilation.
- The grant, assignment or surrender of a major interest in land.
- The transfer of fixed assets or current assets, including transfers to the registered trader whether or not for a consideration.
- Business gifts are taxable supplies unless the transfer is either a gift of goods made in the course or furtherance of the business (which cost the donor not more than £50) or a gift to an actual or potential customer of the business of an industrial sample which is not ordinarily available for sale to the public.
- Goods which were owned by the business and are put to any private use or are used, or made available to any person, including the registered trader, to use for a private purpose are taxable at cost.

- Goods lent to someone outside the business or hired to someone are a taxable supply of services.

A taxable supply is considered to have occurred once the ownership of the asset being supplied transfers from one person to another. This means the actual physical transfer of the asset, if it is a good, may happen after the supply has actually been made and supplies of services will have occurred for VAT purposes once the service has been carried out.

The value of a taxable supply

10.6 If the supply is for a consideration in money, then VAT should be added to the price charged for the good or service. If the supply is for a consideration which is not wholly in money (e.g. involving payment in kind) then, the money value of the consideration is taken to be the VAT inclusive price.

The market value of a supply of goods or services is taken to be the amount which would be payable by a person in an *arms' length* transaction. This means that if a business makes a taxable supply to a *connected person* the VAT will be due on the price that would have been charged on the supply had this transaction been with an unconnected recipient. This rule ensures the correct amount of VAT is charged on all supplies.

The current standard VAT rate is 20%. This amount is added to the value of the sale of a good or service to determine the total amount to be collected from the customer. The VAT proportion of the total consideration is $20 \div (100 + 20) = 1/6$. This proportion is called the *VAT fraction* and can be used to find how much VAT will have been paid on any standard rated supply if you are only given the VAT inclusive amount of the supply.

Input and output tax

10.7 The VAT system operates by registered traders collecting VAT on behalf of the Government from customers they supply to – VAT is therefore an example of an indirect tax. Registered traders can also, however, reclaim VAT they suffer on their purchases. These two parts of the VAT system from the trader's perspective are referred to as *input tax* and *output tax*.

Input tax is the VAT a taxable person has to pay:

- on the supply to him or her of any goods or services;
- on the acquisition by him or her of any goods from another EU member state; or
- paid or payable by him or her on the importation of any goods from a place outside the EU provided that the goods or services are, or will be, used for the purposes of a business carried on by the taxable person.

A taxable person's output tax is the VAT charged on taxable supplies made. The difference between input and output tax is the amount they pay over to the Government on a regular basis. We will shortly see how this works in practice.

The tax point

10.8   VAT is accounted for on a periodic basis, usually quarterly, and so we need to know the date on which transactions occur in order to determine which time period it belongs to. The deemed date of supply of taxable goods or services is called the *tax point*. The basic tax point is the date on which a supply of goods or services is treated as taking place.

A supply of goods will be treated as taking place when:

- the supplier sends the goods to the customer;
- the customer collects the goods from the supplier; or
- the goods are made available for the customer to use. This might be, for example, when the supplier assembles something at the premises of the customer.

A supply of services is any taxable supply which is not a supply of goods. As no physical transfers take place when services are supplied, the supply of services will be treated as taking place at the time when the services are carried out and all the work is finished.

A trader can choose to use these basic tax points, however, if a tax invoice is issued within 14 days of the date on which the supply is considered to have taken place according to the basic rules, the supply can be treated as taking place at the time the invoice is issued instead. This makes the practical process of accounting for VAT more straight forward as it is then linked with the accounting part of the transaction, not the physical movement of goods or supply of the service. HMRC can, at the taxpayer's request, substitute a period longer than the 14 days. For example, many companies generate all invoices at the end of the month and so some invoices may be generated more than 14 days after the basic tax point. If this is the case, then it is likely that this end of month date will be treated as the date of supply.

The impact of VAT on registered traders and final consumers

10.9   The easiest way to illustrate the operation of VAT we have outlined so far in this chapter, and its actual impact on registered traders and their consumers, is to use an example. The following activity illustrates the cascade effect of VAT where traders account for VAT on their value added at each stage in a production process.

Activity

Susan runs a small farm as a business on which she keeps rare breed sheep. She sells fleeces for £200 to a local manufacturer, Country Crafts Ltd, which employs spinners and knitters to produce garments which are sold for a total of £600 to a shop, Country Clothes Ltd, which sells the clothes to members of the public for £1,000. All three businesses are registered for VAT purposes.

None of the above amounts include VAT, which you can assume is levied at the standard rate of 20% on each of the transactions. Calculate the impact of VAT on the transactions described above.

Feedback

Taxable person	Cost (£)	Input tax (£)	Net sales price (£)	Output tax (£)	VAT payable to HMRC (£)
Susan	0	0	200	40	40
Country Crafts	200	40	600	120	80
Country Clothes	600	120	1,000	200	80
					200

Note that the VAT suffered by the final consumer is £200 which is exactly the amount payable to HMRC over the three transactions (£40 + £80 + £80).

Each person has to pay input tax on taxable supplies received and charges output tax on taxable supplies made.

The difference between the output tax charged and input tax paid must be paid to HMRC. This simple example does not illustrate it, but if there is an excess of input tax over output tax the excess can be reclaimed from HMRC.

Notice that as registered businesses collect VAT from their customers, but can deduct (reclaim) VAT they pay on their inputs, these businesses are not affected by the direct cost of VAT. So long as all the input tax is recoverable, the only impact is the administrative cost and any impact on cash flow between when they pay input tax and receive output tax. Some types of input tax are not recoverable, however, and this will be a cost borne by the trader.

Registration and deregistration

10.10 A registered trader is a sole trader, partnership or company who is registered for VAT. Failure to register carries severe penalties as well as a liability to pay the VAT which should have been accounted for.

Initial registration

10.11 A person who makes taxable supplies, but is not already registered for VAT, becomes liable to be registered:

- at the end of any month, if the value of taxable supplies for the preceding 12 months has exceeded £85,000 in 2022/23, or
- at any time, if there are reasonable grounds for believing that the value of taxable supplies in the period of the next 30 days will exceed £85,000.

In determining the value of a trader's supplies for this purpose supplies of goods or services that are capital assets of the business are ignored.

The second of these tests is referred to as the future prospects rule and is designed to capture large, one off transactions that are standard rated. Traders can avoid registration under this rule, however, if HMRC can be persuaded that the business has only exceeded the limit because of unusual circumstances and its turnover will fall below the deregistration threshold once they have passed. In one case, *Mark Mills-Henning v Revenue & Customs Commissioners* [2012] UKFTT 444, the trader had a sudden short period of increased sales that took the business over the threshold, but because the turnover then fell so that it was below the threshold, his accountant didn't seek exemption from registration. The Tribunal found that Mr Mills-Henning should have been registered from the date the business exceeded the registration threshold. The decision whether to allow exemption from registration must be made by HMRC, and not by the trader.

The trader will be registered from the end of the month following the 12-month period in which they exceeded the limit. If HMRC and the trader agree to an earlier date, this will be used instead.

If a trader's taxable supplies will not exceed £85,000, then they are not required to register for but they may choose to do so, as we will see later.

Where a business is split so as to keep each part below the registration threshold, HMRC can treat it as a single business in determining if registration is required.

As soon as it becomes known that a trader is required to register they should keep VAT records and begin to charge VAT on any taxable outputs they supply (although they cannot issue VAT invoices until a VAT registration number is received). During this period the trader should notify customers that the price charged is VAT inclusive and a full tax invoice should be sent within 30 days of receiving the registration number.

Traders who should register, but fail to do so, will still be liable for VAT on taxable supplies made from the date on which they should have registered. If it is not possible to collect the VAT due from customers retrospectively, then they will be liable themselves for the tax they should have collected. This could prove very expensive of course as it could equate to up to 20% of the value of all the supplies made since they should have registered.

Fiscal Fact

The cost to the government of allowing small traders not to register for VAT where their turnover doesn't exceed the registration threshold is estimated to be £1.7 billion for 2020/21. [Source: HMRC Structured relief cost estimates – updated December 2021]

Voluntary registration

10.12 It is possible to register for VAT even if the business' turnover is below the registration limit. There are a number of benefits of voluntary registration:

- input tax suffered can be reclaimed; and
- the trader may appear to be a larger business than they actually are, which may increase their status with customers.

The key disadvantages of voluntary registration are:

- customers who are not VAT registered cannot reclaim the output tax charged on the supply and so the trader may lose their competitive edge with non-registered customers; and
- the administrative burden of registration (e.g. completing quarterly VAT returns and handling queries from HMRC) should not be overlooked.

The tax status of a trader's customers is an important factor when deciding whether voluntary registration is likely to be beneficial. Let's consider this in a little more detail with an example.

Activity

Elaine makes patchwork quilts. She can make a maximum of 40 quilts in a year which she can sell on the open market for £500 each (before VAT). She does not think that customers would be willing to pay any more. Alternatively, she has been made an offer to sell her total production for the year to an exclusive retail outlet, again for £500 a quilt excluding VAT. The materials to make a quilt cost £100 before VAT.

Under what circumstances should Elaine apply for voluntary registration for VAT?

Feedback

Sales to public	If registered £	If not registered £
Value of supply		
40 × (£500 × 120%)	24,000	
40 × £500		20,000
Less output VAT		
40 × (£500 × 20%)	(4,000)	
Net sales	20,000	20,000
Less costs 40 × £120	(4,800)	(4,800)
Reclaimed VAT	800	nil
Profit	16,000	15,200

The difference in the two positions is therefore a result of the extra cost to Elaine of her input tax – if she is a registered trader, this is not a cost she will have to bear. However, if she registers, she will need to start charging her customers £600 (£500 + 20%) for her quilts, rather than £500 if she does not register. She must be certain that her sales will not be offset by this extra price as she only needs to lose 2 sales of her 40 to then have a lower overall profit.

If Elaine took the option of selling to the retailer instead, the numbers would be the same (i.e. a profit of £16,000 if she registered and £15,200 if she did not) but now as long as the retail outlet was also a registered trader, then the extra cost associated with the output VAT charge would not directly affect this transaction. It would just become part of the retail outlet's input VAT which they can then reclaim. It would be up to the retailer how much of this extra cost to pass on to their own customers.

Deregistration

10.13 Deregistration may also be compulsory or voluntary. Compulsory deregistration will occur if the trader ceases to make taxable supplies.

A trader may ask to be voluntarily deregistered if they can satisfy HMRC their taxable supplies, net of VAT, for the following 12 months will not exceed £83,000, the deregistration limit for this year (unchanged from 2018/19). Traders can not claim to be voluntarily deregistered if they intend to cease to trade (it will be compulsory when they do cease to trade) or if there will be a suspension of taxable supplies for a continuous period of 30 days or more in the next 12 months (their registration cannot be suspended therefore by trading inactivity alone).

The date of a voluntary deregistration is the later of the date on which the request is made or an agreed date between the trader and HMRC.

Fiscal Fact

The number of registered VAT traders was 2.445 million in 2021/22. This was compared with 1.961 million in 2008/9 and 978,000 in 1972/3, the year VAT was introduced. [Source: HMRC Statistics - Number of taxpayers and registered traders as at April 2022]

Taxable supplies and exempt supplies

10.14 The example above (Elaine) illustrated the use of the standard rate (20% currently) for calculating the VAT due. There are actually three possible rates of VAT. The standard rate of 20%, a reduced rate (5%) and zero (i.e. 0%). It might appear strange to have a rate of 0%, but it is an important part of the VAT system as we will see later. The general rule is that any supply that is not exempt, reduced rated or zero rated will be taxable at the standard rate. In this section we consider what types of supply fall in these categories and how this classification affects the VAT system.

Exempt supplies

10.15 The exemptions to VAT are contained in Schedule 9 of the VATA 1994. The Schedule contains a number of groups, which are listed here, together with some important examples of exempt goods and services.

Group 1   Land, including:
- granting of any interest in or right over land
- holiday accommodation
- mooring fees including anchoring and berthing.

Group 2   Insurance.

Group 3   Postal services provided by the post office.

Group 4   Betting, gaming and lotteries.

Group 5   Financial services. Including:
- provision of credit
- issue, transfer or receipt of, or any dealing with, any security or secondary security.

Group 6   Education, including:
- provision of education or research by a school, eligible institution or university or independent private tutor
- supply of any goods or services incidental to the provision of any education, training or re-training.

Group 7   Health and welfare, including:
- supply of services by registered medical practitioners, ophthalmic opticians and dentists
- provision of spiritual welfare by a religious institution as part of a course of instruction or a retreat.

Group 8   Burial and cremation.

Group 9   Supplies to trade unions and professional bodies if in consideration for membership.

Group 10   Entry fees for sports competitions (if non profit making).

Group 11   Works of art when disposed of to public bodies.

Group 12   Fund-raising events by charities and other qualifying bodies (this was extended in the 2000 Budget to include participative events and events on the internet).

Group 13   Provision of cultural services (e.g. admission charges for museums, zoos, galleries, exhibitions, etc).

Group 14   Supplies of goods with unrecoverable input tax.

Group 15   Gold purchased as an investment.

A business of making any of these exempt supplies cannot charge VAT on the supply to a customer. If the trader only makes exempt supplies, they cannot register for VAT and therefore cannot reclaim any input tax they pay. Effectively, they become the final consumer in any supply chain and therefore must bear the full VAT costs as part of the costs of their business.

Fiscal Fact

For 2021/22, exempting education from VAT is estimated to cost the Government £5 billion, rent on domestic dwellings £7.3 billion, health services exemption £8 billion, finance and insurance £12.3 billion and betting/gaming/lottery dues £2.5 billion. [Source: HMRC Structured relief cost estimates as at December 2021]

Zero rated supplies

10.16 Zero rated goods and services are defined in Schedule 8 of the VATA 1994. The Schedule has a number of groups, listed below, together with some important examples of zero rated goods and services. This Schedule has been amended since 1994 to add other groups (specifically groups 19 onwards) some of which are only temporarily given this status.

Group 1   Food, including:
- food of a kind used for human consumption
- animal feeding stuffs.

Exceptions include (these are standard rated instead):
- supply in the course of catering, including all food which is consumed on the premises and all hot food
- ice cream, confectionery and chocolate biscuits
- spirits, beer and wine
- pet food.

Group 2   Sewerage services and water for non-industrial use

Group 3   Books, including:
- books, booklets, brochures, pamphlets and leaflets (but not stationery).
- newspapers, journals and periodicals.

Group 4   Talking books for the blind and handicapped and wireless sets for the blind when supplied to a charity.

Group 5   Construction or conversion of buildings, for residential or charitable purposes.

Group 6   Sale by builders of restored 'protected buildings' (i.e. listed) if used for residential or charitable purposes.

Group 7   International services.

Group 8   Transport (apart from those with less than 10 seats which are standard rated, such as a taxi or hire car).

Group 9   Caravans and houseboats.

Group 10 Gold supplied between capital banks (through a new scheme of investment gold was introduced at the start of 2000).

Group 11 Bank notes.

Group 12 Drugs, medicines, as prescribed by a medical practitioner and aids for the handicapped.

Group 13 Certain imports and exports, etc. (see further explanation on export handling later)

Group 14 Tax-free shops.

Group 15 Sales by charities of donated goods and some supplies to charities e.g. some advertising (not for paid staff), etc.

Group 16 Children's clothing and footwear and some protective clothing e.g. crash helmets and bike helmets (children's and adults – latter being added in the Finance Act 2001).

[Groups 17 – 18 are now removed from the legislation]

Group 19 Women's sanitary products.

Group 20 Personal protective equipment (coronavirus) – temporary measure that ended 31 October 2020

Group 21 Online marketplaces

Group 22 Free zones

Group 23 Installation of energy-saving materials – temporary measure from 1 April 2022 to 31 March 2027

The VAT system is complex and full of anomalies, for example, individual knitting patterns are taxable supplies but booklets containing more than one pattern are zero rated. The classification or exclusion of supplies into or from groups gives rise to lots of disputes and litigation between taxpayers and HMRC.

Fiscal Fact

Currently the UK and Ireland are the only EU countries to zero rate food, water, books or children's clothes. It is estimated the cost of zero rating children's' clothes will be £2.07bn in foregone tax revenues for 2021/22. [Source: HMRC Non-structural tax reliefs - December 2021]

A zero rated supply is a taxable supply; the VAT is calculated at 0% – but it is in effect charged, and therefore not the same as an exempt supply. Businesses making zero rated supplies can still register and reclaim input tax as a taxable person. As such, businesses will often prefer to be classed as making a zero rated supply rather than exempt supplies. Traders making only zero rated supplies can request exemption from registration. Traders with this exemption are responsible for notifying HMRC if there is any change in the nature of their supplies.

Zero rating of food has generated numerous disputes. In *Nestlé v HMRC* [2018] UKUT 29, it was found that although chocolate flavoured Nesquik (when sold as a powder) are zero rated, strawberry and banana Nesquik is standard rated. In another case, *Pulsin' Ltd v HMRC* [2018] UKFTT 775, 'Raw Choc Brownies' were found to be cakes and therefore qualify for zero rating.

You will see from the above list that newspapers and books are zero rated. In a recent case, *News Corp UK & Ireland v HMRC* [2019] UKUT 404, it was held that digital newspapers are also eligible for zero rating. The Government decided to extend zero rating not only to digital newspapers but also e-books. In the March 2020 budget, it was announced that this change would take place from 1 December 2020, however following the outbreak of the Covid-19 pandemic, the Chancellor decided to bring forward this date to 1 May 2020 saying 'we want to make it as easy as possible for people across the UK to get hold of the books they want whilst they are staying at home and saving lives'.

These are examples of the complexities in VAT that arise from the attempt to achieve equity by zero rating basic necessities.

Reduced rated supplies

10.17 A handful of items that would normally fall into the standard rated category are, by special exception instead, taxed at a reduced rate of 5%. These are termed reduced rate supplies. This category includes:

- Domestic fuel or power (or for charity use);
- Installation of energy-saving materials in the home or a charity property (e.g. loft insulation);
- Government grant-funded installation, maintenance and repair of central heating systems or water heating system in homes;
- Ground source heat pumps;
- Qualifying security goods installed in the homes of qualifying pensioners (when installed as part of a Government grant funded scheme);
- Renovations and alterations of homes that have been left unoccupied for at least two years;
- Children's car seats, seat bases and booster seats/cushions;
- Certain conversions, alterations or renovations of non-residential property into residential property;
- Contraceptives (although note that prescription contraceptives are a zero rated supply);
- Nicotine patches and gum (and related 'over the counter', non-prescription, smoking cessation products); and
- Housing alterations to provide mobility aids for the elderly, for example, grab rails and stair lifts.

Fiscal Fact

The cost to the Treasury of reduced rated supplies of domestic fuel and power is estimated to be £5.2 billion for 2021/22. [Source: HMRC Estimated costs of non-structural tax reliefs December 2021]

The VAT fraction (for determining VAT exclusive costs from a VAT inclusive price) on reduced rated items is $1/21$ (i.e. $5 \div (100 + 5)$).

 You can now attempt Quick Quiz questions 1-4 and Full question 1.

Accounting for VAT

You next need to understand the principles of accounting for VAT in a business and you need to know the basic legislation and practices which deal with the accounting for VAT.

VAT returns

10.18 Registered traders will pay and collect VAT over a *tax period*. They must submit a VAT *return*, together with any VAT payable, within one month of the end of a tax period.

A tax period is the length of time covered by their VAT return. It is normally three months long and ends on the last day of a month. It is possible to shorten the length of the tax periods to one month. This would be attractive to traders who regularly receive a repayment of VAT (i.e. their input tax regularly exceeds their output tax for reasons we will explore later), and so could decrease the impact of VAT on their cash flow. However, this option carries the penalty of having to complete twelve VAT returns a year. At the other extreme, small businesses can elect to complete only one tax return a year, although they must still pay VAT throughout the year (see below).

A transaction must be accounted for in the tax period in which the tax point occurs. The transaction is subject to the relevant rate of VAT which prevails on the date of the tax point.

A VAT return, called a VAT 100, is completed at the end of each tax period and sent to HMRC (in paper form or also now via electronic submissions if the registered person wants to do it this way – although from April 2008 returns had to be electronically filed for businesses with turnover exceeding £5.6million. Registered businesses with turnover above the VAT registration threshold must keep digital VAT records and submit them to HMRC using Making Tax Digital (MTD) compatible software.

The VAT return includes the following information:

- output tax collected in the period
- input tax paid in the period
- net amount payable or repayable
- value of supplies to other EU countries
- value of acquisitions from other EU countries
- input VAT due on acquisitions from other EU countries.

If an excess of input over output tax exists for the period this is repayable to the business. If the output tax exceeds the input tax (as would be normal for most businesses that are profitable over time) this difference will be paid over to HMRC from the sums collected by the registered person during the period.

Tax invoices

10.19 Invoicing is important to the integrity of the VAT system. Once a person is registered for VAT they must provide a tax invoice to other registered people whenever they make a taxable supply to them. The trader must also retain a copy of the tax invoice (in paper or electronic form) to illustrate what output tax has been charged on the supplies they have made.

A tax invoice must include specified information including the supplier's name address and registration number and a description of the goods or services. Simplified invoices can be issued by retailers where the supply is less than £250.

Invoicing of small businesses and for low valued items is simplified and electronic transfers of VAT invoices is possible in some circumstances.

Cash operated machines, for example in car parks, do not need to provide a tax invoice if the total value of the invoice is less than £25. Purchasers can still reclaim the input tax on these costs even though they do not have a tax invoice, as a practical concession from HMRC.

Mixed supplies

10.20 Sometimes goods and services are sold as a unit but are, in fact, made up of a mixture of standard rated, reduced rated, zero rated or exempt supplies. For example, if a book and cassette tape is sold together, perhaps as a foreign language course, the book is zero rated and the tape is standard rated. This is called making a mixed supply.

In this case the supplier must apportion the value of the supply between the different components using an equitable basis. VAT is then levied on each part at the appropriate rate. The legislation does not offer one method to be used to apportion the value, but acceptable methods are likely to include apportionment using the cost to the supplier of the components and apportionment using the open market value of each component.

Sometimes it may not be possible to apportion the value in this way. It is then necessary to consider the sale as a composite supply and one rate will be applied to the whole of the supply.

Cash discounts

10.21 Prior to 1 April 2015, if a cash discount was offered for early settlement of an invoice (prompt payment discount), then VAT was levied on the value of the supply net of the cash discount. This rule applied whether the discount was actually taken up, or not. With effect from 1 April 2015, this concession has been removed and VAT is now payable on the full consideration paid.

Input tax: more detail

10.22 So far we have assumed that registered traders can reclaim input tax they pay against output tax they charge provided that they have a VAT invoices to prove these amounts. In principle this is correct, but there are a number of special situations that you need to know about where these basic principles of VAT are varied.

We will start by considering capital expenditure, then VAT and cars, and finally list the occasions on which input tax cannot be reclaimed or there are restrictions on reclaiming.

Capital expenditure

10.23 Unlike income tax and corporation tax, VAT does not distinguish between capital and revenue expenditure. All input tax is therefore potentially fully recoverable as it is incurred, and capital items are not spread over several years. When a capital asset is disposed of, VAT is charged on the disposal price just as for any other taxable supply.

VAT and cars

10.24 One exception to the VAT on capital expenditure rules is the treatment of cars. Generally, input tax on cars cannot be reclaimed. Equally, registered traders do not account for output tax when the car is subsequently sold, unless it is sold at a profit, when output tax must be levied on the profit element. However, there are a number of exceptions to these rules. VAT can be reclaimed on cars:

- acquired new and intended to be sold (i.e. if you are a car dealer);
- intended to be leased to or used in a taxi business, a self-drive hire business or a driving school.

Where input VAT on a car is recoverable, output VAT must be accounted for in the usual way when the car is eventually disposed of.

Accessories bought at the same time as the car suffer the same treatment as the car itself, but if they are acquired and fitted after the car was acquired, the input VAT can be reclaimed, provided that the expenditure is for business use.

Travelling and car maintenance costs

10.25 While VAT on the acquisition of a new car is generally not recoverable, what happens to the VAT on petrol and maintenance costs?

By concession, provided that a car is owned by a business and used for some business purposes, the VAT on the full cost of any repair and maintenance costs is reclaimable, even if the car is also partly used for private purposes.

VAT on fuel used for business purposes is reclaimable even if the fuel is paid for by an employee who is then reimbursed, either through a mileage allowance or by repayment of the cost of the fuel.

If a business provides its employees with petrol for private use, and the employee does not fully reimburse the company for the cost of the fuel, the business is considered to have made a taxable supply of that fuel to the employee. VAT car fuel scale charge tables can be accessed from HMRC website to show how this output tax should be charged. However, if the business chooses not to try to reclaim the input tax on the fuel they do not have to account for this special output tax.

If an employee reimburses an employer for the cost of either the use of the car or any private fuel used, then the payment is treated as if it were VAT inclusive provided that the payment is equal to or exceeds the cost of the fuel.

Bad debts

10.26 What happens when a supply is made to a customer, VAT is charged, but the customer doesn't pay, i.e. the debt goes bad? In this situation, the trader can obtain a refund of the amount of tax chargeable on that debt. Where the trader has supplied goods or services and has accounted for and paid tax on the supply, if either the whole or any part of the debt has subsequently been written off in the accounts as an impairment loss, and a period of six months from the date on which payment was due has elapsed, the trader is entitled to a refund of the output tax previously paid.

On the opposite side, registered traders must repay any input VAT which they have reclaimed on supplies for which they have not actually paid and on which bad debt relief is then claimed by the supplier, as we have just discussed. This ensures repayments made to suppliers for their bad debts are collected from the buyers whose debt was not paid and so the Government does not end up 'out of pocket'.

Those who use the annual accounting scheme for VAT (explained at 10.34), and hence only complete one VAT return a year, will be able to account for output tax and claim bad debt relief on the same return.

VAT recovery on registration

10.27 What if a business incurs input tax before registering for VAT, can it be recovered once registered? The VAT regulations allow for recovery of VAT on assets used in the business for resale that were bought in the previous four years and on services received in the six months before registration. The newly registered business can recover this input tax in its first VAT return, or any time within the first four years of registration.

Input tax specifically disallowed

10.28 In addition to non-recoverable input tax on the acquisition of cars discussed above, registered traders cannot reclaim input tax on expenditure on:

- Business entertaining, unless the expense is allowable for income tax or corporation tax purposes e.g. entertaining overseas customers (see Chapter 6.4 for more on this).
- Living accommodation being paid for by the business on behalf of its directors.
- Non-business items which have been recorded in the business accounts.

If the taxable supply is partly for business use and partly for private use, the registered trader may either reclaim all of the input tax, and then account for output tax on the value of the supply taken for private use, or reclaim only the business element of the input tax. If the taxable supply is a service, then only the second method can be used.

Note that non-reclaimable input tax is deductible as an expense for income tax, corporation tax and capital gains tax purposes, just like other expenses, if the related expenditure is deductible for trading income or capital gains tax purposes.

Self-supply

10.29 A self-supply occurs when a trader produces a marketable output and then instead of selling it, uses it during the course of their business instead. For example, a business may own a printing operation which produces stationery which is used by the business.

If a trader makes a supply to themselves, output tax must be charged as if it were a supply to a third party. Input tax charged on the supply is only reclaimable up to the level of output tax they charged themselves on the supply. (i.e. input tax reclaimed cannot exceed output tax on the supply).

Partial exemption

10.30 Input tax is only recoverable if it has been paid on acquiring goods and services which are directly attributable to taxable supplies made by the trader. Remember that taxable supplies covers standard rated, reduced rated and zero rated supplies.

If a trader's outputs consist of both taxable and exempt supplies, then the rule is that only input tax which relates to taxable outputs is recoverable. The trader cannot reclaim input tax on the goods or services they purchased that went into making their exempt output supplies. This type of trader is referred to as 'partially exempt' to recognise this fact.

This necessary matching of inputs and taxable outputs is achieved by firstly determining how much input tax can be related directly to taxable outputs and exempt outputs. The input tax which relates directly to taxable outputs is fully reclaimable and that which relates to exempt supplies is not deductible. The remaining input tax is apportioned between taxable supplies and exempt supplies by using the percentage:

$$\frac{\text{Taxable turnover excluding VAT}}{\text{Total turnover excluding VAT}} \times 100$$

This is then rounded up to the next whole percentage point. The following items are omitted from this calculation:

- goods acquired and sold without any work being done to them.
- self-supplies.
- capital goods acquired for use within the business.

HMRC may be willing to allow an alternative basis to be used to allocate input tax between taxable and exempt supplies but this will not happen automatically and the trader will need to seek approval directly for the use of any alternative method.

As a concession to this allocation rule, if the amount of input tax which is deemed to relate to exempt supplies is less than an average of £625 a month (£7,500 pa) the above apportionment is ignored and all of the input tax is reclaimable anyway. This concession helps to reduce some of the compliance costs that would arise for managing a very small amount of exempt input tax.

The treatment of partial exemption is a complex area of the VAT rules and many cases exist in this area.

It is possible for a registered trader to use last year's annual percentage rather than perform separate calculations for each quarter. A potential problem with using last year's annual percentage is that actual proportions of total to taxable supplies might vary during the year, but it has the advantage of smoothing out seasonal fluctuations and may help the cash flow of the business. An annual adjustment is required in the final VAT return for the year.

 You can now attempt Quick Quiz questions 5-8 and Full question 2.

Special schemes

10.31 You need to be aware of some of the special VAT schemes which are available to registered traders that affect how VAT is accounted for between the trader and HMRC. There are many VAT schemes in use, but here we illustrate only the most commonly used ones. The payments on account scheme (see 10.32) is compulsory for large organisations but other schemes are offered to taxpayers on a voluntary basis. The schemes don't normally alter the amount of VAT which must be paid (the exception being the new flat rate scheme which is deliberately designed to do this); they merely affect either the date of payments to HMRC or the administration of VAT.

In practice the take-up of these voluntary schemes is very low despite the apparent attractiveness of some of them. This may be partly due to the stringent conditions for joining the schemes.

The payments on account scheme

10.32 Companies which have to pay £2 million a year or more to HMRC complete their VAT returns in the normal way once each quarter but are required to make two payments on account in each quarter in addition to the usual end of quarter payment. The first payment is made a month before the end of the quarter and the second at the end of the tax period. The final payment, which is sufficient to cover the remaining VAT liability for the tax period, is made at the usual time, i.e. one month after the end of the tax period. This means, in practice, that the trader will make a payment to HMRC at the end of each month of the year.

HMRC will use the previous twelve months' information in order to determine the monthly payments of the scheme members usually on the basis of 1/24th of the trader's total VAT liability for the previous year. Traders can opt to pay their actual VAT liability instead, however, if they so wish. This may be cheaper for them to do if their activity is less than in the previous year.

The cash accounting scheme

10.33 The cash accounting scheme allows members to bend the normal tax point rules we examined earlier in the chapter. Instead members of this scheme can use the following tax points:

- for output tax; the day on which payment or other consideration is received, or the date of any cheque, if later.
- for input tax; the date on which payment is made or other consideration is given, or the date of any cheque, if later.

This means members of the scheme only pay VAT on actual cash transactions.

This can provide a considerable cash flow advantage to many businesses as it also avoids them having to deduct output tax on a VAT return when they have not yet received the payment from their customer.

Taxable persons are eligible for admission to the scheme if:

- the value of their taxable supplies for the next year after application is not likely to exceed £1,350,000;
- they have made all the returns which they are required to make and all their VAT payments are up to date
- they have not, in the last twelve months up to date of application, been convicted of any VAT offence.

The scheme does not apply to hire purchase agreements, conditional sale agreements or credit sale agreements.

Members of the scheme may remain in the scheme unless at the end of any quarter or relevant accounting period the value of taxable supplies made in the 12 months up to that point has exceeded £1,600,000 and in the year then beginning is expected to exceed £1,600,000. If this is the case, they must notify HMRC and stop operating the scheme on the anniversary of joining it.

Current members can withdraw themselves from the scheme if:

- they want to at any point; or
- they are unable to comply with the requirements of the scheme for any reason (e.g. their accounting systems do not comply).

HMRC can terminate membership of the scheme in certain circumstances.

A person whose membership has been terminated must account for, and pay in the current period, all the tax they owe to return to the normal VAT rules.

The annual accounting scheme

10.34 Under this scheme, members:

- pay 90% of tax liability as estimated by HMRC for that current accounting year. This payment is normally made by direct debit from their bank account in nine equal monthly instalments commencing on the last day of the fourth month of their current accounting year. An option to pay in three larger instalments in the year was also introduced with effect from 25 April, 2002. Payments are then equal to 25% of the previous year's VAT liability.
- supply a return for the year by the last day of the second month following the end of that accounting year, together with any outstanding payment due to HMRC for their liability for tax declared on the return.

Taxable persons are eligible to apply for membership of the scheme if:

- the value of taxable supplies in the year from the date of application to join will not exceed £1,350,000;

- they have made all the VAT returns which they are required to make;
- total credits for input tax did not exceed total output tax in the year prior to application for authorisation; and
- they have not had membership terminated in the three years preceding the date of application for authorisation.

Members can remain in the scheme once they have been allowed to join unless:

- at the end of any current accounting year the value of the taxable supplies made by them in that year has exceeded £1,600,000, in which case their authorisation will be terminated immediately;
- at any time the value of taxable supplies made so far in the current accounting year will exceed £1,600,000 in which case they have 30 days in which to notify HMRC who may then terminate their membership

They are expelled from the scheme for non-compliance with its rules. As with the cash accounting scheme, HMRC can terminate membership in certain circumstances.

Activity

Why may a business choose to use the annual accounting scheme?

Feedback

The annual accounting scheme is useful in managing business cash flows as payments are predictable throughout the year and only one VAT return needs to be completed, helping to reduce compliance costs. However, it does require monitoring of the various membership limits to ensure the turnover maximum is not exceeded as well as some planning to ensure monies are available for payments when they fall due, irrespective of the cash flow position of the business. If you are down-scaling your business, or just having a less profitable year, larger payments may need to be paid than would otherwise be the case as payments due will be based on the previous year's figures. This is of course reversed if you have a better year again the following year.

Retail schemes

10.35 There are a number of special schemes which are used by retailers. The normal VAT legislation requires registered traders to maintain detailed records of every transaction. Retailers who make a mixture of standard rated, zero rated and exempt supplies face particular problems with accounting correctly for VAT.

Retailers are allowed therefore to keep less detailed records by using one of the schemes and calculate output tax in a way which better suits their circumstances. Some of the schemes require totals for different sorts of supply rather than details of individual transactions while others allow the VAT liability to be estimated using purchases and mark-up percentages. The retail schemes are only available to retailers who cannot reasonably be expected to account for VAT in the normal way.

Retail schemes are not just for small traders. Individually agreed schemes for businesses with taxable retail turnover in excess of £100 million per annum have recently been introduced. From 1 April 2009, retailers with a turnover of more than £130million are required to enter into bespoke schemes and are no longer able to use the published schemes.

The second-hand goods scheme

10.36 The second-hand goods scheme is available to traders who buy second-hand goods from individuals who are not registered traders. HMRC can allow a reduction on the taxable supply amounts of such second-hand goods as such traders will typically have to charge output tax but not have any input tax to offset against it. The maximum reduction available is equal to the amount of tax which would have been due had the purchase of the goods been a normal taxable supply. This means that VAT is due only on the trader's profit margin rather than on the total sales price of the goods. Hence the trader has to only account for output tax of $1/6^{th}$ of the difference between their purchase price and their selling price.

Under this scheme the member selling the second-hand goods does not have to create a tax invoice when they make a sale. A registered trader who buys goods from a trader who is using the second-hand goods scheme will not therefore be able to reclaim the input tax because he or she will not have received a tax invoice.

This scheme can apply to sales of all second-hand goods, works of art, antiques and collectors' items. The scheme cannot, however, be applied to precious metals and gemstones.

Flat rate scheme

10.37 The flat rate scheme is for businesses with VAT-exclusive taxable turnover of up to £150,000 per annum.

The scheme allows businesses to account for VAT using a flat rate percentage applied to their tax-inclusive turnover (including exempt or zero rated supplies). The rate that applies depends on the nature of the business as different flat rates will apply to different businesses. To illustrate the range in these rates; the lowest flat rates can be enjoyed by suppliers of food and of children's clothing (flat rate of 4% applies) whereas the highest rate applies to suppliers such as builders who charge for labour only, accountants, architects and IT consultants (flat rate of 14.5% applies).

While many of the rates remain unchanged since the start of the scheme, several have been changed, for example, the rate applicable to accountancy or bookkeeping was 11.5% in 2009, then 13% in 2010 and 2011 and is 14.5% from 4 January 2011. In addition, newly registered businesses are now entitled to an extra 1% discount in their first year of operation.

The government was concerned that the flat rate scheme was being abused by so called 'limited cost traders', for example those who purchase no goods and so suffer limited input tax. Traders that meet the definition of limited cost traders have been liable for a 16.5% rate under the flat rate scheme.

The full range of rates for both levels of VAT can be found on the HMRC website.

Businesses using this scheme still issue VAT invoices to and collect VAT from their customers but don't have to track input or output VAT specifically to calculate their VAT charge or repayment. The only exception to this is for capital purchases in excess of £2,000 (VAT inclusive). For such purchases traders who normally use the flat rate systems can recover the input tax on these purchases directly in the normal way (i.e. as for non-flat rate users). Of course, if these assets are subsequently sold, full VAT must be charged on the sale price and accounted for as output tax in the usual way.

The use of the flat rate scheme could save businesses significant compliance effort by reducing much of the separate accounting that is otherwise needed for recording the input and output VAT appropriately. This scheme needs careful monitoring, however, as it may not produce a lower tax bill for all business depending on the specific make-up of supplies and other inputs they buy.

In one case a mechanical engineer registered for the Flat Rate Scheme and, on advice from his accountant, adopted a flat rate of 12% which applies to activities not listed elsewhere. HMRC argued that he should have been registered under the category 'architect, civil and structural engineer or surveyor' with a rate of 14.5%. The taxpayer challenged this, and won in the first tier tribunal. This further demonstrates the need to take care when entering into this scheme, to make sure the appropriate flat rate is used, and also that HMRC are prepared to argue about the categorisation.

Imports and exports

10.38 Since the creation of a Europe without trade barriers (the 'Single Market') on 1 January, 1993 it has become necessary to differentiate between transactions with traders resident in other countries in the European Union and those resident in countries outside the European Union when a trader completes a VAT return. Since the UK left the EU on 1 January 2021, the special EU rules no longer apply and the non-EU rules apply to all transactions.

Imports

10.39 There are slightly different rules for the import of goods and services.

Goods

10.40 Tax on the importation of goods from overseas will be charged and payable as if it were a customs duty. VAT due and any associated customs duty on imports is often in fact paid at the same time by traders. The rate of the duty is the same as the rate which would apply if the goods were supplied in the home market by a registered trader. The registered trader can then reclaim the duty paid on the goods as input tax in the normal way.

A registered trader can apply for approval to make deferred payments until a fixed payment day once a month. Payment day is the 15th day of the next month following the one in which the amount of duty deferred fell due to be paid. Each period under this scheme commences on the 16th day of a month and ends on the 15th day of the next month. On each payment day an approved person has to pay to the Commissioners the total amount of customs duty deferred.

There are anti-avoidance rules for overseas traders who use online marketplaces to sell goods into the UK. Where they fail to comply with UK VAT rules they will be required to appoint a UK tax representative to deal with their VAT obligations and HMRC will notify their online marketplace of their non-compliance. If they continue to be non-compliant, HMRC will then require the VAT due to be paid by the online marketplace. This, they hope, will encourage the online marketplaces to police the tax compliance behaviour of those they allow to trade via their services more effectively. They are very unlikely to wish to pay over VAT due for their traders that they have not collected!

Services

10.41 If services are supplied to a registered trader who is UK resident by a person resident overseas, the *reverse charge system* is used. The reverse charge system requires the recipient trader to treat the supply received as if they were also the supplier. This means they account for a notional output tax, which then becomes the actual input tax on the supply.

Relevant services include:

- transfers and assignments of copyright, patents, licences, trademarks and similar rights;
- advertising services;
- services of consultants, engineers, consultancy bureaux, lawyers, accountants and other similar services; data processing and provision of information;
- banking, financial and insurance services including re-insurance; any other service supplied to a registered trader provided that it is not exempt.

Overseas companies can register for VAT in the UK if they wish to. If they do so they then follow the usual rules for charging VAT on their supplies we have examined in this chapter. Under this circumstance no reverse charging is then necessary by the recipient of the supply.

Suppliers of broadcast electronic services (e.g. via the Internet) to UK based non-registered recipients are also required to charge VAT at the rate applicable for that sale in the customers' country.

Imports of works of art, antiques and collectors' pieces are subject to VAT at a reduced rate of 2.5%.

Exports

10.42 A supply of goods is zero rated if HMRC are satisfied that the person supplying the goods has:

- exported them to a place outside the EU member states (evidence must be produced); or
- shipped them for use as stores on a voyage or flight to an eventual destination outside the UK, or as merchandise for sale by retail to persons carried on such a voyage or flight in a ship or aircraft.

 You can now attempt Quick Quiz questions 9-10 and Full questions 3-5.

Summary

In this chapter you have read about the operation of VAT, one of the most important taxes in the UK.

VAT has to be paid whenever a taxable person makes a taxable supply of goods or services in the course of business. Unless a supply of goods or services is specifically exempt in the legislation it is a taxable supply. With the exception of domestic fuel and a handful of other supplies, which are taxable at 5%, taxable supplies are either standard rated or zero rated. The standard rate of VAT for the UK was 17.5% for a number of years, but reduced to 15% for the period 1/12/08 to 31/12/09 and then increased to its current rate of 20% from 4/1/11.

A trader must register if turnover exceeds certain limits, for this tax year the limit is £85,000 a year. A trader whose turnover is lower than the registration limit may choose to register voluntarily.

A registered trader is able to reclaim allowable input tax but must account for output tax on taxable supplies.

VAT is normally paid quarterly to HMRC on the basis of invoices received and issued in the quarter. However, there are a considerable number of special schemes, some of which are compulsory for some businesses, which require VAT to be accounted for on a different basis.

There is debate about the acceptability of further increases in the amount of revenue which is raised using indirect taxation. This debate was considered in the first three chapters.

Project areas

Not all countries around the world use a VAT style tax on consumption. Review how other countries tax consumption and discuss the relevant merits/disadvantages of each approach.

Since 1979 there has been a significant shift in taxation in the UK from direct taxation to indirect taxation. A number of titles may apply in this area, for example, is it possible for there to be further shifts from direct taxes to indirect taxes? Alternatively, would a shift back towards direct taxation be possible or desirable?

Reduced and zero rating particular items costs the UK Government lots of lost revenue. Should they instead impose a fixed rate on all purchases to collect as much tax as possible – and to improve fiscal neutrality? What would be the implications of so doing?

Quick quiz

1. Kieran makes taxable supplies of £87,000 p.a. Is he required to register for VAT?

2. Louise offers her customers a 5% discount for prompt payment. She sells a standard rated item for £500 in December 2022 to a customer who does not take up the discount. How much VAT should she charge?

3. Maurice owns a business which makes wholly zero rated supplies totalling £50,000 p.a. Should he register for VAT?

4. Nigella is registered for VAT and is partially exempt. During the year she incurred the following input tax:

– attributable to taxable supplies	£50,000
– attributable to exempt supplies	£5,000
– unattributable	£4,000

   The total value of supplies excluding VAT for the year was £500,000 of which £100,000 was exempt. How much of Nigella's input tax is recoverable?

5. Omnibus Ltd is a company that makes office furniture. It received an order on 30 July, delivered the goods to the customer on 20 August and issued an invoice on 30 August. Payment was received on 13 September. What is the tax point for VAT purposes?

6. Portia uses the cash accounting scheme and in the quarter ended 31 September 2022 invoices sales of £6,000 plus VAT; purchases raw materials for cash of £4,000 plus VAT and receives cash from debtors of £5,525. How much VAT is due?

7. Quentin is a VAT registered trader who prepares quarterly returns for quarters ended 31 March, 30 June, 30 September and 31 December, and does not use the cash accounting scheme. He made a supply of goods on 22 September 2022 with a due date for payment of 10 October 2022 The customer did not pay, and Quentin has written the debt off in his accounts. Which quarterly return is the earliest in which relief can be claimed for the impaired debt?

8. Roxanne is a VAT registered trader. On 14 November 2022, she purchased a motor car for £14,000 (VAT inclusive) to use for both business (70%) and private (30%) purposes. The car was damaged in an accident on 5 November 2021 and repairs cost £2,000 (VAT inclusive). What is the input tax that Roxanne can recover for the quarter ended 31 December 2022?

9. Suzanne has been running a small business for three years and has applied for VAT registration from 1 October 2022. Prior to that date, she had incurred the following expenses:

	£
Legal fees (invoice dated 13 January 2022)	500
Accountancy fees (invoice dated 4 September 2022)	300
Inventory of spare parts on hand on 30 September 2022	250

What amount of pre-registration input VAT can Suzanne recover for these items?

10. Victor commenced trading as a garden centre business on 1 May 2012, and became registered for VAT on the same day. Supplies made (exclusive of VAT) for the 31 October 2022 quarter are:

	£
Standard rated supplies	88,400
Exempt supplies	11,600
Total supplies	100,000

Input tax for the quarter is £24,000, of which £18,000 directly relates to taxable supplies and £1,500 to exempt supplies. How much is Victor's deductible input tax for the quarter ended 31 October 2022?

Questions

Question 1   (based on a CIMA exam question).

A trader started in business, selling mainly foodstuffs which are zero rated for VAT purposes, on 1 January 2022 and the following information was extracted from his records for the year ended 31 December 2022.
The purchases (but not the sales) are inclusive of VAT.

	£
Fixed assets purchased (all standard rated)	9,000
Other standard rated purchases and expenses	4,000
Sales of zero rated foodstuffs	78,000
Sales of standard rated items	9,000

He approaches you shortly after the end of the year and informs you that he does not intend to register for VAT since 'the sales liable to VAT were well below the threshold'.

Required: Advise him on the position regarding VAT registration, and show the final value added tax position which would have applied for the above year if the trader had registered voluntarily at the start of the year.

Question 2   (based on an ACCA question)

Zim has been registered for VAT since 1 April 2010. The following information is available for the year ended 31 March 2023 (all are VAT inclusive where applicable):

(1) Sales invoices totalling £126,000 were issued, of which £115,200 were in respect of standard rated sales. Zim's customers are all members of the general public.

(2) On 31 March 2023, Zim wrote off two impairment losses which were in respect of standard rated sales. The first impairment loss was for £780, and was in respect of a sales invoice which had been due for payment on 15 August 2022. The second impairment loss was for £660, and was in respect of a sales invoice which had been due for payment on 15 September 2022.

(3) Purchase invoices totalling £49,200 were received, of which £43,200 were in respect of standard rated purchases and £6,000 were in respect of zero rated purchases.

(4) Rent of £1,200 is paid each month. During the year ended 31 March 2023, Zim made 13 rental payments because the invoice dated 1 April 2023 was paid early on 31 March 2023. This invoice was in respect of the rent for April 2023.

(5) During the year ended 31 March 2023, Zim spent £2,600 on mobile telephone calls, of which 40% related to private calls.

(6) During the year ended 31 March 2023, Zim spent £1,560 on entertaining customers, of which £240 was in respect of overseas customers.

The expenses referred to in notes (4), (5) and (6) are all standard rated. Zim does not use either the cash accounting or flat rate schemes. He has forecast that for the year ended 31 March 2024, his total sales will be the same as for the year ended 31 March 2023.

Required: Calculate the amount of VAT payable by Zim for the year ended 31 March 2023.

Question 3   (based on an ACCA question)

Anne Attire runs a retail clothing shop. She is registered for VAT and is in the process of completing her VAT return for the quarter ended 30 November 2023. The following information is available (all figures are exclusive of VAT):

(1) Cash sales amounted to £42,000, of which £28,000 was in respect of standard rated sales and £14,000 was in respect of zero rated sales.

(2) Sales invoices totalling £12,000 were issued in respect of credit sales. These sales were all standard rated. Ann offers all of her credit sales

customers a 5% discount for payment within one month of the date of the sales invoice, and 90% of customers pay within this period. The sales figure of £12,000 is stated before any deduction for the 5% discount.

(3) Purchase and expense invoices totalling £19,200 were received from VAT registered suppliers. This figure is made up as follows:

	£
Standard rated purchases and expenses	11,200
Zero rated purchases	6,000
Exempt expenses	2,000
	19,200

(4) On 30 November 2022, Ann wrote off two impairment losses (bad debts). The first was in respect of a sales invoice due for payment on 15 July 2022. The second impairment loss was for £800, and was in respect of a sales invoice due for payment on 10 April 2022.

Anne does not use the cash accounting scheme.

Anne will soon be 60 years old and is therefore considering retirement. On the cessation of trading, Anne can either sell the fixed assets of the business on a piecemeal basis to individual VAT registered purchasers, or she can sell the entire business as a going concern to a single VAT registered purchaser.

Required:
(a) Calculate the amount of VAT payable by Anne Attire for the quarter ended 30 November 2022, and state the date by which the VAT return for this period was due for submission.
(b) State the conditions that Anne Attire must satisfy before she will be permitted to use the cash accounting scheme, and advise her of the implications of using the scheme.
(c) Advise Anne Attire as to what will happen to her VAT registration, and whether output VAT will be due in respect of the fixed assets, if she ceases trading and then (i) sells her fixed assets on a piecemeal basis to individual VAT registered purchasers, or (ii) sells her entire business as a going concern to a single VAT registered purchaser.

Question 4   (based on an ACCA question).

Sandy Brick has been a self-employed builder since 2000. He registered for VAT on 1 January 2023 and is in the process of completing his VAT return for the quarter ended 31 March 2023. The following information is relevant to the completion of this VAT return:

(1) Sales invoices totalling £44,000 (excluding VAT) were issued to VAT registered customers in respect of standard rated sales. Sandy offers his

VAT registered customers a 5% discount for prompt payment and 50% of customers took the discount.

(2) Sales invoices totalling £16,920 were issued to customers that were not registered for VAT. Of this figure, £5,170 was in respect of zero rated sales with the balance being in respect of standard rated sales. In this case, standard rated sales are inclusive of VAT.

(3) On 10 January 2023, Sandy received a payment on account of £5,000 in respect of a contract that was completed on 28 April 2023. The total value of the contract is £10,000. Both of these figures are inclusive of VAT at the standard rate.

(4) Standard rated materials amounted to £11,200 of which £800 were used in work on Sandy's private residence (VAT inclusive).

(5) Since 1 December 2021, Sandy has paid £120 per month for the lease of office equipment. This expense is standard rated (VAT inclusive).

(6) During the quarter ended 31 March 2023, £400 (VAT inclusive) was spent on mobile telephone calls, of which 30% relates to private calls. This expense is standard rated.

(7) On 20 February 2023, £920 (VAT inclusive) was spent on repairs to a motor car. The motor car is used by Sandy in his business, although 20% of the mileage is for private journeys. This expense is standard rated.

(8) On 15 March 2023, equipment was purchased for £6,000 (VAT inclusive). The purchase was partly financed by a bank loan of £5,000. This purchase is standard rated.

Unless otherwise stated, all of the above figures are exclusive of VAT.

Required:
Calculate the amount of VAT payable by Sandy for the quarter ended 31 March 2023.

(Note: answer available via lecturer's website)

Question 5   (based on an ACCA question).

Vanessa Serve is self-employed as a tennis coach. She is registered for VAT and is the process of completing her VAT return for the quarter ended 31 March 2023. The following information is available:

(1) Sales invoices totalling £18,000 (VAT inclusive) were issued in respect of standard rated sales. All of Vanessa's customers are members of the general public.

(2) During the quarter ended 31 March 2023 Vanessa spent £600 (VAT inclusive) on mobile telephone calls of which 40% related to private calls.

(3) On 3 January 2023, Vanessa purchased a car for £12,000. On 18 March 2023, £987 was spent on repairs to the car. The cars used by Vanessa for business, although approximately 10% of the mileage is for private journeys. Both figures are inclusive of VAT at the standard rate.

(4) On 29 March 2023 tennis coaching equipment was purchased for £1,465 (VAT exclusive). Vanessa paid for the equipment on that date, but did not take delivery of the equipment or receive an invoice until 3 April 2023. This purchase was standard rated.

(5) In addition to the above, Vanessa also had other standard rated expenses amounting to £2,200 (VAT inclusive) in the quarter ended 31 March 2023. This figure includes £400 for entertaining customers.

Required:

(i) Calculate the amount of VAT payable by Vanessa for the quarter ended 31 March 2023.

(ii) Advise Vanessa of the conditions she must satisfy before being permitted to use the VAT flat rate scheme, and the advantages of joining the scheme. The relevant flat rate percentage for Vanessa's trade as notified by HMRC is 6%. Your answer should be supported by appropriate calculations of the amount of tax saving if Vanessa had used the flat rate scheme to calculate the amount of VAT payable for the quarter ended 31 March 2023.

(Note: answer available via lecturer's website)

Further questions for this chapter to test your knowledge can be found in the student section of the website at:

https://www.fiscalpublications.com/lymerandoats/2022

Further reading

For more details on the UK's VAT system use the HMRC website at www.gov.uk/government/organisations/hm-revenue-customs. You can also refer to the detailed professional guides such as Tolley's VAT Guide.

For a discussion of VAT systems generally see S. Cnossen, 'Issues in Adapting and Designing a Value Added Tax' in C. Sandford ed. (1993) *Key Issues in Tax Reform*, Fiscal Publications, Birmingham 1993.

For a fuller discussion of how VAT compares with other approaches to general and specific sales taxes, and various approaches used around the world to operating a VAT system (they aren't all identical), see Evans, C., Hasseldine, J., Lymer, A., Ricketts, R. & Sandford, C. (2017) *Comparative Taxation: Why tax systems differ*, Fiscal Publications: Birmingham.

For a chance to review the coverage of this chapter further, and for lots of extra questions to test your knowledge on, see:

Combs, A. (2022), *UK Corporation tax, Capital Gains Tax and VAT Practice Questions (2nd edition 2022/23)*, Fiscal Publications: Malvern.
– a large test bank of questions linked to the content of this chapter that will enable you to thoroughly test your knowledge of this work with exam-level questions. See
https://www.fiscalpublications.com/uk-ct-cgt-vat-practice-questions/2022

Combs, A. & Tutin, R. (2022), *Taxation: incorporating the 2022 Finance Act*, Fiscal Publications: Birmingham.
– use this book for many other examples to further develop and test your knowledge of this chapter's contents. See
https://www.fiscalpublications.com/combsandtutin/2022

11 Tax planning

Introduction

11.1 In Chapter 3 we discussed the concept of tax avoidance and the difference between avoidance and evasion. In this chapter we will first consider tax planning, which involves strategic use of available tax concessions in order to minimise your tax liability, before looking more closely at avoidance and then evasion. The distinction between tax planning and tax avoidance is by no means straightforward, and you might like to think of it as a continuum:

| Tax planning | Acceptable tax avoidance | Unacceptable tax avoidance |

We saw in Chapter 3 that tax planning, which involves availing yourself of legitimate tax concessions, is quite legal and acceptable. Tax evasion involves at least an element of fraud or non-disclosure including, for example, failing to declare income which is taxable. This is illegal activity.

It is the grey area of tax avoidance which is particularly problematic, as exactly where the boundary exists between 'acceptable' tax avoidance and 'unacceptable' tax avoidance is difficult to determine. Tax evasion is clearly different to other forms of non-compliance in that it occurs after a tax liability has already crystallised, i.e. a taxpayer has done something that creates a tax liability such as receiving taxable income or selling a chargeable asset. Tax planning and avoidance, on the other hand take place before a tax liability crystallises. Importantly, the diagram above doesn't take into account the temporal aspect – i.e. that over time, things change and what might be acceptable or not acceptable will fluctuate over time. It is still useful, however, as a way of starting to think about this complex issue. We will come back to this question of the boundary between acceptable and unacceptable tax avoidance later in the chapter, using the illustration of personal service companies to demonstrate the problems associated with this grey area, but we will start by considering tax planning, in the white zone.

At the end of this chapter you will be able to:

- identify some ways in which transactions can be structured so as to minimise tax liabilities;
- discuss the advantages and disadvantages of being an employee as compared to being self-employed;
- compare the tax and national insurance differences of operating a business as a sole trader or a company;
- understand how tax avoidance is dealt with at present in the UK; and
- briefly discuss the concept of tax evasion.

Basic tax planning issues

11.2 A number of earlier chapters covered specific issues of tax planning and you may want to review these at this time. Chapter 4 looked at some basic income tax planning points for couples including shifting income from a high rate taxpayer to a basic rate paying spouse. In Chapter 8 we considered some basic CGT planning issues which relate to controlling the timing of disposals and making sure that any available reliefs and exemptions are used. Chapter 9 looked at basic tax planning for UK resident companies including the use of group relief. In Chapter 10 we considered VAT planning including the use of voluntary registration.

We can now consider some other basic planning issues before considering broader structural issues.

Remuneration packages

11.3 A number of tax planning options are available to employees which will have the effect of reducing their income tax and NIC liabilities. Benefits in kind can be tax effective, even if they do not reduce the amount of income tax payable compared to a salary or bonus. Remember that employee (primary class 1) NICs are not payable on most benefits in kind (although class 1A contributions may need to be paid by the employer), making them a tax efficient way to receive extra remuneration – at least as far as the recipient is concerned.

In addition, pension plans allow for tax savings, you may like to review Chapter 5 for more details of these.

Salary sacrifice

11.4 Salary sacrifice is a technique that can be used to reduce tax liabilities for both employers (secondary Class 1 NICs) and employees (both income tax and NICs). A salary sacrifice is where the employee gives up the right to receive some of his or her salary in return for an agreement from the employer to provide some kind of benefit in kind. To be effective for tax purposes, any arrangement to substitute benefits in kind for cash salary must be a genuine contractual arrangement. There are some potential pitfalls for employees, however, and the 'package' needs to be worked out carefully. For example, reducing the amount of cash payment entitlement under an employment contract may affect pension scheme contributions or entitlement to working tax credit, child tax credit or state pension and other government benefits.

Typically, a salary sacrifice will involve a benefit that is not taxable such as pension contributions, childcare vouchers or mobile phones. The arrangement must be such that it is not possible for the employee to go back to the original salary whenever he or she wishes. This was established in a 1969 tax case *Heaton v Bell* where it was decided that because the taxpayer, who had the use of a car, could give up the benefit at any time, then it had a 'money's worth' that was taxable.

As we saw in Chapter 5, the Government tightened up the rules on salary sacrifice arrangements and from 6 April 2017 they can only be used for employer pensions and pensions advice, childcare, cycle to work and ultra-low emission cars.

Capital allowances

11.5 Capital allowances provide scope for some tax planning for both incorporated and unincorporated businesses. You will recall from Chapter 7 that it is not compulsory to claim capital allowances in any given year. The choice of whether, or how much, to claim is the taxpayer's. Taking less than the maximum allowances available will increase the taxable profit for that year, but also increase the capital allowance claim that can be made the following year. This may be beneficial, for example, where a business has losses to be absorbed in the current year.

Timing is also important when considering capital allowances. Remember that enhanced capital allowances and writing down allowances are not pro-rated if an asset is purchased part way through the period. This means that even if you purchase an asset on the last day of the capital allowance period you still get a full period's allowance for that asset. Also, remember to classify the capital allowances you want to claim carefully to ensure the allocation you decide on gives you the option to claim the maximum allowances.

An example of this occurs where assets qualify for treatment as short life assets. Businesses should consider de-pooling such assets to crystallise a balancing allowance if it is sold at a loss within eight years.

See if you can identify any other planning opportunities that arise in other chapters of the book. Remember these can include making sure that you meet the criteria for special tax treatment such as the special deduction for research and development expenditure that we considered in Chapter 9. In the remainder of this chapter, we will be looking at some structural issues, specifically the tax differences that arise between being an employee, self-employed and incorporated.

Employee or self-employed?

11.6 There are a number of tax planning considerations that apply to the classification of employment status. To illustrate these we will use the following activity to provide a context for discussion.

Activity

Andrea is a management consultant who seeks your advice about the tax implications of being an employee compared to being self-employed. Discuss the issues that you would raise in the course of providing Andrea with advice.

Feedback

There are significant differences in how an individual is assessed for income tax as an employee or as a self-employed taxpayer. Self-employed persons generally enjoy tax advantages including:

- Payment of income tax later, through the payment on account system, than employees who are locked into payment through the PAYE system on a weekly or monthly basis;
- A wider range of deductible expenses. You will recall that to be deductible under the employment rules, expenses generally must be *wholly, exclusively and necessarily* incurred in the performance of the duties of the employment. Under the trading income rules, expenses need only be *wholly and exclusively* for the purposes of the trade or profession, i.e. the *necessarily* requirement does not apply. In practice this means that some items of expenditure may be deductible to someone who is self-employed, but not to someone doing the same work but as an employee.
- Lower national insurance contributions under classes 2 and 4, although this must be weighed against reduced social security benefit entitlements that may then result.

Activity

Andrea (from the previous activity) expects to earn approximately £70,000 for a consultancy project she is to undertake. She will spend £2,000 on furniture for her home office, £1,000 on a computer, and it will cost her £500 to travel from her home to her client. She has asked you to provide some estimates of the different income tax and national insurance contribution liabilities arising if she is an employee or self employed.

Feedback

If Andrea is an employee of the client business, she will be taxed under employment income rules. While she may do some of her work at home, that in itself is not sufficient to make more than a very small amount of her household expenses deductible. The cost of travel between home and work is also not deductible for an employee. Andrea will be taxed as an employee on the full £70,000 salary as follows (assuming she has no other income and is entitled to just the basic personal allowance):

		£
Taxable income	(£70,000 – £12,570)	57,430
Non savings income	37,700 @ 20%	7,540.00
	19,730 @ 40%	7,892.00
Tax liability		15,432.00

As an employee, Andrea will also be liable for class 1 national insurance contributions; primary contributions will need to be paid by Andrea herself, and secondary contributions will be paid by her employer. These contributions are normally calculated on a periodical basis (see Chapter 4), however for simplicity we will calculate it on an annual basis using annual thresholds. The annual thresholds we will use for the purpose of this chapter are as follows:

	£
Primary Class 1	11,908
Secondary Class 1	9,100
Upper profits limit	50,270

Primary Class 1
£38,362 (50,270 – £11,908) @ 13.25%   5,082.96
£19,730 (£70,000 – £50,270) @ 3.25%   641.22   £5,724.18
Secondary Class 1
£60,900 (£70,000 – £9,100) @ 15.05%   £9,165.45

Although secondary class 1 contributions are the legal responsibility of the employer, they can be considered part of the employee's effective tax liability. We will talk more about this idea when we discuss the question of tax incidence in Chapter 14.

Therefore, earning the £70,000 as an employee will cost Andrea £21,156.18 (£15,432.00+ £5,724.18) in income tax and NICs, and her employer £9,165.45 in NICs.

If instead of becoming an employee Andrea becomes self-employed, she will be taxed under the trading income rules. If she can establish that her home is a place of business, there is a case for capital allowances to be claimed for her office furniture and computer. In addition, the cost of travel to the client's premises will probably also be deductible. Her tax adjusted trading profits will therefore be:

	£	£
Gross fees		70,000
Expenses:		
Capital allowances:		
AIA: computer	1,000	
furniture	2,000	
Travel expenses	500	(3,500)
Net profit from business		66,500
Less personal allowance		(12,570)
Taxable income		53,930
Income tax due:		
Non savings income		
37,700 @ 20%		7,540.00
16,230 @ 40%		6,492.00
Tax liability		14,032.00
National Insurance Contributions:		
Class 2		
£3.15 per week x 52 weeks		163.80
Class 4		
£38,362 (£50,270 – £11,908) @ 10.25%	3,932.10	
£16,230 (£66,500 – £50,270) @ 3.25%	527.47	4,459.57
Total		4,623.37

Therefore, Andrea's total income tax and NIC liability is £18,655.37 (£11,666.26 lower than the combined total she and her employer would pay if she were an employee).

Of course, this is an over-simplified example, and in reality, other considerations will come into play. For example, Andrea's remuneration as an employee does not need to be salary only. A range of benefits in kind may be available which could help to reduce her total tax liability. Andrea may well decide to start a pension scheme of one or other type which will give her tax relief. It must also be remembered that the question of whether someone is an employee or self-employed is not a simple one (see Chapter 5) and care must be taken to ensure that the rules relating to personal service income are not invoked. These are referred to as the IR35 rules and will be discussed later in this chapter. As we will see later, Andrea may well have a problem with these rules if she operates as proposed above.

Sole trader or company?

11.7 A taxpayer wanting to carry on business on his or her own account, has to make a decision about how to operate that business, as a sole trader or as a company. It is also possible to operate a business as a partnership, but for the purposes of this chapter we will only be considering the first two options.

Activity

Andrea (from the previous examples in this chapter) has decided that she would rather have the independence of being self-employed, and wants to set up her own management consultancy business. She now seeks your advice on the tax implications of operating her business either as a sole trader or as a company.

Feedback

As a sole trader, Andrea will be liable for income tax on her business profits under trading income rules as well as class 2 and class 4 national insurance contributions, as we saw in the previous activity.

If Andrea incorporates a company, with herself as sole director/shareholder, the company will be liable for corporation tax on the profits, which can then be distributed to Andrea in a number of ways. As a director/shareholder, Andrea can decide how much of the profits should be distributed to her as employment earnings, to be taxed under employment income rules, or as dividends to be taxed under dividend rules. Remember, the profits do not have to be distributed at all, they can be retained in the company which gives Andrea control over whether and when the higher rate of tax will apply.

The dates on which payments to HMRC are due differ between self-employed taxpayers and companies. As we noted earlier (in Chapter 6), for self-employed taxpayers income tax and class 4 national insurance contributions are payable by payments on account. Class 2 national insurance contributions are paid through the self assessment system for most people. Corporation tax, for companies paying less than the full rate of corporation tax, is payable nine months and one day after the end of the accounting period. Income tax and class 1 NICs must be deducted from any director's remuneration and remitted to HMRC on a monthly basis. Tax on dividends in the hands of shareholders will be taxed under self-assessment.

> For a company, the choice of accounting date is not important for tax purposes, however for a sole trader, the current year basis rules may operate in the early years to create overlap profits. If you need to know about the current year basis period rules for unincorporated businesses, you may want to visit the website to refresh your memory of how these rules work in the early years of a new business.

There are also capital gains tax differences between sole traders and companies which you will recall from Chapters 8 and 9. For a sole trader, a flat rate of tax of 10% or 20% applies and an annual exemption is available, currently of £12,300. Some specific capital gains tax reliefs and exemptions are only available to individual taxpayers, for example, the principle residence exemption, gift relief, and business asset disposal relief. For companies, allowable costs are indexed to remove the inflation element and chargeable gains form part of the company's taxable total profits (TTP).

It should be noted that capital gains retained within the company will increase the value of the company's shares. If the shareholder sells the shares, he or she may be subject to further capital gains tax, which means that there is effectively double taxation of the gain.

Activity

Given that Andrea is expecting to earn £70,000, and incur expenses as noted in previous activities, how much corporation tax will be payable if she decides to incorporate her business? How will this change if the company pays her:

(a) £30,000 as a salary or

(b) £30,000 as a dividend?

Feedback

With TTP of £66,500 (in this case there will be the same net profit whether she is trading as self-employed or incorporated) the corporation tax due would be:

	£
Corporation tax on £66,500 @ 19%	12,635.00

Compare this with the income tax and NICs payable as a sole trader on the same amount of profit in the earlier activity.

(a) If £30,000 is paid as a salary, this, together with the secondary Class 1 NICs, will be deductible for the company as follows:

	£
Net profit before salary and NIC	66,500

Less:

	£	
Salary to Andrea	30,000	
Secondary Class 1 NICs		
(£30,000 – £9,100) x 15.05%	3,145.45	(33,145)
Taxable profit		33,355

The corporation tax then becomes: £33,355 x 19% = £6,337.45

There will also be income tax and primary class 1 national insurance to pay by Andrea on the salary of £30,000 as follows:

	£
Taxable income (£30,000 – £12,570)	17,430
Non savings income	
£17,430 @ 20%	3,486.00
Income Tax liability	3,486.00
Primary Class 1:	
£18,092 (£30,000 – £11,908) @ 13.25%	2,397.19
Secondary Class 1:	
£20,900 (£30,000 – £9,100) @ 15.05%	3,145.45

Total tax and NICs payable by Andrea is therefore £5,883.19 (£3,486.00 + 2,397.19), with £9,482.90 (£6,337.45+ £3,145.45) payable by the company.

(b) If £30,000 is payable to Andrea as a dividend, and not a salary, the picture is different. The dividend will not be deductible for the company, and so the corporation tax will still be the same as we calculated earlier, i.e. £12,635.00.

In Andrea's hands, the dividend will then be taxed using the dividend income rules. Assuming she has no other income, her income tax liability will be £15,430 (£30,000 – £12,570 – £2,000 (the dividend tax free allowance)) x the basic rate of tax on dividends (8.75%) i.e. £1,350.12.

Dividends are not subject to NICs, and so the result is the only tax Andrea would have to pay on the dividend payment is the £1,350.12.

Therefore, in this particular case, it will be slightly more tax efficient for Andrea to have her income paid as a dividend, not as a salary, as the total tax cost to Andrea and her company is lower this way i.e. £13,985.12 (£12,635.00 + £1,350.12) compared to £15,366.09 (£5,883.19 + £9,482.90). This may reverse however, as the sums extracted by way of dividend versus salary increase, given the rate of tax on dividends rises to 33.75% then 39.35% as the sums paid go into the higher rate tax band and the additional rate band. It will not always be more tax efficient to use dividends rather than salary.

It can be seen that the advantages of operating a business through a company depend, to some extent, on the amount of profit extracted from the company and the form that the extraction takes. Dividends are only taxed in the hands of basic and starting rate taxpayers at 8.75%, but are not deductible for the company and the corporation tax rate will be 19% on these dividends. Salary is deductible for the company, but taxable on the director under employment income rules.

It must also be remembered that the decision whether or not to incorporate a business, like all commercial decisions, should not be made with only tax in mind. Many other non-tax issues need to be considered. These include quite considerable reporting requirements that exist for companies that don't arise for unincorporated businesses. This extra administrative burden needs to be considered when making the decision whether or not to incorporate as the cost could easily outweigh any tax advantage.

Constraints on the use of companies

11.8 Earlier in this chapter we mentioned some rules that may influence the decision whether to use a company as a vehicle through which to provide personal services to clients. Personal services in this context will include any work a taxpayer may perform for a specific client in return for payment of some kind. As we have seen in this chapter so far, being able to work as an employee, self-employed person or through a company you own can make a significant difference to the amounts of tax you have to pay. We have discussed in previous chapters how the timing of when tax must be paid is also different between these three ways of structuring your business activity. HMRC is concerned that these tax planning strategies are not used to avoid tax.

The use of personal service companies in the UK to avoid employment related tax obligations is by no means a new issue. Indeed, the 1981 Finance Bill contained provisions described by the Revenue then as being introduced to ensure that agency workers were taxed as employees even if they operated through a company. In April 1982, however, the Government decided not to proceed.

The IR35 rules

11.9 IR35, dated 9 March, 1999, was a press release announcing changes to counter avoidance 'in the area of personal service provision'. Clearly the Government saw this as an area of unacceptable tax avoidance, in the grey zone of the continuum we discussed at the start of the chapter.

The stated aim of the changes was "to ensure that people working in what is, in effect, disguised employment will, in practice, pay the same tax and national insurance as someone employed directly". This is an attempt by the Government to increase equity in the tax system so that all "employees" are taxed the same whether or not they consider themselves to be an employee.

A new set of rules was then introduced to look at whether a worker, who wants to be taxed as a self-employed person, would have been considered to be an employee of a client, using the usual tests of an employment relationship for tax purposes (which we looked at in Chapter 5). This will be clear in many cases by looking at the terms and conditions of the particular engagement. So, if a taxpayer "pretends" to be in self-employment to benefit from the kinds of tax advantages we discussed earlier in this chapter, and particularly if they offer their services through an intermediary (usually a company) to disguise the fact that they are really an employee under the usual rules to test for this, IR35 will be applied.

The IR35 rules operate so that the fee received by the intermediary for duties a taxpayer performs and to which the rules apply (net of specified deductions) is treated as having been paid to the taxpayer in the form of salary and wages subject to PAYE and NICs. All services provided through an intermediary are potentially subject to these rules. Corporate intermediaries account for PAYE deductions and NICs as usual for any salary paid to the worker throughout the year and reconciliation is then required at the year end. Any shortfall between the actual salary paid and the amount to which the rules apply is then deemed to be paid to the worker on the last day of the year. The personal services company then has to remit PAYE and NICs to HMRC to cover this deemed payment.

Because the aim of the IR35 rules is to make sure that taxpayers do not avoid tax by disguising an employment relationship, the intermediary can deduct expenses otherwise deductible under employment income rules, as well as employer pension contributions, when working out the amount of the year end deemed payment to the worker. In addition, because the Government recognises that running a company involves extra administration costs, the company can deduct a further flat five per cent of the gross payment in working out the deemed payment. If the interposed personal services entity fails to deduct and account for PAYE and NICs, the normal penalties for employer default apply.

This means that taxpayers like Andrea need to be careful about the nature of the contracts their companies enter into with clients. If they are really contracts *of* service, rather than contracts *for* services, IR35 may come into play so that extra tax and NICs are payable.

The introduction of the IR35 rules led to some further developments in subsequent years. Concern that a new form of arrangement, managed service companies was also unacceptable tax avoidance, the Government introduced more rules that now sit beside the IR35 rules and aim to remove the tax advantage of providing personal services through a company rather than directly as an employee.

There have been many cases on the application of IR35 which revolve around determining the employment status of taxpayers. One recent case involves TV presenter Lorraine Kelly (*Albatel Ltd v HMRC* [2019] UKFTT 195].

Settlements and income splitting

11.10 Another potential problem area from a tax planning perspective is the settlement legislation. This was first introduced in the 1920s as a tax avoidance rule, but for many years had not been invoked by HMRC. In the early 2000s, however, the rule was used to challenge husband and wife companies. The rules require that if income from property arises under a 'settlement', and the settlor has an interest in the property, then the income is taxed as income of the settlor. In a key case, *Arctic Systems* (2007), Mr and Mrs Jones each owned one share in a company which earned fees by providing Mr Jones' services to clients. After drawing a small salary, the remaining profits were distributed as dividends to Mr and Mrs Jones. HMRC argued that this was an arrangement which came under the settlement rules and attempted to tax Mr Jones on the dividends distributed to Mrs Jones. After a series of cases, the House of Lords finally found in favour of the taxpayers.

Following the lack of success in the *Arctic Systems* case, HMRC tried to bring in new rules to prevent income shifting, but these were found to be unworkable and in 2009 were postponed indefinitely.

In a 2013 case, *AJ Bingham v HMRC* [2013] TC2528, family tax planning involving joint bank accounts were attacked by HMRC using the settlements rules. The First Tier Tribunal went against the taxpayer, which means that even interest on joint bank accounts is not automatically taxed 50:50.

IR35, the settlements legislation and the failed income splitting rules all deal with the tension in the tax system between acceptable tax planning and unacceptable tax avoidance. In the next section we will consider some of the court decisions dealing with the question of whether an activity constitutes unacceptable tax avoidance.

In 2013, the Government set out a number of measures to clarify the distinction between employment and self-employment. Further, from April 2017 the rules for engaging 'off payroll' workers through their own companies in the public sector have been tightened to make the public sector body responsible for determining the correct status of these workers.

An extension to these rules to private sector engagements commenced in April 2021. The rules give concessionary treatment for an end client who is a small company, in which case they do not have to check the status of their contractors and it is up to the contractor to address IR35 in their own self-assessment return.

The Loan Charge

11.11 A good example of how attitudes towards tax planning and tax avoidance change over time, and the difficulties associated with drawing a line between acceptable and unacceptable tax avoidance in the UK, is the loan charge. New rules in 2017 brought employment related loans made by third parties to tax if they remained outstanding on 5 April 2019. Employment related tax avoidance has been a problem for HMRC for many years, as shown above in the discussion of IR35 and Settlements. In the 1990s and 2000s, one scheme involved providing funds to an employment benefits trust which then loaned them back to the employees. The disguised remuneration rules were introduced in 2010 to curb the use of employee benefits trusts, although arrangements that pre-dated these rules were being challenged in the courts. A high profile case involved Glasgow Rangers football club [*RVC 2012 Plc (in liquidation) v Advocate General for Scotland* [2017] UKSC 45], found that HMRC succeeded not because the loans were taxable, but rather that the original contribution to the employment benefits trust was taxable. In response, HMRC introduced the loan charge under the disguised remuneration rules.

The employee benefit schemes were highly artificial, however the loan charge challenges arrangements from the last 20 years, to before the disguised remuneration rules were introduced and effectively treats taxpayers involved in the same way as people who deliberately cheated.

In 2019, following an independent review, it was decided to change the date from which the loan charge applies to outstanding loan balances to 2010. Another change is to provide that the loan charge will not apply if the taxpayer made reasonable disclosure on a tax return of a loan.

A loan charge action group was formed to support taxpayers caught by the loan charge. Concessions have been made by HMRC in light of the Covid-19 outbreak. HMRC have also issued a warning to returning National Health Service workers who are being targeted by promoters of schemes.

There is an argument that if HMRC had taken action sooner, the loan charge rules would not have been needed.

Tax avoidance

11.12 Over the past 75 years there has been a shift in the attitudes of the courts in relation to the question of what constitutes tax avoidance. Earlier in the twentieth century the courts adopted a strict interpretation of taxation laws: they looked at what the words of the legislation said and only considered the legal nature of any avoidance scheme, not any underlying issues. This has now evolved into looking beyond the legal form of transactions and arrangements and considering the purpose of the relevant legislation.

In this section we will look at some of the more significant cases involving tax avoidance and trace the development of the courts' attitudes. Note, however, that we present here only a very simplified discussion of the case law to illustrate the developments over time.

Tax avoidance case law

IRC v Duke of Westminster (1936)

11.13 The early, strict, interpretation is illustrated by the case of *IRC v Duke of Westminster* (1936). In this case an arrangement was entered into so that domestic servants were not paid wages but instead received an income under a deed of covenant. A deed of covenant produced a tax deduction for the person executing the deed and was valid only if no valuable consideration was provided by the recipient in return. However, the Duke of Westminster and his servants had an understanding, that so long as the deed of covenant operated the servants would not claim the wages due to them. The scheme enabled the Duke to claim tax relief for the amounts paid to his servants whereas payment of wages to servants would not have been an allowable deduction Today such a scheme could not be used because payments made under deeds of covenant are no longer tax effective when paid to individuals. However, at the time, the House of Lords found for the Duke, declaring that they would only consider the legal nature of the transaction, that is, they were more concerned with the form of the transaction than its substance. Until the mid-1980s this case remained an important precedent and the Inland Revenue were rarely successful in challenging tax avoidance schemes in the courts.

WT Ramsay Ltd. V IRC (1981)

11.14 In *WT Ramsay Ltd v IRC* (1981) the House of Lords took a completely different view of an avoidance scheme. The case involved an artificial scheme which was used to create a large capital loss. The company had realised a capital gain and intended to set the artificially generated loss against the capital gain to avoid paying tax on the gain. The scheme was artificial because it was made up of a series of preordained steps which were to be carried out in rapid succession. The scheme required that all steps be completed once the first one had been made. At the end of the series of steps the taxpayers would be in the same position as they had been at the beginning and any loss created would not be a real financial loss – just a paper loss. In fact the only real losses which had been suffered were the professional fees which were paid for the scheme's operation. The House of Lords decided that although each step in the scheme was a separate legal transaction, it was possible to view the scheme not as a series of separate legal transactions, but as a whole, by comparing the position of the taxpayer in real terms at the start and finish of the scheme. When this was done no real loss was incurred and the scheme was self- cancelling.

Lord Wilberforce explained the decision as follows:

> 'While obliging the court to accept documents or transactions, found to be genuine, as such, it does not compel the court to look at a document or a transaction in blinkers, isolated from any context to which it properly belongs. If it can be seen that a document or transaction was intended to have effect as part of a nexus or series of transactions, or as an ingredient of a wider transaction intended as a whole, there is nothing in the doctrine to prevent it being so regarded; to do so is not to prefer form to substance, or substance to form. It is the task of the court to ascertain the legal nature of any transaction to which it is sought to attach a tax, or a tax consequence, and if that emerges from a series, or combination of transactions, intended to operate as such, it is that series or combination which may be regarded.'

Furniss v Dawson (1984)

11.15 The *Ramsay principle* established in the previous case was extended in *Furniss v Dawson* (1984). This time the objective was to defer capital gains tax by using an intermediary company based in the Isle of Man. The scheme was not circular or self-cancelling. However, the House of Lords decided that the scheme should still be set aside for tax purposes because once again the scheme required a series of artificial steps to be carried out in quick succession just to save tax rather than with a real business purpose in mind.

Craven v White (1989)

11.16 Later the case of *Craven v White* (1989) was used by the House of Lords to limit the application of the *Ramsay* principle somewhat. Once again an intermediary company in the Isle of Man was used to defer a capital gains tax liability. The key difference between *Craven v White* and *Furniss v Dawson* was that when the shares were transferred to the Isle of Man based company, their final disposal had not been agreed. Hence no preordained series of steps existed at the time that the first transaction was undertaken. Consequently the House of Lords refused to view the series of transactions as a whole and the scheme was successful this time in reducing the tax liability. This case has great significance for anti-avoidance schemes generally. It makes planning well in advance critical. If transactions are undertaken before the final step is known with certainty, there is a greater likelihood of the scheme being successful if challenged by HMRC as tax avoidance activity – although of course, not being certain of the full outcome makes such schemes inherently more risky.

IRC v McGuckian (1997)

11.17 IRC *v McGuckian* (1997) dealt with an issue in which there was a transfer of company shares to a non-resident trustee of a settlement, followed by the rights to a dividend being assigned to a resident company for consideration. The UK resident company then paid an amount of dividend less commission to the trustee. The question was whether this constituted a tax avoidance scheme, and the House of Lords were of the view that it did. The case raised some important issues, not so much because *Furniss v Dawson* was again applied, but from comments made by their Lordships in the course of the decision. They appeared to adopt a more purposive approach to interpretation which means the courts will look at what legislation is designed to achieve, rather than just what it says.

McNiven v Westmoreland Investments Ltd (2001)

11.18 In *McNiven v Westmoreland Investments Ltd* (2001) the House of Lords had to consider whether steps inserted into a transaction had any commercial purpose or were present simply to affect the tax outcome. The case involved a company with accrued unpaid interest. To be deductible for corporation tax at the time, the interest had to be paid. The lender, which was the parent company, made a loan to Westmoreland that was then repaid in discharge of the outstanding interest. It was a preordained, circular, arrangement, designed purely so as to secure a tax deduction. The House of Lords found, however, that the company had incurred a real economic outlay and that this was tax mitigation to take advantage of a statutory tax relief. It was therefore legitimate tax avoidance.

Barclays Mercantile Business Finance Ltd. v Mawson (2005)

11.19 In 2005, the House of Lords delivered its decision in *Barclays Mercantile Business Finance Ltd v Mawson* [2005] STC 1. In this case, the Barclays group purchased a gas pipeline from the Irish Gas Board for £91million and leased it back to them. By a series of transactions, the £91million found its way back into the group as a deposit. The bank claimed capital allowances on the pipeline, however the Revenue was of the view that the money was spent on "financial engineering" rather than plant and machinery qualifying for capital allowances. The House of Lords affirmed the decision of the Court of Appeal that whether or not an expense is incurred is a legal question and so the arrangement did not constitute unacceptable tax avoidance.

Tower MCashback (2011)

11.20 In this complicated case, a software company, MCashback, owned software that it licensed to third parties. The company wanted to raise funds, and so with the help of a finance company, Tower, agreed to sell an exclusive royalty free license to a limited liability partnership, the partners of which were high net worth individuals. The investing partners provided some of the funds, and borrowed the rest from a special purpose vehicle set up by Tower Finance. The Supreme Court found that not all of the funds spent on the license were eligible for capital allowances, because some of it (the part provided by Tower) was not incurred on the acquisition of software rights. The case is different to Barclays Mercantile Business Finance Ltd (above) mainly because in that case the asset was bought and the funds borrowed on normal commercial terms, which was not the case here.

The question of where the boundary is between acceptable and unacceptable tax avoidance will continue to be debated, and subject to further subtle shifts, as a result of a number of forces. These will include the constitution of the courts and prevailing attitudes in HMRC, government and of society at large.

Tower Radio Ltd v HMRC (2015)

11.21 In this case (TC02784) a company entered into a scheme devised by an accountancy firm that was designed to pay the managing director a substantial bonus without having to pay PAYE or NIC. The scheme involved awarding shares in a subsidiary company that was subsequently liquidated and the assets distributed to the managing director. The First Tier Tribunal (FTT) upheld the view of HMRC that the Ramsay principle (see above) applied and the interposition of the subsidiary company could be ignored. The Upper Tribunal, (UKUT 0060) however, subsequently upheld the taxpayer's appeal against the FTT decision in 2015. The judges found that the employees were given shares, not money, and said 'However unattractive the result may be, it seems to us that the appeals before us must be allowed". Therefore, no income tax or NIC liability arose, and the purposive approach could not be used to overcome a deficiency in the legislation.

UBS AG v HMRC (2016)

11.22 The UBS case, together with the Deutsche Bank case heard at the same time, also involved employees being given shares instead of cash, in this case bankers' bonuses. The Supreme Court handed down its decision in April 2016 finding in favour of HMRC and overturning the previous Court of Appeal decision, and applied a purposive Ramsay approach, albeit a narrower version. The case involved a large sum: UBS paid £91,880,000 to acquire the shares that were then given to the employees, and the arrangement to sidestep income tax and NICs was quite complex involving several steps. Some commentators have suggested that this decision means that what was once a popular way of avoiding tax cannot be guaranteed to work in the future.

You have seen in this section that under the UK's common law system the law is developed by judges whose decisions become binding for similar cases in the future. Some principles that emerge from the various tax avoidance cases are:

- Substance over form – the courts will look at what has actually happened, rather than taking what is documented at face value;
- The courts have increasingly used a purposive interpretation of tax law to look at what the legislation is designed to achieve, not just what the words say; and
- The courts are generally hostile to artificial tax avoidance arrangements but are also bound by what the legislation says and sometimes even a purposive approach cannot overcome defective legislation.

Tackling tax avoidance in the UK

11.23 The question of whether a transaction or arrangement is tax avoidance, and how to distinguish avoidance and planning, is a difficult one. Graham Aaronson, QC, in evidence to the House of Lords Economic Affairs committee in January 2013 said:

'Avoidance' is a rather unfortunate word... because avoidance can be regarded as a particularly nasty thing to do or, if it is an accident, it is a very sensible thing to do – you avoid an accident. So I would rather use words that are less emotive when describing the intellectual process in determining whether you should be paying a smaller amount of tax than you would otherwise pay. You can call that tax planning because it is planning. Where it is good planning or bad planning, whether it is abusive or innocent planning, it is planning. Tax avoidance is a very dangerous expression to use if you want to have a serious debate because one person's avoidance is another person's perfectly reasonable planning.

HMRC define tax avoidance as "exploiting the tax rules to gain an advantage that Parliament never intended. It often involves contrived, artificial transactions that serve little or no commercial purpose other than to produce a tax advantages. It involves operating within the letter, but not the spirit of the law."

The UK currently has a multifaceted approach to tackling tax avoidance that has been developing over a number of years. In the previous section we saw how the judiciary play a role in changing their approach to interpretation and are now looking at the purpose of the legislation and not just its strict wording. Another facet is to deal with specific transactions by specific legislation introduced to curtail new schemes. These are referred to as Targeted Anti Avoidance Rules (TAARs). The difficulty that arises with this approach is that there is an ongoing incentive for the creation of new schemes not covered by existing legislation. It is also often the case that specific measures leave room for new tax planning opportunities.

Finally, in Chapter 2 we saw that tax advisers who are members of professional bodies are bound by a professional code of conduct. In 2016 this was revised to give some clarity around tax planning. The new standard states:

'Members must not create, encourage or promote tax planning arrangements or structures that (i) set out to achieve results that are contrary to the clear intention of parliament in enacting relevant legislation and/or (ii) are highly artificial or highly contrived and seek to exploit shortcomings within the relevant legislation.'

Disclosure of tax avoidance schemes (DOTAs)

11.24 The DOTAS rules require those who sell tax avoidance schemes, and those who use them, to disclose them to HMRC if they fit certain 'hallmarks' that may indicate they would come under these rules.

There is anecdotal evidence that the rules put a brake on the mass marketing of generic tax avoidance schemes. Many of the TAARs referred to in the previous section have been introduced as a result of disclosure of tax avoidance schemes, and their introduction is adding significantly to the length and complexity of the tax legislation in the UK.

In 2014, the Government introduced rules that may require taxpayers who have used a disclosable (see above) tax avoidance scheme to make a payment of the amount that relates to their use of the scheme, even though the final amount has yet to be determined. HMRC can issue an 'accelerated payment notice' (APN) if a tax enquiry or tax appeal is in progress involving an arrangement which has been given a DOTAS number. It operates like a payment on account.

Specific schemes identified by HMRC for examination are also now detailed in a series of 'Spotlights' published on their website – see: https://www.gov.uk/government/collections/tax-avoidance-schemes-currently-in-the-spotlight.

Promoters and enablers of tax avoidance

11.25 There are special rules designed to tackle tax advisers who promote tax avoidance schemes and allow HMRC to closely monitor such advisers and require them to provide additional information. The Promoters of Tax Avoidance Schemes (POTAS) legislation aims to stop promoters of schemes from marketing schemes to clients.

In addition, new legislation was introduced in 2017 to deal with 'enablers' of abusive tax arrangements that are later defeated in the courts. This legislation is designed to change the behaviour of the small number of tax advisers and others who benefit from designing, marketing and facilitating tax abusive arrangements.

The General Anti Abuse Rule

11.26 In the UK there was for many years no general anti-avoidance rule (GAAR), as there is in some other countries, such as Canada and Australia.

Following extensive consultation, a General Anti Abuse (rather than avoidance) Rule was introduced in 2013 and is designed to apply where HMRC judge that taxpayers enter into an arrangement that has obtaining a tax advantage as one of its main purposes. An independent Advisory Panel examines arrangements to see if they fall within the GAAR. Only after the Advisory Panel issues its opinion can HMRC make any adjustments, which can then be appealed against in the normal way. A penalty of up to 60% of the avoided tax can be imposed.

The GAAR therefore allows HMRC to counteract tax advantages where it is found that an arrangement is abusive. It does not override the DOTAS rules or TAARs. Rather it is another piece of equipment available to HMRC in its quest to tackle tax avoidance.

Tax evasion

11.27 As we noted earlier, tax evasion is illegal activity, and in recent years it has become an important area of academic research, particularly in the fields of economics and psychology. Researchers around the world are trying to work out what factors affect people's decisions to evade payment of taxes, including attitudes and norms, both personal and social. This research has led tax authorities to develop new strategies for dealing with taxpayers who evade taxes. For a list of references, see the end of this Chapter.

One recent example of tax evasion on a very large scale is referred to as 'missing trader' fraud where huge amounts of VAT have effectively been stolen. A version of this fraud, referred to as 'carousel' fraud, involves evasion of VAT in trade within the European Union taking advantage of the zero rating of cross border transactions within the EU. Importers of goods are able to receive them without paying VAT, but charge VAT on their resale without remitting it to the revenue authority.

Fiscal Fact

In a press release dated 5 July 2010, HMRC announced that two members of a 21-strong criminal tax fraud gang have been ordered to pay £92.3m in the biggest ever confiscation order secured by HMRC. The gang stole £37.5m in VAT tax fraud involving import and export of computer processing units through a chain of companies using sham invoices. They used the cash to invest in luxury properties.

Summary

We opened this chapter with a brief look at the difference between tax planning, tax avoidance and tax evasion. We then considered a limited number of different basic tax planning strategies for both employees and businesses. From a structural viewpoint, we considered the differences in the tax system for employees, self-employed taxpayers and incorporated taxpayers. We found that there are some clear differences, with employees generally paying more tax than self-employed taxpayers and unincorporated businesses paying more than incorporated businesses on the same amount of profits. We noted, however, that the decision of how to structure an income earning activity is not just a tax issue, there are other commercial considerations involved.

We also considered how the attitudes of the courts towards tax avoidance have changed over time and looked at some current developments in this area.

Project areas

The issue of tax planning provides lots of opportunities for projects as it is a subject that can be approached from a number of different directions. The boundary between tax planning and unacceptable tax avoidance for example raises questions about the different attitudes of the revenue authorities, taxpayers and their professional advisers and can also raise some interesting moral and ethical questions.

The incorporation of tax considerations into strategic management decision making is another area of potential project topics as is considering the tax policy questions of providing opportunities for tax planning in the first instance.

Discussion questions

1. The treatment of corporations separately from their shareholders for tax purposes can lead to tax avoidance, particularly where there is a significant difference between the rate of tax applicable to corporations and that applying to high income individuals. What measures can the Government put in place to prevent high income taxpayers from sheltering profits behind the corporate form?

2. How can a government fairly determine the difference between employment and self-employment to ensure legitimate tax planning is allowed to continue but abuses of the system are minimised?

3. Discuss how tax planning can occur for other taxes, such as inheritance tax, stamp duty or VAT. Does the interaction of these taxes and income tax provide any opportunities for tax planning?

4. Do you think the decision in *WT Ramsay v IRC* was the right one?

5. How effective do you think the General Anti Abuse Rule is?

6. Is the current approach of HMRC – requiring tax avoidance schemes to be disclosed– an effective way to limit tax loss to the Government or an 'over-the-top' solution that prevents acceptable tax planning which would otherwise be allowed by the law?

Questions

Question 1

Zainab is employed by a company that does not currently contribute to her pension scheme, and she pays £80 per month to a pension scheme from her net (after tax) pay. What would be the effect of entering into a salary sacrifice arrangement so that the company pays pension contributions on her behalf?

Question 2 (based on an ACCA question)

Andrew Zoom is a cameraman who started working for Slick-Productions Ltd on 6 April 2018. The following information is available in respect of the year ended 5 April 2023:

1.   Andrew received gross income of £50,000 from Slick Productions Ltd. He works a set number of hours each week and is paid hourly for the work that he does. When Andrew works more than the set number of hours, he is paid overtime.

2.   Andrew is under an obligation to accept the work offered to him by Slick-Productions Ltd, and the work is carried out under the control of the company's production manager. He is obliged to do the work personally, and this is all performed at Slick-Productions Ltd's premises.

3.   All of the equipment that Andrew uses is provided by Slick-Productions Ltd.

Andrew has several friends who are cameramen, and they are all treated as self-employed. He therefore considers that he should be treated as self-employed as well in relation to his work for Slick-Productions Ltd.

Required:

(a)   List those factors that indicate that Andrew Zoom should be treated as an employee in relation to his work for Slick-Productions Ltd rather than self-employed.

(b)   Calculate Andrew Zoom's income tax liability and national insurance contributions for the tax year 2022/23 if he is treated:

(i) as an employee in respect of his work for Slick-Productions Ltd (note, you are not required to calculate employer's national insurance contributions);

(ii) as self-employed in respect of his work for Slick Productions Ltd.

Note: for NIC purposes you can use an annual threshold of £11,908.

Question 3 (based on an ICAS question)

You are a tax partner for Chic Ltd ('Chic'), a designer clothing manufacturing company jointly owned by Mr and Mrs Style. Mr Style is the managing director. Chic has no associated companies. The management and work force total 45 people. The company has a year end of 31 March and owns the existing premises which cost £100,000 in 1992.

The projected management accounts for the year to 31 March 2023 show turnover of £1,800,000 and allowable trading expenses of £1,400,000. Capital allowances on existing assets for the accounting period will amount to £90,000. The company will also receive the following income:

1.   Dividends from UK companies of £9,000;

2.   Annual royalties of £15,600; and

3.   Loan interest of £4,000.

You have had a meeting with Mr Style regarding year-end planning for capital expenditure. The Styles are thinking of selling the existing factory premises to a developer for £400,000. With the proceeds, the Styles are planning to:

(a)   purchase new fixed plant and machinery at a cost of £250,000 to allow the company's production to expand;

(b)   upgrade the computer system at a cost of £70,000 to improve the efficiency in production, stock control and accounting functions, and to launch the company on to the internet; and

(c)   build a 'granny annex' to the Styles family mansion by borrowing £50,000 from the company. The loan will be repaid when Mrs Style's mother sells her own flat after moving into the annex.

Mr Style is concerned about the timing and tax implications of these transactions and the effect of any tax liabilities on the company's cash flow.

Required:

1. Calculate the corporation tax that would be payable by Chic for the year ending 31 March 2023 assuming that none of the proposed capital expenditure took place. State when the corporation tax is due.

2. Prepare notes for a meeting with Mr and Mrs Style:
    (a) detailing the tax implications for the company of the proposed sale of the factory and of each of the three capital transactions which will follow; and
    (b) revising the corporation tax that will become payable for the year ending 31 March 2023 after the capital expenditure.

Indexation factors:	April 1992	138.8
	December 2017	278.1

(*Note: answer available via lecturer's website*)

Question 4 (based on an ACCA question)

You work as a Tax Senior and your manager has received a letter from Ziti. Ziti owns and runs an unincorporated business which was given to him by his father, Ravi. Extracts from the letter and from an email from your manager are set out below.

Extract from the letter from Ziti:
"I have decided that, due to my father's illness, I want to be able to look after him on a full time basis. Accordingly, I am going to sell my business and use the proceeds to buy a house nearer to where he lives. My father started the business in 1999 when he purchased the building referred to

in the business assets below. He gave the business (consisting of the goodwill, the building and the equipment) to me on 1 July 2014 and we submitted a joint claim for gift relief, such that no capital gains tax was payable. I have no sources of income other than this business.

I have identified two possible methods of disposal:

(i)   My preferred approach would be to close the business down. I would do this by selling the building and equipment on 31 January 2023, at which point I would cease trading.

(ii)   My father would prefer to see the business carry on after I sell it. For this to occur, I would have to continue trading until 30 April 2023 and then sell the business to someone who would continue to operate it.

In each case I would prepare accounts for the year ending 30 April 2023 and then to the date of cessation or disposal. I attach an appendix setting out the information you requested in relation to the business.

Appendix: Business assets (all figures exclude VAT)

	Goodwill £	Building £	Equipment £
Original cost of assets	nil	60,000	18,000
Market value as at 1 July 2014	40,000	300,000	9,000
Expected value 31/1/23 and 30/4/23	40,000	330,000	10,000

Financial position of the business

The tax adjusted trading profits for the year ended 30 April 2021 were £55,000. From 1 May 2021, it can be assumed that the business generates trading profits of £5,000 per month. The only tax adjustment required to this figure is in respect of capital allowances.

The tax written down value of the main pool as at 30 April 2021 was nil. I purchased business equipment for £6,000 on 1 August 2021. There have been no disposals of equipment since 30 April 2021.

Extract from an email from your manager:

- Ziti was born in 1967 and both he and his father are resident and domiciled in the UK.
- All of the equipment is movable and no item has a cost or market value of more than £6,000.

The business is registered for VAT and no election has been made in respect of the building in relation to VAT.

Required:
- a) Calculate Ziti's taxable trading profits from 1 May 2021 onwards, the income tax thereon and any capital gains tax payable, assuming the income tax and capital gains tax rates and allowances remain as the 2022/23 rates in the future.
- b) Compare the financial implications of the alternative methods for disposing of the business (you may ignore national insurance contributions).
- c) Explain whether or not VAT would need to be charged on either or both of the alternative disposals

(*Note: answer available via lecturer's website*)

 Further test questions for this chapter to test your knowledge can be found in the student section of the website at:

http://www.fiscalpublications.com/lymerandoats/2022

Further reading and examples

Aaronson, G. (2011), GAAR Study available at:
   http://www.hm-treasury.gov.uk/d/gaar_final_report_111111.pdf

Bowler, T. (2009), *Countering Tax Avoidance in the UK: Which Way Forward?* Institute for Fiscal Studies, Tax Law Review Committee Discussion Paper No. 7

Evans, C., Hasseldine, J., Lymer, A., Ricketts, R. & Sandford, C. (2017), Tax compliance in *Comparative Taxation: Why tax systems differ*, Fiscal Publications: Birmingham.

HMRC (2013), *Tackling Tax Avoidance*, available at
   http://www.gov.uk/government/publications/tackling-tax-avoidance

Kirchler, E. (2007), *The Economic Psychology of Tax Behaviour*, Cambridge University Press.

Seely, A. (2020), *The 2019 Loan Charge*, House of Commons Briefing Paper No 8811.

Seely, A. (2020), *Personal Service Companies and IR35*, House of Commons Briefing Paper No 5876.

Seely, A. (2020), *Tax Avoidance: A General Anti-Abuse Rule*, House of Commons Briefing Paper No 6265.

For a chance to review the coverage of this chapter further, and for lots of extra questions to test your knowledge on, see:

Combs, A. (2022), *UK Corporation Tax, Capital Gains Tax and VAT Practice Questions (2nd edition 2022/23)*, Fiscal Publications: Malvern.
    – a large test bank of questions linked to the content of this chapter that will enable you to thoroughly test your knowledge of this work with exam-level questions. See
        https://www.fiscalpublications.com/uk-ct-cgt-vat-practice-questions/2022

Combs, A. & Tutin, R (2022), *Taxation: Incorporating the 2022 Finance Act,* Fiscal Publications: Malvern.
    – use this book for many other examples to further develop and test your knowledge of this chapter's contents. See
    http://www.fiscalpublications.com/combsandtutin/2022/

12 International tax

Introduction

12.1 The UK tax paid by an individual or company is influenced by the residence or domicile of the taxpayer.

As a general rule, an individual who is closely connected with the UK will pay tax in the UK on his or her income no matter where in the world it comes from. If an individual only has a vague connection with the UK, however, he or she will be taxed in the UK only on income arising in the UK. A similar principle applies to companies, although the system is becoming increasingly territorial for companies as you will see later.

With increased globalisation, more and more UK-based individuals and companies are conducting business or earning income outside of the UK. It is important to know how the returns from these activities will be taxed. Overseas investments also allow scope for tax planning, particularly as there are a number of countries with much lower tax rates than the UK.

International tax is an extremely complex area and in this chapter we will only cover some of these issues at a level that will give you an overview of the key issues involved. We will also have a brief look at how some of the special tax rules work that are related to international activity.

At the end of this chapter you will be able to:

- explain the terms residence and domicile;
- outline the general rules concerning whether an individual or company is liable to UK income and corporation tax;
- explain how payment of tax overseas can affect a UK tax liability and the measures available to prevent double taxation; and
- identify some international tax avoidance practices and the legislation which seeks to prevent them.

Residence of individuals

12.2 Residence rules are important as they determine a taxpayer's likely exposure to UK tax legislation; for both individuals and companies there are different liabilities arising depending on whether a taxpayer is considered to be tax resident or not.

Your residence status will determine how much of your income will be taxed in the UK and also when it will be taxed. If you are a UK resident you normally pay UK tax on all your income, whether it is from the UK or abroad. If you are not a UK tax resident you will only pay tax on any UK income you earn and or on any UK based assets you own.

Some income is taxed on an *arising basis*, that is the amount that is earned during the tax year, even if it is not brought over to the UK. This rule applies to all UK residents normally. Other income is taxed on a *remittance basis*, that is so long as it remains overseas it will not be taxed in the UK, but will attract tax as soon as it is remitted, or brought into the UK. This basis can be used by 'non-doms' as we explain below.

There is, since 2013, a statutory residence test to provide clear, objective tests that will give certainty as to whether you are UK tax resident or not in most cases.

The rules have three components:

1. An *automatic overseas* test. This test means that an individual meeting the following conditions will be a non-resident for UK tax purposes. The conditions are that they were:
    - not resident in the UK for the previous 3 tax years and they are present in the UK for fewer than 45 days in the current tax year; or
    - resident in the UK in one or more of the previous 3 tax years, and present for fewer than 16 days in the current tax year; or
    - leave the UK to carry out full-time work overseas, provided they are present in the UK for fewer than 91 days in the tax year and fewer than 31 days are spent working in the UK in the tax year.

2. An *automatic UK* test. This test provides that an individual will be a UK tax resident if they:
    - Are present in the UK for at least 183 days in a tax year; or
    - Have a home in the UK for more than 90 days, spend at least 30 separate days in that home, there are 91 consecutive days during which they don't have an overseas home or if they do, they spend fewer than 30 separate days in each of them; or
    - Work full time in the UK for a period of 365 days with no significant breaks.

3. A *sufficient UK ties* test. This test looks at the ties the individual has to the UK and specifies the number of days they can spend in the UK without becoming tax resident. The ties are:
    - UK resident family;
    - Accessible accommodation in the UK;

- Substantive work in the UK;
- UK presence in the previous tax years (more than 90 days in the UK in either of the previous 2 tax years;)
- More time in the UK than in any other single country.

If your course requires you to understand these rules in more detail, HMRC has published guidance, including detailed worked examples at: www.gov.uk/government/publications/rdr3-statutory-residence-test-srt

Non-domiciles

12.3   There are special rules for taxpayers who meet the tests for UK residency but who they have their 'permanent' home (their 'domicile') elsewhere. They will be subject to some UK tax but not necessarily on all of their worldwide income or capital gains as other UK residents are.

A person's domicile is generally either where he or she is born, or the place where the person intends to settle permanently. An individual has a domicile of origin from the moment of birth. Once the individual is aged 16 or over they may choose their domicile. To do this the individual must maintain a physical presence in the country concerned and must have evidence that he or she has an intention to remain there indefinitely. You can only have one domicile at any one time, although it may be possible to be tax resident of more than one country.

Most people who are UK tax resident will also have a UK domicile. For such the rules are simple – as outlined in the previous section – you are subject to UK tax on your worldwide income. However, if you are UK resident, but not UK domiciled (referred to as a 'non-dom') you only have to pay UK tax on your UK income and gains. You do not have to pay UK tax on your foreign income or gains provided it is either less than £2,000 in the tax year, or if you don't bring it back to the UK (i.e. have it paid to a UK bank account).

This concession for non-doms however, does not continue indefinitely and after a few years being present in the UK with this status the rules change. An annual charge (the Remittance Basis Charge or RBC) of £30,000 applies to non-UK domiciled adults resident in the UK for the year and also at least 7 of the previous 9 years (the charge does not apply to children). A higher charge applies of £60,000 where the person has been resident at least 12 in the last 14 years. In all cases a period of 6 years of non-residence is required to reset each clock.

The RBC applies when a non-dom claims the right to be taxed on their foreign income and gains on a remittance basis, that is, not as they are earned, but when the income or gains are brought into the UK (which they may never be, of course).

This charge is in addition to whatever UK tax is also due but the charge will not apply if the unremitted foreign income is £2,000 or less in any tax year.

Non-domiciled adult residents in the UK in the tax year who claim the remittance basis do not have the right to UK income tax personal allowances against their remitted income (including the personal allowance itself, blind person allowance and tax reductions for married couples or civil partners). They also cannot use the capital gains tax AEA against capital gains remitted to the UK. However, a £2,000 de minimus rule also applies so that if unremitted income does not exceed this sum, non-domiciles will be allowed to keep their allowances to offset their remitted income for both income and capital gains taxes.

Fiscal Fact

Approximately 5,400 individuals paid the remittance basis charge in its year of introduction (2008/09). By 2019-20 there were an estimated 75,700 individuals claiming non domiciled status (the vast majority of whom are UK residents), although only 1,800 of these paid the remittance basis charge (down from over 5,000 when the new RBC rules were introduced). In 2019/20 non-doms paid £7.8bn in income tax, NIC and CGT via the remittance basis and those paying the RBC paid £914m (including the RBC charge itself).
[Source: Statistical commentary on non-domiciled UK taxpayers, available at https://www.gov.uk/government/statistics/statistics-on-non-domiciled-taxpayers-in-the-uk - version 30 July 2020]

Since April 2012, non-domiciled individuals have been able to bring foreign income and capital gains into the UK without the need to pay the remittance charge where this money is used for commercial investment. This is called Business Investment Relief.

Permanent non-dom status ceased from April 2017. After this date, anyone who has been resident in the UK for more than 15 of the last 20 years is deemed domiciled in the UK and subject to normal rules for taxation of their income and wealth. Further, (also from April 2017), anyone born in the UK, to UK domiciled parents, would no longer be able to leave the country and later return as a non-dom.

Where an individual becomes a 'deemed domicile' under the 15 year rule, they become subject to income tax and CGT on a normal arising basis and their worldwide estate becomes subject to Inheritance Tax. A person wishing to avoid becoming a deemed domicile must cease to be resident in the UK in year 14.

Employment income

12.4 As we saw in Chapter 5, earnings from employment or pensions are assessed on an arising (taxed in the year it is received) basis. This applies to any employment earnings for any year of assessment in which the person holding the office or employment is resident in the UK.

These rules also detail how to tax income, also on the arising basis, for UK-based duties performed by a person who is not a resident. In this circumstance, the taxpayer is charged tax only on income generated in the UK.

As we also saw in 12.3 above, a person who is resident but not domiciled in the UK, may pay UK income tax on a remittance basis. This means they only have to pay income tax if they bring their income into the UK, subject to payment of the remittance basis charge.

Capital taxes

12.5 Capital gains tax is charged on individuals if they are resident in the UK. If they are also domiciled in the UK, this charge is on gains made anywhere in the world and tax due is reported and collected via the usual processes, as we saw in Chapter 8. If individuals are not domiciled in the UK then only gains arising in the UK, or remitted here, are taxed in the UK. Use of the remittance basis is subject to payment of the £30,000 or £60,000 charge.

Resident status does not affect inheritance tax. If you are domiciled in the UK, when you die you pay UK inheritance tax on your worldwide property. If you are not domiciled here you only pay inheritance tax on your UK property. Finance Act (No. 2) 2017 extended inheritance tax to UK residential property held by a non-dom through an overseas structure such as a company.

From 6 April 2015, non-residents who dispose of residential property will be potentially liable to capital gains tax. Such taxpayers will be entitled to claim principal private residence relief, but subject to some new conditions: the property must be located in the same country as where the taxpayer is resident for tax purposes and the taxpayer spends at least 90 midnights in the property in the tax year.

From April 2017, all non-doms who are deemed to be UK domiciled under the changes to the remittance basis charge rules outlined above will have their assets rebased to April 2017 values. It is possible for taxpayers in this situation to opt out of rebasing. This might be beneficial, for example, where an asset was in a loss position relative to its base cost as at 5 April 2017.

Rates of tax

12.6 For UK residents any foreign income earned is simply added to the other, UK-sourced, income as part of the tax computation. It is then taxed at the same rates as if it had arisen in the UK. If tax has been paid overseas on this income already however, a reduction may be available in the UK tax computation to compensate for the tax already deducted by another Government. We will look at when this might apply later in this chapter.

Individuals who are only charged tax on amounts they remit in the UK, pay tax on all foreign sourced income (including foreign savings and dividend income) at UK rates for non-savings income (i.e., 20% 40% or 45% based on the usual bands).

Residence of companies

12.7 Companies do not have a domicile, only a residence status for tax purposes. UK resident companies used to be liable to corporation tax on their total worldwide profits arising in an accounting period regardless of whether those profits are remitted to the UK – the same rule as applies to resident individuals. More recently, however, there has been a shift away from a 'worldwide' system to a 'territorial' system, so that in many cases foreign profits are exempt from UK tax.

A company is deemed to be a UK resident if it is either incorporated in the UK or, if it is not incorporated here, its central management and control is exercised in the UK. This is generally where the key operational decisions are made, often the place where directors' board meetings are held.

In addition to having subsidiary companies, i.e. where a parent company owns shares in another company which may be located in another country, many companies operate in other countries through what is known as a *permanent establishment (PE)*. A PE is a fixed place of business; the most common form of which is a branch. A PE represents a minimum level of activity that is required in order to give taxing rights to the country in which it is located. If the level of activity falls below the threshold for creating a PE, then no tax will be charged in the country where the activity takes place and only UK tax will be payable.

Non-resident companies are liable to UK corporation tax if they trade in the UK through a UK-based PE which usually involves staff, and often premises of some kind, based in the UK but owned by the non-resident company. The trading profits arising, directly or indirectly, from the UK-based PE are liable to UK tax, whether or not they are fully earned in the UK. The question of whether a foreign company has a PE in the UK is very complex and depends on the facts of the particular case. The recent controversies over multinationals such as Google and Amazon have brought to public attention how complex this area of tax law can be.

Income from property or rights either used by, or held by, the UK PE of a foreign company is chargeable to corporation tax as are any chargeable gains on the disposal of assets situated in the UK.

Double taxation relief

12.8 It is possible, because of the way tax systems in different countries interact, that a UK resident can pay tax in two countries on the same income source; in their country of residence and the country in which the income or profit arises (referred to as the source country). A UK resident (individual or company) is sometimes taxed on worldwide income and so may have to pay tax, for example, on foreign business profits in both the UK and the source country where the business is being carried on. This situation is called *double taxation*. Fortunately, the problem of double taxation is well recognised by tax authorities around the world and, in most cases, the full effects of double tax can be avoided.

There are two main methods for reducing double taxation on overseas income. One is a credit system, where the home government taxes the overseas income but then allows a credit, or reduction in tax payable, for at least some of the tax paid overseas (a worldwide system). The second is the exemption system where the home government chooses not to tax foreign income at all, i.e. it is treated as exempt from home country taxation (a territorial system).

In the UK, as in many other countries, double tax is reduced by a system of double tax reliefs. These reliefs are outlined in a series of agreements between countries on how they will each handle this problem. These agreements are called *double tax treaties*. The UK has a large number of double tax treaties with other countries that contain provisions explaining exactly how double tax is to be relieved and how taxable activities between their countries are to be reported. As a general rule, until recently, the UK tax was calculated on gross worldwide income and then double tax relief was deducted from that liability.

What if the country you pay tax to does not have a treaty with the UK? This does not mean that you will have to suffer double taxation. The UK tax rules also contain provisions which allow for unilateral (one sided) relief for at least some of this double tax for such cases. These provisions require that the foreign income is first included in the taxable income of an individual (or TTP of a company in some cases), grossed up for any foreign tax suffered.

The double tax relief under these relief provisions is usually the lower of the foreign tax suffered on the overseas income or profits, and the UK tax liability on that overseas income. More relief can be available where a double tax treaty exists, but this basic rule is true in most circumstances.

Since 2011, UK companies can make an election to exempt foreign PE profits and losses from UK taxation. The election is permanent, so companies will have to be careful about making this election. If the location of the foreign PE has a lower rate of tax than the UK, and the PE makes profits, there will be a tax saving. However, if the PE is making a loss, then the election will mean that the loss cannot be offset against UK profits. If the foreign PE is in a location with a higher tax rate than the UK, then making the election to treat it as exempt will have no effect on the UK tax burden.

Activity

Aristotle Ltd is a UK resident company with no associated companies. During the year ended 31 March 2023, Aristotle had the following income:

	£
Tax adjusted trading profits from UK business	2,500,000
Tax adjusted trading profits from overseas branch office (PE) (net of 35% foreign tax)	208,000

Calculate Aristotle Ltd's UK corporation tax liability for the year, assuming the company does not opt to use the PE profits exemption.

Feedback

First, in calculating total taxable profits, it is necessary to gross up the foreign profits by the amount of foreign tax paid to determine the total overseas income.

	Total £	UK Income £	Overseas Income £
Tax adjusted UK profit	2,500,000	2,500,000	
Foreign profit (£208,000 × 100/65)	320,000		320,000
TTP	2,820,000	2,500,000	320,000
Corporation tax @ 19%	535,800	475,000	60,800
Less double tax relief:			
Foreign tax paid:			
£320,000 @ 35%	112,000		
UK tax on foreign income			
£320,000 @ 19%	60,800		
Relief is the lower of the two	(60,800)		(60,800)
Corporation tax payable	475,000	500,000	nil

Note: In this case £51,200 (£112,000 – £60,800) of foreign taxes payable cannot be offset against Aristotle's UK tax bill. Unrelieved foreign tax can be either:

- Carried back to accounting periods beginning not more than 3 years before the period in which the unrelieved tax arises; or
- Carried forward indefinitely.

In both cases the unrelieved foreign tax is treated as if it was paid in respect of the same source of income and may be relieved against corporation tax payable on that source of income, in the earlier or later accounting period.

Dividend income from foreign companies

12.9 The UK has an exemption system for companies that receive dividends from foreign subsidiary companies in which they own more than 10% of the shares. This means that dividends from such subsidiaries are generally not taxed in the UK.

Where the exemption does not apply, the UK shareholder will be entitled to double tax relief. When a foreign company pays dividends to a UK resident shareholder, the country where the foreign company is located (the source country) is likely to levy what is called *withholding tax*, which is a tax at a fixed rate on dividends leaving that country to go to foreign shareholders. UK resident companies receiving dividends from foreign companies will usually be entitled to double tax relief for withholding tax paid.

International tax planning and avoidance

Branch or subsidiary?

12.10 When a company is considering expanding overseas, a decision must be made about how best to establish its foreign activities. The most common options are to either set up the foreign business as a branch, or PE, of the existing business, or to incorporate a separate subsidiary company in the foreign country. This is a complex decision and, of course, does not only involve tax considerations. However from a tax point of view, we can note the following that must be considered at the minimum:

- A branch office of a UK business is not treated as a separate taxpaying entity. The profits of a branch will need to be included in the UK head office's trading income and so will be liable for UK corporation tax in the year in which they are earned in the same way as the profits of a UK based business are, unless the company elects for the branch profits exemption to apply. Similarly, losses incurred by a branch will generally be able to be offset against the company's UK profits.

- A subsidiary company is a separate legal entity and for tax purposes, and there is no consolidation of profits required as there is for accounting reporting to stakeholders. Losses made by subsidiaries cannot generally be surrendered for group relief and so may not be able to offset UK profits. Dividends from overseas subsidiaries are generally exempt from UK corporation tax.

12.11 Double taxation of profits by two or more countries is an added cost of doing business overseas. Minimising worldwide taxes paid and, where possible, eliminating double taxation has led to the development of a large international tax planning community. This is of some concern to governments who want to protect their taxing rights and so the grey area between tax planning and unacceptable tax avoidance, which we discussed in Chapter 11, also arises in the international context. Some tax avoidance practices of multinational enterprises entail the use of tax havens, which are countries where little or no tax is imposed on the profits of organisations resident or doing business there.

In the UK, there are some specific anti-avoidance provisions which aim to protect the Government's tax revenue from what they consider to be unacceptable international tax avoidance. Here we will consider three common avoidance practices and see how the UK provisions operate to prevent their inappropriate use to artificially reduce taxes due to the UK Government. Specifically they are the transfer pricing rules, thin capitalisation rules and the rules dealing with controlled foreign companies.

Transfer pricing

12.12 Transfer pricing refers to the process of determining the price to be charged for goods or services flowing between related or associated enterprises. Where goods or services are bought or sold between unrelated enterprises, the parties will agree what is known as an *arm's length price*, which is the market price for the item being traded where both parties seek to get the best price they can from their perspective. Where the two enterprises are related to one another, through common shareholding or some other arrangement, it is possible to agree to set a price for trades between them which is not the same as an arm's length bargain. The way in which transactions are structured may then allow for some tax planning, particularly where the parties are in different countries and there is a difference in the tax rates in force in those two countries.

To illustrate how transfer pricing could be used to affect global tax liabilities, take the case where a company resident in the UK sells goods to a subsidiary company resident in France, which then sells the product to French customers. The product cost £1,000 to manufacture, £100 to ship to France and retails for £2,100 in France.

Depending on how the parties wish to price the transaction, the profit can appear to be made in either the UK or France or partly in both. For example, the UK company can sell the product to the French associate for £2,000 leaving a £900 profit in UK and a £100 profit in France. Alternatively, it can sell the product for £1,100 leaving £100 profit in UK and £900 profit in France.

The companies could also introduce a third party through which to trade to place the profits somewhere else again. For example, the company could create a wholly owned subsidiary, perhaps in a tax haven where there are no taxes on business profits. If this new company then charge say £900 to arrange the transport of the goods, £800 of the profit is shifted from either UK or France to the tax haven.

Given the flexibility transfer pricing across tax borders offers to companies, HMRC has been given the power under UK law to substitute an arm's length price for any prices they consider to be artificial, in situations where:

- Sales are made by a UK company to an overseas company at what they consider to be an undervalue; or
- Purchases are made by a UK company from an overseas company at an overvalue.

The legislation applies not only to trading activities but also to:

- Sales or purchase of fixed assets
- Letting or hiring of property
- Loan interest
- Patent royalties
- Management charges

Transactions between related companies also have to be at arm's length prices even when they are both residents of the UK. There are, however, some exceptions to these rules for small and medium companies.

There are comprehensive guidelines, published by the OECD, that advise how an arm's length price should be calculated, and the UK transfer pricing rules draw on these guidelines. There are several methods available and companies have a certain amount of choice about what method to use. This can lead to disputes with HMRC, and the tax authorities overseas if the transactions are with foreign companies or branches. Transfer pricing is therefore an area of considerable uncertainty and gives plenty of scope for disagreement.

It is possible for companies to enter into advance pricing agreements (APAs) with HMRC under which an agreed method can be used without being challenged for a certain period of time. Often these agreements are entered into bilaterally, that is not just with HMRC but also with another tax authority e.g. the US Internal Revenue Service, so that both countries commit to accepting the companies method for working out its transfer prices. This reduces the uncertainty for both the taxpayer and the tax authorities concerned.

Fiscal Fact

In 2020/21 transfer pricing enquiries generated additional revenue of £2.16b. The average age of settled enquiries is 36 months and there were 124 cases settled.

[Source: HMRC Transfer Pricing Statistics]

Thin capitalisation

12.13 Thin capitalisation refers to a company's gearing; a thinly capitalised company is one which has a high proportion of debt financing compared to equity. The fact that dividends paid to holders of equity are not tax deductible, whereas interest payments to creditors are, means that there is a tax induced incentive for companies to finance operations through debt. The UK government, along with others, is concerned that companies may artificially inflate the amount of debt, and therefore interest payable, in order to get an extra tax advantage, which is viewed as a form of tax avoidance.

The rules restricting interest deductions are complex and beyond this scope of this introductory chapter so we provide no further information here, but if you are interested, the HMRC website has useful details on these rules.

Controlled foreign companies

12.14 We saw earlier that differences in the tax situation result from the choice of earning foreign profits through a branch office as compared to a separately incorporated subsidiary. Having a subsidiary company, where the UK parent company has a controlling interest, presents opportunities for at least the deferral of some tax, and maybe some tax savings. Remember that the profits of a subsidiary will not attract UK corporation tax until such time as they are remitted to the UK, although since 2009 dividend payments from subsidiaries are usually exempt as we saw above. If that overseas subsidiary is also located in a country where the tax rate is low, considerable overall tax savings can be made, so long as the profits are left in the hands of the overseas subsidiary.

When taken to extremes, this is viewed by the UK Government as being unacceptable tax avoidance, and so provisions are contained in the UK legislation to make deferring tax by leaving profits in the hands of some foreign companies less attractive. These rules specifically refer to what are called *Controlled Foreign Companies* (or CFCs). If the controlled foreign company rules are applied, then HMRC has the power to apportion the profits of the CFC between its corporate shareholders and charge those profits to corporation tax in the UK even though they have not yet been actually remitted to the UK as either dividends or in another form. The UK's CFC rules are quite complex, and here we will only provide an overview of how they work. The rules are designed to identify and bring to tax artificially diverted profits.

Under the current rules, a CFC is a company which is:

- resident overseas but is controlled by UK residents, and
- subject to taxation in its country of residence where the tax rate applicable is less than 75% of the corresponding UK tax rate.

In deciding whether or not an overseas company is controlled by UK residents, the rules look at legal, economic and accounting assessments. For example, shareholdings, voting power, other rights which give control and whether consolidated accounts are required under accounting rules. The foreign company does not need to be controlled by just one UK resident, a combination of UK residents can cause the foreign company to be classified as a CFC.

There are several entity level exemptions. If any of these apply, then all the profits of the CFC will be exempted from a CFC charge. These include:

- Exempt period– for the first 12 months of coming under UK control;
- Excluded territories exemption – where the CFC is resident in a specified territory with a headline corporation tax rate of not less than 75% of the UK main rate;
- Low profits exemption – where the CFC's profits are not more than £50,000, or not more than £500,000 of which nor more than £50,000 is non-trading profits;
- Low profit margin exemption – where the CFC's profits are no more than 10% of its operating expenditure;

If the entity level exemptions do not apply, then a series of 'gateway' provisions operate to define the profits which are considered to have been artificially diverted from the UK and to which the CFC charge will apply. Where the profits do not fall within the gateway provisions, they are excluded.

Under self-assessment, UK companies are required to calculate their own liability to tax on the profits of CFC's. This is an onerous requirement, especially given the need to compute the CFC's profits as if they had been liable to UK corporation tax. Given, however, that the provisions only apply to UK companies with at least a 25% interest in the CFC, and then only if one of the exemption provisions does not apply, the rules do not have wide application.

The OECD BEPS project

12.15 Important work has been undertaken since 2013 by the OECD in relation to various aspects of the potential for international tax avoidance. This is primarily being undertaken under a project entitled 'Base Erosion and Profit Shifting' (BEPS). A number of working groups were set up to look into different problematic aspects of international taxation including the digital economy and the increased use of intangible assets. These groups reported on their considerations at the end of 2015 and 15 different Action Plans were proposed to implement their recommendations. Countries around the world are gradually introducing measures recommended by the BEPS project and in the longer term it is hoped that there will be greater consistency in the global rules.

The UK Government has started a process of implementing these Action Plans into UK legislation following consultations. Most of these changes are beyond the scope of this book.

In 2020, the OECD launched proposals for BEPS 2.0 to deal primarily with the digital economy. There are two Pillars to the proposals. Pillar One is designed to make sure that the profits of large digital service companies are fairly taxed, taking into account where those services are consumed. Pillar One identifies a 'residual profit' component of large multinationals total profit that is generated by automated digital services, and allocates that to relevant countries using a formula based on where revenues are generated.

Pillar Two proposes new rules to make sure that multinationals pay a minimum rate of tax globally. It is designed to combat base erosion and tax competition. While broad agreement to move these proposals forward has been reached, there is still a lot of work to do to design laws to put them into effect.

For current information about the progress and recommendations of these working groups, you should refer to the OECD website: https://www.oecd.org/tax/beps/.

Diverted Profits Tax

12.16 The diverted profits tax (DPT) came into operation in 2015. Some have called this the 'Google' tax because it is directed at the type of arrangements that Google entered into that left it paying little or no tax in the UK. The tax is at the rate of 25% on diverted profits that relate to UK activity.

The DPT is a highly complex tax and, according to HMRC, is designed to catch contrived arrangements used by large corporate groups to erode the UK tax base. There are some concerns among practitioners, however, that the scope of the tax is wider than HMRC suggested. The tax is a departure from the usual principle that the UK will not attempt to tax the profits of foreign companies doing business in the UK unless they have a PE here. It was introduced largely in response to public concerns that technology multinationals like Google were avoiding UK tax through artificial arrangements.

Fiscal Fact

The new diverted profits tax was expected to bring in additional revenue to the UK government of £355m by 2019/20 however, current estimates for 2020/21 show a yield of only £1517m. [Source: HMRC Diverted Profits Tax TIIN; HMRC Transfer Pricing and Diverted Profits Tax Statistics]

Digital Services Tax

12.17 The Digital Services Tax (DST) commenced in April 2020. The OECD is currently trying to work out some global rules in relation to taxing digital services, but the UK Government, along with several other countries, decided to act in advance of the OECD conclusions, which may take some time to reach. It was estimated that the UK DST could raise over £400m a year by 2021/22.

The DST will apply to businesses that provide to UK users a social media platform, search engine or an online marketplace. It is targeted towards large multinationals, where the group's worldwide revenues from these digital activities are more than £500m and more than £25m is from UK users. The tax itself is at the rate of 2% on revenues, although the first £25m of revenues from UK users will not be taxed. The tax applies from 1 April 2020 and is paid annually.

This is a novel form of tax, and the Government is committed to removing the tax once an international solution is implemented.

Fiscal Fact

The digital services tax is expected to raise £70m in 2019/20, rising to £515m in 2024/25.

[Source: https://www.gov.uk/government/publications/introduction-of-the-digital-services-tax/digital-services-tax]

Information access and exchange

12.18 A further anti-avoidance tool HMRC regularly uses is information access rights and information exchange agreements. HMRC has the power to obtain information from taxpayers to determine the extent to which they are telling the truth about their taxable activity overseas. The information can be supplemented by information from those with whom the UK has a tax treaty or tax information exchange agreement. Although such agreements do not exist with all countries, these agreements do cover a large number of the major trading countries where individuals or companies are likely to invest their wealth.

The question of information exchange is particularly sensitive in the case of dealings with countries that are tax havens, and the UK government, along with others, are concerned about the possibility of tax evasion through the use of offshore tax havens. In response to the G20 group's calls for more tax transparency throughout the world, to combat tax evasion, the OECD has been obtaining reports from countries about their exchange of tax information, including bank information. It released a report in March 2011 entitled *The Global Forum on Transparency and Exchange of Information for Tax Purposes*, which provides an in-depth analysis of 18 countries and is continuing to work to ensure that all jurisdictions adopt international standards on transparency and the exchange of information.

The release of the Panama and Paradise papers, which revealed information about monies placed in tax havens, has led to increased public pressure to tackle tax evasion through tax havens.

Summary

In this chapter you have read a basic introduction to how the UK taxation system works in an international setting. The application of the UK income and corporation tax rules depends on whether the taxpayer concerned is a resident of the UK for tax purposes. In some cases, taxpayers may be subject to tax in more than one country on the same income or profits. When this happens, the UK tax laws provide for a credit to be allowed for the foreign tax paid in order to mitigate, if not eliminate the double taxation.

For companies setting up an overseas business, there may be different tax consequences depending on whether it is established as a branch operation or a subsidiary company.

The existence of countries with considerably lower tax rates than the UK allows scope for tax planning, and HMRC is concerned about the boundary between tax planning and unacceptable tax avoidance this opportunity offers. In this chapter we have considered three examples of special rules that allow HMRC to combat international tax avoidance, the transfer pricing rules, the worldwide debt cap and the controlled foreign company rules.

The international tax rules for companies are in the process of being changed following extensive consultation over a period of more than three years. The most significant change has been the shift to an exemption system, away from a credit system, that is consistent with developments in other parts of the world.

Project areas

This area of tax study is complex, but provides plenty of opportunity for projects. You may wish to explore some of the issues we have touched on in more depth, for example, the decision whether to adopt a branch or subsidiary structure for a new foreign operation.

The UK offers both a tax credit for foreign taxes paid (under treaty agreements or unilaterally) and exempts some forms of returns from UK taxation as we have discussed. However, other countries offer double tax relief in other ways. You might like to explore how these other methods work and compare the use of these different methods to the use of credits.

The UK Government is not the only one to tackle issues like transfer pricing, thin capitalisation and controlled foreign corporations, you could compare the approaches taken by governments in other jurisdictions to the question of international tax avoidance.

You might also like to review the work of the OECD in the area of co-ordinating international activity in this area, in particular the BEPS project which is gaining in profile and is likely to lead to significant changes in the tax rules for companies in the future in the UK and elsewhere.

Questions

Question 1

Petra is a resident in the UK, but is non-domiciled and has claimed to be taxed on a remittance basis. In the year ended 5 April 2023, she had income from the following sources:

i.   Bank interest paid on an account held in Jersey and not remitted to the UK

ii.   Salary paid by a UK employer for work performed in the UK, but paid directly into an Australian bank account.

Required: Explain how Petra's income will be taxed in the UK

Question 2

Andromeda Ltd is a company that is incorporated in France. Three of the four directors of the company are based in the UK and they hold their board meetings in London.

Required: Explain how Andromeda Ltd will be treated for UK corporation tax purposes.

Question 3

Zanzibar Ltd is a UK company that has a wholly owned overseas subsidiary, company called Zeus, located in a country with a lower corporation tax rate than in the UK. Zanzibar exports goods to Zeus at a price for tax purposes that is less than market price.

Required: Explain the consequences of the under-pricing of goods exported from Zanzibar to Zeus.

Question 4

Gerald is resident and domiciled in the UK and is employed by Pied Piper Ltd earning a salary of £42,000 for the year ended 5 April 2023. Gerald owns an overseas property which he rents to tenants earning gross rental income of £7,000 from which tax is paid overseas of £3,150.00. What will be Gerald's UK tax liability if the maximum double tax relief is claimed?

Question 5

Abacus Ltd is a UK resident that has two branches overseas. The results for the year ended 31 March 2023 are as follows:

	Abacus £	Branch 1 £	Branch 2 £
Trading profits	1,500,000	58,000	376,000
Overseas tax paid	n/a	5,800	112,800

Required:
(a) Calculate both the global and UK corporation tax payable by Abacus Ltd if Abacus does not elect for the PE profits exemption to apply.
(b) What difference would taking the PE profits exemption make to the global and UK tax liabilities?

(Note: answer available via lecturer's website)

Further reading and examples

Evans, C., Hasseldine, J., Lymer, A., Ricketts, R. & Sandford, C. (2017), *Comparative taxation: Why tax sytems differ*, Fiscal Publications: Malvern;
James, S. & Nobes, C. (2018), *The Economics of Taxation (18th edition)*, Fiscal Publications: Malvern;
Lymer, A. & Hasseldine, J. (2002), *The International Tax System*, Springer: Boston;

Oats, L,. (2021), *Principles of International Taxation (8th edition)*, Bloomsbury
   Professional: Haywards Heath, UK.
– all four books provide further explanation of international taxation issues.

On the new digital services tax, see House of Commons Briefing Paper Number
   8719, updated in February 2021.
Further information on the Automatic Exchange of Tax Information can be
   found on the OECD website at:
   www.oecd.org/tax/transparency/automaticexchangeofinformation.htm

Appendix A: 2022/23 Tables of tax rates and allowances

The current rates and allowances for income tax, corporation tax, capital gains tax, inheritance tax and other taxes are set out below.

Income tax rates***

	Non-savings	Savings	Dividends
£0 – £2,000	–*	0%*	0%**
£0 (or £2,000) – £37,700	20%	20%	8.75%**
£37,701 – £150,000	40%	40%	33.75%**
Over £150,000	45%	45%	39.35%**

* 0% rate on savings only available up to £5,000 of savings income if non-savings income does not exceed this sum. In addition, a £1,000 personal savings allowance is available to basic rate taxpayers (£500 for higher rate taxpayers and nil for additional rate taxpayers).
**Dividend allowance of £2,000 (unchanged from 2021/22)
*** These rates apply in England, Wales and Northern Ireland only.
Scottish IT rates: £1–£2,162=19%, £2,163–£13,118=20%, £13,119–£31,092=21%, £31,093–£150,000=41%, over £150,000=46%

Personal income tax allowances

	2022/23 £	2021/22 £	Increase £
Income tax allowances:			
Personal allowance	12,570	12,570	0
Income limit: personal allowance	100,000	100,000	0
Transferrable tax allowance (married couples)	1,260	1,260	0
Income limit: transferable tax allowance	31,400	30,400	1,000
Dividend allowance	2,000	2,000	0
Personal savings allowance:			
Basic rate taxpayers	1,000	1,000	0
Higher rate taxpayers	500	500	0
Blind person's allowance	2,600	2,520	80

Car and fuel benefits in kind

(round reported CO_2 g/km down to find the correct percentage)

Company car benefit charge –

Table 1: For *non-hybrid* cars or where a *hybrid* car has CO_2 emissions more than 50g/km:

CO_2 g/km	Taxable % Petrol	Taxable % Diesel	CO_2 g/km	Taxable % Petrol	Taxable % Diesel	CO_2 g/km	Taxable % Petrol	Taxable % Diesel
0	2		85	22	26	130	31	35
1	14	18	90	23	27	135	32	36
51	15	19	95	24	28	140	33	37
55	16	20	100	25	29	145	34	37
60	17	21	105	26	30	150	35	37
65	18	22	110	27	31	155	36	37
70	19	23	115	28	32	160+	37	37
75	20	24	120	29	33			
80	21	25	125	30	34			

Note – no Diesel supplement applies if car meets Euro standard 6d (RDE2) and car registration dates do not affect charge rate from 2022/23. Hybrid cars should use the petrol rates listed whether they are petrol/electric or diesel/electric hybrids.

Table 2: Fully electric or hybrid cars with CO_2 <51g/km (otherwise use above):

CO_2 g/km	Electric only mileage range	Taxable %
0		2
1 to 50	130 +	2
1 to 50	70 to 129	5
1 to 50	40 to 69	8
1 to 50	30 to 39	12
1 to 50	< 30	14

	£
Car fuel benefit charge	25,300
Van benefit charge	3,600
Zero emissions van benefit charge	0
Flat rate Van fuel benefit charge	688

Approved mileage rates

	Business Miles	Allowance rate per mile
Cars and vans	0 – 10,000	45p
	10,000+	25p
Motor cycles		24p
Bicycles		20p

Excess payments over these rates are taxable. Shortfalls can be claimed as tax relief by the employee. If the employee carries another employee in their own car or van on a business journey, an additional tax-free payment of 5p per mile applies for each passenger.

Income tax reliefs and incentives: annual limits

	2022/23 £	2021/22 £
Individual Savings Account (ISA)	20,000	20,000
Junior ISA	9,000	9,000
Lifetime ISA	4,000	4,000
Child Trust Fund	9,000	9,000
Enterprise investment scheme (EIS)	2,000,000	2,000,000
Seed Enterprise investment scheme (SEIS)	100,000	100,000
Venture capital trust (VCT)	200,000	200,000
Social investment tax relief (SITR)	1,000,000	1,000,000
Pension scheme allowances:		
Lifetime allowance	1,073,100	1,073,100
Annual allowance	40,000	40,000
Money purchase annual allowance	4,000	4,000
..Tapered annual allowance	240,000	240,000

National Insurance Contributions

Item	2022/23*	2021/22
Class 1:		
Lower Earnings Limit – LEL (per week)	£123	£120
Primary (employees) Threshold (per week)	£242	£184
Primary (directors) Threshold (per annum)	£11,908	£9,568
Secondary (employers) Threshold (per week)	£175	£170
Upper Earnings Limit – UEL		
(per week – employees only)	£967	£967
Upper Secondary Threshold		
(per week – <21yr old)	£967	£967
(per week – <25yr old apprentices)	£967	£967
Employment allowance (per employer)	£5,000	£4,000
Employee's contributions	13.25**%	12%
(£242pw to £967pw +3.25**% over £967pw)		
Employer's Contribution Rates	15.05**%	13.8%
(all earnings over £175pw)		
Class 1A and 1B	15.05**%	13.8%
Class 2: Self-employed Contribution (per week)	£3.15	£3.05
Small Profits Threshold (per annum)	£6,725	£6,515
Class 3: Contribution (per week) (voluntary)	£15.85	£15.40
Class 4: Contributions – Upper Profits Limit	£50,270	£50,000
Contributions – Lower Profits Limit	£11,908	£9,568
Contribution Rate	10.25**%	9.0%
(£11,908pa – £50,270pa then 3.25**% over £50,270pa)		

*Changes to the thresholds detailed apply from 6 July 2022 following revisions announced in the Spring Statement 2022
** Rates include a 1.25% Health and Social Care Levy from 6 April 2022

Apprenticeship Levy

	2022/23	2021/22
Apprenticeship Levy Allowance (per employer)	£15,000	£15,000
Apprenticeship Levy rate (gross employee earnings)	0.5%	0.5%

Capital taxes: Individuals

	2022/23 £	2021/22 £	Increase £/%
Capital gains tax annual exempt amount			
Individuals, etc.	12,300	12,300	0
Capital gains tax standard basic rate	10%*	10%*	0
Capital gains tax standard higher rate	20%*	20%*	0
Business Asset Disposal/			
Relief limit	1 million	1 million	0
Relief rate	10%	10%	0
Investors' Relief limit	10 million	10 million	0
Investors' Relief rate	10%	10%	0
Inheritance tax threshold	325,000	325,000	0
(each if couple/partner)			
Residence nil rate band limit	175,000	175,000	0
Inheritance tax rate	40%	40%	0
Lower rate (10%+ of estate left to charity)	36%	36%	0
Stamp Duty/Stamp Duty Reserve Tax**	0.5%	0.5%	0

* An 8% surcharge applies in respect of residential properties and carried interest
** Duty payable on share purchase over £1,000 only and rounded up to nearest £5

Capital allowances

	2022/23	2021/22
Plant and machinery: Main rate	18%	18%
Special rate	6%	6%
Annual investment allowance	£1,000,000*	£1,000,000
Structures and Buildings Allowance	3%	3%

* applies to investments made 1.1.19 to 31.03.23 then rate of £200,000 will apply

Corporation tax, allowances and reliefs

	2022/23	2021/22
Corporation Tax rate	19%	19%
R&D tax credits SME scheme	230%	230%
R&D SME repayable credit	14.5%	14.5%
R&D Expenditure credit	13%	13%
Patent box	10%	10%
Film, High end TV and videogame tax relief	25%	25%
Diverted Profits Tax	25%	25%
Digital Service Tax	2%	2%
Bank Surcharge	8%	8%
Bank levy: 1.1.21 onwards – equity and LT liabs	0.05%	0.05%
ST liabs	0.1%	0.1%

Corporation tax on chargeable gains: indexation allowance

Retail prices index (January 1987 = 100.0)

	Jan	Feb	Mar	Apr	May	Jun	Jul	Aug	Sep	Oct	Nov	Dec
1982	–	–	79.44	81.04	81.62	81.85	81.90	81.90	81.85	82.26	82.66	82.51
1983	82.61	82.97	83.12	84.28	84.64	84.84	85.30	85.68	86.06	86.36	86.67	86.89
1984	86.84	87.20	87.48	88.64	88.97	89.20	89.10	89.94	90.11	90.67	90.95	90.87
1985	91.20	91.94	92.80	94.78	95.21	95.41	95.23	95.49	95.44	95.59	95.92	96.05
1986	96.25	96.60	96.73	97.67	97.85	97.79	97.52	97.82	98.30	98.45	99.29	99.62
1987	100.0	100.4	100.6	101.8	101.9	101.9	101.8	102.1	102.4	102.9	103.4	103.3
1988	103.3	103.7	104.1	105.8	106.2	106.6	106.7	107.9	108.4	109.5	110.0	110.3
1989	111.0	111.8	112.3	114.3	115.0	115.4	115.5	115.8	116.6	117.5	118.5	118.8
1990	119.5	120.2	121.4	125.1	126.2	126.7	126.8	128.1	129.3	130.3	130.0	129.9
1991	130.2	130.9	131.4	133.1	133.5	134.1	133.8	134.1	134.6	135.1	135.6	135.7
1992	135.6	136.3	136.7	138.8	139.3	139.3	138.8	138.9	139.4	139.9	139.7	139.2
1993	137.9	138.8	139.3	140.6	141.1	141.0	140.7	141.3	141.9	141.8	141.6	141.9
1994	141.3	142.1	142.5	144.2	144.7	144.7	144.0	144.7	145.0	145.2	145.3	146.0
1995	146.0	146.9	147.5	149.0	149.6	149.8	149.1	149.9	150.6	149.8	149.8	150.7
1996	150.2	150.9	151.5	152.6	152.9	153.0	152.4	153.1	153.8	153.8	153.9	154.4
1997	154.4	155.0	155.4	156.3	156.9	157.5	157.5	158.5	159.3	159.5	159.6	160.0
1998	159.5	160.3	160.8	**162.6**	163.5	163.4	163.0	163.7	164.4	164.5	164.4	164.4
1999	163.4	163.7	164.1	165.2	165.5	165.6	165.1	165.5	166.2	166.5	166.7	167.3
2000	166.6	167.5	168.4	170.1	170.7	171.1	170.5	170.5	171.7	171.6	172.1	172.2
2001	171.1	172.0	172.2	173.1	174.2	174.4	173.3	174.0	174.6	174.3	173.6	173.4
2002	173.3	173.8	174.5	175.7	176.2	176.2	175.9	176.4	177.6	177.9	178.2	178.5
2003	178.4	179.3	179.9	181.2	181.5	181.3	181.3	181.6	182.5	182.6	182.7	183.5
2004	183.1	183.8	184.6	185.7	186.5	186.8	186.8	187.4	188.1	188.6	189.0	189.9
2005	188.9	189.6	190.5	191.6	192.0	192.2	192.2	192.6	193.1	193.3	193.6	194.1
2006	193.4	194.2	195.0	196.5	197.7	198.5	198.5	199.2	200.1	200.4	201.1	202.7
2007	201.6	203.1	204.4	205.4	206.2	207.3	206.1	207.3	208.0	208.9	209.7	210.9
2008	209.8	211.4	212.1	214.0	215.1	216.8	216.5	217.2	218.4	217.7	216.0	212.9
2009	210.1	211.4	211.3	211.5	212.8	213.4	213.4	214.4	215.3	216.0	216.6	218.0
2010	217.9	219.2	220.7	222.8	223.6	224.1	223.6	224.5	225.3	225.8	226.8	228.4
2011	229.0	231.3	232.5	234.4	235.2	235.2	234.7	236.1	237.9	238.0	238.5	239.4
2012	238.0	239.9	240.8	242.5	242.4	241.8	242.1	243.0	244.2	245.6	245.6	246.8
2013	245.8	247.6	248.7	249.5	250.0	249.7	249.7	251.0	251.9	251.9	252.1	253.4
2014	252.6	254.2	254.8	255.7	255.9	256.3	256.0	257.0	257.6	257.7	257.1	257.5
2015	255.4	256.7	257.1	258.0	258.5	258.9	258.6	259.8	259.6	259.5	259.8	260.6
2016	258.8	260.0	261.1	261.4	262.1	263.1	263.4	264.4	264.9	264.8	265.5	267.1
2017	265.5	268.4	269.3	270.6	271.7	272.3	272.9	274.7	275.1	275.3	275.8	278.1

Note – no further indexation allowance will apply for disposals after 1 Jan 2018 – the Dec 2017 rate should be used for all subsequent sales.

VAT

	after 1 April 2022	after 1 April 2021
Standard Rate	20%	20%
Reduced Rate*	5%	5%
Annual Registration Limit	£85,000	£85,000
De-registration Limit	£83,000	£83,000
VAT Fraction – standard rate	1/6	1/6
Maximum turnover to join:		
Cash Accounting Scheme	£1,350,000	£1,350,000
Annual Accounting Scheme	£1,350,000	£1,350,000
Flat Rate Scheme (ex VAT)	£150,000	£150,000

* Including temporary reduced rate for hospitality and tourism sector from 15 July 20 to 30 September 21. This rose to 12.5% from 1 October 21 to 31 March 22.

Stamp Duty Land Tax

Value of property (£)	Stamp duty rate (%)
Residential property**	not buy to let
0 – 125,000	0*
125,001 – 250,000	2*
250,001 – 925,000	5*
925,001 – 1.5m	10*
remainder (over £1.5m)	12*

* 3% supplement on additional dwelling purchased over £40,000.

Value of property (£)	Stamp duty rate (%)
Non-residential property	
up to 150,000	0
150,001 – 250,000	2
over 250,000	5

Annual Tax on Enveloped Dwellings

Value of property (£)	ATED charge (£)
500,000 – 1,000,000	3,800
1,000,001 – 2,000,000	7,700
2,000,001 – 5,000,000	26,050
5,000,001 – 10,000,000	60,900
10,000,001 – 20,000,000	122,250
20,000,000	244,750

Scottish Land and Buildings Transactions Tax

Value of property (£)	LBTT rate % (>1 Apr 21)
*Residential property***	
0 – 145,000*	0*
145,001 – 250,000	2*
250,001 – 325,000	5*
325,001 – 750,000	10*
Over 750,000	12*

* 4% supplement on additional dwelling purchased priced at over £40,000.
** LBTT relief for 1st time purchasers up to £175,000.

Non-residential property (on or after 25 Jan 19)	
0 – 150,000	0
150,001 – 250,000	1
over 250,000	5

Welsh Land Transaction Tax

Value of property (£)	LTT rate %
*Residential property***	
0 – 180,000*	0*
180,001 – 250,000	3.5*
250,001 – 400,000	5*
400,001 – 750,000	7.5*
750,001 – 1,500,000	10*
Over 1,500,000	12*

* 4% supplement on additional dwelling (was 3% before 22 December 20)

Non-residential property	
0 – 225,000	0
225,001 – 250,000	1
250,001 – 1,000,000	5
over 1,000,000	6

Environmental taxes

	2022/23 (2021/22)
Landfill tax (England and NI):	
Standard rate (per tonne)	£98.60 (£96.70)
Lower rate (inactive waste per tonne)	£3.15 (£3.10)
Aggregates levy (per tonne)	£2.00 (£2.00)
Climate Change Levy (main rates):	
Electricity	0.775p/kwh
Natural Gas	0.568p/kwh
LPG	2.175p/kg
Plastic packaging tax	£200 per tonne

Insurance Premium Tax

Standard Rate	12%
Higher Rate (travel, appliances, some vehicles)	20%

Air Passenger Duty

Band	Reduced rate (lowest class of travel)	Standard rate (other than lowest class of travel)	Higher rate
A (0–2000 miles)	£13	£26	£78
B (>2000 miles)	£84	£185	£554

HMRC interest rates

	Late Payment (%)	Repayment (%)
All taxes (since 24/05/22)	3.5	0.5
Average Official rate for 2022/23	2.0%	

(These rates change occasionally – see the HMRC website for details)

Tax credits:

Working tax credit

	£ per year
Basic element	2,070.00
Couple and lone parent element	2,125.00
30 hour element	860.00
Disability element	3,345.00
Severe disability (additional) element	1,445.00
Childcare element:	£ per week
Maximum eligible cost for 2 or more children	300.00
Maximum eligible cost for 1 child	175.00
Max. percent of eligible costs covered	70%

Child tax credit

	£ per year
Family element	545.00
Child element (each child)	2,935.00
Disabled child element	3,545.00
Severe disabled child (additional) element	1,430.00

Tapering

	£
Income thresholds & withdrawal rates	
First income threshold	6,770.00
First withdrawal rate	41%
First threshold for child tax credit entitlement only (where no WTC claimed)	17,005.00
Income rise disregard	2,500.00
Income fall disregard	2,500.00

Pension credit

	£
Standard Minimum income guarantee credit: (per week)	
Single	182.60
Couple	278.70
Capital:	
Amount disregard	10,000.00
Amount disregard – care homes	10,000.00
Deemed income:	
£1 per week for every £500 (or part thereof) in excess of these amounts	

Personal benefit rates

	2022/23 £	2021/22 £
Old State Pension (per week):		
– Single Person (based on own NIC)	141.85	137.60
– Single Person (based on spouse's NIC)	85.00	82.45
– Non-contributory (over 80 pension)	85.00	82.45
New State Pension	185.15	179.60
Child Benefit (per week):		
– First Eligible Child	21.80	21.15
– Each Extra Child	14.45	14.00
– Guardian allowance	18.55	18.00
Statutory Sick Pay (per week):		
– normally receive £123 per week or more	99.35	96.35
Statutory Maternity Pay (per week):		
Average Weekly Earnings of £123 or over		
– Higher Weekly Rate (first 6 weeks)	90% of weekly earnings	
– Standard Rate (remaining 33 weeks)	156.66	151.97
Statutory Paternity/Adoption Pay (per week)	156.66	151.97
Job Seekers Allowance (income based – per week):		
– Single Person (over 25)	77.00	74.20
– Married Couple (both over 18)	121.05	117.40
National Living/Minimum Wage (per hour from Apr 22):		
– ages 23 and over	£9.50	£8.91
– ages 21 to 22	£9.18	£8.36
– ages 18 to 20 (Development rate)	£6.83	£6.56
– ages <18 (Young worker rate)	£4.81	£4.62
– Apprentice rate (under 19 or in first year)	£4.81	£4.30
Employment & Support Allowance (per week):		
– Single under 25 (first 13 weeks)	61.05	59.20
– Single 25 and over (first 13 weeks)	77.00	74.70
Universal Credit (per month):		
– Single under 25	265.31	257.33
– Single 25 and over	334.91	324.84
– Couple one at least over 25	525.72	509.91
– Child element:		
– First child (born > 6.5.17)	244.58	237.08
– Second/subsequent child	244.58	237.08
Benefit Cap (per annum) (inside Greater London totals in brackets)		
– Single claimant (no children)	13,400.00 (15,410.00)	
– Single claimant (children living with them)	20,000.00 (23,000.00)	
– Couple (with or without children)	20,000.00 (23,000.00)	

These rates are selected from a complex list of benefits available based on personal circumstances and therefore are provided in basic outline only – and rates are subject to regular changes. For a full list of benefits see the www.gov.uk website.

Suggested solutions to questions

Chapter 4

Quick quiz answers

Answers provided below are not given using the full computation format. You are, however, advised to use the full computation in producing your answers before checking them here, at least initially, to ensure you have followed the necessary steps correctly and fully understand how these answers are arrived at.

1. Deirdre is entitled to a regular personal allowance (£12,570) to offset her total income for the year. Her income tax computation is therefore:

    total income = £36,700 – her personal allowance of £12,570= £24,130.

    This would all be taxable at 20% as non-savings income as this only partly fills her basic rate tax band and so her tax liability = £4,826.
    As an employee she probably paid all of this via PAYE throughout the year. However, she should check this against her payslips or annual summary document form her employer (called a P60) to check this is the case.

2. Benson is entitled to a personal allowance of £12,570. His taxable income is (£28,650 + 1,500) – 12,570 = £17,580 (remember that his pension income is taxable just like most other sources of income). The personal allowance should be deducted from his non-savings income making his taxable non-saving income £16,080 (i.e. £28,650 – £12,570)

Tax due:	£
Non-savings	
16,080 @ 20%	3,216.00
Savings	
1,000 PSA @ 0%	-
500 @ 20%	100.00
Tax liability	3,316.00

3. Candice has a taxable income comprising savings income of £18,870; dividend income of £2,500 less a personal allowance of £12,570 i.e. a total taxable income of £8,800. Remember the personal allowance can be offset in any order. As she has no non-savings income, it would benefit Candice to use her personal

allowance first against savings income ahead of dividend income, so she will be able to benefit from the Personal Savings Allowance and part of the Dividend Allowance.

Tax due:	£
Savings	
5,000 @ 0%	–
1,000 PSA @ 0%	–
300 @ 20%	60.00
6,300	
Dividends	
2,000 @ 0%	–
500 @ 8.75%	43.75
Tax payable	103.75

4. Taxable income comprises non-saving income of £23,850 less personal allowance of £12,570 and less the patent royalty (grossed up at 100/80) of £250 i.e. £11,030.

Tax due:	£
Non-savings:	
11,030 @ 20%	2,206.00
Add: Tax withheld patent royalty	
250 @ 20%	50.00
Tax liability	2,256.00

5. Erica is entitled to a personal allowance of £12,570. Her taxable income is £13,350 less her personal allowance of £12,570 plus savings income of £500. Remember the personal allowance can be used to reduce the non-savings income first and the savings rate band is available to Erica as her non-savings income is below £5,000.

Tax due:	£
Non-savings	
780 @ 20%	156.00
Savings	
500 @ 0%	–
Tax payable	156.00

The charitable gift does not affect Dominic's calculation as he has paid sufficient basic rate tax to cover the repayment to the charity and is not a high rate taxpayer. Dominic will probably have paid this tax payable fully through the PAYE system as he is an employee.

6. Geoffrey's taxable income (and adjusted net income) comprises of his non-savings income of £110,500. His personal allowance of £12,570 will be reduced by ½ (£110,500 - £100,000) i.e. £5,250 so he has a taxable income of £103,180 (£110,500 - £7,320).

Tax due:	£
Non-savings	
37,700 @ 20%	7,540.00
65,480 @ 40%	26,192.00
Tax payable	33,732.00

7. Dominic's taxable income comprises employment earnings of £21,215 less the personal allowance of £12,570 i.e. £8,645.

Tax due:	£
Non-savings:	
8,645 @ 20%	1,729.00

8. Hillary's taxable income comprises non-savings income of £73,850 less a personal allowance of £12,570. She therefore has a taxable income of £61,280.

Tax due:	£
Non-savings	
37,700 @ 20%	7,540.00
23,580 @ 40%	9,432.00
	16,972.00
Less:	
Tax reducers	
EIS 30% x £50,000	(15,000.00)
Tax payable	1,972.00

If Hillary's investment had qualified for Seed EIS, then the tax reducer would have been 50% i.e. £25,000.

9. Frank's taxable income comprises non-savings income of £33,350 less a personal allowance of £12,570 plus dividends of £3,000 i.e. a total taxable income of £23,780.

Tax due:	£
Non-savings	
20,780 @ 20%	4,156.00
Dividends	
2,000 @ 0%	–
1,000 @ 8.75%	87.50
Tax payable	4,243.50

National Insurance contributions: this is only due on his trading income (not dividend income) at Class 2 and Class 4:

Class 2:	£3.15 x 52	=	£163.80
Class 4:	(£33,350 – £11,908) x 10.25%	=	£2,197.80

10. Ivan will have to pay class 2 NICs of £3.15 per week for 52 weeks i.e. £163.80. He will also have to pay Class 4 NICs at 10.25% on £46,000 - £11,908 i.e. £34,092 = £3,494.43.

11. If we assume the NIC thresholds and rates applicable after 5 July 2022 applied for the whole year, Josephine will have to pay primary Class 1 NICs of £500 – £242 x 13.25% = £34.18.

12. Kamran does not have to pay primary Class 1 NICs on his benefit in kind. His employer will need to pay Class 1A NICs at the rate of 15.05% i.e. £60.20

Full questions

Question 1

Personal tax computation for Sam for 2022/23

	Non-savings £	Savings £	Dividends £	Total £
Employment earnings	27,570			27,570
Savings income:				
Building society interest		2,000		2,000
Dividend income			3,000	3,000
Net Income	27,570	2,000	3,000	32,570
Less personal allowance	(12,570)			(12,570)
Taxable income	15,000	2,000	3,000	20,000

	£
Income tax due:	
Non-savings income	
15,000 @ 20%	3,000.00
Savings	
1,000 PSA @ 0%	–
1,000 @ 20%	200.00
Dividend income	
2,000 @ 0%	–
1,000 @ 8.75%	87.50
Tax liability	3,287.50
Less: tax credits:	
PAYE	(3,080.00)
Tax payable	207.50

Note: The charitable donation does not affect the calculation as Sam has paid sufficient basic rate tax and is not a higher rate taxpayer.

Question 2

Personal tax computation for Jasper for 2022/23

	Non-savings £	Savings £	Dividends £	Total £
Employment earnings	68,150			68,150
Savings income:				
Bank interest		3,000		3,000
Dividend income			6,000	6,000
Net Income	68,150	3,000	6,000	77,150
Less personal allowance	(12,570)			(12,570)
Taxable income	55,580	3,000	6,000	64,580

Income tax due:	£
Non-savings income	
37,700 @ 20%	7,540.00
17,880 @ 40%	7,152.00
Savings	
500 PSA @ 0%	–
2,500 @ 40%	1,000.00
Dividend income	
2,000 @ 0%	–
4,000 @ 33.75%	1,350.00
Tax liability	17,042.00
Less: tax credits:	
PAYE	(15,000.00)
Tax payable	2,042.00

Question 3

Personal tax computation for Janet for 2022/23

	Non-Savings £	Savings £	Dividends £	Total £
Income:				
Employment earnings	39,850			39,850
Bonus	3,000			3,000
Savings income:				
Building society interest		5,375		5,375
Property income				
2/4 × £8,000 4,000				
Less expenses (1,000)	3,000			3,000
Net income	45,850	5,375	0	51,225
Less personal allowance[1]	(7,695)	(4,875)		(12,570)
Taxable income	38,155	500	0	38,655

Tax due:

Non-savings income

37,700 @ 20%	7,540.00
455 @ 40%	182.00

Savings income

500 PSA	–
38,655	
Tax liability	7,722.00
Less: tax credits	
PAYE	(6,500.00)
Tax payable	1,222.00

Note:

The premium bond winnings are exempt and do not need to form part of Janet's tax computation. Do not forget that the property was only rented for half the year so only 2 payments will have been received in the tax year.

The approach shown here to include rental income in Janet's tax computation is called the 'cash basis' – i.e. reporting what she has actually received for tax purposes. This is opposed to using an 'accruals basis' and allocating this month-by-month to determine taxable income received more closely linked to the rental periods it relates to. A cash basis is very commonly used in situations like this as it is simple to use, but larger businesses would probably use the accruals basis. We will show you how this works and its implications in Chapter 6).

1 Janet is a higher rate taxpayer – you can see from the total column that £955 (£38,655 – £37,700) of her taxable income falls into the higher rate band. This means she is entitled to a £500 personal savings allowance. If we allocate all of the personal allowance to the non savings income, then £955 of the savings income will be taxed at 40%. However, by allocating enough of the personal allowance to the savings income to reduce it to £500, and the balance to non savings income, we can reduce the exposure to the higher rate band to £455. This saves Janet £100 tax (£500 x 20%).

Personal tax computation for Dave for 2022/23

	Non-Savings £	Savings £	Dividends £	Total £
Income:				
Employment earnings	37,650			37,650
Savings income:				
Bank deposit account		3,750		3,750
Dividend income:			9,760	9,760
Net income	37,650	3,750	9,760	51,160
Less personal allowances[1]	(12,570)			(12,570)
Taxable income	25,080	3,750	9,760	38,590

Tax due:	£
Non-savings	
25,080 @ 20%	5,016.00
Savings	
500 PSA	–
3,250 @ 20%	650.00
Dividends	
2,000 @ 0%	–
6,870[1] @ 8.75%	601.12
890 @ 33.75%	300.37
37,590	
Tax liability	6,567.49
Less: tax credits	
PAYE	(4,780.00)
Tax payable	1,787.49

1   Dave is also a higher rate taxpayer, but he has dividends which changes the way we think about allocating the personal allowance. Because the higher rate for dividends is only 33.75% compared to 40% for savings and non savings, it makes more sense to allocate the personal allowance to either savings or non savings. It doesn't actually matter which in this case because in total they are within the basic rate band. So, £37,700 – £25,080 – £3,750 – £2,000 = £6,870 of dividends falls into the basic rate band and £9,760 – £8,870 = £890 of dividends will be taxed at the higher rate.

Chapter 5

Quick quiz answers

1.   Helena's bonus is taxable on the earliest of the time the payment is made or the time of entitlement. In this case, the entitlement arose on 31 March 2023, so the bonus will be taxed in the 2022/23 year.

2.   Iain can fully reclaim the cost of business calls (£125) against his employment income – although he must keep detailed records of these calls to prove they were wholly, exclusively and necessarily for his employment. However, he won't be able to reclaim any of his line rental costs as these are not for a dedicated business line.

3.   Julia's mileage allowance is exempt as it is less than 45p for the first 10,000 miles. She will actually be able to claim a deduction from her employment earnings for the shortfall of 3,000 miles @ (45p – 30p) = £450.

4.   Assuming the house is not job related, Keith will be taxed on the annual value of the house of £10,200, plus the extra charge which arises because it is an expensive house of 2% × (£250,000 – £75,000) plus the value of the running costs of £2,500 i.e. a total of £16,200.

5. With this emission rating, Lorna will be taxed on £27,000 at the maximum rate of 37% i.e. £9,990.

6. Michael cannot deduct the cost of the golf club subscription. Although he might be able to argue it is wholly and exclusively for his job, he would not be able to argue that it is *necessary*.

7. The annual value for the use of the family computer is 20% x £1,500 = £300. For this year, however, the machine is only available for 6 months so the taxable benefit in kind is 6/12 x £300 = £150.

8. Pauline's use of the bicycle is an exempt benefit. When it is transferred to her, however, she will have a taxable benefit equivalent to the market value of the bicycle at the time, i.e. £500.

9. Quentin's removal expenses are an exempt benefit in kind because they are below the threshold of £8,000. Note, however, that if the new job is within a reasonable commuting distance from his old house, the exemption does not apply.

10. Ravi's employer making a parking space available does not give rise to a taxable benefit.

11. Sumo's tax liability will be:

	£
Trading income	85,500
Personal allowance	(12,570)
Taxable income	72,930

The gross (£7,200 x 100/80 = £9,000) pension contribution will increase the basic rate band to £46,700 (£37,700 + £9,000).

46,700 @ 20%	9,340.00
26,230 @ 40%	10,492.00
72,930	
Tax liability	19,832.00

12. As an employee, Tiffany's contribution to the workplace pension scheme will simply be deducted from her gross salary (under the net pay arrangement rules) before PAYE is calculated. No further adjustment to her tax computation is needed as this will give her full tax deduction available at her marginal tax rate. The employer's contribution is not a taxable benefit to Tiffany. Her tax liability (before PAYE) will therefore be:

Employment income (30,850 – 5,000)	25,850
Personal allowance	(12,570)
Taxable income	13,280
Tax liability:	
13,280 @ 20%	2,656.00

Full questions

Question 1

Employment income for Serene Volley

	£
Salary	26,400
Pension contributions (£26,400 x 5%)	(1,320)
	25,080
Car benefit £16,400 @ 29%	4,756
(no fuel benefit arises)	
	29,836

Personal tax computation for Serene Volley for 2022/23

	Non-savings £	Total £
Earnings from employment	29,836	29,836
Interest is exempt		
Total income	29,836	29,836
Less personal allowance	(12,570)	(12,570)
Taxable income	17,266	17,266

		£
Income tax due:		
Non-savings		
17,266 @ 20%		3,453.20
Tax liability		3,453.20
Less Tax credits		
PAYE		(4,190.00)
Tax payable/(repayable)		(736.80)

Question 2

Employment income for Kim White

	£
Salary	21,600.00
Beneficial loan[1]	312.50
	21,912.50
Expense claim[2]	(4,625.00)
Employment income	17,287.50

Notes:

1   The taxable benefit from the beneficial loan is £312.50 (18,750 @ 2% x 10/12)

2   Ordinary commuting (travel between home and the permanent workplace) does not qualify for relief. The travel to a temporary workplace

qualifies as it is for a period lasting less than 24 months. Kim can therefore make an expense claim based on 10,500 miles as follows:

10,000 miles at 45p	£4,500
500 miles at 25p	£125

3   The loan interest paid of £140 is eligible for relief since the loan was used by Kim to finance expenditure for a relevant purpose. It is paid gross.

Personal tax computation for Kim White for 2022/23

	Non-savings £	Savings £	Dividends £	Total £
Earnings from employment	17,287			17,287
Building society interest		750	0	750
Total income	17,287	750	0	18,037
Interest paid[3]	(140)			(140)
	17,147			17,897
Less personal allowance	(12,570)			(12,570)
Taxable income	4,577	750	0	5,327

Income tax due:	£
Non-savings	
4,577 @ 20%	915.40
Savings	
423 @ 0% (Starting rate relief band)	
327 @ 0% (basic rate PSA £1000)	–
5,327	
Tax liability	915.40
Tax payable (before PAYE)	915.40

Question 3

(a) Personal tax computation for Domingo Gomez for 2022/23

	Non-savings £	Savings £	Dividends £	Total £
Pensions (6,082 + 3,480)	9,562			9,562
Building society interest		18,160	0	18,160
Total income	9,562	18,160	0	27,722
Less personal allowance	(9,562)	(3,008)		(12,570)
Taxable income	0	15,152	0	15,152

Income tax due:	£
Savings	
5,000 @ 0%	0.00
PSA 1,000 @ 0%	0.00
9,152 @ 20%	1,830.40
15,152	
Tax liability	1,830.40
Tax payable	1,830.40

Notes:

1. No tax relief is available in respect of the charity donations as they were not made under the gift aid scheme.
2. Interest from the savings certificate is exempt from income tax.
3. As there is no non-savings income left after his personal allowance Domingo gets the benefit of the full £5,000 savings nil rate band, and as his income falls into the basic rate tax band he receives £1,000 personal savings allowance.

Employment income for Erigo Gomez

	£
Salary	36,000
Pension contributions (36,000 x 6%)	(2,160)
Charitable payroll deductions (12 x 100)	(1,200)
	32,640
Relocation costs (Note 1)	3,400
Mileage allowance (Note 2)	(2,900)
	33,140

Personal tax computation for Erigo Gomez for 2022/23

	Non-savings £	Savings £	Dividends £	Total £
Earnings from employment	33,140	0	0	33,140
Total income	33,140	0	0	33,140
Less personal allowance	(12,570)			(12,570)
Taxable income	20,570	0	0	20,570

Income tax due:	£
Non-savings 20,570 @ 20%	4,114.00
Tax liability (before PAYE)	4,114.00

Notes:

1. Only £8,000 of the relocation costs are exempt, and so the taxable benefit is £11,400 – £8,000 = £3,400.

2. The mileage allowance received will be tax free, and Erigo can make the following expense claim:

10,000 miles at 45p	4,500
8,000 miles at 25p	2,000
	6,500
Mileage allowance (18,000 at 20p)	(3,600)
	2,900

(b) Tax returns

Unless the returns are issued late, the latest date that Domingo can file paper self-assessment returns for 2022/23 is 31 October 2023.

If Domingo completes a paper return by 31 October 2023, then HMRC will prepare a self-assessment computation on his behalf.

As Erigo is willing to submit an electronic form he has until 31 January 2024 to do this.

(c) Record keeping

1. Domingo and Erigo were not in business during 2022/23, so their records must be retained until one year after 31 January following the tax year, which is 31 January 2025.

2. A failure to maintain records for the tax year could result in a penalty of up to £3,000. However, the maximum penalty will only be charged in serious cases.

Question 4

Employment income assessment for Edward King

	£
Director's remuneration	179,000.00
Pension contributions (£179,000 x 4%)	(7,160.00)
Charitable payroll deductions (12 x £200)	(2,400.00)
	169,440.00
Beneficial loan (£87,000 x 4/12 @ 2%)	580.00
Home entertainment system[1]	2,200.00
Mileage allowance[2]	(800.00)
Professional subscription	(240.00)
Employment income	171,180.00

Notes:

1. Edward will have been taxed on the use of the home entertainment system totalling £3,120 (£5,200 x 20% x 3) for the tax years 2019/20,

2020/21 and 2021/22. The benefit for the acquisition of the home entertainment system in 2022/23 is the market value at the date of the gift of £2,200, as this is greater than £2,080 (£5,200 – £3,120).

2.

	£
Mileage allowance received 12,000 @ 35p	4,200
Less 10,000 miles @ 45p + 2,000 miles @ 25p	(5,000)
	800

Personal tax computation for Edward King for 2022/23

	Non-savings £	Savings £	Dividends £	Total £
Earnings from employment	171,180	0	0	171,180
Total income	171,180			171,180
Less personal allowance	(nil)	0	0	(nil)
Taxable income	171,180	0	0	171,180

	£
Income tax due:	
Non-savings	
37,700[1] @ 20%	7,540.00
150,000 – 37,700 @ 40%	44,920.00
171,180 – 150,000 @ 45%	9,531.00
Tax liability	61,991.00
Less:	
PAYE	(61,600.00)
Tax payable/(repayable)	391.00

Note:
1. No extension to the basic rate band (or higher and additional rate bands) is needed for charity donations made by Edward as his gifts were made via the payroll deduction scheme. As such, full relief has already been provided for this in his salary deduction (see section 4.38).

Chapter 6

Quick quiz answers

1. The staff loan written off and the increase in general provision are not deductible for tax purposes and so Matthew must add back £400 in his adjustment of profits.

2. None of this £800 deduction would be allowed under the cash basis. The income would not have been recorded, as the sums have not been received.

3. We need to know the CO_2 emission levels. If they are more than 50g/km, then only 85% of the lease payments will be deductible, i.e. £3,570. If its emissions were less than 50g/km then all 100% of this sum would be deductible.

4. Both the T shirts and the Christmas party are fully deductible for tax purposes. Note, however, that as the cost of the Christmas party exceeds £150 per head, a benefit in kind may arise for Orlando's employees.

5. As £90 has been recorded as a cost of sale expense, Pauline must add £115 to her profit for tax purposes (i.e. sales value not cost price must be added back).

6. Quentin's landlord will be taxed under the property income rules on £10,000 − (£10,000 × 14 × 2%) i.e. £7,200. Quentin can therefore deduct this amount over the term of the lease i.e. £480 (£7,200 ÷ 15) per annum.

7. The cost of debt collection is deductible. Both the acquisition of new premises and the patent registration are capital transactions and so on face value the fees associated with these are not deductible. However special provision allows the cost of patent registration to be deducted and so Rachel can claim £230.

8. Assuming Gerald does not own multiple properties that provide him with an income over £150,000 a year, HMRC will assume that Gerald will be using the cash basis for his computations of taxable property (unless he expressly opts otherwise to use the accruals basis). On that basis he will be assessed on actual income receive in the year i.e. 5/12×£8,400 + 7/12×£8,600 = £8,516. If he instead opted to be assessed under the accruals basis he would be assessed on 6/12×£8,400 + 6/12×£8,600 = £8,500.

9. Using the formula for short lease premiums, Heather will be assessed on: £48,000 − (48,000× (40 − 1) ×2%) = £10,560

Full questions

Question 1

The treatment of each of the items, for tax purposes, is as follows:

(a) *Reconstruction of the roof*
The expenditure was incurred to renovate an asset soon after it was acquired and the asset, a building, was not in a usable condition immediately after acquisition. Following the decision in *Law Shipping* the expenditure will be deemed to be capital and hence will be disallowable for tax purposes.

The expenditure on the roof should be added back to the net profit in order to determine the tax adjusted trading profit.

(b) *Embezzlement by the director*
Defalcations by directors are not allowable deductions for trading income purposes. Hence the expense should be added back to the net profit in order to determine the tax adjusted trading profit. (Embezzlement by a staff member

(not a partner or director), however, is an allowable tax expense). All payments in connection with criminal offences (e.g. fines or bribes) are explicitly excluded as deductions.

(c) *Redundancy payment to a works manager*
Redundancy payments made wholly and exclusively for the purpose of trade are allowed without limit, provided that the business continues to trade. If Jones ceases to trade there is a limit on the amount of any redundancy payment of the statutory amount plus up to three times the statutory amount. In the case of the works manager the maximum deductible is £48,000 (£12,000 × 3 + £12,000). Since the actual payment is lower than this it will be an allowable expense even if Jones ceases to trade. Hence no adjustment needs to be made to determine the tax adjusted trading profit.

(d) *Salary of senior manager seconded to a charity*
Such a payment is specifically allowable for tax purposes and hence no adjustment needs to be made in order to determine the trading profit.

(e) *Costs of the crèche*
The construction costs are capital expenditure and as such are not allowable for tax purposes
The running costs of the crèche are incurred in order to provide a benefit in kind for employees and as such are allowable deductions for tax purposes. Hence the construction costs should be added back to the net profit in order to determine the tax adjusted trading profit while no adjustment is required for the running costs.

(f) *Receipt from insurance company*
The cost of repairing the asset is an allowable expense. The receipt from the insurance company will reduce the allowable expenditure by £18,000 because the business has been reimbursed for its costs.
The receipt of £6,000 in compensation for loss of profits is taxable. Since the business has already reduced the balance on the repairs account by £18,000 and increased the balance on the profits and loss account by £6,000 no adjustments in respect of these items are necessary.

(g) *Gain on the sale of investments*
Capital gains are not taxed under trading income rules. Hence the gain of £30,000 should be deducted in order to calculate the tax adjusted trading profits. We will see in Chapter 8 how capital gains are dealt with.

(h) *Sales to X Ltd*
Drawings in the form of goods or services made by sole traders or partners have to be dealt with at market prices. This includes selling goods to an associate for less than market value. The sales figure should therefore be increased by £30,000.

Question 2

Sam – trading profit for the year ended 5 April 2023

	£	£
Net profit		50,000
Add		
Depreciation	7,600	
Motor expenses (8,800 x 20%) (Note 1)	1,760	
Patent royalties (Note 2)	–	
Personal capital gains tax advice	320	
Gifts to customers (560 + 420) (Note 3)	980	
Own consumption	1,480	12,140
Less		
Use of office (5,120 x 1/8)	640	
Private telephone (1,600 x 25%)	400	
Capital allowances	6,100	(7,140)
Tax adjusted trading profit		55,000

Notes:

1. Of the 25,000 miles driven by Sam during the year ended 5 April 2023, (25,000 - 5,000 = 20,000) x 75%) = 15,000 were for U.K. business journeys. With the addition of the 5,000 miles driven for business in Europe, this means 20,000 of the 25,000 miles driven are for business. The business proportion is therefore 80% (20,000/25,000 x 100).
2. Patent royalties are allowed as a deduction when calculating the trading profit so no adjustment is required. Remember there is a requirement to withhold income tax on patent royalty payments, which is why they receive special mention here.
3. Gifts to customers are an allowable deduction if they cost less than £50 per recipient per year, are not of food, drink, tobacco or vouchers for exchangeable goods and carry a conspicuous advertisement for the business making the gift.

Question 3

a) Tax-adjusted profits for year ended 31 January 2023 (using the accruals basis)

	£	£
Surplus per cash book		8,412
Adjustments to get profit calculated on accruals basis:		
Accounts receivable and work done not invoiced		
(£2,900 + 1,300)	4,200	
Accrued costs (interest)	(74)	
		4,126
Profit per accounts (accruals basis)		12,538

Tax adjustments:

Ben's wages	12,000	
Capital items [1]	7,227	
Entertaining	2,103	
Motor expenses [2]	212	
Lunch costs [5]	246	
Clothing [6]	680	
		22,468
Less: Capital Allowances [3]		(6,830)
Tax-adjusted trading profits – accruals basis [4]		28,176

Note:

1. Capital items comprise computer (£1,855), machinery (£4,122) and repairs to machinery before able to be used (Law Shipping) (£1,250).
2. Motoring expenses – only two-thirds of the costs are for business purposes therefore one third must be added back as is not a business expense.
3. Because you have not yet covered capital allowances, the question gives you this figure – a total of £6,830. Once you have studied capital allowances in Chapter 7, you will be able to see how this is worked out.
4. Because you are given the cash figures in the question, we should really take into account the VAT implications. However, because you haven't yet covered VAT, we have ignored it in this answer. To make the question complete, you would need to know the VAT payable on the purchases (input tax) and the VAT payable on the sales (output tax). The difference would then be removed to reach the profit figure and hence taxable figure, as for a registered company this excludes the VAT impact for recoverable transactions.
5. The food costs are not reclaimable at all as only meals related to overnight stays are allowable – even if he is incurring more costs when travelling on business than we would otherwise (see Caillebotte v Quinn [1975] 50 TC 222 and Watkins v Ashford, Sparkes and Harward [1985] 58 TC 468).
6. Even though the suits are used only for work, they are conventional (not special) clothing and therefore not deductible.

Tax-adjusted profits for year ended 31 January 2023 (using the cash basis)

	£	£
Surplus per cash book [1 and 2]		8,412
Tax adjustments [3]:		
Ben's wages	12,000	
Entertaining [4]	2,103	
Motor expenses [5]	212	
Lunch costs [6]	246	
Clothing [6]	680	
Interest deduction cap [7]	464	
		15,705
Tax-adjusted trading profit – cash basis [8]		24,117

1. No adjustments are made for accounts receivable and un-invoiced work as these are recorded under the cash basis only when they occur.
2. No adjustment is made for accrued expenses when using the cash basis.
3. Rent paid in advance at 11 months x £3,000 also deductible under the cash basis.
4. Entertaining costs are not allowable deductions for tax purposes under either basis.
5. The motor expenses will only be allowable for the business element. Ben may opt to use the fixed rates (i.e. 45p/25p for business miles driven) but the question says that he does not wish to use this.
6. Clothing and lunch costs are not allowable deductions for either basis.
7. Interest as a tax deduction is capped under the cash basis to £500. Therefore, we must disallow (£964 – £500) = £464.
8. Charges for capital items are only included under the cash basis in the periods in which purchases or disposals occur. Capital allowances will therefore not be allowed. All other items are deductible under the cash basis as legitimate expenses incurred and paid within the tax period.

It is often helpful to create a reconciliation to show how the differences arise between the two trading profit figures you have computed using the different bases:

		£
Tax-adjusted profit – accruals basis		28,176
Minus :	debtors and work done not invoiced	(4,200)
	Capital items (inc. capitalised repairs)	(7,227)
Add:	accrued interest costs	74
	capital allowances	6,830
	interest deduction cap	464
Tax-adjusted profit – cash basis		24,117

Chapter 7

Quick quiz answers

1. The car is a high emissions car and so must go into the special rate pool where it will receive a 6% writing down allowance. It does not qualify for either the AIA or FYA. There is no apportionment for the length of ownership within the accounting period and no private use reduction as it is used solely for business purposes.

2. Theresa will need to allocate this car to the main capital allowances pool as it doesn't qualify as a low emission car (0g/km) for FYA purposes (and AIA doesn't include car purchases). The car is deemed a 'medium' emissions vehicle under the current car capital allowance rules (see section 7.13). She would get 18% capital allowances for this a year as part of the pool computation for annual writing down allowances. (Note that , had she bought this before 6 April 2021 it would have qualified for 100% FYA as acceptable emissions levels before that were 50g/km). We will need to check if there was any private usage to restrict capital allowances by that she can then claim each year.

3. In 2022/23 Umut would be entitled to the maximum level of AIA of £1,000,000 as his year end is 31 December 2022. Therefore, he can claim the full £1,000,000, with the £450,000 excess expenditure added to the main rate pool for which the writing down allowance will be 18%, i.e. £81,000. This gives Umut a total capital allowance entitlement of £1,081,000 for the year to 31 December 2022.

    While the transition rules are fairly complicated, in essence, had Umut's year-end been 5 September 2023, part of his year would have fallen into the period when the AIA cap fell to £200,000 (i.e. after 1 April 2023). If he bought the same machine on the same date, his capital allowances would have been:

    AIA cap = (7/12 x £1 million) + (5/12 x £200,000) = £666,666

    The excess purchase value therefore over the cap would have £783,334 (£1,450,000 – £666,666) on which capital allowance at 18% would have been eligible for the year of acquisition i.e. £141,000, giving Umut £807,666 (£666,666 + £141,000) allowances in an accounting period ended 5 September 2023.

4. Vivian is entitled to a 100% capital allowance for this purchase using the AIA available for this part of the year. This maximum entitlement is £1,000,000 for the accounting period ended 30 September 2022.

    If Vivian has used up some, or all her AIA for the year, and she expects to sell the computer within eight years and realise a loss (i.e. if it is expected to fall in value faster than the 18% main pool capital allowance rate, both of which are quite likely) then it may be worth de-pooling the asset and keeping it separate as a short life asset so as to get the benefit of the balancing allowance that is expected as soon as possible.

5. Walter has sold the car for less than its tax written down value and so for tax purposes has a balancing allowance of £5,000. He can only claim 75% of this (£3,750), however, as he uses the car 75% for business purposes.

6. Xanthe y/e 31.03.23

	Main	CAs
	£	£
Opening balance	15,000	
Disposals		
Plant *(lower of cost/proceeds)*	(14,200)	
	800	
WDA (small pool <£1,000)	(800)	800
WDV c/f	nil	
Total allowances		800

7. As Norma's work was undertaken after 29 October 2018 and relates to construction work on a commercial building, her expenditure is eligible for SBA. However, as £5,000 of this spend qualifies as integral features, only £20,000 can be used to base her SBA on.

As she used the building from 1 January 2022, she can claim 3% for the 11 months to the end of the accounting period.
SBA = £20,000 x 11/12 x 3% = £550 that is claimable against the profits from her shop for the year ended 30 November 2022
(Note that strictly, the number of days in each period should be used for this computation rather than rounding to months - months are used here for simplicity).

The £5,000 spent on integral features would be claimable under her AIA so is likely to be claimable in full in 2022/23 (unless she fully used up this allowance on other purchases).

8. Yolande's accounts are for 3 months so the AIA cap for her claim is 3/12 x £1,000,000 AIA = £250,000. The excess of her expenditure over this can have capital allowances applied at the main pool rate (nothing in the question indicates the machine purchased should be anything other than allocated to the main pool) i.e. 3/12 x 18% x (£400,000 – AIA cap already applied of £250,000) i.e. a total of £256,750.

9. Zeus For y/e 31.3.22:

	£
Trading profit	12,000
Property business income	250,000
	262,000
Less loss relief against general income	(77,500)
Net income	184,500

In 2021/22, the loss relief cap applies to relief against non-trading income i.e. 25% x £262,000 = £65,500. The relief against trading income is not capped, so the total relief available is £65,500 + £12,000 = £77,500.

Full questions

Question 1

For each new asset, we need to think about whether it qualifies for either ECA or the AIA.

Looking at the new assets acquired by Luke we can say:

- The new van (purchased 29/7/21) qualifies for AIA (remember vans are not treated the same as cars and do qualify for AIA).

- The car purchased 25/10/21 has CO_2 emissions of only 0g/km and so will qualify for first year allowances (i.e. 100% in year of purchase).

- The plant disposed of must be deducted from the relevant pool at the lower of cost or the value it is sold for. It will have been added to the main pool when acquired and so should be deducted from there.

- The new plant (purchased 1/05/22) qualifies for AIA.

- Cars don't qualify for AIA and so the second new car (purchased 15/5/22) is put into either the main or special rate pools depending on their CO_2 emission levels. Here the car is 180g/km, and so must go into the special rate pool. No hybrid rate needs to apply to this WDA as the applicable rate did not change in the relevant period.

- The new lift (purchased 30/5/22) is an integral feature that also qualifies for AIA.

- The AIA cap of £1,000,000 applies throughout this accounting period and therefore the available AIA is much more than the amount Luke spent.

y/e 30/6/22	£	Main £	Sp rate £	CAs £
Opening balance		10,000		
Additions qualifying for FYA				
1st new car (25/10/21)	6,000			6,000
Additions qualifying for AIA:				
New van (29/7/21)	4,000			
New plant (1/5/22)	15,000			
New lift (30/5/22)	8,000			
AIA (cap £1 million)	27,000			27,000
Balance to main pool		nil		
Other Additions				
2nd new car (15/5/22)			20,000	
Disposals				
Plant		(7,000)		
		3,000	20,000	
WDA (18%)		(540)		540
WDA (6%)			(1,200)	1,200
WDV c/f		2,460	18,800	
Total allowances				34,740

Question 2

	£
Net loss as per accounts	(56,400)
Add back accounting depreciation	12,340
Less capital allowances (see below)	(148)
Tax adjusted trading loss	(44,208)

	Main pool £	Short life Asset £	Special rate pool £	CAs £
WDV b/f	21,600	8,800		
Additions				
Car			11,800	
Disposals				
Short life asset		(11,700)		
Lorry	(8,600)			
	13,000		11,800	
Balancing charge		(2,900)		(2,900)
WDA (18%/6%)	(2,340)		(708)	3,048
WDV c/f	10,660	nil	11,092	
Total allowances				148

The new Ford Focus car must go into a special rate pool as it is a high emissions car (CO_2 emissions exceed 50g/km).

The net loss from Jogger can be dealt with in a number of ways as he uses the accruals basis. Phil can use it to reduce his current year's income, i.e. offset it against other income sources he may have for the year such as property income or savings income. He can carry it back to the previous year, or he can carry it forward to future years. If he carries it forward to future years, it can only then be offset against subsequent 'Jogger' profits.

Question 3

Capital allowances	Main £	Special £	Mercedes £	CAs £
Balance brought forward		59,400	14,200	26,300	
Additions qualifying for ECAs					
Electric charging points	3,000				
ECA 100% (Note 1)	(3,000)				3,000
Additions qualifying for AIA:					
Air conditioning	28,000				
Sewing machines	15,000				
AIA (Note 2)	(43,000)				43,000
Disposals (5 x £250)	(1,250)			
	58,150	14,200	26,300	
WDA (18%)	(10,467)			10,467
WDA (6% - Note 3)		(852)	(1,578)x50%	1,641
WDV c/f	47,683	13,135	24,722	

SBA		
(£500,000 x 3% x 6/12 (see Note 4)		7,500
Total allowances for the accounting period		65,608

Notes:
1. The value used for the electric charging points is the net value, after deducting the government grant.
2. The AIA cap has been constant throughout the tax year (it changes from April 2023), so no transitional cap needs to be applied in this year's computation. The purchases are more than covered by this threshold and so can be fully claimed under AIA.

3. The Mercedes should normally be placed in the relevant pool – in this case it would be the special rate pool as it has emissions exceeding 50g/km. However, as there is private use it must be given its own pool, and the special pool rate be used for the WDA, with a restriction (at 50% in this case) for the allowable part of the capital allowance. The applicable WDA rate is 6% with no need to compute a hybrid rate as it didn't change in the relevant period of assessment. Note that if it was an employee of the business (not the owner) using the car then no private usage would be deducted. Instead the employee would be taxed on the company car as a benefit in kind.

4. The new factory extension will qualify for SBA. As Stitched up started to use the new building from 1 January 2022 it can claim six months' worth of SBAs in the accounting period to 30 June 2022.

Chapter 8

Quick quiz answers

1. Andrew will have a chargeable gain as follows:

	£
Disposal proceeds	5,000
Cost	(1,700)
Chargeable gain	3,300

He will have to add this gain to any others in the year to see if he has to pay any CGT on this transaction. If he has no other gains he'll not have to pay CGT on this as it comes under his AEA for 2022/23.

2. A hearse may be exempt from capital gains tax as a motor vehicle, however, the exemption is for passenger vehicles and arguably a hearse is not constructed to carry passengers (of the kind implied by the rule anyway). However, assuming Barbara is not carrying on a business as an undertaker, the hearse will be exempt as a wasting chattel (estimated life less than 50 years) and so Barbara will not pay capital gains tax on the profit.

3. The £12,200 capital loss generated in 2022/23 must first be set against the £24,800 capital gain in 2022/23. The capital loss brought forward will then be set against the £12,600 net 2022/23 gain, but the loss relief can be restricted to protect the £12,300 2022/23 AEA so only £300 of the brought forward loss will be used in 2022/23 (£12,600 - £12,300). This leaves £6,800 capital loss to carry forward to the following tax year.

4. A painting is a chattel and since it was sold for less than £6,000, it will be exempt from capital gains tax.

5. As Davina's gain of £450,000 is fully available for entrepreneurs' relief, it will simply be subject to a 10% charge after deducting the AEA.

6. Eddie will be able to claim a loss of £6,950 based on deemed disposal proceeds of £50.

7. When part of an asset is sold, the formula A ÷ (A+B) is used to determine how much of the cost is attributable to the part of the asset that has been sold. In this case 200,000 ÷ (860,000 + 200,000) of the original cost is attributed to the part sold i.e. £94,340 and so the gain is £105,660. This is then reduced by the AEA of £12,300. Because Felicity is a higher rate taxpayer, her capital gains tax liability is therefore £93,360 x 20% = £18,672.00.

8. Gregory must acquire the new asset between August 2021 and August 2025 in order to qualify for rollover relief, unless HMRC allows an extension. HMRC will do this if he can show a firm intention to acquire a new asset within the time limit, but was prevented from doing so by circumstances beyond his control, and that he acquired the new asset as soon as he reasonably could.

9. The part of the gain attributable to the consideration in shares is £50,000 x £80,000/£100,000 = £40,000. This is the part of the gain that can be deferred using incorporation relief. The cost of the shares for any future disposal will therefore be £80,000, reduced by the deferred gain of £40,000 i.e. a cost base of £40,000. Helen may be liable to tax on the balance of the gain of £10,000 for the year 2022/23, depending on how much of her AEA is available to reduce the gain.

10. £143,000. The proceeds of the old warehouse exceeds the investment in the new warehouse by more than the value of the chargeable gain, so there can be no rollover in this case and all of the chargeable gain will be taxable.

Full questions

Question 1

Net chargeable gains for 2022/23 are:

	£
Antique table [1]	6,500
Cottage [2]	0
Plot of land [3]	1,357
Ryft plc shares [4]	0
PK plc shares [5]	2,125
	9,982

Because this is below the AEA, no capital gains tax will be payable.

1 – The table is a chattel whose proceeds and cost both exceed £6,000.

	£
Net sales proceeds (£35,000 – £3,500)	31,500
Less: cost	(25,000)
Gain	6,500

2 – Holiday cottage – disposed of to a connected person and therefore deemed proceeds of market value used. The loss arising can only be used against gains on disposals to the same person and is computed as follows:

	£
Proceeds – market value	45,000
Less: incidental costs of disposal	(1,100)
	43,900
Less cost	(47,500)
Loss – only use against gains on disposals to the same person	(3,600)

3 – Plot of land

	£
Proceeds	13,000
Less: incidental costs of disposal	(500)
	12,500
Less: Cost	
£24,000 x (£13,000/ (£13,000 + £15,000))	(11,143)
Gain	1,357

4 – Ryft plc shares – exempt as sold within an ISA.

5 – PK plc shares – sale proceeds must be matched with cost of shares purchased within the following 30 days.

	£
Proceeds	8,500
Less: cost – £8,500 x 1,200/1,600	(6,375)
Gain	2,125

Question 2

Jointly owned property

(a) Cars are exempt from CGT

(b) The chargeable gain on the house is calculated as follows:

	£
Disposal proceeds	381,900
Cost	(86,000)
	295,900
Principal private residence exemption (PPR)	(236,720)
	59,180

David and Angela are assessed on half the gain each – and remember that the rates applicable to residential property are 18% or 28%.

The total period of ownership of the house is 300 months (240 + 60) of which 240 months qualify for exemption as follows:

465

	Exempt	Chargeable
1/10/97 – 31/3/01 (occupied)	42	
1/4/01 – 31/12/04 (working in UK)	45	
1/1/05 – 31/12/16 (occupied)	144	
1/1/17 – 31/12/21 (unoccupied)		60
1/1/22 – 30/9/22 (final 9 months)	9	
	240	60

The exemption is therefore £236,720 (295,900 x 240/300).

David Brook

(a) The antique table is a non-wasting chattel, but is exempt from capital gains tax because the gross sale proceeds were less than £6,000.

(b) The transfer of 20,000 £1 ordinary shares in Bend Ltd to Angela does not give rise to any gain or loss, because it is a transfer between spouses.

(c) Ordinary shares in Galatico plc

Deemed proceeds (15,000 x £2.95)	44,250
Cost (15,000 x £1.96)	(29,400)
	14,850

Using the quarter up method (see section 8.9 under Gross Disposal Proceeds) to determine the market value, the shares in Galatico plc are valued at £2.95 (£2.90 + ¼ (3.10 – 2.90)

Using weighted average, the cost of the shares disposed of is £1.96 per share (£39,200/20,000)

	£	£
Capital gains tax liability:		
House (59,180/2)	29,590	
AEA*	(12,300)	
	17,290	
Capital gains tax at 18%		3,112.20
Galatico plc shares	14,850	
AEA (all used on the House sale)	(0)	
	14,850	
CGT at 10%		1,485.00
Total CGT Tax due		4,597.20

* You are allowed to apply the AEA in whatever way best suits the taxpayer. It will be better here to assign it to the house sale first as that incurs CGT at a higher rate.

Angela Brook

(a) The antique cabinet is a non-wasting chattel. The gain is restricted to £2,000 (7,200 – 6,000 = 1,200 x 5/3) as this is less than £3,500 (7,200 – 3,700).

(b) Bend Ltd shares

Disposal proceeds	62,400
Cost (48,000 x 15,000/20,000)	(36,000)
	26,400

David's original cost is used in calculating the capital gain on the disposal of shares in Bend Ltd.

Capital gains tax liability:	£	£
House (59,180/2)	29,590	
AEA*	(12,300)	
	17,290	
Capital gains tax at 28%		4,841.20
Antique cabinet	2,000	
Ordinary shares in Bend Ltd	26,400	
Chargeable gains	28,400	
AEA (all used on the House sale)	(0)	
	28,400	
Capital gains tax @ 20%		5,680.00
Total Capital Gains Tax due		10,521.20

House sale CGT is due 60 days after disposal (i.e. 31 January 2022), balance is due 31 January 2024

*Again, the AEA should be applied to the house sale for Angela as this gives her the lower CGT bill.

Question 3

(a) Freehold office building

	£
Disposal proceeds	246,000
Cost	(104,000)
Potential Chargeable gain	142,000
Less amount not reinvested (£246,000 – £136,000)	(110,000)
Gain eligible to be rolled over	32,000

The chargeable gain is £110,000 as this is the amount not re-invested and is lower than the gain calculated.

(b) Retail business: Goodwill

	£
Disposal proceeds	120,000
Cost	nil
	120,000
Rollover relief (120,000 – 36,000)	(84,000)
Chargeable gain	36,000

Note:
The proportion of the gain relating to the cash consideration cannot be rolled over, so £36,000 (120,000 x 60,000/200,000) of the gain is immediately chargeable to capital gains tax.

(c) Ordinary shares in Gandua Ltd

	£
Deemed proceeds	220,000
Cost	(112,000)
	108,000
Gift relief	(90,000)
Chargeable gain	18,000

Note:
Gift relief is restricted to £90,000 (£108,000 x £150,000/£180,000) being the proportion of chargeable business assets to chargeable assets.

(d) Antique vase
The insurance proceeds of £68,000 received by Wilson have been fully reinvested in a replacement antique vase. The disposal is therefore on a 'no gain, no loss' basis, with the capital gain of £19,000 (insurance proceeds of £68,000 less original cost of £49,000) being set against the cost of the replacement antique vase.

(e) Land

	£
Disposal proceeds	85,000
Cost	(68,000)
	17,000

Note:
The cost relating to the ten acres of land sold is £68,000 (120,000 x 85,000/150,000 (85,000 + 65,000)).

Chapter 9

Quick quiz answers

1. Grotius Ltd will have two accounting periods for tax purposes, the year ended 31 August, 2022 and the four months ended 31 December, 2022.

2. The dividends do not form part of taxable total profits and so are not taxed as part of Helvetius' income.

3. Justinian Ltd must include £4,875 in its total taxable profits under trade profits (£3,900 × 100 ÷80). The income tax withheld on the patent royalties by the payer of £975 (£4,875 - £3,900) can be offset against any income tax withheld on payments made by the company, and any surplus can be reclaimed against the corporation tax liability.

4. The non-trading loan relationship profit will be £7,000 - (£5,650 + £1,200) = £150. The loan to purchase plant is a trading loan relationship, not a non-trading loan relationship.

5. New Money Ltd's research costs are deductible so no adjustment is required to the accounting profit for the £11,000. The special R&D deduction for tax purposes gives an *additional* deduction of £11,000 x 130% i.e. £14,300. At a corporation tax rate of 19% this will mean a reduction in corporation tax of £2,717.

6. Isocrates Ltd can claim 4% per annum as a deduction in calculating trade profits, as this exceeds the rate used for accounting purposes which is 3%.

7. When Quay Ltd pays corporation tax for the year ended for the accounting period ended 31 July 2022 the company can recover 50% of the penalty tax, as 50% of the loan has been repaid, i.e. £4,875. The remaining penalty tax can be recovered if the shareholder repays more of the remaining loan, or if the company writes the remaining loan off.

8. Because Ranch Ltd is a close company and a benefit has been provided to a non-director, non-employee participator, the company cannot deduct any costs, including capital allowances in respect of the car. Billy is taxed on the value of the benefit as if it were a dividend.

9.

Proceeds	14,600	
Cost		(5,000)
Unindexed gain		9,600
Indexation allowance		
$\frac{278.1 - 179.3}{179.3}$ $0.551 \times 5,000$		(2,755)
Indexed gain		6,845

10. Origami Ltd has total taxable profits of £11m for the year ended 30 June 2022. After deducting the £5m allowance, the remaining £6m is multiplied by 50%, i.e. £3m. This means £5m + £3m = £8m can be offset this year, leaving £2m loss to be carried forward to the next year.
11. Time, Verity and Wallace are related companies for the purposes of quarterly instalments limits.
12. Lychophron Ltd is a large company for instalment payment purposes because with tax of £650,000 its profits are deemed "large" as they exceed the relevant threshold (£1.5m x 5/12 = £625,000). As such it will have instalments due on 14 July, 2022 and 14 September, 2022 for this short period.

Full questions

Question 1

Ultimate Upholsterers Ltd, Corporation Tax computation for the 12 months to 31 March 2023

		£
Trading Profit (Note 1)		324,960
Non-trading loan relationships:		
Loan interest receivable	12,000	
Less Debenture Interest payable	(10,000)	
		2,000
Chargeable gain (Note 2)		16,810
Taxable total profits		343,370
Corporation tax: £343,370 × 19%		65,316.30

Note 1: calculation of trade profits

In order to calculate the trading profits we need to calculate the capital allowances. The writing down allowance is given in the question. Capital allowances are not available on buildings constructed before October 2018. However, tax relief will be available for the lease premium paid. The landlord will be assessed on £26,000 i.e.

£50,000 – £24,000   (£50,000 × (25 – 1) ×2%).

Ultimate Upholsterers will be able to claim relief of £1,040 (£26,000 ÷ 25).

	£
Adjustment of Profits:	
Trading profit	375,000
Less Capital Allowances:	
Plant and machinery	(49,000)
Less relief on lease premium paid	(1,040)
Adjusted trading profits	324,960

Note 2: calculation of chargeable gain on land

	£
Proceeds	47,410
Less cost	(10,000)
Unindexed gain	37,410
Less indexation allowance:	
$\dfrac{278.1 - 90.87}{90.87}$	
£10,000 × 2.060	(20,600)
Indexed gain	16,810

Question 2

With two related companies the applicable limit is £750,000 (£1.5m ÷ 2). With augmented profit of £1.2million ABC Ltd and a tax liability over £10,000, the company is required to make instalment payments of their tax liability.

a) Instalment dates will be

1st instalment	31 Oct 2021 + 6 months + 14 days	14 May 2021
2nd instalment	14 May 2022 + 3 months	14 Aug 2022
3rd instalment	14 Aug 2022 + 3 months	14 Nov 2022
Final instalment	14 Nov 2022 + 3 months	14 Feb 2023

Amounts due on each date above:

$$\frac{3 \times 228,000}{12} = £57,000$$

b) Instalment dates

1st instalment	31 Oct 2021+ 6 months+ 14 days	14 May 2022
2nd instalment	14 May 2022 + 3 months	14 Aug 2022
3rd instalment	(not due as falls beyond final instalment date)	
Final instalment	30 Jun 2022 + 3 months + 14 days	14 Oct 2022

Amounts due each instalment

$$\frac{3 \times 228,000}{8} = £85,500$$

Balance due in final instalment £57,000.

Question 3

In order to answer this question, first we must perform a trading profit adjustment. As part of this process, we will need to compute the capital allowances that are available to the company.

1 Capital allowances

Plant and machinery		*Main pool*	*Allowances*
Additions eligible for super deduction:			
31/1/23 Plant	10,500		
super deduction@130%	(13,650)		13,650
31/1/23 Low emission car			
(private use n/a)	13,000		
FYA 100%	(13,000)		13,000

Writing down allowance			
1/4/22 Balance brought forward		263,504	
Disposal 1/8/22		(9,400)	
		254,104	
WDA @ 18%		(45,738)	45,738
WDV c/f		208,366	
Total allowances			72,388

2 Trade profits

Net profit as per accounts			127,663
Add back:			
Depreciation (not deductible)		43,150	
Non trading loan interest payable (reclassify)		700	
Entertaining (not deductible)		730	
Charitable donation (reclassify)		5,000	
Trading expenses disallowable:			
Gifts of alcohol		280	
Legal expenses for non-trading loan (reclassify)		500	50,360
			178,023
Less			
Debenture interest (reclassify)		1,200	
Building society interest (reclassify)		759	
Capital allowances		72,388	(74,347)
Adjusted Trading profits			103,676

Corporation Tax computation

Trading Profits			103,676
Non trading loan relationships:			
Debenture interest		1,200	
Building society interest		759	
Less non trading loan interest		(700)	
Legal costs re non trading loan		(500)	759
			104,435
Less charitable donation			(5,000)
Taxable Total Profits			99,435

Corporation tax
£99,435 @ 19%   £18,892.65
Payable 1 January 2024

Chapter 10

Quick quiz answers

1. Yes, Kieran will have to register for VAT as his 12 month turnover exceeds the threshold which is £85,000 .

2. The value of the supply is £500 so the standard rated VAT is £100.00 A settlement discount is only taken into account when the customer actually takes advantage of it.

3. Maurice does not have to register as his taxable supplies are less than the threshold. He could, however, register voluntarily so that he can reclaim his input tax.

4. The input tax attributable to taxable supplies is £50,000. Nigella can also recover a portion of the unattributable input tax i.e. 80%, since 80% of her supplies are taxable ((£500,000-£100,000)÷£500,000). This means that a total of £53,200 is recoverable and the balance of £5,800 is not recoverable. Do not forget the de minimus test though, £5,800 spread over the whole year is £483 per month which is less than the de minimus of £625 and so Nigella can in fact recover all of her input tax.

5. The basic tax point is 20 August as this is when the goods are made available to the customer. Do not forget though that this basic tax point can be altered if an invoice has been issued within 14 days of the basic tax point. That is the case here, and so the actual tax point will be 30 August, the date of issue of the invoice, even though the customer did not pay until 13 September.

6. Under cash accounting we are only concerned about cash received and paid, not invoices issued. Portia has received £5,525 from her debtors, so we can use the VAT fraction of 1/6 to work out the VAT i.e. £920.83. She has paid £4,000 to suppliers before VAT and so the tax on that is @20% i.e. £800.00. Portia must therefore pay HMRC the difference between these two figures i.e. £920.83 minus £800.00 which is £120.83.

7. The earliest quarterly return in which relief can be claimed for the impaired debt is the quarter ended 30 June 2023, i.e. the quarter in which the debt has been outstanding for six months (10 April 2023).

8. Roxanne can recover £333 i.e. all the tax on the repairs @ 1/6 x £2,000. Input tax is not recoverable on the car itself because it is partly used for private purposes.

9. Goods acquired within 4 years prior to registration and held on registration date, services supplied within six months prior to registration qualify for input tax recovery. Suzanne can therefore recover £550 (accountancy fees and spare parts).

10. Deductible input tax – quarter ended 31 October, 2022

	£
Input tax attributable to taxable supplies	18,000
Proportion of remaining input tax	
£88,400 ÷ £100,000 = 89% (rounded)	
89% × (£24,000 – £18,000 – £1,500)	4,005
	22,005

(Non deductible of £1,995 exceeds *de minimus* of £625 per month.)

Full questions

Question 1

A person who makes taxable supplies becomes liable to be registered for VAT:

- at the end of any month, if the value of his or her taxable supplies in the period of one year then ending has exceeded £85,000, or
- at any time, if there are reasonable grounds for believing that the value of his or her taxable supplies in the period of thirty days then beginning will exceed £85,000.

Taxable supplies are made up of both standard rated and zero rated supplies. Since the trader's taxable supplies of £87,000 (£78,000 + £9,000) exceeds the annual limit of £85,000, the trader is liable to register for VAT. The trader must notify HMRC within 30 days of the end of the month in which the limits were exceeded. The trader will then be registered from the first day of the following month.

Had the trader voluntarily registered from the beginning of the accounting period his VAT position would have been:

	£
Output tax:	
Standard-rated supplies £9,000 × 20%	1,800
Less input tax:	
(9,000 + 4,000) × 1/6	(2,166)
VAT recoverable	(366)

Question 2

VAT for the year ended 31 March 2023

	£	£
Output VAT		
Standard rated sales (£115,200 x 20/120)		19,200
Zero rated sales		0
Input VAT		
Impairment losses (£1,440 x 20/120)	240	
Standard rated purchases (£43,200 x 20/120)	7,200	
Zero rated purchases	0	
Rent (£1,200 x 13 x 20/120)	2,600	
Telephone (£2,600 x 60% x 20/120)	260	
Entertaining UK customers	0	
Entertaining overseas customers (£240 x 20/120)	40	(10,340)
VAT payable		8,860

Question 3

(a) VAT Return Quarter ended 30 November 2022

	£	£
Output VAT		
Cash sales (28,000 x 20%)		5,600
Credit sales		2,292
Input VAT		
Purchases and expenses (11,200 x 20%)	2,240	
Impairment loss (800 x 20%) [2]	160	(2,400)
		5,492

The VAT return for the quarter ended 30 November 2022 should be submitted by 31 December 2022, being one month after the end of the VAT period.
Note:
1. The calculation of output VAT on the credit sales takes into account the discount for prompt payment, but only for the customers who took it:

90% x £12,000 x 95% x 20% = £2,052

10% x £12,000 x 100% x 20% = £240

2. Relief for an impairment loss is not given until six months from the time that payment is due. Therefore, relief can only be claimed in respect of the invoice due for payment on 10 April 2022. Relief is based on the amount of output VAT that would have originally been paid.

(b) Anne can use the cash accounting scheme if her expected taxable turnover for the next 12 months does not exceed £1,350,000. In addition, Anne must be up to date with her VAT returns and VAT payments. Output VAT on most credit sales will be accounted for up to one month later than at present, since the scheme will result in the tax point becoming the date that payment is received from her customers. However, the recovery of input VAT will be delayed by two months. The scheme will provide automatic bad debt relief should a credit sale customer default on payment of a debt.

(c) (i) Sale of assets on a piecemeal basis: upon cessation of trading, Anne will cease to make taxable supplies, so her VAT registration will be cancelled on the date of cessation or an agreed later date. Output VAT will be due in respect of the fixed assets at the date of de-registration on which VAT has been claimed (although output VAT is not due if it totals less than £1,000).

(c) (ii) Sale of business as a going concern: Since the purchaser is already registered for VAT, Anne's registration will be cancelled as above. A sale of a business as a going concern is outside the scope of VAT and therefore output VAT will not be due.

Chapter 11

Question 1

Without a salary sacrifice, Zainab has a gross pension contribution of £100 per month, because the incentive system to encourage pension contributions adds basic rate tax (currently 20%) to the pension contribution, so her £80 net pay contribution becomes a gross contribution of £100. Assuming she is a basic rate taxpayer, Zainab could sacrifice £119 of gross (before tax and NIC) pay each month, which would be worth £80 of net pay after deduction of basic rate tax and national insurance (80 x 100/100–(20+12.8). The employer contributes this sacrificed salary of £119 to Zainab's pension, so pension contribution increases by £19 compared to the previous arrangement. Zainab's net (take home) pay is the same, but she has now put more each month into her pension. Her employer saves £16.42 in national insurance contributions (£119 x 13.8%).

Question 2
(a)
- Andrew is under the control of Slick Productions Ltd
- Andrew is not taking any financial risk
- Andrew works a set number of hours, is paid by the hour and is paid for overtime
- Andrew cannot profit from sound management
- Andrew is required to do the work personally
- There is an obligation to accept the work that is offered
- Andrew does not provide his own equipment.

(b)
Treated as an employee:

	£
Employment income	50,000
Personal allowance	(12,570)
Taxable income	37,430
Income tax	
37,430 @ 20%	7,486.00
Income tax liability	7,486.00

Class 1 NIC will be (using annual thresholds):
(50,000 – 11,908) @ 13.25% = £5,047.19

Treated as self-employed:
Andrew's trading profit for 2022/23 will be £50,000 so his income tax liability will be unchanged at £7,486.00.

Class 2 NIC will be £163.80 (£3.15 x 52)
Class 4 NIC will be (50,000 – 11,908) = 38,092 @ 10.25% £3,904.43.

Chapter 12

Question 1

Petra's income will be subject to UK tax as follows:
i.   Bank Interest – not taxable as not remitted to the UK;
ii.   Employment income – taxable, since it was paid by a UK employer for work performed in the UK and would get relevant personal allowances for this income.

As a non-domiciled but resident and ordinarily resident taxpayer, Petra will also have to pay the relevant annual remittance based charge to keep her remittance basis of assessment – unless she has foreign income of less than £2,000 or has not been in the UK as a non-domicile for seven of the last ten years. The size of this charge may mean it is more tax effective for her to give up this tax status and instead be taxed on her worldwide income as if she was domiciled in the UK (with relief then potentially available for foreign taxes paid).

Question 2

Even though Andromeda is incorporated in France, its central management and control is located in the UK, because most of the directors live here and this is where the board meetings are held. This means that Andromeda must pay UK corporation tax. If France also treats Andromeda as a resident company for tax purposes, then the double tax treaty between them will determine which country has priority, usually the country where the effective management is carried out, in this case probably the UK.

Question 3

The under-pricing of goods exported by Zanzibar to Zeus means that the UK profits of Zanzibar will be understated, and this will attract the operation of the transfer pricing rules. These require Zanzibar to use arm's length prices to compute its UK profit for tax purposes. The company will have to look to the OECD guidelines to determine which method best fits its situation, and be prepared to justify the choice to HMRC, which includes keeping documentation to show how the arm's length price was calculated.

Question 4

	Non-savings £	Savings £	Dividends £	Total £
Income:				
Employment Income	42,000			42,000
Overseas rental income	7,000			7,000
Total Income	49,000			49,000
Less Personal Allowance	(12,570)			(12,570)
Total Taxable Income	36,430			36,430
Tax Due:				
Non-savings income 36,430 @ 20%				7,286.00
Tax Borne				7, 286.00
Less:				
Double tax relief (^{1})				(1,400.00)
UK Tax Payable				5,886.00

Notes:
1. The double tax relief is the lower of the overseas tax paid and the UK tax on the overseas income.

The rents are taxed at a higher rate overseas than the UK tax. We need to calculate the amount of UK tax attributable to the rent.

Without the rental income, Gerald's taxable income would be £29,430 and the UK tax at 20% would be £5,886.00. Therefore, the UK tax on rents is £7,286.00 – £5, 886.00 = £1,400.00. This is lower than the £3,150 overseas tax paid, so the UK income tax liability is reduced by £1,400.00.

Index

Index of cases

Subject index

Notes:

App A/B = See Appendix A or B
G = Defined in Glossary
W = See Website chapters for more details
Supp = see online supplement for more details

Ability to pay 3.14, 3.24, 3.28, 4.30, G
Accelerated payments, tax avoidance 11.25
Acceptable tax avoidance 11.1
Accommodation 8.28, 12.11
  benefit in kind 5.9, 5.27, 5.28, G
  employer provided/job related 5.27, G
  VAT 10.28
Accounting date 4.26, 6.42, 9.5, W
Accounting period 2.3, 10.33, G
  capital allowances 7.8, 7.10
  corporation tax 9.4, 9.5, 9.6, 9.22, 9.24,
    9.27, 11.7, 12.7, W
  trading income 6.2, 6.12, 6.42
Accruals basis 4.3, 4.14, 4.25, 4.26, 5.4, 6.2,
  6.12, 6.38, 6.44, 6.46, 6.48, 6.49, 7.2, 9.6,
  9.7, 9.11, 14.21, G
Actual basis 9.6
Addington, Henry W
Additional property/dwelling supplement 8.37,
  8.42
Additional rate of tax 1.14, 3.31, 4.17-4.20,
  4.38, 5.38, 6.3, 8.3, 8.4, 9.3, 11.7, 14.18
Additional tax 2.6, 4.12
Adjusted net income 4.35
Adjustment of profits 6.11-6.40
Administrative Burden Advisory Board 2.10
Administrative efficiency 3.20, 3.24
Advanced pricing agreements (APAs) 12.11, G
Age related allowance (AA) 4.35, G
Agents 2.12
Aggregates levy 1.14, 13.9, App A, B
Agricultural buildings & works, Capital
  allowances 7.2
Agricultural property relief, IHT 8.49
Air passenger duty 1.14, 2.2, 13.5
Alcohol 1.2, 3.3, 3.11, 14.6, App A
Allocating profits,
  IT 6.42
  CT 9.6
Allowable costs, CGT 8.3, 8.11, 8.18, 8.22, G
Allowable expenses/deductions
  CGT 8.8, 8.11, 11.7
  chargeable gains, CT 9.21, 11.7
  corporation tax, 9.6, 9.11, 9.15
  employment income 4.15, 5.6-5.11

IHT 8.46
  property income 4.25, 6.45, 6.47
  rent-a-room scheme, 6.50
  trading income 4.15, 4.26, 6.17-6.38
Allowances (see Tax allowances)
Alternative dispute resolution (ADR) 2.8
Alternative tax bases 3.27-3.38
Amortisation 9.18
Animation tax relief (ATR) 9.17
Annual accounting scheme, VAT 10.26,
  10.34, G
Annual exemption amount (AEA), CGT 8.8,
  8.14, 8.19, 8.50, 9.13, G
Annual investment allowance (AIA) 7.4, 7.11,
  7.14, 7.15, 11.6, G
Annual payments 4.31, 4.33
Annual tax on enveloped dwellings (ATED)
  8.43, App A, G
Annuity 4.19, 4.23, 4.33, 5.40, 8.7, G
Anti-avoidance 4.23, 8.18, 8.34, 10.40, 11.26,
  12.13, 12.18, G
Appropriations 6.37, 6.40
Approved mileage allowance payments
  (AMAP) 5.10, App A
Arising basis 4.14, 12.4, G
Arm's length price 8.9, 10.6, 12.11, G
Associated companies 9.26, 9.27, 12.11, App
  A, G, W
Augmented profits, CT W
Automatic overseas/UK tests 12.2
Availability condition 6.49
Average rate of tax 3.5, 4.35, 14.8, 14.12, G, W

Bad debts
  expense deduction 6.37, 6.40, 6.41, G
  VAT 10.26
Badges of trade 6.3, 6.5-6.10, G
Balancing allowances and charges 7.19, 7.22,
  7.24, 7.25, 8.19, 9.6, 11.5, G
Bands (see Tax bands)
Bank accounts 3.17, 4.5, 4.19, 4.27, 9.6, 10.34
Bank levy 1.14
Base cost 8.11, 8.30, 8.31
Base erosion and profiting shifting project,
  OECD, 12.15

480